A History *of the* New York Juvenile Asylum *and* Its Orphan Trains

VOLUME ONE

CHILDREN IN NEED

Clark Kidder

Front cover photo: "Boys En Masse." (New York Juvenile Asylum. *Forty-Eighth Annual Report* (1899), 48.)

Cover design by Clark Kidder.

First Edition
© 2021 by Clark Kidder

All rights reserved. International copyright secured. No part of this book may be reproduced, stored in a retrieval system, or transmitted in any form or by any means—electronic, mechanical, photocopying, recording, or otherwise—without the prior written permission of the author, except for the inclusion of brief quotations in an acknowledged review.

Library of Congress Control Number: 2021900548

ISBN-13: 978-1-7364884-1-6

Contents

Preface v
Acknowledgments vii
Abbreviations viii
Introduction ix

Part I: The New York Juvenile Asylum

Chapter One: History of the New York Juvenile Asylum 3
An Institution is Born 3
Early Years 4
America's First Orphan Train 6
A New Home for the Asylum 9
House of Reception 12
Fire! 16
Growing Pains 17
A New Philosophy 17
"An Ideal American Village" 19
The Move to Dobbs Ferry 20
Official Name Change 26

Chapter Two: NYJA Procedures 27
Admissions 27
Notification of Parents or Guardians ... 27
Reasons for Commitments 28
Parental Surrenders 33
Society for the Prevention of Cruelty to Children ... 36
Children's Court 36
Indentures 39
Discharges 42

Chapter Three: The Children of the NYJA 45
Immigrants 45
Integration 46
Visiting Day 48
Escapes 51

A Bad Influence 54
Asylum Boys in the Civil War 55

Chapter Four: Life in the Asylum 61
Education 61
Employment 65
Discipline 67
Recreation 71
Holidays 72
And the Band Played On 74
Kitchen and Dining 75
Hygiene 77
Bedtime 80

Chapter Five: Life in The Children's Village 83
Education 83
Intelligence Quotient Testing 83
Cottage Living 87
Agriculture 88
Recreation 90
A Beautiful Title 91
A Visit from President Taft 93

Part II: Orphan Trains of the New York Juvenile Asylum

Chapter Six: History of the Orphan Trains 97
Orphan Trains to Illinois 97
Western Indenturing Agent 102
Western Indentures 103
An Act of Legislature 107
Western Agency Established 108
Greener Pastures 111

Chapter Seven: All Aboard the Orphan Train! 113
Candidates for the West 113

Investigation of Children 114
Preparing for the Journey 114
Prior to Departure 117
Beginning of the Journey 120
Journey to the West 122
Arrival at Their Western Destination 124
Chapter Eight: Challenges and Successes 129
Placement Challenges 129
A Matter of Religion 130
A Matter of Nationality 132
A Matter of Race 132
Follow-Up Visits and Communication 133
Seeking Relatives 139
Removals 140
Abuse and Tragedies 142
Runaways and Returns 146
Happy Endings 149
Chapter Nine: Partners in Placements 153
Passing the Torch 153
Renewed Collaboration 158
The End of an Era 159

Appendix A: Superintendents of the NYJA and The Children's Village 167
Appendix B: Presidents of the NYJA and The Children's Village 169
Appendix C: Directors of the NYJA and The Children's Village 171
Appendix D: Matrons of the NYJA, The Children's Village, and the House of Reception 177
Appendix E: County Agents of the NYJA 189
Appendix F: Civil War Service Roster 191
Appendix G: Spanish-American War Roster 201
Appendix H: Admission Percentage Table 203
Appendix I: Nativity of Children in Foreign Countries Table 205
Appendix J: Nativity of Children in USA Table 209
Appendix K: Whether Parents Are Living Table 213
Appendix L: Records of the NYJA and The Children's Village 215
Appendix M: Bibliography 217
Notes 219
Index 235
About the Author 247
Other Works by the Author 249

Preface

My objective in writing this book was twofold. I wanted to present a general history of the New York Juvenile Asylum, from its beginning through the end of its participation in America's orphan train movement, and a compendium of source material on the Asylum's orphan train children. The book is written from the perspective of a historian with a personal connection to both the institution and the movement.

The journey that led me to writing this book began many hundreds of miles away from New York—on my family's farm in Milton, Wisconsin. I was in my late teens when I complained to my paternal aunt, Mildred (Kidder) Yahnke, about being bored one day. It must have been during the winter months as we always had plenty to do on our farm during the other seasons. Mildred was a retired rural school superintendent, so creating an assignment for me came easily for her.

I heeded her advice and began interviewing my paternal grandparents, Earl and Emily Kidder, who were in their eighties and shared our farmhouse with us. Grandfather Earl was a natural storyteller, so I was able to obtain a wealth of information from him on my Kidder lineage. The Kidders settled in Fulton, Wisconsin in 1846.

My grandmother Emily's lineage was quite another story. I learned she was born Emily Reese on March 28, 1892 in Brooklyn, New York, and that she and her older brother, Richard, were placed in an orphan asylum when they were very young. I later learned the name of the institution was the Home for Destitute Children at 217 Sterling Place in Brooklyn.

Grandmother lamented the fact that her brother Richard was adopted by "a rich family" during their stay at the Home and she never saw him again. She wasn't so lucky, as she was not adopted, and remained in the Home for many years until she eventually, as we now call it, "aged out" of the system. "They kick you out when you turn thirteen," she proclaimed, and proceeded to tell me about how she was sent west on a train, accompanied by a minister named Reverend Mr. Herman D. Clarke. "He placed children in homes," she said, and explained how she was placed in several homes after being brought west. She took a nursing course in Chamberlain, South Dakota before her marriage to my grandfather in 1912, which lasted an incredible seventy-four years.

My grandmother was able to provide me with the names of her parents and all of her siblings, but that was about all. She briefly reconnected with several siblings in the 1920s, but all of them had long since passed away. It would require a great deal of sleuth work to find out the details of her lineage.

Grandmother passed away in 1986 at age ninety-four, and I continued my search. I read an article about a new organization called the Orphan Train Heritage Society of America and how its members were gathering information on all of the estimated two hundred thousand orphan children sent west from New York City and Boston, Massachusetts on what they were now calling "orphan trains." It immediately occurred to me that my grandmother Emily could have been one of these children they were dubbing "orphan train riders."

As luck would have it, my aunt Mildred was approached by a woman in our hometown who asked

Mildred to pay her a visit as she had some old record books that contained the name of Midred's mother, Emily. The books turned out to be the journals and scrapbooks kept by Reverend Mr. Herman D. Clarke—the minister who brought my grandmother out on the train from New York. Mildred, aware of my interest in the family tree, told me about her discovery immediately.

Reverend Mr. Clarke kept in touch with my grandparents for many years, and even had their wedding photo glued in one of his scrapbooks. He recorded my grandmother's file number and case history as well. I learned that Reverend Mr. Clarke was employed by the New York Children's Aid Society. The Society didn't operate a brick and mortar orphan asylum, but instead facilitated the placement of children in private homes who had been obtained from various orphan asylums and lodging houses in New York City and other asylums in New York state.

One of the siblings my grandmother spoke of was a brother named Clarence Reese. I found Clarence on the 1880 federal census in New York, age eleven, listed as a "pupil" at an institution called the New York Juvenile Asylum. This was the first I'd heard of the New York Juvenile Asylum. Fortunately, many of the old records of the Asylum survived, so I hired a researcher to send me copies of the admission and discharge records for Clarence. They revealed that Clarence was admitted to the Asylum by his parents for "disobedience."

After several years of research I published a book about my grandmother's life, titled *Emily's Story: The Brave Journey of an Orphan Train Rider* (2001), which in turn was the basis for a documentary I co-wrote/produced in conjunction with Iowa Public Television titled *West by Orphan Train* (2014). My interest in America's orphan train movement deepened, and I began speaking throughout the Midwest on the subject, both independently and as a member of the Wisconsin Humanities Council Speakers Bureau. I always meant to delve deeper into the history of the New York Juvenile Asylum but didn't have time until recently, when I was finally able to turn my attention to it.

Due to my job, I was unable to spend long periods in New York to do the research in person. I decided to take it upon myself, at considerable expense, to hire a number of Columbia University students to scan the vast majority of the original records of the New York Juvenile Asylum, which are held at the University's Butler Library.

As I perused the records I was surprised to find that another of my grandmother's brothers, Lewis Reese, was also placed in the Juvenile Asylum for disobedience. Like the New York Children's Aid Society that sent my grandmother west on an orphan train, the Asylum sent children west in much the same manner. The most notable difference was that the Asylum indentured its children to learn a trade.

Many of the orphan train riders took on the last name of their foster parents without being legally adopted. As a result, descendants have no idea what the surname of their ancestor was originally before being sent west. The importance of family medical histories also makes it increasingly imperative to ascertain the correct lineage. It is my hope that this set of books will assist those in search of their roots to connect with long lost family members, and finally be able to add that missing branch to their family tree.

Acknowledgments

I owe very special thanks to the many librarians and archivists who so graciously and efficiently assisted me with a vast array of requests. I am, indeed, indebted to their professions at large. I would also like to extend my gratitude to various genealogical societies in Illinois, including the Stephenson County Genealogical Society, Tazewell County Genealogical and Historical Society, Iroquois County Genealogical Society, Bond County Genealogical Society, Champaign County Historical Archives, and Will County Historical Museum. I will be forever grateful to the officials at The Children's Village who made the decision to donate its original records to Columbia University's Rare Book and Manuscript Library (Butler Library). This book (especially the volumes dealing with the orphan trains) would not have been possible without the research assistance of the following Columbia University students: Xavier Dade, Ashley Brown, Bernadette Bridges, Jillian Carroll, Ivana Moore, and Suzen Fylke. I would also like to recognize the Danville (Illinois) Public Library staff for their assistance with records relating to Reverend Mr. Enoch Kingsbury.

Abbreviations

AICP: Association for Improving the Condition of the Poor
CAS: Children's Aid Society
ICHAS: Illinois Children's Home and Aid Society
NYJA: New York Juvenile Asylum
NYSPCC: New York Society for the Prevention of Cruelty to Children

Introduction

In the late 1840s, a crisis involving children began to unfold on the streets of New York City. Immigrants were pouring into the city at the rate of one thousand per day in this period, primarily from Germany and Ireland.[1] Abandoned babies were being found on doorsteps, in vestibules, even in ashcans and vacant lots. For those still alive, the only refuge was the almshouse. Few survived there.

At the time the city's population was about five hundred thousand, and the police estimated that ten thousand boys and girls were living on the streets.[2] In 1849, New York City's chief of police, George Washington Matsell, sounded an alarm about the "constantly increasing number of vagrant, idle and vicious children of both sexes, who infest our public thoroughfares, hotels and docks." His numbers were far more conservative than those of social reformers, who commonly put the number of vagrant children at up to thirty or forty thousand.[3]

Although orphan asylums were not unknown in colonial America, they were few and far between. The sheer numbers of displaced children in New York City and other large eastern cities necessitated the building of more and more institutions to warehouse the children. One of the first was the New York House of Refuge, built in 1825.[4] Other institutions were known by names such as Almshouse, Workhouse, and Poorhouse.

These places were far from humane in their treatment of children and provided appalling living conditions. A New York State commission noted: "The great mass of poor houses are most disgraceful memorials of the public charity. Common domestic animals are usually more humanely provided for than the paupers in some of these institutions."[5] Eventually, private orphan asylums such as the New York Juvenile Asylum were built to house the children as officials began to comprehend the scope of the inhumane conditions in the poorhouses and similar institutions.

During the period following the Civil War the population of the United States grew rapidly, and the problems of juvenile reform became greater and more dynamic.

In 1865 the New York State Legislature enacted a bill to control the "disorderly child." The act provided that, upon complaint of a parent or guardian, a magistrate or justice of the peace could issue a warrant to apprehend an offender. The court was required to commit a child found to be disorderly to the House of Refuge. Though the Disorderly Child Act hinged on parental complaint, it represented a move away from parental authority. Under the Act, a child did not need to have committed a crime— disorderly conduct was sufficient justification for placement.[6]

The problem of unsupervised children only worsened with the advent of the industrial age. Thousands of people moved from rural areas into New York City to obtain work at one of the many new factories. The huge number of job applicants allowed factory owners to pay them a mere pittance for their labor. Labor unions were nonexistent. There was a housing shortage due to the influx of thousands of immigrants competing with farmers for the factory jobs, allowing landlords to demand high rent for places that were barely habitable. Even in families where the mother, father, and several children were working, there was still not enough money to subsist. Children as young as five or six would often labor long hours and receive just pennies a day.

Starting in the 1880s, immigrants from Italy and Eastern Europe began to dominate New York's cultural landscape. With poor parents working long hours, children had more opportunities to get into mischief on the city streets. Few parents could count on a structure of extended families as there was back in the mother country. Thousands lived in familial isolation, unable to rely on a grandparent, or an aunt or uncle, to help care for their young children.

When mothers went to work in factories, many would leave their children locked in rooms all day or free to roam the streets. Some of these children prostituted themselves. Others shined shoes, peddled newspapers, sold matches, ran errands, or scoured the streets for wood chips and rags to sell.

By 1890, day nurseries were established throughout the city, but poorer families could not afford to take advantage of them. A family's survival depended entirely on the ability of the parents to stay healthy and maintain a steady income. This fact was especially true of families living in the inner city, without the resources that an extended family might have otherwise provided. Diseases such as tuberculosis, smallpox, yellow fever, typhus, and measles were rampant and spread easily in the overcrowded tenement buildings where several families often shared a single apartment. It was not uncommon for poultry and livestock to inhabit the same quarters with families, increasing health risks.

Part I: The New York Juvenile Asylum

Part 1 of this book covers the history of the New York Juvenile Asylum from its incorporation in 1851 through the early 1920s, explaining why and how it evolved, like similar New York City institutions, from the typical congregate-style facility of the day into a modern cottage plan, which almost always coincided with moving operations to a rural area outside New York City.

Chapter One, "History of the New York Juvenile Asylum" begins with the early history of the NYJA and describes the functions of the Asylum's House of Reception, as well as the several moves that took place for the Asylum proper and the separate House of Reception. In September 1854 the Asylum partnered with the Children's Aid Society to send what would be America's first orphan train to Dowagiac, Michigan. The Asylum made the move from its congregate-style facility in New York City to a new cottage plan in Dobbs Ferry, Westchester County, New York, in 1905. The new location later became known as The Children's Village—the name it still operates under to this day

Chapter Two, "NYJA Procedures" chronicles the day to day operating procedures of the Asylum, including the admission and discharge of children, and the reasons for doing so. Many children were sent to the Asylum by the Society for the Prevention of Cruelty to Children after it was founded in 1875. A special Children's Court was established in New York City in 1902, and was responsible for the commitment of many children to the NYJA. The Asylum indentured children to tradesmen and families in a system fashioned after the New York House of Refuge, which dated to 1825. Applicants for children were to provide several character references from such people as a minister, justice of peace, or superintendent of schools. At the termination of the indenture the child was to receive a single payment of cash, some new clothes, and a new bible.

Chapter Three, "The Children of the NYJA" describes the children themselves and how immigration and integration affected the children housed in the Asylum. Children were allowed visitors on a given day each month, under close supervision. The Asylum contended with both attempted and successful (some very dramatic) escapes from its very beginning. The ramifications of placing more hardened offenders in the same Asylum as children who were simply destitute or truant is explained in this chapter. Several hundred of the Asylum's boys answered Lincoln's call to arms and in the Civil War. Some of them perished during the conflict—others lived to tell their stories of heroism.

Chapter Four, "Life in the Asylum" covers the day to day lives of the NYJA children in Washington Heights, including their education, an example of lesson plans, and the high regard the children often had for their teachers. The children were employed at the Asylum and made thousands of articles of shoes and other clothing during their average two-year stay. Some were employed in the garden, which produced large quantities of produce to be consumed by the children throughout the year. Discipline was essential in maintaining order in the Asylum, and varied in method and severity over the decades. Solitary confinement and a dungeon featured prominently in the early years. Later, prolonged marching became the norm. It was not all work and no play for the kiddies. A large yard allowed for ample room for playtime, including a "Girl's Croquet-Ground." A large gymnasium was built in later years. The Asylum sported its own band, which participated in parades and events throughout the city and surrounding communities.

Chapter Five, "Life in The Children's Village" covers the day to day lives of the children who lived in The Children's Village after the Asylum moved operations to Dobbs Ferry in Westchester County, New York, including their education. The Children's Village implemented Intelligence Quotient Testing, which became popular in America in 1912. The children aided in building many new cottages at the new location, utilizing lumber sawn from trees harvested on the property. An athletic field provided ample space for baseball games, which consisted of teams formed at each cottage. Tournaments were held amongst teams from the various cottages and from surrounding communities, and even other New York institutions. A special visit from a *New York Times* reporter declared "The Children's Village" a "Beautiful title" in an article written in 1908 after his visit to Dobbs Ferry. He describes his interaction with the children, and walk around the property—during which he would have encountered a flock of sheep tended to by one or two Asylum boys. The chapter concludes with a visit and special message from the President Taft.

Orphan Train Movement

Almost as soon as the orphan asylums sprang up, they became as overcrowded as the tenements and streets from whence the children came. A plan to reduce the numbers of children on the streets and in the asylums gave birth to America's orphan train movement.

Part II of this book chronicles the role the New York Juvenile Asylum played in the movement, including the Asylum's inaugural experience, which involved supplying funds and the majority of children for America's very first company of orphan train children sent west.

It is estimated that about 6,620 children were sent west from the NYJA between September 1854 and circa 1922, placing it in the top four (based on the number of children sent) of institutions known to have taken part in the movement. The others, in order of numbers sent, were the New York Children's Aid Society, the New York Foundling Asylum (also called New York Foundling Hospital), and the New England Home for Little Wanderers of Boston, Massachusetts.

Chapter Six, "History of the Orphan Trains" covers the history of the NYJA's orphan trains. The Asylum was approached by Reverend Enoch Kingsbury of Danville, Illinois in 1855 and asked to allow him to take what would be several hundred children west to indenture them to farmers in and around Danville. The Asylum later cut ties with Kingsbury, but continued sending children west for over six more decades. A permanent Western indenturing agent was employed to help facilitate indentures of the children in Illinois, and a Western Agency house purchased in the state for the agent to reside in. A special Act of the Illinois Legislature was voted into law in 1861 and officially recognized the indentures of the NYJA as a legal document. By 1898 the Asylum began placing the majority of their children in the state of Iowa.

Chapter Seven, "All Aboard the Orphan Train!" describes the preparations for the journey west, the procedures for notifying the parents and guardians, and obtaining proper permissions. Reason for the commitment of the children sent west on orphan trains is covered. Special words of encouragement were given to the children by directors of the Asylum and prominent members of the community. Songs were sung just prior to leaving and during the journey west. The journey itself and the arrival of the children at western destinations are outlined in detail. The only surviving application for a child by a farmer in Illinois is shown.

Chapter Eight, "Challenges and Successes" chronicles the challenges and successes of the orphan trains of the NYJA, including placements, removals, race, religion, abuse and tragedies, runaways, and happy endings. Prejudices against the children sent out from New York became an issue as the years went by. Motives for taking in a child were not always good. Catholics and Protestants sparred with each other over the fact that Catholic children were placed in Protestant homes and vice versa, which culminated in Catholic priests spiriting away several children from a distribution in Peru, Illinois before they could be placed in homes. Some children were abused—others did the abusing. Many ran away, worked for a neighbor, joined the circus, or returned to New York. Siblings and families were separated from each other and later placed ads in newspapers looking for their lost kin.

Chapter Nine, "Partners in Placements" explains why the NYJA stopped indenturing children out of its Western Agency and partnered with other organizations to take children for the purpose of placing out instead. The Illinois Children's Home and Aid Society began handling all western placements for the Asylum in 1903. In 1908 the Asylum renewed its collaboration with the Children's Aid Society of New York, which would send the last of the Asylum's children west. Changing attitudes on how to best care for needy children, as well was laws passed by several western states prohibiting children from being placed within their borders, or requiring large bonds to be posted before doing so, eventually led to the end of America's orphan train movement.

Records of the Children

Sadly, not all records for the NYJA have survived. Perhaps the greatest loss is the numerous bound volumes containing thousands of letters and accompanying photos sent to the Asylum from the children and their foster parents out west.[7] The volumes of records that have survived are substantial, however, and provided valuable information for the compilation of this series. In most cases a number of different ledgers had to be consulted, and the information combined, to form the complete record of each orphan train rider.

Subsequent volumes of this set include a comprehensive list of thousands of the children known to have been sent west from the NYJA. Over three hundred companies are documented, listing the date sent, where to (for most), and the names and addresses of all known foster parents to whom the children were indentured to or placed with in Illinois and other midwestern states. This is the most complete list of orphan train riders from any one institution that has ever been compiled.

There are undoubtedly many lessons to be learned by studying the individual lives of the children who took part in America's orphan train movement. Though most of the stories of the individual children have been lost in the attic of history, this book manages to rescue many of them through the use of the Asylum's surviving records and its annual reports. Magazine accounts have also been utilized to unearth new information to tell the story of the NYJA, the children it housed, and those sent west on the orphan trains.

Through trial and error, the orphan train movement evolved into today's modern foster care system, which is still evolving. At a program I once presented about the orphan trains in Chicago, I was told by a social worker that even today the average child is placed in as many as six or seven homes before a "good fit" is found. It brings to mind the old saying, "The more things change, the more they stay the same." It is my fondest wish that this book, even in the smallest way, may assist today's foster care workers striving to find that "good fit" for a child in their care.

PART I
The New York Juvenile Asylum

CHAPTER ONE

History of the New York Juvenile Asylum

An Institution is Born

Responding to the sheer extent of poverty that became evident in the financial Panic of 1837,[1] a group of prominent Protestant New York City businessmen and professionals organized the Association for Improving the Condition of the Poor (hereafter, AICP) in 1843. It was subsequently incorporated in 1848 to coordinate family visiting, collect funds, and distribute them for the relief of the poor.[2]

Members of the Association believed these services could alleviate the basic causes of poverty. The AICP Home Visitors' Manual advised its volunteers,

> You will become an important instrument of good to your suffering fellow creatures, when you aid them to obtain this good from resources within themselves. To effect this, show them the true origin of their sufferings, when these sufferings are the result of improvidence, extravagance, idleness, intemperance, or other moral causes which are within their own control; and endeavor, by all appropriate means, to awaken their self-respect to direct their exertions, and to strengthen their capacities for self-support.[3]

At the time, punishment for adolescents was often indiscernible from that of adults. In the New York City penitentiary, children convicted of the most serious crimes were incarcerated alongside

Boys in their cell at the Tombs (prison) in New York City. (*Harpers Weekly, 1870/Drawing by Julian Scott*)

much older, more hardened criminals. As late as 1851, there were still four thousand inmates under the age of twenty-one years in New York's adult prisons. Eight hundred were fourteen or younger, and 176 were under ten years old.[4]

Motivation for the establishment of a new juvenile asylum came in the form of a semi-annual report to Mayor Woodhull by Chief of Police George Washington Matsell, in October 1849 which described a "deplorable and growing evil":

> I allude to the constantly increasing numbers of vagrant, idle and vicious children of both sexes, who infest our public thoroughfares, hotels, docks, etc. Children are growing up in ignorance and profligacy, only destined

to a life of misery, shame and crime, and ultimately to a felon's doom. Their numbers are almost incredible, and to those whose business and habits do not permit them a searching scrutiny, the degrading and disgusting practices of these almost infants in the schools of vice, prostitution and rowdyism, would certainly be beyond belief. The offspring of always careless, generally intemperate, and often times immoral and dishonest parents, they never see the inside of a schoolroom.[5]

New Yorkers were also horrified by a Grand Jury report on serious crimes. "Of the higher grades of felony, four-fifths of the complaints examined have been against minors. And two-thirds of all complaints acted on during the term have been against persons between the ages of 19 and 21."[6]

On October 8, 1849, Benjamin F. Butler, Robert Milham Hartley, Luther Bradish, Joseph B. Collins, Apollos R. Wetmore, Thomas Denny, and Frederick S. Winston met to consider the establishment of an institution to provide moral training and character-building for the growing population of homeless and destitute children in the city.[7] They were also motivated by the need to establish a corrective institution as an alternative to the New York House of Refuge, which was a more punitive institution for young criminals.

In November 1849, Dr. John D. Russ, corresponding secretary of the Prison Association, and Solomon Jenner, of the Society of Friends, announced their intention of securing a charter for a juvenile asylum.[8] On March 1, 1850, after the failure of the first application to the Legislature for a charter to establish the asylum, the Association of Ladies for an Asylum, with thirty managers and seventeen boys, opened a facility at 109 Bank Street. Here, they "continued to labor with marked success, in this inviting field of philanthropic effort, under the appellation of the 'Asylum for Friendless Boys.'"[9] On November 14, the directors organized and elected officers.

Early Years

Senator Beekman reintroduced the bill to incorporate the asylum in Albany on February 11, 1851.[10] The New York Juvenile Asylum (hereafter, NYJA) was subsequently incorporated by an act of the Legislature:

> AN ACT to incorporate the New York Juvenile Asylum. Passed June 30, 1851, three-fifths being present.
>
> The People of the State of New York, represented in Senate and Assembly, do enact as follows:
>
> Section 1. Robert B. Minturn, Myndert Van Schaick, Robert M. Stratton, Solomon Jenner, Albert Gilbert, Stewart Brown, Francis R. Tillon, David S. Kennedy, Joseph B. Collins, Benjamin F. Butler, Isaac T. Hopper, Charles Partridge, Luther Bradish, Christopher Y. Wemple, Charles O'Conor, John D. Russ, John Duer, Peter Cooper, Apollos R. Wetmore, Frederick S. Winston, James Kelly, Silas C. Herring, Rensselaer N. Havens, John W. Edmonds, and their associates, are hereby constituted a body corporate, by the name of "New York Juvenile Asylum."[11]

The legislators reported, "This provides for the safe keeping of such neglected or destitute children of that City by law or by the voluntary act of parents as are committed to them. It received a unanimous vote."[12] Asylum officials added:

> It should ever be borne in mind that our Institution is intended to be preventive, as well as reformatory, in its character; that we design simply to withdraw those who have been surrounded by vicious and degrading associations, from the contamination to which they were exposed—to eradicate evil tendencies, and to surround them with such circumstances as may elevate and ennoble them.[13]

Luther Bradish. He served as the first president of the NYJA. (*Library of Congress/Luther Bradish. [Between 1855 and 1865] photograph. https://www.loc.gov/item/2017896763/*)

Luther Bradish, lieutenant governor of New York from 1839 to 1842, was the first president of the NYJA. Benjamin F. Butler and Peter Cooper served as vice presidents. John D. Russ served as secretary, and Frederick H. Wolcott as treasurer.[14]

Volunteers collected a "subscription fund" of fifty thousand dollars as of January 1, 1853.[15] The City of New York contributed another fifty thousand and agreed to pay forty dollars per year for each child committed to the institution "from the city's streets and slums."[16]

The NYJA was almost immediately established in the rented building already in use at 109 Bank Street in lower Manhattan. A House of Reception was opened there on January 10, 1853, "succeeding to the property and work of the Association of Ladies for an Asylum, which association had been in existence three years." Fifty-seven children were received into the new Asylum by transfer on that opening day.[17]

The Asylum's leadership established standing committees composed of three members each to cover finances, supplies, indenturing, correspondence, visiting, instruction, employments, buildings and repairs, and applications.[18]

Efforts were soon underway to "obtain, within the county, a suitable building for a temporary Asylum, and an eligible site for a permanent Institution."[19] The search was successful, and on April 25, 1853 the Asylum, with some two hundred children, was moved to a new location at the foot of East Fifty-fifth Street, above the Shot Tower, near the East River.[20]

By the end of the year, Asylum officials reported that only eighteen of the 623 children received were able to "read, write and cipher." In the Eleventh Ward, where the majority of the city's immigrants resided, the numbers of unschooled youth were staggering. A study conducted in the ward during the prior year found that seven thousand out of a total of twelve thousand children between the ages of five and fifteen did not attend school.[21] Conditions slowly changed over the next fifty years, and by 1902, the Asylum was reporting that 690 of 861 of children received could read, write and cipher.[22]

Chief of Police George Washington Matsell, who previously sounded the alarm about vagrant children in the streets of New York, granted the Asylum "a platoon of officers, and informed Asylum officials that they were clearing the streets of these children."[23]

In 1854 Apollos R. Wetmore began his tenure as president of the NYJA—a position he held until his death in 1881.

Wetmore was born in Huntington, Long Island on November 11, 1796.[24] His father, Noah Wetmore, was Superintendent of the New York Hospital for about thirty years.[25] After attending Columbia College for a few years, in 1819 Apollos went into business with his brother, David, opening a hardware and iron store on the corner of Canal and Hudson Streets.[26] Apollos married Mary Carmer on April 30, 1822. They had six children.[27] In the revival of 1831 he became a member of Dr. Cox's Presbyterian

Apollos Russell Wetmore, an original founder of the NYJA who served as its president for nearly thirty years. (*NYJA Annual Report, 1880*)

church on Laight Street, and soon joined the City Tract Society "for the distribution of religious truth among the neglected, and personal efforts for the conversion of individuals." He became a visitor in a district of about one hundred families where he supplied the destitute with Bibles.[28]

Wetmore was an ardent supporter of the NYJA and raised a large amount of money for its establishment and operation. On one occasion, while soliciting a donation from a prominent citizen, he was met with the response, "I should think you would find it disagreeable business to beg and be refused." Wetmore replied, "It is my Master that is refused, not I. I am only his agent." The gentleman gave him his check for the desired amount.[29] Wetmore's good nature undoubtedly played a factor in his philanthropic success. It was said he "spent his life in making people laugh."[30]

Wetmore visited the Asylum at least 348 times in addition to his weekly and monthly attendance in meetings at the House of Reception.[31]

In 1853, responding to pressure from AICP leaders, the New York State Legislature passed a law providing for the arrest and detention of vagrant children.[32] Many children arrested under the new law were sent to the NYJA. At that time the Asylum was reporting that 18 percent of the children admitted were orphans, 50 percent were natives of Ireland, and 56 percent were illiterate.[33]

Once again, the Asylum quickly outgrew its quarters. Finding themselves in cramped quarters in an old building, Asylum officials declared in 1854:

> In the present condition of our House, it has been an object of primary importance to get a situation for every child that was thought competent to fill one.
>
> Effort has, therefore, been made to provide them with homes as early as may be, in the country. For this purpose we have *advertised repeatedly* [emphasis added] and directed and sent circulars all over our own and the neighboring States: and we would invite all those who need active and intelligent boys or girls, between the ages of seven and fourteen, to make application, and we have no doubt but we shall be able to supply the demand. Whatever may be the future policy of the Institution in regard to this subject, while it remains in its present location, there can be no doubt about the course necessary now to be pursued.[34]

Asylum officials added, "The propriety of such a measure, under different circumstances, might admit of a doubt by some, but when the alternative is, the streets of New-York or a good place in the country, there is no room for hesitation."[35]

America's First Orphan Train

One of the parties who read the Asylum's advertisement in 1854 was Charles Loring Brace, founder of the Children's Aid Society (hereafter, CAS), which had just been established in New York City 1853.[36] The NYJA entered into an arrangement with the CAS "to send an agent to the West with such children as the Asylum and the Society might furnish at their mutual cost."[37]

Before embarking for Dowagiac, Michigan on Wednesday evening, September 20, 1854, CAS officials stopped by the NYJA and "thirty-one boys and six girls were intrusted to the care of E. H. [E. P.] Smith, Esq.," who was at that time an assistant secretary of the CAS, for what was then very much an experimental program.[38] It would become known as "placing-out" (later called "free-home placing out", and collectively known as orphan trains). While perusing the early records of the Asylum, this writer came across the names and ages of the children sent west on this very first orphan train.[39]

> John Bennett, age 9
> Christina Calla, age 10
> George Duncan, age 9
> Thomas Early, age 11
> John Fitzgerald, age 11
> Michael Gillan, age 14
> Bridget Gilmartin, age 12
> John Gray, age 10
> Anna M. Honey, age 7
> Frederick Johnson, age 9
> James Kelly, age 11
> Henry Knight, age 9
> Michael Larkin, age 10
> Eugene Leake, age 12
> Hannah Long, age 7
> Michael Martin, age 10
> Caleb McColen, age 10
> Mary Ann McLaughlin, age 8
> Mary McLaughlin, age 11
> Thomas McQuinn, age 10
> James Meagher, age 12
> William Morris, age 13
> Edward Murphy, age 14
> Isaac E. Munger, age 14
> George F. Pointon, age 10
> Patrick Philip Punch, age 10
> William H. Rathbun, age 15
> Edward Smith, age 10
> James Smith, age 10
> John Smith, age 11
> John Sneider, age 9
> William Trump/Trumpp, age 12
> George Walker, age 12
> Thomas Walker, age 8
> Nathaniel J. Williams, age 10

There was a single placement of a twelve-year-old girl named Rosina Flara that may have been part of the Dowagiac, Michigan company above and just placed later—perhaps by Reverend Mr. Charles Collins Townsend of Iowa City, Iowa who took other children to Iowa with him from the Dowagiac company.

Forty-six boys and girls were sent to Dowagiac. The ages of those from the Asylum were seven to fifteen, with most ten to twelve.[40] The company (group) of children and their adult escorts departed New York on the steamship *Isaac Newton* with emigrant tickets for Detroit.[41] They were accompanied by a CAS agent named Reverend Mr. E. P. [Edward Parmelee] Smith, who was undoubtedly referring to the children from the Asylum when he said, "The majority of them orphans, dressed in *uniform* [emphasis added]—as bright sharp, bold, racy a crowd of little fellows as can be grown nowhere out of the streets of New York," adding, "The other ten were from New York at large—no number or street in particular."[42] Smith later recalled the trip:

You can hardly imagine the delight of the children as they looked, many of them for the first time, upon country scenery. Each one must see everything we passed, find its name, and make his own comments: 'What's that, mister?' 'A cornfield.' 'Oh, yes, them's what makes buckwheaters.' 'Look at them cows (oxen plowing); my mother used to milk cows.' As we whirled through orchards loaded with large, red apples, their enthusiasm rose to the highest pitch. It was difficult to keep them within doors. Arms stretched out, hats swinging, eyes swimming, mouths watering, and all screaming—'oh! oh! just look at 'em! Mister, be they any sich in Michigan? Then I'm in for that place—three cheers for Michigan!' We had been riding in comparative quiet for

Edward Parmelee Smith. Smith was an agent for the New York Children's Aid Society and escorted the first company of children sent West, in September 1854. (*Image courtesy of the Trustees of Reservations, Fruitlands Museum*)

nearly an hour, when all at once the greatest excitement broke out. We were passing a cornfield spread over with ripe, yellow pumpkins. 'Oh! yonder! look! Just look at 'em!' and in an instant the same exclamation was echoed from forty-seven mouths. 'Jist look at 'em! What a heap of mushmillons!' 'Mister, do they make mushmillons in Michigan?' 'Ah, fellers, aint that the country tho'—won't we have nice things to eat?' 'Yes; and won't we sell some, too?' 'Hip! hip! boys; three cheers for Michigan!'[43]

NYJA officials deemed the venture a success: "Smith, in less than a fortnight, succeeded in finding homes for not only those that he took from our Asylum, but for those belonging to the Aid Society; scattering them some in Michigan, some in Indiana, some in Illinois, and others in Iowa." Brace came to a similar conclusion: "On the whole, the first experiment of sending children West is a very happy one, and I am sure there are places enough with good families in Michigan, Illinois, Iowa, and Wisconsin, to give every poor boy and girl in New York a permanent home. The only difficulty is to bring the children to the homes."[44]

The CAS reported taking a total of forty-two children from the NYJA by the end of 1854.[45] The final destination for the five children who did not go to Dowagiac, Michigan is not known.

In the following May the NYJA sent a small company of eight children to Andover, Ashtabula County, Ohio. It is not known why they were sent to that particular location or if the company was again sent in conjunction with the CAS, with an individual, or with another organization. A large orphan asylum was in operation in Andover at the time and may have been involved in some way; however, no subsequent companies of children were sent to Andover from the NYJA. The Asylum also sent several large companies of children to Maryland in the fall of 1855.[46]

The history of the NYJA's orphan trains is chronicled in Part Two.

A New Home for the Asylum

The deteriorated condition of the frame building the Asylum was housed in was summed up by Census Marshal David B. Scott when he arrived to take the census at the Asylum on July 14, 1855: "no value—old & dilapidated."[47]

Asylum officials continued their search for an "eligible site for a permanent Asylum," which culminated in the purchase of twenty-three acres of land (later expanded to twenty-nine) at a cost of thirty-three thousand dollars in a semi-rural area of the city near High Bridge in Washington Heights, on 176th Street between Tenth and Eleventh Avenues.[48]

The plans for the new Gothic-inspired building were drawn by Thomas & Son, architects. The structure was built of blue granite (blue trap rock) mined on Manhattan Island, and officially opened for the reception of the Asylum children on April 2, 1856.[49]

The children were loaded into wagons to make the half-hour journey from the old location up to the new Asylum in Washington Heights. A little boy named Peter Haley, about eight years of age, was the first child to jump in the first wagon, and he thereafter boasted of being the first inmate in the new building.

Peter's story was a rather tragic one:

> He went out with his little sister one evening to play on the streets & staying so late that they were afraid to go home they laid down in an alley & fell asleep. When he awoke in the morning his little sister was gone. He went and told his mother and she at once commenced search for her, visiting all the institutions, advertising, & using every means for her discovery, but all without avail. At last worn out & broken hearted, she fell sick, was taken to the hospital & died. Peter now left alone in the world was taken to the Asylum, where he remained till he was 12 yrs. old & was then brought West in 1860, & bound to Mr. John Thompson of Vandalia [Illinois].[50]

The New York Juvenile Asylum, built in 1856, showing the "wide, well-groomed carriage road" in front. This engraving is likely the one the Asylum commissioned in early 1856 for the express purpose of inserting in each bible given to the children they sent west. (*NYJA Annual Report, 1868*/Lithograph by G. Schlegel, New York, New York)

The new building was a vast improvement over the prior one, which Asylum directors described as "dreary, comfortless, inconvenient and insecure as can well be imagined." However, the *Times* described the new building as being "somewhat too prison-like in appearance." The building was in the form of a T, with a front of 150 feet. The center was fifty feet in width by sixty-two feet in depth. The two wings were each seventy-five feet in length and forty-six in width, and a central extension in back from the center of the building was eighty-two feet deep and forty-three feet in width. A brick wall enclosed playgrounds for both sexes.[51]

A description of the building and grounds in 1870 also made reference to a prior prison-like appearance: "The twenty acres about their pleasant home, barren and bleak enough twelve years ago, are made fertile and beautiful. Rocks have been blasted away, and the flower-beds put in their place; trees have been planted, and the gray lintels and cornices of the stone-buildings tinted, so as to do away with the old prison look."[52]

The location was described as "one of the finest on the Island, commanding a view of the Hudson River and Palisades for many miles, Harlem River and Long Island Sound, and the whole country for miles around."[53]

The new building accommodated one thousand children, but the Asylum's chronic problem of overcrowding did not go away for very long.[54] On October 6, 1859, Asylum officials wrote letters to the Leake & Watts Orphan Asylum and the New York Orphan Asylum, asking them to take some of the NYJA children. Leake & Watts subsequently selected only nine of the forty children presented to them for consideration.[55] By October 25, efforts were being ramped up to cull the population of the Asylum: "The Chairman wrote to Supt. [of the] Asylum directing him to consummate arrangements with Messrs. Pell of the N. Y. Orphan Asylum and Guest of the Leake & Watts Orphan House for the transfer of all children

Chapter One

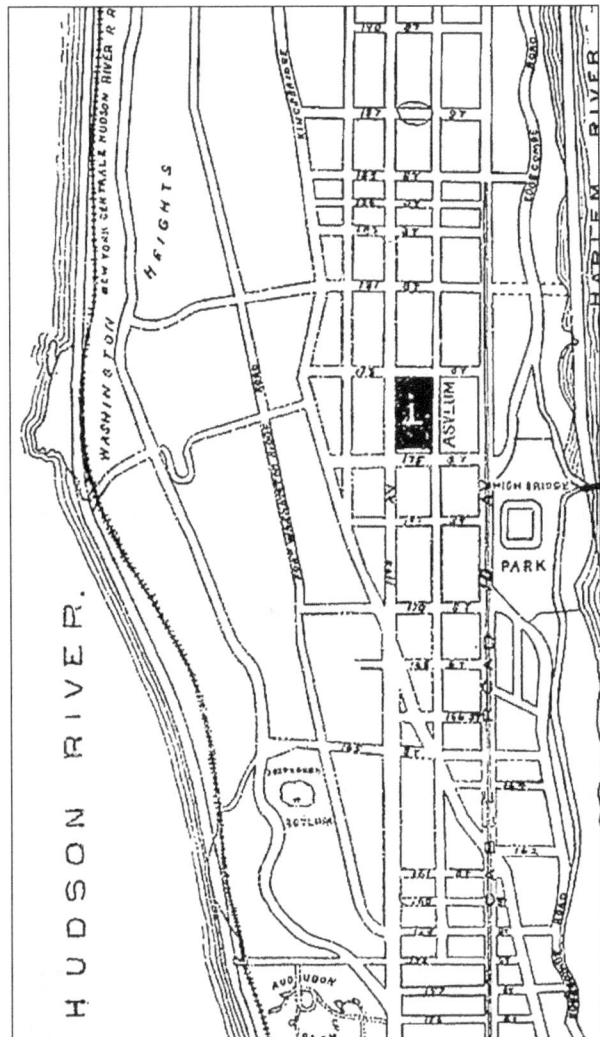

Map showing the location of the Asylum in Washington Heights. (*NYJA Annual Report, 1900*)

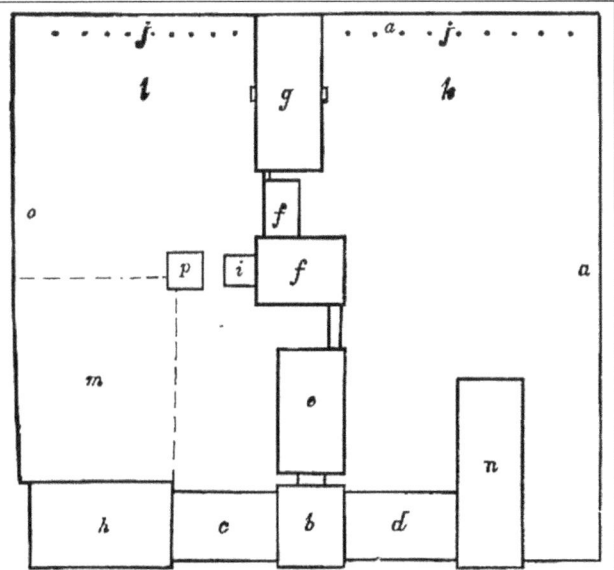

Plan of buildings at the NYJA. See key for each letter below. (*NYJA Annual Report, 1900*)

that they can receive, and to send such children to the H. R. [House of Reception]."⁵⁶

Apparently, the overcrowding situation improved as reflected in the minutes of May 31, 1860: "Resolved that no children be sent out of this Institution to any place except upon Indenture."⁵⁷

The transfer of children between institutions was somewhat in flux as surviving records reveal that the NYJA was often asked to take in a child or siblings from other New York City institutions as well. Many were received from the American Female Guardian Society and Home for the Friendless, with a few coming from the Brooklyn Industrial School Association.

An unidentified institution sent the Asylum's Superintendent a letter in 1870 requesting as much:

NEW YORK, July 28, 1870.
DR. [Samuel D.] BROOKS:

DEAR SIR: —There is a boy under my care who needs stricter discipline than we can exercise in this Institution. What steps can I take to have him placed under your care? He is 10 or 11 years old, lies, swears, fights, and flings missiles at any one who attempts to control him. If you can manage to take him, if only for a short time (although I would like you to keep him altogether), I should be much relieved. Pray take him, if possible.⁵⁸

The largest number of children the NYJA received in one year was 1,160 in 1863, of whom 65 percent were "dependents." Overcrowding resulted in some children sleeping "3 or 4 in a bed."⁵⁹

a. Enclosure wall of brick, 400 ft. rear, 585 ft. deep, and 8 ft. high.

b. Centre front building, 50x60, containing Reception-rooms, Library, Officers and Teachers' Apartments, and Boys' Ward on fourth floor.

c. West wing, 45x75, containing Girls' Dining-room in the basement, Sewing-room and Teachers' Rooms on first floor, Girls' Ward on second and third floors.

d. East wing, 45x75, containing a Cellar, two Kitchens in the basement, Officers' Dining-room and Teachers' Rooms on first floor, and Boys' Wards on the second and third floors.

e. North wing, 44x83, containing the Boys' Dining-room in the basement, Assembly room on the first floor, and Boys' Wards on the second and third floors.

f. School building, 40x66, and wing, containing a Cellar, a Laundry and Bakery on first floor, four School-rooms, a Tailor-shop and Mending-room on the second floor and a four on the third.

g. Gymnasium building, 42x108, containing a Cellar, a Bath-room and Play-room on first floor, two School-rooms, a Tailor-shop and Mending-room on the second floor, and the Hospital and Shoe-shop on third floor.

h. Wetmore Hall, 60x94, containing the Girls' play-rooms and Bath-room in the basement, Kindergarden Class rooms and Teachers' Rooms on the first floor. Girls' School rooms and Ward on the second floor, and Chapel on the Third floor.

i. Officers' Laundry and Engine-room in basement.

j. Sheds in Boys' Yards, 200 and 150 feet long and 14 wide.

k. Boys' Play-ground, first division.

l. Boys' Play-ground, second division.

m. Girls' Yard.

n. House of Reception and Dormitories.

o. Retaining wall surmounted by an iron railing eight feet high.

p. Boiler-house.

The amount of acreage was sufficient for three playgrounds (for the boys' first and second divisions, and for the girls) as well as the establishment of a farm for growing produce and livestock. A steward was hired for this purpose: "He shall be the farmer, and have charge of all the implements and cattle, and all other necessary articles pertaining to the farm, and shall be responsible for the economical use and preservation of same." In addition, he was to "keep correct and methodical accounts of all the labor performed on the farm by the pupils of the Asylum."[60]

House of Reception

Before being officially admitted to the Asylum, children were processed through the Asylum's House of Reception. The functions of the House of Reception were explained in detail in the Asylum's 1855 annual report:

> The Charter provides that all children committed to this Corporation by Magistrates shall be detained in the House of Reception for ten days before a final commitment to the Asylum, unless previously discharged by the proper authority. Within these ten days, the parents or guardians, if to be found, are to be notified of the arrest of the child, and that they may appear and show cause for his discharge. Failing to do this, the law deprives them of all custody of the child, and transfers their rights to this Corporation, who thenceforth stand to him in loco parentis [in place of a parent].
>
> But the ten days or less, for which the child is in the House of Reception may be, and doubtless often is, the turning period of his life. Immediately on his delivery to the Su-

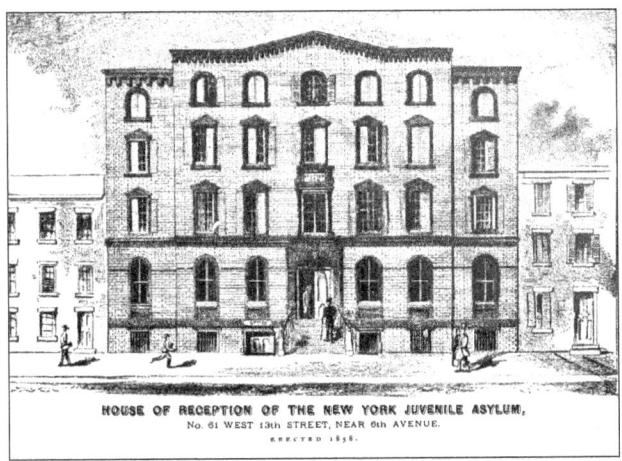

The Asylum moved its House of Reception from 23 West 13th Street to this building at 61 West 13th Street, near 6th Avenue, in 1859. (*NYJA Annual Report, 1883*)

perintendent, he is taken to the bathing room. All his clothes are removed; and if, as is frequently found to be the case, they are either worthless as garments, or are infested with vermin [lice], they are burned or otherwise disposed of. The child is thoroughly cleansed; is examined by the physician of the House; is furnished with new clothing suited to the season of the year; and is provided with ample and wholesome food. He is then examined as to his education, and is at once assigned to his proper place in the school. The idea, that, as he may be retained for but three or five days, or at the most, for ten days under our control, it is useless to attempt his improvement, is not admitted. However brief the period for which he may be under our influence, we mean, if it be possible, that an impression shall then be made upon him, of an elevating, improving and permanent character.

Moreover, it is not unfrequently necessary that children should be retained in the House of Reception for more than ten days, their cases requiring a somewhat necessarily protracted investigation. Others again are temporarily committed by their parents, for restraint and discipline. And others still, to be removed to the country, as soon as suitable homes can be found for them. Thus there are generally so many at the House, that the rules for its government are framed, as nearly as may be, as for a permanent family. The hours for rising, for daily ablutions, for worship, for meals, for school, for play, and on the Sabbath for Sunday school and religious services, are all fixed. The children are thus at once taught to do right things and at the right time. An examination of the statistics of the House will show more accurately what has here been accomplished of good.[61]

The House of Reception was also where meetings of the Asylum's committees and board were held.[62] In 1855 it was determined to be advantageous to establish a new House of Reception, but at a location separate from that of the Asylum proper. The board of directors leased a three-story brick building at 77 Grand Street for the purpose. It wasn't long before the building was found to be inadequate, and operations were moved to a rented building at 23 West Thirteenth Street on March 24, 1855.[63]

Early in 1859, it was again deemed necessary to move the House of Reception to a new location on the same street—at 61 West Thirteenth Street. An author visited the House of Reception in 1862 and described it as follows:

> Taste and refinement modify the necessary severity of its surroundings, and a pleasanter school-room and chapel combined is rarely to be met with even in this city of model school edifices. The green-washed walls and inside Venetian blinds of the same color are particularly grateful to any eyesight, but especially so to the little victims of sore or weak eyes, a disease [ophthalmia] apt to prevail for a time in all institutions for children. Pictures and large gaily-colored maps relieve the uniformity of the walls.
>
> Here the street children are not only re-

ceived, cleansed, and prepared for the asylum, but they are, after a sojourn there, and when it is decided to send a company of chosen ones to the West, again transmitted to the House of Reception in companies of forty or fifty, consisting of both sexes, and are marshalled, outfitted, and accompanied upon their journey of day and night travel by the indenturing clerk, who chooses each home with a view to the well-being of the child."[64]

The building could accommodate 130 children.[65] One of the children sent to this particular House of Reception was a little girl named Mary Ryan. In February 1860 Mary was arrested and charged for begging. She was taken before a magistrate at the Jefferson Market Police Court. A policeman entered the courtroom,

> leading by the hand a little girl, about ten years old. She was barefoot, had neither bonnet nor shawl, and the only garment upon her body was a faded calico dress, a world too large, which trailed on the floor about her feet. Even this was torn from the bottom upward half its length, and afforded no protection from the cold; on the contrary, it had dragged in mud and wet, and flapped about her tiny limbs till they were as wet and muddy as the streets themselves. This was her only covering on that frosty day, and the little sufferer was crying with the cold.

The magistrate "spoke kindly" to Mary, and ascertained that her father was a "drunken Irish laborer, and her mother a more drunken scold." They lived in a tenement house, "where they quarreled most of the time." The magistrate learned that the parents made Mary go out and beg, and if unsuccessful, they'd beat her when she returned home. The day before Mary's arrest it seems a "kind lady" that lived in a "big brick house" called Mary into the basement and "warmed her by the fire." The lady also fed Mary, and gave her "shoes and stockings, and a dress and a petticoat and a nice little bonnet, and a piece of money to take home." When Mary returned home later her father "took the two shillings and bought gin, and he and his wife and some of the neighbors got drunk."

When the gin was all gone they made Mary take all of the clothing the "kind lady" had given her to "one of the low grog shops and pawn them all for more gin." Mary resisted, and started crying. Her parents then "beat her till she was so sore she couldn't sleep all that night."

Mary pleaded with the magistrate, "Oh! Please, sir, I don't want to be sent home again." She sobbed "as if her little heart would break, and the Magistrate winked both his eyes as he filled out the paper, which read something like this:

> This to command you, John Doe, policeman of the City of New-York, to take charge of Mary Ryan, a child under 14 and above 5 years of age, who has been proved to me by competent evidence to be a vagrant, and to deliver the said child to the officers of the New-York Juvenile Asylum at their House of Reception, and for so doing this shall be your sufficient warrant. – PELEG BUNGAY, Committing Magistrate."

Mary dried her eyes and "joyfully trotted along by the side of the comfortable blue coat that had been a friend to her," to the Asylum's House of Reception. Here, Mary was "warmed, and washed, and combed, and dressed, by the kind-hearted matron, and she came out of the crucible a real jolly, pretty, intelligent-looking little girl." Mary thus became "a regular inmate of the house, and now takes her chances with the hundreds who are sent here under similar circumstances."[66]

By 1889, the leadership decided another move was in store for the Asylum's House of Reception. The old building was sold for $150,000.00.[67] The NYJA's account books were moved to temporary quarters at 30 West Twenty-fourth Street, and a new site was eventually purchased at 106 West

The NYJA established its new House of Reception in this building at 106 West 27th Street near Sixth Avenue, in 1891. (*NYJA Annual Report, 1906*)

Twenty-seventh Street, near Sixth Avenue, at a cost of $125,000.00.[68]

A newspaper described the new House of Reception, as well as an escape made by a boy on the first night it opened in 1891:

> The new reception house was thrown open for inspection yesterday. The building is of brick with red sandstone trimmings. [...] It is fitted with every contrivance which modern ingenuity can devise for the comfort and health of children. It is steam heated, and has cement flooring in the basement, where boys and girls from 7 to 14 years old, surrendered by parents or committed by Police Justices to the institution, are received. There are big and little porcelain-lined bathtubs in the basement. A score of boys and a dozen girls have been inmates of the reception house about a week. On the first night of the commitment of one of the boys he climbed down the fire escape from the dormitory into an inner courtyard, and thence, by shinning up a water pipe, got on a fence twenty feet high, jumped to a telegraph pole, and finally dropped to the street. He was recaptured, and the fence has since been built up so that no one can get over it. There is a chapel and school room in the rear of the second floor, and the children's dormitories are on the third floor, the girls' in front and the boys' in the rear. There is a hospital room on the top floor in the rear, and the kitchen is on the top floor in front. While the front of the house is like an ordinary city dwelling, the rear is divided from it by strong, locked doors and barred windows. The rear, in fact, though fitted up with comfort and cleanliness, is a jail.
>
> The children, in uniform, yesterday sat in the chapel and listed with wonder in their eyes to speeches by President [Ezra M.] Kingsley, the Rev. Isaac Sturges, and the Rev. Antonio Arrighi, pastor of the Italian church.[69]

This site was occupied until March 1909 when NYJA moved its "City office" to 103 Park Avenue.

Fire!

A few minor fires affected either the House of Reception or the Asylum proper over the years. A fire on the evening of July 15, 1878 occurred at the House of Reception on West Thirteenth Street. At 1:30 a.m. "the cry of fire rang through the building." Its origin was in one of the dormitories where nearly eighty boys, of all ages, slept in small iron bedsteads. One of the bedsteads was on fire, with "flames leaping up from under the pillow." Three officers "who specially watch over the youthful prisoners during the night" quickly sprang to action from their rooms, which adjoined the dormitory. Both adults and children brought in water from other rooms to extinguish the flames. Two officers from the Fifteenth Precinct were in the vicinity and heard the commotion. They demanded admittance, and "helped restore order." The Superintendent learned that the eleven-year-old boy occupying the bed that caught fire had carried a bunch of matches in one pocket of his trousers, and, "according to the custom of the place, he had placed the trowsers under his pillow." The Superintendent accepted "the stout denial of the lad" of any wrongdoing as he was the son of a very respectable grocer downtown. The boy had been committed on a charge of truancy at the request of his father. The Superintendent commented, "The class of boys from whom such things might be expected were not sent to the Juvenile Asylum, but to the New York House of Refuge." He made the following statement to the *New-York Tribune* reporter covering the story, blaming "trashy literature" for corrupting the boys:

> I wish to enter the strongest protest against the evil that sends seven-eighths of these boys here. THE TRIBUNE has often assailed it, and it never did better work. Almost the first question I put to the unfortunate lads is 'What have you been reading?' and

the answer invariably shows that my surmise was right. The horrible, trashy literature these boys feed on is what corrupts their minds.

The other day a boy was brought here in whose pockets were found a toy pistol, three revolvers, three boxes of cartridges, a gold watch, and three large new jackknives. With this display before me, I asked the usual question, and the answer came promptly, 'I read *The Boys of New-York.*'

The boy had an uncle in Connecticut, from whom he had run away after stealing his money and the watch.[70]

Growing Pains

Until 1875, many children in the state of New York were sent to almshouses. In that year, the New York Legislature passed what became known as the Children's Law, which ordered the removal from poorhouses of all children between the ages of three (amended in 1878 to two) and sixteen.[71] This law was the start of several half-hearted attempts during the latter part of the nineteenth century to more clearly define the functions of New York's various institutions.

As a consequence of the new law, many children previously destined for placement in an almshouse now found themselves being sent to one of New York's private institutions, such as the NYJA. The population of the Asylum grew from 623 in 1875 (when it received $77,894 from the city) to 778 a year later.[72] However, the law was not rigidly enforced until about 1884.[73] By 1885, the population of the Asylum grew to 911, for which it received $105,026 from the city.[74]

By 1901, the State Board of Charities decided the public should not be charged for the maintenance of children in institutions under private control when voluntarily surrendered by a parent. Instead, it dictated that each child was to be committed by a "public officer," and made the following amendment:

No child between the ages of 2 and 16 years, unless convicted of crime, shall be received into any such institution as a public charge, unless committed thereto, or placed therein, by a court or magistrate having jurisdiction, or by the superintendent of the poor of a county, or overseer of the poor of a town, or commissioner or commissioners of charities, or other local officer or board legally exercising the powers of an overseer in the county, city, town or village sought to be charged with the support of such child, and authorized by law to commit children to such institution or to place them therein.[75]

A New Philosophy

Over the course of time, attitudes about how to best care for needy children changed in America. In 1896, the State Board of Charities began making annual inspections of congregate-style orphan asylums like the NYJA.[76] New laws dictated that in order to receive payment from the city for the support of children committed to the Asylum, written authorization from the local Department of Public Charities was required, and the authorization had to be renewed annually for each inmate living in the institution. In addition, the department had to approve each charge an orphan asylum presented to the city before the comptroller could pay it.[77]

In 1897, Mornay Williams, president of the Asylum's board of directors, responded to the growing criticism of congregate-style orphan asylums in a "Memorandum as to the Development of the Asylum Work," which he shared with other members of the board. He called attention to "critics of our institution and kindred institutions" who "are not few nor are they uninfluential." He also emphasized the serious financial difficulties the Asylum was facing at the time. Even after all monies received from the city, endowment income, and private donations, the Asylum spent forty-seven thousand dollars more than it took in.[78]

Williams, an attorney who specialized in estate

management, suggested the board take measures to correct the situation that amounted to a very radical departure of previous policies:

> All of the sources of expenditure can be materially reduced by the aggregating of large numbers of children under one roof. The clothing can be made in bulk; the heating and lighting carried on at a less per capita cost, and the number of attendants reduced, but it is more than questionable whether this method of training subserves the best interests of the children. Institutional life, at the best, is a poor substitute for the home. The further removed the mode of life is from the home life, the more objectionable it becomes. The larger the number of children maintained under one roof, the less of the home atmosphere.[79]

Ironically, the Asylum's western indenturing agent, Ebenezer Wright, had drawn much the same conclusion nearly three decades earlier in an 1870 monthly report:

> The following letter [...] concerning a boy of the April company, 14 years old, shows up the inside character of one reported at the Asylum "well behaved."
>
> "Daniel has run away. He is a very wicked boy. He has learned my little boys more ugliness than they ever knew before. He will swear, lie & steal & I do not think any one can ever make any thing of him. My family have tried to make a good boy of him but there is no use."
>
> I state these unpleasant facts because they are suggestive & deserve consideration. Do they not seem to teach that a reformatory system that deals with its subjects in a mass, & but little with individuals separately; that relies upon a sort of machinery more than upon the power of personal influences, must fail to accomplish its purposes? Or must we conclude that these children are beyond all power of reclamation.[80]

Other congregate-style institutions in New York began drawing similar conclusions as they evolved.

Solomon Lowenstein, Superintendent of the Hebrew Orphan Asylum, expressed his concerns: "It is manifestly impossible that only one person shall be acquainted with the lives and personalities of over 1,000 children. It is absolutely necessary, for purposes of proper order and discipline, that the children be dealt with in large masses."[81] He conceded that some of the children were receiving individual attention, albeit under Darwinian circumstances. "The children of greatest ability, most forward, and the children of least ability, most backward, the best behaved and the ablest, the worst behaved and the least capable are those who receive the most special consideration."[82] He was undoubtedly alluding to the fact that the plethora of children in between were simply forgotten.

Williams argued for "devising an entirely new plan of work" at the NYJA.[83] He proposed two options. The first was to convert the current operation into a "Day Industrial School [...] to which truant children and disobedient children should be sent for instruction and manual training during the hours of the day, but which would not board any children; only giving them a mid-day meal."[84] The second option he proposed was taking advantage of the huge increase in the value of the Asylum's property at its present location.

A description of the grounds appeared in the Asylum's Annual Report for the year 1899:

> The Asylum grounds contain somewhat less than twelve acres, extending from Amsterdam Avenue to Broadway, and are enclosed by a substantial stone wall and picket fence. On the part adjoining Amsterdam Avenue is a fine Oak Grove of four acres and a double cottage for the use of employees. The buildings and yards occupy four acres, which form an eminence near the central part of the grounds, and are enclosed on three sides by a brick wall eight feet high. The Asylum is easily

> **PETER F. MEYER, Auctioneer**
> will sell at auction on
> **Thursday, May 11, 1899,**
> at 12 o'clock, at the New York Real Estate Salesroom, 111 Broadway.
> By order of the Board of Directors
> OF THE
> **NEW YORK JUVENILE ASYLUM,**
> **85**
> **CHOICE AND VALUABLE LOTS**
> ON
> **Kingsbridge Road,**
> **Wadsworth and Eleventh Aves.,**
> **176th, 177th and 178th Streets.**
> 70 per cent. may remain on Bond and Mortgage for 1, 2, or 3 years at 4½ per cent. Titles guaranteed free of charge to each purchaser by
> **LAWYERS' TITLE INSURANCE CO.**
> For book-maps and further particulars apply at the Auctioneer's office, 111 Broadway, or at the offices of the following directors: Mornay Williams, 59 Wall St.; Theron G. Strong, 45 William St.; Randolph Hurry, 58 William St.; Edmund Dwight, jr., 51 Cedar St.; Alfred E. Marling, 64 Cedar St.

In preparation for the move to Dobbs Ferry, NYJA directors began to sell off land surrounding the Asylum building in New York City. (*New-York Tribune, April 30, 1899*)

reached by the Elevated Roads to 125th Street, thence by electric cars to Asylum gate.[85]

The value of the organization's property in Washington Heights, originally purchased for thirty-three thousand dollars, had risen in value to more than a million. The grounds were "cut up by the opening of new avenues, so that the tract extending from the old Kingsbridge Road to Amsterdam Avenue, is now intersected not only by Eleventh Avenue (as it has been for a number of years), but by Audubon and Wadsworth Avenues."[86] The Asylum could be "easily reached by Third or Sixth Avenue Electric Cars"[87] and was no longer the secluded location that afforded much needed elbow room for the many hundreds of young residents.

Williams suggested that the land be sold and used as an endowment fund for a smaller institution—housing about three hundred children—to be located on less expensive land beyond the island of Manhattan.[88]

The latter proposal was in keeping with the new era of more progressive social reform. The nineteenth century's morally uplifting method of child care was giving way to a more educational model. It was generally believed that it was beneficial to remove children from the inner city to more rural "fresh air" locations, providing a more familial atmosphere in contrast to the mass incarceration of children in the institution-like orphan asylums of America's larger cities.

"An Ideal American Village"

It took several more years for the Asylum to locate and proceed with the purchase of a suitable tract of land. Finally, in 1901, the Asylum's directors acquired 277 acres of farm land in Dobbs Ferry, New York, in Westchester County, at a location known as Echo Hills. The site overlooked the Hudson River (just as the Asylum's former location did) "thirteen miles from the One Hundred and Fifty-fifth street station of the Manhattan Elevated Railway." The property extended thirty-six hundred feet along the New York and Putnam Railroad at Chauncey, running "westerly about half a mile," and consisted of "nearly all wild land with steep hillsides and a fine growth of trees." It adjoined the Cochrane and Villard estates, and its highest point was 430 feet above the tide water of the Hudson.[89] An article in the *Times* explained a bit of the property's history: "Several years ago it was purchased by a syndicate, which planned to develop the tract and resell large plots as sites for handsome country residences. This undertaking, however, proved too large for those who had gone into it."[90] All five houses on the premises required remodeling.[91]

Such a move was a trend followed by several other orphan asylums in New York City in response to the new "cottage plan" in vogue at the time, as Williams explained to the press:

> It became evident some years ago that the institution would do well to follow the

example of [...] other [New York City] institutions and move northward, and we have long been looking for the best place to go. We shall not move at once, nor perhaps for several years. We have 1,200 children to house, and it will take time to build accommodations for the institution at its new site. Moreover, there will have to be a good deal done to the land itself at Chauncey.[92]

The cottage style institution was not a new idea. The first such institution in the United States, the State Industrial School for Girls at Lancaster, Massachusetts, had opened in 1856—the same year that the NYJA moved to its location in Washington Heights.[93] The Lancaster facility was itself built after a study of several European precedents.[94]

Similar institutions converted to the cottage plan and relocated in close proximity to Dobbs Ferry. They included the New York Orphan Asylum, which had moved to Hastings-on-Hudson in the early twentieth century; the Leake & Watts Orphan Asylum in Yonkers; St. Christopher's Home, which had moved to Dobbs Ferry in 1890; the Hawthorne School in May 1906 and Cedar Knolls School in 1912—both in Hawthorne, New York.[95]

The State Industrial School at Rochester changed its name to the State Agricultural and Industrial School in 1902 and moved outside Rochester to fourteen hundred and forty-eight acres of land in Industry, New York, where it too converted to the cottage plan.[96] A 1904 report to the New York Legislature on the New York House of Refuge recommended abandonment of its Randall's Island location and the purchase of one thousand acres within fifty miles of New York City, for a new institution under the cottage plan. Although the recommendations were incorporated into legislation, the selection of the site and construction of the buildings ran into delays, which included obstacles put in place by Vassar College, so the move did not take place until the 1930s.[97]

The trustees of the NYJA subsequently held an architectural design competition for its new suburban facility. A request for bids was printed and sent to five architect firms in New York City in May 1902. The winning design would create, on the new tract of land, "an ideal American village for the occupancy of these children and their successors."[98] The Asylum invited the firms of Walker & Morris, Parish & Schroeder, York & Sawyer, Howells & Stokes, and Butler & Rodman to enter the competition.[99]

The selection committee was very meticulous in its review of proposals submitted. By late June, the firm of York & Sawyer emerged as the winner. Referring to the York & Sawyer plan, the superintendent acknowledged that costs for construction of the cottage plan would be high:

> The striking beauty and desirability of this village, with its attractive central parks and other stately and symmetrical features, would easily outweigh the [financial] objection. [...] An institution founded on the lines of liberality you have adopted will not only call for a larger original investment but for increased outlay for maintenance. Cottages containing small numbers are more homelike and desirable than those heretofore adopted by the managers of American institutions, but the system creates positions and thus enlarges the expenditure.[100]

The Move to Dobbs Ferry

The move to the new quarters could not happen fast enough, as the condition of the old building was deteriorating badly. The plumbing was outdated and required frequent repair. And then there were the rats. Assistant Superintendent Edwin C. Burdick was tasked with obtaining a quote for "clearing the building from rats." In the meantime, he had prepared a rather diverse cuisine in his attempt to lure them into his traps:

> At present I am setting nightly about

thirty-eight traps, using various kinds of bait such as toasted cheese, bacon rinds, etc., but without very great success, the rats having grown weary and leaving the traps strictly alone. I have also had the carpenter nail tin over such holes as he could find, but nevertheless the rats are very numerous and bold. Only the other day one of the boys had his trousers bitten through in several places, absolutely ruining them.[101]

An invasion of flies and mosquitoes caused a cry for help from those affected by them in the hospital, dormitories, and the officers and teacher's sleeping apartments:

> There is at present in the hospital a boy who was so badly bitten by mosquitoes at night that he is unable to see and his face and hands and legs are greatly swollen. Also a number of the teachers and officers have been asking for screens saying that they are unable to sleep at night because of the insects. [...] I made a thorough search but have been unable to find a sufficient number of screens to fit out the offices and reception room.[102]

In 1903, Charles T. Wills was hired as agent for a period of five years, for "assembling men and materials for the building operations at Dobbs Ferry." McCabe & Duffy was hired to "carry out all specifications relating to grading, landscape effects, road-making, sewerage and water distribution."[103]

Superintendent Hilles soon announced specifics on the plans to move to Dobbs Ferry: "Under the terms of the contract executed in the autumn, possession must be given June 1, 1905, to the syndicate that purchased the existing Asylum and the outlying lots on Washington Heights. This means the advance upon Dobbs Ferry and the retreat from Manhattan Island must be simultaneous."[104]

Asylum Directors explained their rationale for the move to Dobbs Ferry in their 1903 Annual Report:

> The ancestry of the congregate school is not to its credit; advanced opinion is unfavorable to dull, forbidding and convent-like walls. Aside from the unedifying environment, the old system is incapable of reproducing the atmosphere of even an average home. It cannot give an adequate amount of individual attention; character development is necessarily neglected, and classification of children under it is a figment of the imagination. Classification is decidedly one of the desiderata of such an institution, and this is possible only where there are many groups, affording opportunity to take into consideration not only character, but stature and educational advancement.[105]

The cost of building each cottage was estimated at $15,000.00.[106]

Former Asylum Superintendent Dr. Samuel D. Brooks learned of the Asylum's intention to relocate in Dobbs Ferry at his home in Springfield, Massachusetts, as reported in his local newspaper:

> No one has read of the improved methods of the New York Juvenile Asylum with more interest than the venerable Dr. S. D. Brooks of this city. He was at the head of that valuable institution from 1858 to 1871 and the fatherly guardian of the children who were rescued from misfortune and set in the way of good and often distinguished citizenship. As an example of its work, it is worth telling that in Dr. Brooks' day from 175 to 200 children were annually located in Illinois, where the Asylum had its home and an agent who kept supervision over boys and girls placed in that state. Since leaving the Asylum Dr. Brooks has kept in touch with boys of his time who have risen to distinction—a governor of Kansas, commissioners of schools and prisons.[107]

The new grounds were ready to be occupied in May 1905. There was one catch. The winning architectural design accommodated one thousand children, but when the new facility was finally completed it had space for just three hundred. Nearly one thousand had been admitted to the Asylum during 1904 alone. The daunting task of reducing the Asylum's population was begun. Arrangements were made for the transfer of hundreds of the children to other institutions in and around Manhattan—similar to when the Asylum was overcrowded back in the 1860s. It was decided that female, African American, Jewish, and Catholic children would not be sent to the new facility in Dobbs Ferry. In addition, arrangements were made to send fifty-eight children to farms in the West through the Illinois Children's Home and Aid Society (hereafter ICHAS), the Asylum's partner at the time to facilitate the majority of supervision over western placements.[108]

The Superintendent commented, "The elimination of seven hundred children in four months, pursuing a policy determined by the Board of Directors without injustice to the children or to society, required patience, industry, courage and intelligence of no mean order."[109]

After consulting with the "well-trained staff of the United Hebrew Charities," the Asylum dispersed "about three hundred children to their homes, or transferred [them] to the Hebrew Orphan Asylum or to the Hebrew Sheltering Guardian Society."[110]

The Asylum explained, "In other cases, where children were eligible to discharge, but their parents were unwilling or unworthy, transfers were made to the Colored Orphan Asylum, the Howard Colored Orphan Asylum, the State Training School [for Girls], Five Points House of Industry, Brace Farm School, Protestant Half-Orphan Asylum and Catholic Home Bureau. Sixty-nine were placed in homes in Iowa and Illinois through the western agency of the Asylum."[111]

Housing only boys at the new location in Dobbs Ferry was in keeping with many similar institutions, which completely segregated boys from girls. For instance, the girls were removed from the New York House of Refuge on Randall's Island, and from the State Industrial School at Rochester.[112] The New York House of Refuge for Women at Hudson, which had previously taken women from sixteen to thirty, had re-opened as the New York State Training School for Girls up to age sixteen, so several NYJA girls were sent there.[113]

Asylum leadership decided to make the last Christmas celebrated in the old asylum on Washington Heights an extra special event:

> One of the largest Christmas parties in this great city this year will be held in a stone building on Washington Heights, where over 1,000 little folks will gather around two great Christmas trees laden with toys and the good things appropriate to the season. After these gifts have been distributed, there will be entertainment in which very likely a slight-of-hand performer or ventriloquist will be the central figure. To many of this regiment of children, the gathering will be the first Christmas party in which they have been included among the guests. They have come mostly from the crowded East Side to be made into good Americans by the New York Juvenile Asylum.[114]

On December 31, 1904 the superintendent reported, "ten cottages are now complete and the interior wood-work of five others is being put in place. The school house and power house have been plastered and are receiving the trim." In addition, a great deal of the landscaping was completed, and the athletic field was underway.[115]

Hilles began contacting parents and telling them to come and get their children. In a letter dated March 30, 1905, Hilles wrote Mr. Adolph Blum of New York City:

Dear Sir:

If you will call at the Asylum and bring clothing for your son Louis, he will be discharged to you.

Very truly yours,

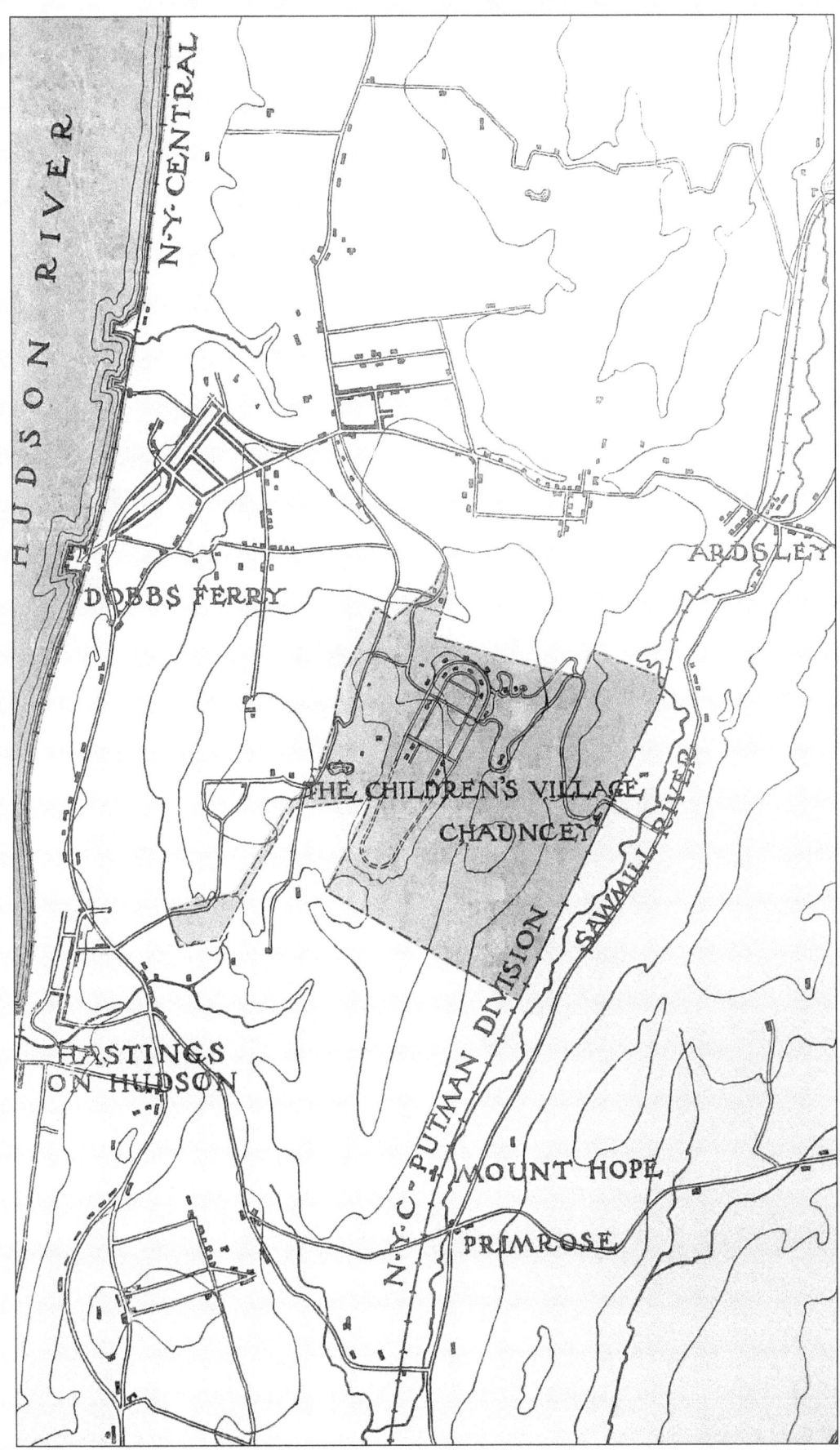

Circa 1905 map of The Children's Village. (*NYJA Annual Report, 1905*)

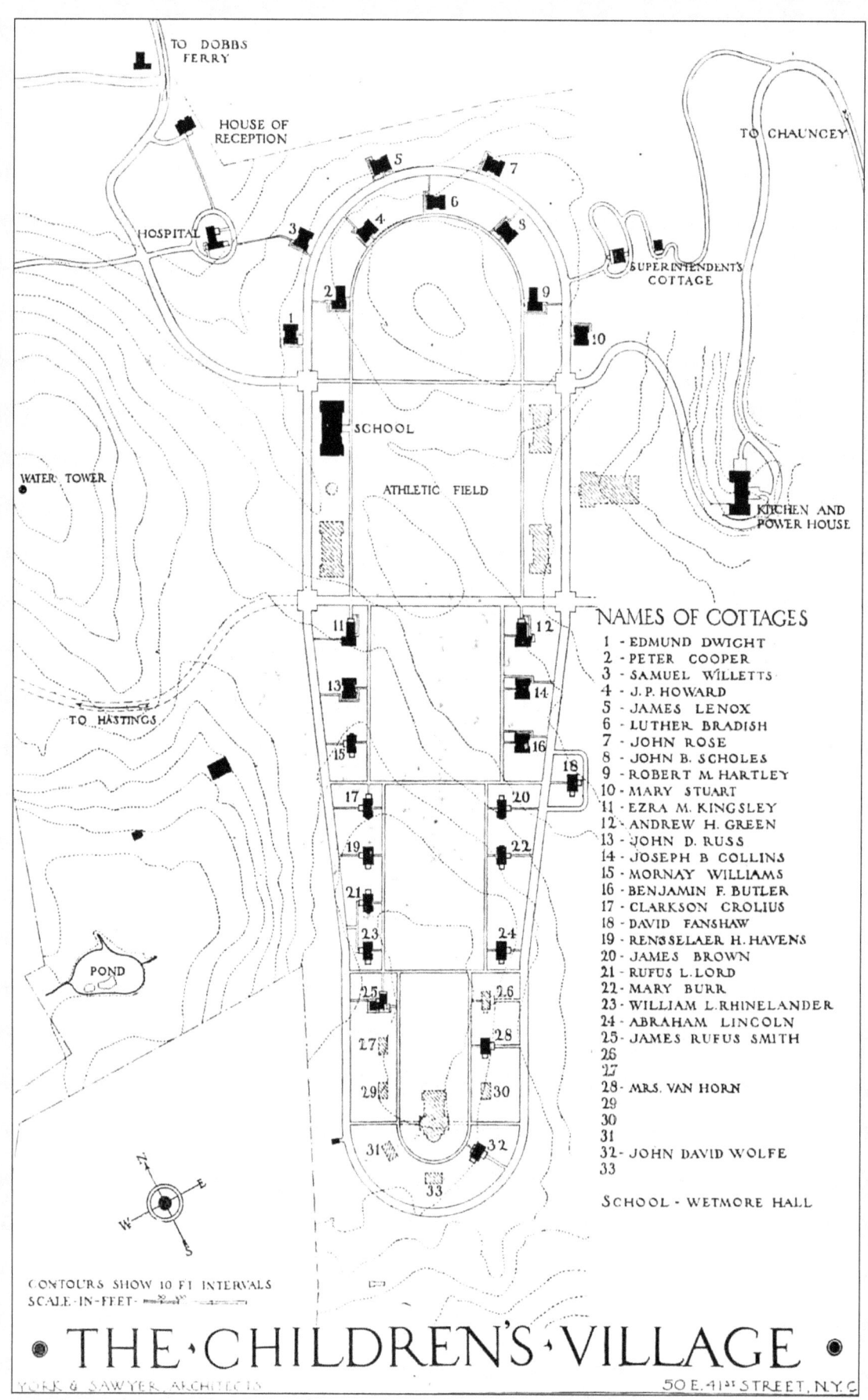

Circa 1916 architect's map of The Children's Village. (*NYJA Annual Report, 1916*)

Chauncey Station (Putnam Division), ca. 1895. The NYJA children arrived here from Manhattan and proceeded up the hill and through the trees to the new cottages that awaited them. (*Health and Pleasure on America's Greatest Railroad, 1895*)

Charles D. Hilles[116]

A few days later, Hilles realized that he had been perhaps a little too thorough in his reduction of the Asylum's child population: "I desire to make the emphatic statement now that unless we limit the discharges in April and May to the girls and the Jewish and colored boys, we will not have enough children to fill the cottages at Dobbs Ferry in June."[117]

In addition to his NYJA position, Hilles was chairman of the Children's Section of the National Conference of Charities and Correction, and responsible for arranging the speakers and literature for the 1905 conference. He was also tasked with making arrangements for the National Conference on the Education of Delinquent, Truant, and Backward Children, which he served as secretary.[118]

A week before the move to Dobbs Ferry, Hilles expressed his views, in harmony with the nationwide views on juvenile reform at the time: "Having exploded the theory that all evil is traceable to bad birth, and substituted the theory that environment is more at fault than heredity, I think we must insist on attractive, wholesome, cheerful surroundings for the children while they are with us."[119]

A farewell service was held at the 176th Street and Amsterdam Avenue location on Sunday afternoon, April 16, 1905.[120] President Mornay Williams presided over the ceremony. The mass exodus of three hundred children and sixty employees began on May 16 and after continuing over the course of two weeks, was completed on May 30: "Two grand divisions of children were subdivided again and again, producing sixteen carefully classified groups." First to be moved were the nursery and kindergarten children, to Collins and Butler Cottages. Others, in groups of twenty, "crossed High Bridge merrily, went by special cars to Chauncey and ascended from the station in the Saw Mill river valley to their respective homes on the plateau."[121]

They commenced walking west up the incline from the station with all of their baggage on wagons, making their way through several tree-shaded switch-backs to the new site. Three days after their arrival, Superintendent Hilles, clearly frustrated with the contractors, lamented:

> I have been literally overwhelmed with petty details incident to the start. Notwithstanding all the promises to us, or warnings

and pleadings, the contractors are not yet out of the houses. Plasterers are in all of them, with their dirt. Electricians haven't all their equipment in position, we haven't hot water nor heat, nor light. Our treatment has been really cruel and in the effort to make our people comfortable we have been driven to the extreme. I hope it will be all right shortly.[122]

The old buildings in New York City were abandoned on May 30.[123]

A shortage of children to fill the cottages in Dobbs Ferry was not a problem for very long. The courts continued to commit children well into 1906. More than two hundred were turned away, but for more than three months some children were temporarily detained at the Asylum's city office at 106 West 27th Street. Superintendent Hilles proclaimed, "The waiting list threatens to become an irresistible force."[124]

Official Name Change

In 1920, during a reorganization that promoted a more therapeutic model of care then in vogue, the institution's name was officially changed to The Children's Village. Children did not stay at the facility indefinitely; after six to twelve months, as a rule, they were returned to their families or placed in foster care. The logic of this policy (seemingly ahead of its time) had been expressed by Superintendent Dr. Samuel D. Brooks to Mary E. Dodge, a reporter for *Scribner's Monthly*, back in 1870.

> He spoke of institution life as a necessary evil at best, allowing, as a governing principle, that as soon as it can be safely done, asylum children should be removed to the more natural conditions of a private home. Above all, he deprecated any set system that unfitted inmates for subsequently mingling with the outside world. Rules and fixed regulations are entirely thrown out of his scheme of management; he prefers to deal with the individuality of the children, creating and acting up to a high public sentiment among them.[125]

❧ CHAPTER TWO ❧

NYJA Procedures

Admissions

As a general rule, children accepted by the NYJA were between the ages of seven and fourteen, but younger or older children were occasionally accepted at the discretion of the Board.

During 1854 less than 50 percent of children admitted to the House of Reception were transferred to the Asylum. The Superintendent of the House of Reception gave this explanation:

> Those of whom no reasonable hope of reformation could be entertained, have been returned to the magistrates, to be sent to institutions [most often the New York House of Refuge] more directly calculated to take charge of the hardened, although youthful offender. And a larger number have been of that class, upon whom the legal term for which they could be held in the House of Reception, had an effect so salutary in its character, as to afford a strong hope that they would not again be found in circumstances such as would warrant a second committal.[1]

Children arrived at the House of Reception, whether with parents, truant officers, officers of the court, or on their own accord, at all hours of the day and night. A reporter observed, "Sometimes several small children are brought in during the morning; and often it happens that a solitary wretched, frightened little vagrant, taken in all his rags and dirt by one of the truant-police force, finds himself standing in the reception-office a prospective victim, as he believes, of every horror this side of hanging."[2]

By the 1890's the City of New York was stipulating that the Asylum was only eligible to receive city monies if a child was a resident of the borough of Manhattan or the Bronx for at least one year and their families could not afford to support them. As a result the Asylum had to delve deeper into the background of each child surrendered, prior to deciding on whether or not to admit them.[3]

Notification of Parents or Guardians

The legislative act that incorporated the NYJA spelled out the duties of the Superintendent of the House of Reception regarding notification of the parents or guardians of children who came under his care.

> Whenever, after careful and diligent search by the policeman arresting the juvenile delinquent, he shall not have found either the child's father, mother, or legal guardian, it shall be the duty of the Superintendent of the House of Reception to cause the following notice to be posted up in a conspicuous place in the Police Station-House nearest the alleged residence of the child:
>
> NOTICE. – This is to certify that A. B., a child of about the age of ___ years, ___ hair, ___ eyes, ___ complexion, ___ in height, and said to be of ___ descent, was on the ___ day

Little street peddlers brought before the New York City Commissioners of Charity. (*Harper's Weekly, January 1869*)

of ___ 18__ , committed by ___ to the House of Reception of the New-York Juvenile Asylum, No. 23 West Thirteenth street, and that after careful search and inquiry made by ___, neither the parents, legal guardians, or persons with whom said A. B. is alleged to have resided can be found. New York, ___, 18__. A. C. PEARCY, Superintendent.

And the posting of said notice as above required shall be deemed as equivalent to having duly served it on the parent or guardian in cases where they or either of them could not be found.[4]

Reasons for Commitments

Children were usually sent to the Asylum's House of Reception by a public authorities, such as court magistrates. Many were voluntarily surrendered by their own parents for being disobedient or for deserting their homes. Commitments were often made under the eighteenth section of the Law of 1833, which allowed for the commitment of children found "in a state of want and suffering, or being abandoned, or improperly exposed, or neglected by their parents or such other person as may have them in charge, or soliciting charity from door to door, or in any street, highway or public place within said City."[5]

In 1878, B. T. Morgan of the Third District Police Court sent a fourteen-year-old boy to be admitted to the House of Reception, along with a letter of introduction:

STATE OF NEW YORK,
CITY AND COUNTY OF NEW YORK. } ss.

FREDERICK W. KORNMANN, of Bedford Park, New York City, being duly sworn, deposes and says that he is an officer of the Municipal Police Force of said city, detailed for duty at The New York Juvenile Asylum, that he personally knows   that said   is a minor under the age of sixteen years, and at present an inmate of The New York Juvenile Asylum. That deponent has made diligent search and inquiry to ascertain whether or not the said minor   has any home or other place of abode, or proper guardianship, and has found that said minor has no home or other place of abode other than said Asylum, and no proper guardianship, and that said minor is in a state of want and suffering, and destitute of means of support in violation of the provisions of the Statute in such cases made and provided. Wherefore deponent prays that said   may be dealt with as the law and justice may provide.

Sworn to before me, this   day
of September, 1895.

After admitting a child to the House of Reception, authorities attempted to locate and notify the parents or guardians of the child. If they showed cause for the child's discharge, the child was then released. If not, all rights were given to the Asylum to serve in loco parentis. (*NYJA Records; Rare Book and Manuscript Library, Columbia University Library*)

MAGISTRATE'S COMMITMENT.

NEW YORK JUVENILE ASYLUM.

To.. one of the Policemen of the City of New York.

You are hereby commanded to take charge of *Charles Schwartz* .... a child under the age of fourteen and above the age of seven years, who has been proved to me, by competent evidence, to be embraced within the eighteenth section of the act entitled, "An act relative to the powers of the Common Council of the City of New York, and the Police and Criminal Courts of said city, Approved January 23d, 1833," and who also appears, to my satisfaction, to be a proper object for the care and instruction of the Corporation created by an act entitled, "an Act to Incorporate the NEW YORK JUVENILE ASYLUM," passed June 30th, 1851, and to deliver the said child, without delay, to the said Corporation at its House of Reception in this City, and for so doing this shall be your sufficient warrant.

Dated this *19th* day of *January* 1876

B. H. Bixby —Committing *Magistrate*.

House of Reception, 61 West 13th Street

Magistrate's commitment of a boy named Charles Schwartz, dated January 19, 1876. (*NYJA records; Rare Book and Manuscript Library, Columbia University Library. Minutes. Admissions, Indentures, Discharges with Invoices, 1873-1880, Box 8*)

Mr. Carpenter, Dear Sir:

This boy is just past 14 years of age. He is in need of discipline and I send him to you in the hope that the salutary influence of your Institution may divert him from the error of his ways.

His Father who I have known for years—he was formerly a Currier in the N. Y. Post Office—when I was Assistant Postmaster—and I had trouble with him then and since. I hope that this boy may not go in the same path as his Father—a reckless man.[6]

Children sent by public authorities included those committing the lesser crimes of petty theft, vagrancy and truancy; orphans without means of support; children whose parents were found to be habitual criminals; children discovered in the company of thieves or prostitutes; and those found in "concert saloons, dance houses, theatres, museums, or other places where wine, malt or spirituous liquors are sold, without being in charge of parents or guardian."[7] After a child was taken to the NYJA,

by any policeman of the City of New York, before the Mayor or Recorder, or any Alderman or other magistrate of said city, upon the allegation that such child was found in any way, street, highway, or public place in said city, in circumstances of want, suffering, or abandonment, or exposure, neglect, or beggary: and it shall appear from the examination of the child that these circumstances were induced by the neglect, habitual drunkenness, or other vicious habits of the parents or legal guardians of said child, and that it is a proper object of the care and instruction of this Corporation, the magistrate before whom such child is brought, may, in his discretion, instead of committing the child to the Alms-House of said city, commit such child to this Corporation.[8]

The minimum length of time each child was committed to the Asylum was two years, regardless of the reason for commitment. Almost 8 percent of the Asylum's children were sent for vagrancy in 1853, and only eight children for being "bad and disorderly."[9]

By the early 1860s, the reasons children were admitted to the NYJA began to shift. Vagrancy began to decrease while truancy, disobedience, and "unfortunate" began to increase, with simple dependency or neglect accounting for about one fifth of the admissions.[10] About one third to one half (through the end of the nineteenth century) were able to "read, write, and cipher."[11]

In 1879 the Asylum commented on another common reason for admissions:

Step-parentage is the *direct* cause for the surrender of many children we have, while *disobedience* is the reason assigned by the surviving parent, in order to gain their admission. As fast as the new brood come on to the carpet, there is no peace at home with the older chicks, so "off to an institution." We have succeeded in getting a *full* surrender in many of these cases, much to the peace of the household, and greatly to the benefit of the children.[12]

Such appears to be the case with a boy named William Masterson, surrendered to the NYJA by his mother in 1883 at the age of eight for being disobedient. William was sent west by the Asylum and indentured to a German farmer in Illinois. Nearly two decades later, William penned a letter to his sister Ida, who remained in New York, alluding to the fact that a male acquaintance of his mother helped influence her decision to put William in the Asylum.

I have worked from day light till dark when the day were about 16 hours long and fared worse and received less than the soldiers did in Cuba, but as small as I was when I was put in the Asylum I have never forgot the one that encuraged [*sic*] my mother to put me there. And if he got what he deserves he would be in Sing Sing. Well there will be a settlement some day [he] will answer for my banishment and his hair will be reder [*sic*] than it is.[13]

Of the 245 commitments during 1913, sixty children were "disobedient and truant," sixty-four were "bad and disorderly," and another sixty-three had been caught "pilfering." Of the remainder, most were simply "unfortunate."[14]

A twelve-year-old girl named Minnie Anthes was representative of one reason some girls were sent to the NYJA. Minnie was committed to the Asylum by Judge Bixby in 1877 for stealing fourteen dollars from a bureau drawer in George S. Cannon's house at 791 Ninth Avenue. She used the money to buy "a wax doll, pair of bracelets, jewelry and gaudy finery." Her classmates had been making fun of her in Sunday school for not being dressed "as finely as they." She declared she took the money to "dress up."[15]

Another example of an admission to the Asylum was a fourteen-year-old boy named William who was apprehended by police for vagrancy on May 29, 1881. In his pockets were found "one horse pistol, one revolver, two silver watches, three pawn tickets, one opera glass, one magnifying glass, and one tobacco box." He claimed to be an orphan boy from Jersey City; however, his father appeared in the Asylum's office on June 11, 1882.[16]

One of the younger offenders sent to the Asylum was Charles Harriman, age seven. He was arraigned in the Jefferson Market Police Court on the charge of burglary. The newspaper said of him: "Charles is one of the band. He is a bright little fellow, unusually intelligent, and the possessor of a frank, open countenance. In appearance he is the last person one would suspect of being a thief." It seems his crime was entering the Theological Seminary at Ninth Avenue and 22nd Street and stealing a set of pool balls from the table. He didn't deny several other charges leveled against him; instead he told an apparently straightforward story of how "he and his confederates worked the rackets."[17]

One example of an Italian boy admitted to the Asylum was little Romillo. He was described as having "abandoned his home and mother." Romillo was fluent in "certain branches of English." The asylum's Visitor showed up at his East Side home one day and found his mother, described as a tiny woman whose "bright eyes are the one lovely feature of an expressionless face—could still speak no language but that of her peasant home." She wanted to hear about her boy, though. She called in an interpreter, a neighbor. The two women, "with their broods of little Giovannis and Francescas clinging about their skirts, stood talking with the visitor in the only spot in the kitchen not cluttered with delapidated furniture, unwashed kettles, pans and dishes, refuse rags and papers, or dirt pure and simple." When the Visitor asked what "Romi's" father was doing for a living, the group chorused, "Father drunk." The reply brought about a "specially imperative call for silence and a particularly pointed menace of a fistcuff."[18]

In addition, "pupils" could be received into the Asylum from any city or town in the state of New York, provided the locality would become responsible for their maintenance and support during their "continuance in the Asylum, and provided they shall not be charged less than sixty dollars per annum for each pupil."[19]

Mornay Williams, President of the Board of Directors of the NYJA, described one type of child (the street boy) who often found himself in the hands of the law and subsequently sent to the Asylum:

> There are two main types of street boy. The first is physically small, lean, wiry and nervous, alert of eye and lithe of limb, a young nomad with not a few of the characteristics of the American Indian, somewhat callous to pain but fond of inflicting torture, revengeful, with flashes of generosity, despising work, manual or intellectual, and intolerant of control, content to starve one day if he may gorge another. This boy is lawless, but not in any proper sense a criminal, and generally quite capable with

proper training of being converted into an upright citizen, but left alone or stupidly interfered with he can be easily turned into a boy of the second type. This second type of boy is dull, embruted, cunning but not clever, hateful and hating others—a criminal in little. The street boy is naturally alert and has received a very complete education in the school of the street. The street is not only his playground, but also his home. But beyond all this the street is his school. It is there that he has learned all the simple maxims of his code—that he who fights and runs away may live to fight another day; that the blunder of being caught "with the goods on" is far worse than the crime of stealing: that the blackest offense possible is "to squeal on a pal," and so on.[20]

One twelve-year-old German boy named Philip, who made the street his playground, found himself admitted to the NYJA as a result. A Visitor employed by the Asylum found his mother at home in three rooms of a tenement on the upper East Side. The rooms were described as "bare, but they are clean and wholesome; there is even an attractiveness about them." His mother was described as "distressfully thin and sad," with a "touching tenderness of manner toward her children." Philip's father was found to be "a sober, hard worker, who uses his authority with his family justly and kindly." His mother, who cried over Philip daily, explained, "He vas not a bad boy, my Philip," she said to the Visitor, "only he has cursed so hart und vas always mit de bad boys. Nights he vould stay oud unt den, because he is afraid of getting a vipping off his papa, he don't dast come back. Sometimes he comes back unt sleeps in der hall outside; but he vouldn't never come in.

She continued, "Den, one morning, ven he had been away t'ree nights, he comes in unt says, 'ama,' he says, 'von't you gif me a cup of coffee?' Unt I tell him I must take him to der judge to put him away because I vas not able to keep him from der bad boys. But he has broke my heart."[21]

The Asylum found that one of the "casual fac-

School-age boys selling newspapers on the Brooklyn Bridge at 3 a.m. on February 23, 1908. (*Library of Congress Prints and Photographs Division Washington, D.C. 20540 USA http://hdl.loc.gov/loc.pnp/nclc.03189. Photo by Lewis Hine*)

tors" of delinquency was factory and street employment of young children—those children who were "prematurely employed in shops or on the streets." The Asylum examined 625 boys of the Asylum as to street careers in 1902. Thirty-five were under age seven so inquiry was not made. Of the remaining number, 325 had been employed prior to their commitment. They averaged eleven years and nine months old at the time they commenced work—the youngest at age four.

One hundred and five were employed as newsboys, forty as messengers, fifty-five in factories, sixty-eight in stores, twenty-eight as peddlers, eleven as hall boys, and six as bootblacks. Of this number, 72 percent were committed for delinquency,

Parent Surrender Form for the author's eleven-year-old great-uncle, Clarence Reese, surrendered to the NYJA on September 9, 1879 for the standard two years due to being disobedient. (*NYJA Records; Rare Book and Manuscript Library, Columbia University Library; Parent Surrender Forms (1878-1880); Box 59; Folder 2*)

with newsboys making up 32 percent of those employed. The Asylum noted a "surprisingly insignificant percentage (less than 2 percent) of the boys were employed as bootblacks, which was perceived as "confirmation of the statement that adult Italians have driven the boy bootblacks out of business."[22]

Parental Surrenders

When parents or guardians surrendered a child they were essentially voluntarily relinquishing all parental rights to the child. The surrender form nearly always spelled out a set period of time the asylum would retain such rights. In the case of the NYJA the term was two years.

The author's great-uncles, Clarence and Lewis Reese, were admitted to the NYJA in the 1880s. In both cases their parents surrendered them to the Asylum due to "disobedience."[23]

Parents or guardians could also elect to board a child in the Asylum and "pay in whole or in part for his maintenance and education."[24]

When parents themselves approached the Asylum and asked if one or more of their children could be admitted, the Asylum usually investigated the family's circumstances by conducting interviews with the parents, neighbors, or employers. Such investigations became more common in the latter years of the nineteenth century. In 1898, the Asylum hired Louise A. Husted, M.D., as its official Visitor. Husted was tasked with visiting and reporting on those families who applied for the admission or discharge of a child, those who wished to have a child sent west, and all persons given as references. She reported on the conditions she found in homes visited in 1898: "The surroundings of truants and unmanageable children are as pitiful as those of the destitute. The evidences of lack of control, mismanagement or cruelty are often plain. One truant boy of eight years was kept fastened by an iron dog chain when not at school."[25]

One of the requirements for an applicant's eligibility was a year's residence in the borough of Manhattan or the Bronx, as required by the city before a child could be supported with city funds. Husted explained, "This residence is sometimes proved by papers in the parents' possession, their passport, insurance papers or old rent receipts, and sometimes it is necessary to trace the family through its journeys from one house to another during the previous twelve months."[26]

In cases where destitution was claimed, the agent found the reason to be "sickness, death, loss of work, intemperance or desertion." She described finding a family of six in a rear tenement, deserted by the father, the mother sick and unable to work, assisted only by the sewing of a girl of thirteen. Another father supported his children by driving an old horse and wagon and assisting his neighbors in their frequent removals. The death of the horse reduced him to ask for help. When parents were able to pay, they were asked to pay as large a proportion as possible for their child's board.[27]

Not all applicants were granted admittance to the Asylum. Out of 350 applications for parental surrender made in 1898, only 235 children were admitted. Reasons for refusal included "because non-resident, too young, unable to pass the doctor's examination, or because the parents were unwilling to pay a portion of the board, although able to do so, or because the parents withdrew their request."[28]

Officers of the Asylum maintained "a constant vigilance against an abuse of the Asylum's hospitalities." The Indenturing Committee was instructed by the superintendent to "guard against improper admissions, also to winnow out such as are allowed to remain an unreasonable time."[29]

It was often very difficult for parents to come to grips with surrendering one or more of their children for the minimum stay of two long years. In 1875 Martha Murphy appeared at the Asylum's House of Reception with her two children, Catherine, age ten, and Edward, age eight, with the intention of surrendering them. The surrender forms, completely filled out (minus the signature of Mrs. Murphy), still appear in the record book, with a handwritten note in the margin that reads: "These children cried so hard that the mother thought best to take them away again."[30]

It was also often very hard on the Superintendent of the House of Reception, or his subordinate, when children were handed over by their parents. When Superintendent Charles Dewey Hilles made an address at the New York City Conference of Charities and Corrections, he alluded to the issue:

> In one of his letters, [Thomas] Arnold of Rugby [a school in England] wrote: "If ever I could receive a new boy from his father without emotion, I should think it high time to be off." These are tremendous words. And yet I believe there are hundreds of good men and women who are today the guardians of the delinquent and dependent children of New York City who are as conscientious as Arnold was, and whose souls tremble at the responsibility of their vocation.[31]

In 1901, responding to the ever-increasing criticism of institutions such as the NYJA, the State Board of Charities ruled that parents could no longer simply surrender their children. In doing so, the Board hoped to reduce what it deemed unnecessary commitments. Directors of the Asylum voiced their objection, arguing that if there were too many dependent children requiring care, restrictions on immigration should be tightened but access to institutions should remain an option.[32] The Asylum challenged the decision in court, but was unsuccessful due to "the rules of the State Board of Charities which provide that no child under the age of 16 years, shall be received as a public charge in any private institution unless committed thereto by some public official."[33] The court added, "This imposes no great hardship on the asylum and it protects the city from the fraud that may be practiced upon it

New York Society for the Prevention of Cruelty to Children Wagon at the Tombs (prison) in New York City. (*NYSPCC. Twenty-Fifth Annual Report, 1899*)

by those who are able to support and educate their own children."[34]

In 1903, Mrs. Charles J. Holt of the St. James Rectory in Fordham, New York, wrote to the Asylum and asked how children were generally received into the NYJA. The Asylum's Assistant Superintendent, Edwin C. Burdick, responded:

First, by their parents, guardians or friends, giving a full surrender and executing a bond agreeing to pay $2.00 per week for maintenance of each child. Second, by being committed to us by the Department of Charities [if the child was destitute, according to another letter he wrote on the same subject]. Third, by being committed to us by the court.[35]

The standard two-year term of commitment could be extended at the discretion of Asylum managers in the case of indeterminate sentences, as Burdick wrote to a boy's father: "Your son Morris was committed here for petty larceny and under the rules of the institution, it will be impossible for us to release him before he has been here at least two years. If he does not show signs of improvement at the expiration of that time, it is possible we may keep him even longer."[36]

Morris subsequently attempted to escape, and his father was informed via letter: "I am very sorry to tell you that your son Morris attempted to escape from here last night by climbing out of a window and down a water leader to the ground, and in so doing, he slipped and fell breaking his arm and I think his leg also. The boy is now in the hospital where he will receive the best of care and attention."[37]

Society for the Prevention of Cruelty to Children

The source of children committed to the Asylum fluctuated over the years as new agencies were formed. One of these agencies, the New York Society for the Prevention of Cruelty to Children (hereafter, NYSPCC), was established in New York City in 1875, with a Brooklyn branch established in 1880. The Society, which was often referred to as the Gerry Society after its co-founder, Elbridge Thomas Gerry, proved to have a significant impact on new admissions to the Asylum. The NYJA began receiving children from the NYSPCC almost immediately. In 1879 the Asylum reported that it had "received a large number of children the past year, among whom were two leading juvenile acrobats from the theatrical stages of our city. They have apparently lost their desire to return again to that vocation, and are being trained with a view to increase the 'sturdy yeomanry' of the West."[38]

By 1892, no less than 15 percent of all children committed to the NYJA came through the NYSPCC. Of these children, 17 percent were committed on account of vagrancy or depravity, 45 percent for truancy and disobedience, and 23 percent for destitution.[39]

In the same year, there was sufficient progress in New York's juvenile court system to provide for separate trials and dockets for child offenders.[40]

Children's Court

In 1902, another phase of development culminated in the establishment of the first children's court in the United States to have a separate building and administrative independence from any other court, as a division of the New York County court of general sessions in Manhattan.[41] In the first year of its existence, 76,647 children, most "arrested by policemen without warrants," were arraigned before the court. An observer described the court room in 1905:

An agent with the Brooklyn Society for the Prevention of Cruelty to Children poses with two boys rescued from an abusive home, ca. 1903. (*BSPCC Annual Report, 1903-04/Case No. 37,061*)

The general appearance of the room is much like that of an ordinary police court. Outside the railing which divides the room into two unequal parts and separates the justice, agents, missionaries and offenders from the spectators, sit several scores of men and women, silent for the most part and manifestly anxious. Many of the faces are those of foreigners, some are stupid, some are prepossessing, not a few hard and vicious. As the justice enters all rise while he takes his seat on the bench. He is a smooth-shaven, keen featured, kindly-appearing man, looking in his black gown like a bishop—but one who knows more of the world than most bishops.

The clerk calls a name, and the court constable brings in a boy by a small side door. He is taken up to the "bridge" before the bench, Mr. [Howard] Townsend and the Gerry soci-

Brooklyn Children's Court in Session, ca. 1910. (*Hastings H. Hart*)

Judge Wilkin hearing a boy's case in chambers—Brooklyn Children's Court, ca. 1910. (*Hastings H. Hart*)

ety [NYSPCC] agents close round him, while the two missionaries stand near. A man and woman from the audience are called up. Not a word is audible ten feet away from the group. After a few minutes the boy is taken out again. Outside the rail no one has the slightest idea what he was accused of, whether he was accused of anything at all, and still less of what has become of him. This is intentional. There is no wish either to make a hero of a bad boy by giving publicity to his case or to parade the misfortunes of a good one. One might spend the whole forenoon in court and go away no wiser than one came.[42]

Court proceedings were described as "more like family council than a trial." Those present in the court included "the justice, the agents of [the] Society for the Prevention of Cruelty to Children, [...] two women missionaries, who care for the interests of Catholic and Hebrew children, and Howard Townsend, vice president of the New York juvenile asylum." The group talked over each case as it came up, "more anxious to do the best for the culprit than to find some clause in the penal code to hold him on." Townsend had legal training and devoted every morning of the weekday to the Children's Court. One case that came before the court was described in this way:

> A pale lad, with a drawn, frightened face is brought up on his stepfather's application to have him committed to an institution because his mother has taken to bad ways. The stepfather is discovered asleep on a settee, is awakened with difficulty and shoved up to the bench in a half dazed state, plainly "under the influence." The justice gives one quick look at the man's dirty countenance, and sees there only an additional argument for taking the little fellow away from his parents. A brief consultation with Mr. Townsend, and the boy is committed to the juvenile asylum, where he will get his first fair chance for improvement.[43]

Another example of a boy committed to the Asylum by the Children's Court was a little German boy named Hermann, who stole a gold watch. The Asylum's Visitor paid Hermann's mother a visit at her tenement home one day. His mother explained Hermann's actions: "Hermann will do anything to get money—always must he haf money." She continued, "He will come by me first, und w'en he gets all I have, he will go out und stole some. Once he took a wash which gave a bill of seven dollars und sold it for ein dollar. Dat boy was crazy mit de theaytre. Dere ain't no night what he ain't went dere since a long time."[44]

At this point in time, the city was paying the Asylum $110.00 towards the support of each child committed. The Asylum estimated that its annual expense for maintaining a child was $131.00.[45]

In time, the Children's Court implemented a system of probation. The judges were interested in giving some of the minor offenders a little taste of what commitment to an institution would be like. The policy resulted in both fewer and shorter commitments to the NYJA and went against the grain of what Asylum officials had been promoting for many years—that commitment to the Asylum was something other than punishment and was more like an educational experience. In addition, the policy caused many disciplinary problems.

To offset this trend, the Asylum expanded its use of indeterminate sentences. The institution's officials decided when the children should go home, and therefore put an end to "ridiculously short commitments" by the magistrates.[46] Furthermore, the Asylum refused to admit boys for shorter terms, a decision that proved to have negative consequences for the Asylum. As time went on, fewer and fewer boys were committed to the Asylum by the magistrates until, in 1915, three cottages were closed at The Children's Village for lack of inmates. The Asylum reluctantly reversed its policy by 1917, when it began to put particular emphasis on its educational platform.

Indentures

The NYJA adopted a system of indenturing children as apprentices to masters. A very similar program of indenturing children had been practiced by the New York House of Refuge since 1825. The Asylum considered the indenture of children in harmony with its prescription of education, work, discipline, and religion in the reformation of its charges. It was the Asylum's hope that the masters would not only teach the children a trade that would be useful when they became of age and entered the working world, but would also subject the child to certain moral and religious influences while under quasi-parental surveillance. The NYJA addressed the terms of indenture in Section 18 of their Charter:

> The said corporation shall have power, in its discretion, to bind out or indenture, as clerks or apprentices, to some profession, trade, or employment, the children entrusted or committed to its charge; and for a shorter or longer period, not exceeding, however, in the case of girls, the age of eighteen years; and, in that of boys, the age of twenty-one years.[47]

On April 5, 1855 New York passed an Act stating:

> 1. The trustees, directors, or managers of any incorporated orphan asylum, may bind out any orphan or indigent child, if a male, under the age of twenty-one years, or if a female, under the age of eighteen years, which has been or shall be surrendered to the care and custody of said society by the parent or guardian thereof, or placed therein by the superintendent of the poor of the county, or the overseers of the poor of any city or town in the county within which said asylum is located, to be clerks, apprentices or servants, until such child, if a male, shall be twenty-one years old, or if a female, shall be eighteen years old, which binding shall be as effectual as if such child had bound himself with the consent of his father.
>
> 2. In case of the death of the father of any indigent child, or in case the father shall have abandoned his family or neglected to provide for them, the mother shall be the guardian of said child for the purpose of surrendering the said child to the care and custody of said society; and in case of the death of both parents, the mayor of the city within which the said asylum may be located, shall be ex-officio the guardian of said child, for the purpose of enabling said trustees, managers or directors, to bind out such child.[48]

The NYJA established an Indenturing Committee to handle this task. The duties of the committee were

> to inquire into the history, character and condition of the pupils, in reference to the propriety of discharging them from the Asylum, and also into the character and fitness of all persons who may propose to take a pupil as an apprentice or servant, and decide on such applications; but no pupil shall be bound to any trade or occupation unless, in the opinion of the Committee, his or her constitution is physically and mentally fitted for such trade or occupation.[49]

The duties of the Superintendent of the Asylum in relation to indenturing required him to "lay before the indenturing Committee all applications for Clerks or Apprentices, and the names of such of the pupils as he thinks may properly be discharged from the Asylum, or apprenticed."[50]

The Asylum required the following of prospective foster parents:

FORM OF APPLICATION FOR APPRENTICE.

To the Superintendent of the New York Juvenile Asylum.

SIR,—The undersigned, a resident of   township,   County, in the State of   , is desirous of obtaining from the Institution under your charge, a   , aged about   years, to serve as an apprentice to the   business, whose color must be

> Here give such other special directions as may be thought necessary, especially noting any particular requirements desired, as well as any insurmountable objection which might be made to an otherwise unobjectionable child.

Dated   185   Signed

CERTIFICATE OF CHARACTER.

To the Superintendent of the New York Juvenile Asylum.

The undersigned having been acquainted with   of   , in the County of   , and State of   for several years, believes   to be a person of a well regulated and amiable temper, of sober, honest, and industrious habits, and not addicted to the use of profane or vulgar language, and that   he is in a fair and profitable business, and in all respects such a person as might, advantageously to the Asylum and the child, be intrusted with the care and management of one or more of its pupils.

Signed,

{ *Justice of Peace.*
  Town Clerk.
  Minister of Gospel. }

Post Office Address,

[The above Certificate of Character must be properly filled up and signed by a Justice of the Peace, a Town Clerk, or a Minister of the Gospel, or any two of them in the town where the applicant resides, and the fact that the persons so signing are what they purport to be, attested by the County Clerk, with the county seal. The Application having been also filled up and signed by the applicant, must be forwarded with the Certificate to the Superintendent of the Asylum, who, on its receipt, will, if he has a child answering the description, immediately fill up an indenture, and forward it for the signature of the applicant. The applicant having signed it, and caused his signature to be properly attested, must inclose the same, with a sufficient amount of money (unless he prefers to send some one or come himself for the child) to pay the expenses of the child to its new home, and direct the same to the Superintendent of the New York Juvenile Asylum, New York.]

This Form of Application, in use as of 1856, was to be filled out by each applicant for a child. See next page for the second page of the Form.

Applicants for a child had to procure suitable references in the city, and shall bring besides a certificate of character from a minister of the gospel, a justice of the peace, a town superintendent of Common Schools, or any two of them, testifying to moral character, his temper, disposition, and habits, and fitness in their opinion to have the management and control of a child.[51]

In 1855 the Asylum indicated that the indentures could be cancelled by magistrates "for cause, on complaint of the children."[52]

In connection to the Indenturing Committee, the Committee on Correspondence was to

> keep themselves advised of the state and condition of the pupils who may have been apprenticed, and for such purpose, semi-annually at least, shall correspond with the master of each apprentice, and with the apprentice himself, and thus inform themselves of his health, condition, and progress; preserve a record, and when required, report such correspondence to the Board.[53]

The Asylum routinely ran examples of the letters received from both the masters and the apprentices in its annual reports.

> July 10, 1855
> J. [John] D. Russ Esq
>
> Sir
> I wish the Board of Directors at the Juvenile Assylum to know that I am well. contented. and happy. and in answering your questions I would say 1st My health is good 2d I never in my life before had better food. clothing and lodging. 3d I have attended Sabbath School & Public Worship every Sabbath except one (when I had the Fever & Ague) since I came here. 4th I have improved in reading some but not in Arithmetic or much in writing. 5th I am improving in pegging boots & I learn some in Farmer's work. I feel contented to live with Mr. & Mrs. _____ and I want to stay with them until my time is out I have been sometimes a good boy and sometimes a bad boy, but I am agoing to try to grow better. I would like to know whether that boy by the name of Johnson is at the Assylum whose number was _____.[54]

In addition to corresponding with the masters, the directors occasionally visited the children, "either personally or by a suitable agent, especially where a considerable number are placed in the same neighborhood."[55]

Beginning in 1856, the Asylum greatly expanded its western indenturing program (orphan trains), and very few children, with the exception of African American children, were indentured in New York or any of the other eastern states. In a 1903 letter written to a prospective foster mother applying for a girl from East Rockaway, New York, the Asylum explained the terms of the indenture:

> Children are sent on three months trial, and, if at the end of that time both parties are satisfied the girl is indentured until she is eighteen years of age, during which time you will bind yourself to care for the child properly, clothe her and give her a certain amount of schooling each year. When the indenture expires you are to give the girl a new bible, two complete outfits of wearing apparel and $50.00 in cash.[56]

Section 21 of the Asylum's Charter stipulated that the masters could not prevent the child indentured to them from applying the trade they were taught upon the conclusion of the indenture:

> No person shall accept from any journeyman or apprentice, indentured as aforesaid,

any contract or agreement, nor cause him or her to be bound by oath or otherwise during his or her term of service, that such journeyman or apprentice shall not set up his or her trade, profession or employment in any particular place, ship or cellar; neither shall any person exact from any journeyman or apprentice, after his or her term of service is expired, any money or other thing for using or exercising his or her trade, profession or employment in any place.[57]

Discharges

If a child was committed by a court magistrate, the parents could make an immediate appeal to the courts for the release of the child and obtain a magistrate's discharge. Magistrates could not only commit a child to the Asylum, but for twenty days had the "unconditional right of discharge."[58] At the expiration of the twenty days the Asylum's Charter stipulated "sole authority over the children reverts to the Directors of the Asylum, who detain them until in their judgement it is proper to discharge them."

Exceptions were made to the standard two-year commitments, but only after a parent, guardian, or legal representative made an official application for the child's discharge. Once accepted into the Asylum, it was unusual for such early discharge requests to be granted, unless the child had an exemplary record since being admitted.

A case in point was a boy named Jacob Friedman. When an attorney wrote the Asylum on May 7, 1903, requesting Jacob's discharge, the Assistant Superintendent replied: "The boy Jacob Friedman was sent here for six months on April 25th upon conviction by trial for stealing some stockings. Since the boy has been here, while not vicious in any way, at the same time he has caused considerable trouble by his disobedience and I would advise that for the boy's own sake if for no other reason you allow him to remain until his sentence is completed."[59]

A clearly distraught mother of a little girl placed in the Asylum wrote passionately, if not grammatically, requesting her daughter's discharge in 1879:

Mr. [Apollos R.] Wetmore,

I hope you will pay attenshon to this & try by all means to get my child back to me & relieve my distressed mind. She will be a comfort & a companion to me. Work will then be a pleasure to me wheare now I can neather work eat nor sleep. In fact I am a miserable woman with out her. Don't deprive me of my dear little daughter.

I have plenty of clothes for her & enough for her to eat & I will do my best to try to bring her up right. Do try & comply with my wishes & receave a Mother's Blessing & may you be rewarded in heaven ten fold for it.

Respectfully,
Your Humble Servant
Sarah

P.S. I will pay all her expenses coming home.[60]

In all applications for discharge, the "physical, mental and moral surroundings which the home offers the children" were studied. The Asylum checked to see if the factors that caused a child's truancy or destitution still remained or had indeed improved enough to warrant the child's discharge. The intention of the parents in regard to the child was also evaluated. One of the Asylum's Visitors noted, "There is a decided tendency to take the children home and make use of their recently acquired English by giving them employment while still below the legal age for working."[61] The Visitor was alluding to the fact that many children of recent immigrants were admitted to the NYJA and taught to speak English during their stay.

The Visitor described the conditions she found in many of the homes and families during her investigations:

The homes of applicants for discharge

A Magistrate's Discharge granted to a mother for her son, William, from the New York Juvenile Asylum's House of Reception in July of 1867. (New York Juvenile Asylum records; Rare Book and Manuscript Library, Columbia University Library)

present much better conditions than those of applicants for admission. Some of our children come from cellars lighted only by the stairway and coal shaft; some from garrets approached only by a ladder; some families had pawned all furniture, preserving only a soapbox as a seat, and in three instances the children slept upon a heap of rags in the corner of the room. Some are found shivering without a fire, and some are absolutely homeless, and sheltered by the charity of neighbors almost as poor as themselves. In one case all that the friends had to offer was space upon the bare floor for a mother and five children to sleep. Among the Italians the evils of overcrowding are especially manifest. In three rooms may be found as many families, aggregating ten or more individuals, or a family of five may be found crowded into one small room.[62]

When a Mrs. Smith wrote to the Asylum asking for the early release of her son, Julius, in May of 1903, she included a letter of recommendation from Morris H. Gottlieb, whose relation to Mrs. Smith is not noted. Her son had been committed for petty larceny on May 13, 1902. The Assistant Superintendent, Edwin C. Burdick, replied with words of skepticism, but also left the door open to the possibility of discharge: "Under the circumstances I can see no reason why the boy should be released until the expiration of the regular term of two years, but if there are any good reasons why the boy should be released, if they are presented to the Committee it is possible that they may consider the application."[63]

The following week Burdick replied to another concerned party inquiring on behalf of Julius, explaining, "His sentence is an indeterminate one and we have the power to keep him until he is twenty-one years of age, but the Board of managers have decided that children who have behaved themselves and have a good record in the institution may be discharged at the end of two years, provided, of course, that there is a responsible person to whom they may be discharged."[64]

The Children's Village devised a system of credit marks in Dobbs Ferry. Children had to earn a certain number of credits to be released. The length of time it took to attain the number of credits amounted to what had been the standard two-year sentence that had always been in place. Superintendent Guy Morgan, replying to two parents requesting release of their sons, wrote:

Dear Madam:

I have your letter making application for the release of your son from this school. All boys who come here are required to earn a certain amount of credit marks before they are eligible to go out. This usually takes them 24 months.

———

Dear Sir:

I have your letter making application for the release of your son from this institution. All boys committed to this school are required to remain 24 months from the time of their commitment.[65]

The system of credits was replaced with a system of parole in 1918. Children were released on parole for a twelve-month period, remaining under the legal control of the The Children's Village. Parolees were supervised by "visitation, correspondence and monthly report." Between 150 and 250 inmates per year left the The Children's Village under parole. In 1919, there were 191 children out on a trial term, nineteen of whom were returned for violation of their parole. A grand total of 214 were out on parole and under supervision as of December 31, 1920.[66] The practice was abruptly discontinued in 1924 after a new superintendent took the helm.[67]

In 1898, the NYJA decided to hire a person to "ascertain the whereabouts and occupations of children who had been discharged to their parents and guardians" in New York City "after a detention of two years in the asylum." The names of several hundred children were selected from 1893 through 1897 (five hundred in all). Care was taken to choose those who "had seemed to be the least promising." Louise A. Husted, M. D., was hired to complete the task, which she did between April 10 and December 31. Husted had varied success. Some of the parents could no longer be located as they had moved and left no forwarding address. Of those found and reported, the Asylum concluded that 77 percent were "doing well and were a credit to the institution." Children under fourteen were attending school. Some were found at work at various trades, such as carpentering, shoemaking, and painting. The Asylum was quick to point out that the children were taught such trades during their stay at the Asylum. Twenty-three cases were deemed "unfavorable." Of those, some were "incorrigible" and "on account of their bad behavior had been sent to the New York House of Refuge and the Elmira Reformatory." There were no females in the "unfortunate" class.[68]

❧ CHAPTER THREE ❦

The Children of the NYJA

Immigrants

There's no doubt that the flood of immigrants into New York City contributed greatly to the numbers of children admitted to the NYJA. By 1855, the population of New York City had grown to 630,000—up from 166,000 in 1825.[1] Of the immigrant children, Asylum officials later said, "The boys, many of them, took to the streets. They became waifs, beggars, scamps, rowdies, loafers, roughs and toughs, and not a few became criminals."[2]

The Asylum kept track of the nationality of each child admitted, and reflected in their records are the early immigrants from Europe. For instance, during 1854, 50 percent of the 1,050 children committed to the Asylum were natives of Ireland.[3]

Much of the Irish immigration during the Asylum's early years was due to the Irish potato famine that created two million refugees. About one million died, and about one million emigrated. A large majority were tenant farmers evicted by their landlords during the crisis. They fled Ireland and arrived in America, children in tow—many with little more than the clothes on their backs. The Irish immigrants in particular tended to congregate in the poorer districts of New York City (the Lower East Side), unable to afford to travel outside of the city to look for higher paying jobs. Many of the fathers set out on their own to seek jobs building the canals and railroads of the West. Their wives, left behind to care for their offspring, took jobs as servants and

Immigrants arriving at Castle Garden. (*Frank Leslie's Illustrated Newspaper, 1878*)

laundresses to make ends meet. Some of the fathers never returned, having died of canal fever or other diseases related to their work, or simply deserted their family back in New York.

Cholera was another reason many Irish children lost one or both parents. The disease took its biggest toll on highly concentrated populations, struck particularly hard in the Irish neighborhoods. In 1850, out of the 2,742 persons who died of cholera in New York City, 1,086 of them were Irish. Although the Irish-born constituted 30 percent of the population, they accounted for forty out of every one hundred persons who died of cholera in the city. Foreign-born people constituted 55 percent of the cholera deaths in New York City.[4]

The mid-1890s brought a wave of Italian immigrants, and from the late 1890s to the early 1900s, waves of Russian and Polish Jews as well as Syrians. Twenty-one percent of the children admitted to the NYJA in 1896 were of Italian descent. Russian children led by 1898 with 16 to 18 percent of admissions.[5]

Fourteen million immigrants arrived in America between 1900 and 1914.[6] In 1900, just 21 percent of the 1,073 commitments to the Asylum were "Americans." In 1902, NYJA reported that "sixty-four percent of the children committed to the Asylum were born in America and a large percentage of this number was born of foreign parentage." The number of Russian children who immigrated equaled 23.5 percent of the total number of children born in the United States.[7]

In 1903, Asylum President Mornay Williams, comparing the Asylum's tables of nativity with those issued by the Census Bureau for the year 1902, deduced that the number of foreign-born children cared for by the Asylum was equivalent to 1 percent of all juvenile immigrants received at the port of New York.[8]

A fund-raising pamphlet distributed by the NYJA alluded to what amounted (intended or not) to its attempt to Americanize the immigrant children:

> The children come, for the most part, from the dense districts [of New York City] that have been invaded by and have capitulated to the immigrant—districts having less than twenty-five percent native-born white population at the 1900 census [...]. It has been pointed out that the reason for the immigrant population crowding in the great cities is the inability to make themselves understood outside their circle. The uplifting process can never come while immigrants are bound to what is practically a European environment. The Juvenile Asylum makes a fundamental education in English compulsory and in this one respect is a potential force as it aids in the assimilation of the foreign born element. [...] If they are to know high ideals and are to adjust themselves to normal social relations, they must be removed from the contamination to which they are exposed, and transplanted while they are in the formative period. Generally, their removal must be permanent—there must be a literal effacement of the old haunts and hindrances and they must be disciplined and trained before entering new homes or assuming new tasks. The molding medium is the institution and it is of vital importance that the conditions within the institution shall not be such as to unfit the wards for the work that lies before them in life.[9]

Integration

Following the total abolition of slavery in New York in 1827, New York City emerged as one of the largest pre-Civil War metropolitan concentrations of free African Americans.

On June 27, 1861, the Indenturing Committee acted on its concern over the ever-growing population of African American children in the NYJA:

> Mr. [Apollos R.] Wetmore stated that a large number of colored children had accumulated at the Asylum, many of whom had been there a long time, and requested the Committee to consider the expediency of requesting the Magistrates not to send any more colored children to the Asylum. Also to adopt some measures for the disposal of those now in the Institution.
>
> The Supt. of the House [of Reception] was instructed to notify the friends of said colored children that they would be speedily Indentured unless other provisions of a satisfactory character are made for them.[10]

At its July 18, 1861 meeting, the Indenturing Committee voted to "advertise in several city papers that the Asylum has a number of desirable colored boys for whom it wishes to find good homes with farmers in the country."

> To FARMERS.—The N. Y. Juvenile Asylum have now a number of desirable *colored boys* to be indentured as apprentices. Parties applying for them must furnish satisfactory certificates of character and ability. On personal application at the House of Reception, No. 71 West 13th street, full information will be given as to the conditions of indenture. The children, who are at the Asylum near the High Bridge, can be seen on an order obtained at the House of Reception. S. D. BROOKS,
> Sup't. N. Y. Juvenile Asylum.

The NYJA ran this advertisement in the *New York Observer* on August 1, 1861.

At the September 19, 1861 meeting, the directors decided to post handbills in trains in Long Island and New Jersey and send them to postmasters. The handbills stated that there were numerous "colored boys" at the NYJA desirable for apprenticeship.[11]

By November 1861, the Asylum was receiving applications from western New York and as far away as Michigan due to ads placed in "country newspapers."[12] Many of its African American children were subsequently placed in rural New York State and rural areas of surrounding states.

In 1864, for reasons that were not explained, the Indenturing Committee voted to not indenture a child (white or black) in New York City "if any other suitable situation could be found."[13] The decision was likely due, at least in the case of the Caucasian children, to the success of NYJA's western indenturing program.

A reporter for *Scribner's Monthly* who visited the Asylum in 1870 described some of the African American children she encountered, most notably the office boy at the House of Reception:

> We noticed here and there a colored child studying or reciting with the others—attentive pupils they seemed to be, though larger than the average of the white children in the same classes. The Institution has had some very bright negroes in charge, chief among whom stands an orphan boy, who, with his brother and sister, found a home in the Asylum some years ago. He was unusually clever, and had so remarkable a memory, that though only about ten years of age, he could call by rote the school-roll of over five hundred names. When requested, he could as correctly call it off, including in their regular order the names of those who had left within the past year or so—the whole amounting to one thousand names. The brother and sister were, after a while, settled in good places, and he was installed as office-boy in the House of Reception, where he renders excellent service. He writes a fine hand, and is moreover a living directory of the names and residences of all the managers and patrons of the Institution, as well as of almost every one whose address he has ever known. Often he is left in sole charge of the office. I have seen him lately, a fine, clear-browed fellow, very boyish, with a good face, yet full of true negro playfulness. It is hard to say whether he is happier laboring at his book-keeping duties, or when out on the side-walk driving his dog before a little wagon.[14]

By 1888, the policy of the NYJA shifted regarding the indenture of colored children to one *favoring* homes closer to New York City: "Colored children who have no homes are placed in families in the vicinity of New York."[15]

However, the policy remained the same for white children. When Mrs. E. L. Whitney of Jersey City, New Jersey, applied for a white child in 1903, Assistant Superintendent Edwin C. Burdick replied, "The Board of Managers will not allow us to place children in or near New York City. I would suggest that you apply to some of the orphan asylums in the City or to the Nursery and Hospital on Staten Island."[16] Burdick replied to a request from Helen F. Clark of New York City similarly, albeit more hope-

The "colored" office boy at the House of Reception, who had a remarkable memory. (*Mary E. Dodge, "A Day with Dr. Brooks," Scribner's Monthly, November 1870, 46.*)

fully, when she asked for a girl on behalf of a friend the same year: "We do not, as a rule, make a practice of placing white girls in the East and of course any home which may be endorsed by you, would be considered an exceptional chance for any young girl."[17]

As aforementioned, when the NYJA moved operations to Dobbs Ferry, New York, the lack of space dictated that many children would have to either be discharged or transferred to other institutions. The Asylum made the decision not to take female, African American, or Jewish children to the new Dobbs Ferry facility.

It was not until 1909 that the Asylum decided to accept African American boys once again; however, a separate cottage was designated for them:

> Under Mr. [Guy] Morgan's supervision five of the new cottages have been opened, and a further departure from recent practice made by the opening of one of them for the reception of colored boys, a number of whom,

though of Protestant parents, it had been necessary to commit to the New York Catholic Protectory, because of the fact that there was no New York institution of the Protestant faith capable of receiving such boys when committed by the courts.[18]

The first group of African American boys to occupy the special cottage was transferred from the Catholic Protectory.[19] By 1910, a second cottage was assigned, "owing to the crowded conditions in institutions for colored children and to the many appeals from the courts."[20]

Visiting Day

According to the Asylum's policy in 1853, citizens could obtain permission to visit the Asylum on "Fridays only, between three and six o'clock in the afternoon, in summer; and from two to four o'clock, in winter," with the only exception being to accommodate "strangers temporarily in the city."[21]

An author who visited the Asylum circa 1863 happened to arrive on visiting day, and she described the scene:

> At a dizzy speed we are whirled along the banks of the beautiful Hudson—taking the railroad for convenience—and are set down in very short order at a neat little station, where carriages await to convey us to the Asylum.
>
> We notice, as we wind up the romantic hill-side avenue, that knots and companies and single individuals, having each and all a family look, and generally well dressed, are bound institution-ward like ourselves.
>
> "What does this mean?" some one asks of the entertainer and friend who is guiding us. His benevolent face lights up. "Ah, I had forgotten. We have happened upon *visiting-day*, the last Thursday in every month, when all the papas and mammas have the privilege of visiting their little ones, and bringing them goodies," etc. "It will be all the pleasanter," for we

This photo of the NYJA was featured in its Forty-Sixth Annual Report (1897) and shows the various additions made over the years.

shall probably be treated to an extra feature in reformatories."

We now alight at the spacious portal, and passing the vestibule are introduced to the delightful shades of the reception-parlor and to the register nearly at the same time. Upon the pages of this register each visitor is requested to inscribe his name and the date of his visit.

As the visitors departed, the sweet evening chant of some five hundred youthful voices—a chant which closes each day's scholastic exercises—floated softly in rich harmony over the grassy lawn and along the shady avenue, and lingered with them on their homeward way, till it sounded only in memory, a memory which made each one feel like looking upward as a little child, and asking, "What is *my duty*, Lord?"[22]

By 1880, the last Thursday in January, April, July, and October, "from one o'clock until five o'clock in the afternoon," was designated as the day parents and friends could visit the children at the Asylum. The ordinary routine was suspended for the day to accommodate the visitors who were known to "throng the avenues leading to the Asylum like an invading army."[23] A room was appropriated for the visitors. Personal inspections of the classrooms, hospital, dining room, and dormitories were also allowed during these visits. It was the policy of the Asylum that on these visiting days, "No conversation respecting the discipline of the Institution shall be allowed in the presence of the children, and no visitor shall be allowed to speak to a child without permission of an officer."[24]

The Asylum declared that such visits remedied misconceptions about the Asylum: "Suspicions, born of malice or of calumny, are thus quite disarmed, and complaints, which formerly were frequent, through ignorance or fear of imagined neglect or cruelty which they had no means of measuring, have well nigh disappeared."[25]

The Children of the NYJA

Parents or friends of the children often asked to visit the children outside the normal visiting days and hours, but the Asylum rarely granted such requests. When J. Moe Cohen asked to visit his brother at the Asylum some "evening," the Asylum replied, "This is strictly against our rules. We have a visiting day once a month at which time we give up the entire day to visitors, closing shops and taking the children from school, so I do not see my way to grant your request. However, I shall be glad to have you come here on next visiting day, which will be May 31st [1903]."[26]

While still at the House of Reception (before being transferred to the Asylum), children could be visited once a week on any day but Sunday, between the hours of 9 a.m. and 12 p.m. and 2 to 4 p.m.[27]

In preparation for the move to Dobbs Ferry, Asylum Superintendent Charles Dewey Hilles sent a letter to George H. Daniels at Grand Central Station regarding transportation for parents visiting their children:

> We expect to move in May to the ridge between Dobbs Ferry and Chauncey. Our children are the street boys and girls of New York. They are not orphans. It has been our custom to have their parents visit them on the last Thursday in the month. Could we not secure through you a special rate for that day—or some other day if you prefer—so that parents and others could go and return on regular trains? We would prefer to have them arrive at and depart from Chauncey and the rate could apply from 155th Street or from Highbridge. Unless we get a rate for these poor people, many of them will go up by trolley to Hastings, notwithstanding the great loss of time.[28]

In 1906, the Asylum noted: "At the old Asylum on Washington Heights, there were months when only 36 per cent. of the children were visited."[29] In 1911, the Asylum reported that the average number of children receiving visits each month was "about sixty per cent. of the enrollment."[30]

William Masterson. He was sent west by the NYJA in 1885 and indentured in Illinois. (*Courtesy of Patricia Bastianelli*)

Not being visited by a parent had to have been a huge disappointment to the children. Such was the case with a boy named William Masterson who was sent west from the Asylum in 1885 and indentured in Illinois. Four years later, William wrote to his sister, Ida, who remained in New York City:

> I would give anything to know what has become of mother and what she is doing. I expect that she is married again and don't care whether she sees I or you any more or not. The last time I saw her was when I went to the Asilum. She could have come to see me if she

wanted to, but I guesse that when she got rid of us that was all she cared for.³¹

By 1913, visiting day was changed to the afternoon of the first Sunday of each month. Asylum officials pointed out that it was "a day to which the boys look forward in pleasant anticipation and a visit from their relatives often serves to dissipate homesickness as well as preserve intact the family ties."³²

The only other contact children were allowed with their parents and friends was by letters, either written or received. In 1903, the Asylum's letter policy, which was likely in place from the beginning, alluded to letters being censored: "Letter writing day only comes on the 14th of the month. Children are allowed to receive letters at any time, although all letters are subject to supervision in the office."³³

Escapes

Both attempted and successful escapes occurred at the House of Reception and the Asylum proper with some frequency from the very beginning.

One of the earlier escapes was made by a boy named Christian Hickey. Born in France, Christian was cared for by his brother, Joseph, at his home on Thames Street, as their parents were deceased. Christian was "put out in the country" to "go to work on a farm." He lasted five or six months, and was then sent back to New York City, presumably by his employer. Upon his return, his brother put him in the NYJA, at the age of fifteen. Christian ran away, but was soon caught and sent to the New York House of Refuge on June 12, 1852 "for greater security." The Refuge noted in his case file, "He is a rather wild boy."³⁴

The 1854 annual report reported that 137 children had escaped from the NYJA. Another thirty-nine fled in 1855. In 1857, it was said that one in every six had escaped.³⁵ The directors of the Asylum explained, "The children, before their surrender to us, have generally been as unfettered in their movements as the wild Arab. [...] Can it be surprising that children, with such habits, should be restive under the restraints and forms of a disciplinary institution."³⁶

If recaptured, escapees were subject to discipline: "The rod has been used in several cases of returned runaways, not only as a punishment, but in the hope of preventing future attempts at escape."³⁷ During the early years the Asylum reported that runaways were "kept in bed-tick petticoats and their ankles shackled with the ordinary handcuffs." Asylum officials declared, "It is encouraging to know that the large majority soon discern their past errors, and quietly submit to the discipline to which they are necessarily subjected. Many, again, of the runaways, on their re-arrest, succumb, and conduct themselves with propriety."³⁸

Some of the more notable escapes made the papers over the years:

In 1868:

> JUVENILE FUGITIVES—This morning about five o'clock James O'Connor, fifteen years of age, and Thomas Driscoll, thirteen years of age, got out of the Juvenile Asylum, One Hundred and Sixty-first street and Bloomingdale Road, by lowering themselves with sheets tied together from the fifth story. They were retaken, after an exciting chase, by a police officer.³⁹

In 1891:

> Boys sent to the New York Juvenile Asylum at 176th street and Tenth avenue generally seem to be contented, and attempts to escape are rare, but three small boys eluded the vigilance of their guardians at 1 o'clock yesterday morning.
>
> They are Isaac Marks, 12 years old, Harry Most, 13 years old, and George Frash, 15 years old. They sleep in a dormitory on the sixth floor, and when they went to the room on Tuesday night they managed to carry a rope to bed with them. They had found it about the

tool rooms during recess. The rope was a long one, but it still lacked many feet of reaching the ground when they tried it, and they made up the deficiency by twisting sheets together and adding them to the rope.

Then they fastened the rope to the window frame, and one by one they slid down to the ground. They had forgotten to provide anything to conceal the gray asylum uniform. They easily scaled the walls surrounding the asylum, but their escape was quickly discovered, and word was sent to the East 152d street police station.

Capt. Cortwright sent out policemen, and three of the reserves came across the runaways travelling down Tenth avenue as fast as they could run. Long before daylight they were back in the building which they had risked their necks to escape from.[40]

One of the larger groups escaping in 1902 made the papers nationwide:

> Twenty-four boys of the New York juvenile asylum broke down an old door in the asylum yard today and escaped in the direction of the speedway. A call was promptly sent in for police help, and when the patrol wagon reached the speedway the boys were seen watching the racing from benches. With a glance at the patrol wagon the boys scattered like quail. The reserves jumped from the wagon and gave chase, but managed to capture only fourteen of the young fugitives. The ten who had alluded the policemen came back one by one in the afternoon. "Nothing will be done to punish them," said Supt. Galbrandt [Aaron P. Garrabrant], who has charge of the asylum. "They are mostly destitute boys committed for their own welfare. The reason for their escape was that they wanted to take a run in the fine weather and see the speedway races."[41]

Garrabrant's statement about the boys not being punished was apparently just for the benefit of the newspaper as just five months later, Edwin C. Burdick, Assistant Superintendent, wrote about two boys (Philip Ziegler and John Thompson) who attempted to escape by "hiding among the steam pipes on the walls of the cellar under the lavatories" and were "only found after a search of two hours." For their attempted escape, Burdick proclaimed, "Both boys are now undergoing punishment in the drill squad." He concluded by surmising, "If these boys are transferred to the New York House of Refuge I think the precedent so established will deter the other boys from attempting to break away for at least some months."[42]

Burdick followed through on his plan to set an example by transferring a few boys who attempted to escape to the New York House of Refuge. A boy named Henry—the ringleader of a group of no less than forty-two boys in an escape orchestrated in early May of 1903—was transferred, along with one of his cohorts—to the House of Refuge.

The frequent attempted and successful escapes begged the question of what would happen after operations were moved in 1905 to Dobbs Ferry, New York, where there was no wall or fence designed to keep the children from escaping? The Asylum's Superintendent, Charles Dewey Hilles, expressed his views on this risk:

> There are those who look with incredulity upon the experiment of an institution without a high wall. They think that during the early months the boys will indulge their taste for freedom. Even so, history will only be repeating itself. When the Asylum was organized, it was with a view to the removal of children from the close confinement and degrading tutelage of the prisons. The first years on Washington Heights were memorable for the large numbers who deserted. The founders were paying the penalty of pioneers, yet they did not return to the system whose ideality was zero—the system that could not distinguish,

> STATE OF NEW YORK—STATE BOARD OF CHARITIES
> [To be placed on file in the institution to which the child is transferred]
> (Form of application and approval of transfer of children, under the Rules adopted by the Board, pursuant to Article VIII, Section 1, of the Constitution.)
>
> No._____
>
> *APPLICATION IS HEREBY MADE*
>
> For approval of the transfer of _Henry N_____ (alias S____)_
> Record No. _7657_, from the _New York Juvenile Asylum_
> to the _House of Refuge_
> for the following reasons: _Being ringleader in escape of forty two (42) boys. Generally incorrigible._
>
> Dated _May 4_ 1903, _Edwin C. Burdick_
>   SUPT. OR PRESIDENT
>
> We hereby consent to receive the said _Henry_ (alias S   )
> as an inmate of the **House of Refuge**
> Dated _May 6._ 1903
>   SUPT.
>
> On the foregoing application and consent the undersigned, Commissioner of the State Board of Charities for the **Kings County**, hereby approves of the transfer of the said _Henry_ (alias S   )
> Dated _May 6,_ 1903.
>   COMMISSIONER

A boy named Henry was transferred from the NYJA to the NYHOR on May 6, 1903 for being the "ringleader in escape of forty two (42) boys. Generally incorrigible" Such transfers had to be approved by the New York State Board of Charities at the time (*New York House of Refuge, Case Files, Series A2064, Vol. 60 (1902-1903); New York State Library Archives, Cultural Education Center, Albany, New York.*)

in its treatment, between mischievous youngsters and vicious adults. Where a movement goes forward by leaps and bounds, some time must be spent in making adjustments.[43]

There were twenty-four attempts at escape during the first three months after the move to The Children's Village and seventeen during the succeeding three months, culminating with one in December.[44] In 1906, the total reached fifty-five, the attempts being made "largely by the boys in the House of Reception," which was by that time located on the same premises.[45]

In 1915, six boys made a daring escape from their third-floor dormitory at midnight by tying blankets together: "[. . .] slipping to earth in the most approved dime novel fashion. Their only clothes were flannel pajamas. In this costume they made their way into Hastings and broke into the basement of Morris Rosenbaum's shoe store, where

The Children of the NYJA

they opened a case and provided themselves with rubber boots. Three were caught, and the others escaped by swimming the Hudson river."[46]

In 1916, a thirteen-year-old boy, whose name was not given, was recaptured by trustees after he escaped. Armed, he "fired on his pursuers with a pistol he had obtained, but hit no one."[47]

Apparently there was an issue with children breaking into, as well as out of, the Asylum. In 1903, Burdick penned a letter to James T. Barrow of New York City regarding the Asylum's plans to fortify the fence surrounding the playgrounds of the Asylum "to prevent not only the inmates from planning to run away, but also the outsiders from getting over." The fortification called for the fence to be "heightened three feet and the overhang into the yard will be about the same." As an added deterrent, Burdick declared that "barbed wire will be strung at intervals of a few inches." Burdick concluded by speculating, "I think that this will make it impossible for the boys to get over." The total cost was projected at "about $75.00, exclusive of labor, which will be done by the institution carpenter."[48]

A Bad Influence

One of the great downfalls of institutions such as the NYJA was the fact that children convicted of very serious crimes were housed alongside those who were simply truant or destitute—not guilty of ever having committed a crime. As a consequence, many of the innocent children were taught the vices of the more criminally inclined. The Asylum's managers began to realize this dichotomy fairly early, expressing concern that "the class we are all trying to influence for good, when collected in numbers in a large institution, almost of necessity corrupt one another."[49]

When a visitor at the Asylum suggested all of the children there were "little vagrants, more or less criminal," Dr. Samuel D. Brooks, who served as both Superintendent and Physician at the Asylum from 1858 to 1871, acknowledged this mix of "classes" in his response: "The parentage of some of our inmates would astonish you. We have had the children of lawyers, merchants, clergyman, and high dignitaries here, to say nothing of descendants of noted men, all voluntarily sent from comfortable homes for reform. Again, a number of our children are innocent of any known offence. They are brought simply on account of destitution, and are sent away as fast as suitable homes can be obtained."[50]

In 1903, Minnie M. Rathburn of Poultney, Vermont, inquired about boarding her son at the Asylum, which ran $2.00 per week at the time. Edwin C. Burdick responded to her very honestly, indicating his awareness of the hazards of mixing the innocent with the criminally inclined:

> I would advise you not to send the boy here, but to endeavor to find a place for him on some farm away from your home, or, if that will be impossible to send him to some institution in your own state.
>
> If the boy be sent here he would be associated with a number of boys who have lived all their lives in the City and who are thoroughly acquainted with all the tricks which can be learned by boys who have no other playground than the street, and sending him here would really do more harm to him than good.[51]

A former inmate of the Asylum named Jack Rose recalled his experience with what Burdick was alluding to during his ten-month stay:

> In my case the fact that I lost all my hair as the result of an attack of scarlet fever when I was 5 years old was responsible for my playing truant. Other boys play truant for different reasons. The reason doesn't matter [...]. I was sent to the New York Juvenile Asylum. There I associated with boys who were even then confirmed criminals and who readily imparted what they knew of criminal methods to the rest of us and filled our willing ears with wonderful tales of the "soft money" to be made by picking pockets and snatching handbags. [...] Many of them were adept

pickpockets, others had had considerable experience with breaking in stores, still others were thoroughly familiar with firearms, while the majority of those who had lived in the underworld had associated with criminals of every stripe, and had listened with interest to stories of their exploits and were familiar with their methods, if they had not already put them into practice. [...] From these new associates I learned more of criminal ways and methods in the 10 months during which I was an inmate of the asylum than I have learned in the 20 years I have lived in the underworld.[52]

A good example of Rose's reference to some boys being "familiar with firearms" was the case of Maitland Jarvis, a twelve-year-old "boy scout" from the Bronx. After shooting and killing Harry Luckhardt, age nine, Jarvis was committed to the NYJA by Justice Mayo of the Children's Court on a charge of being "incorrigible."[53]

It was not until 1907 that the State Board of Charities finally ruled that delinquent and dependent youth could not be maintained in the same institution. The directors of The Children's Village had to decide which group (delinquent or dependent) they would take in. They chose the latter, but complained quite bitterly about it:

> The Asylum has become almost exclusively a reformatory institution. That is to say, its wards are no longer drawn both from the class of children technically labelled as dependents and the class technically labelled as delinquents, but are, by the action of city authorities, and by the desire of the State Board of Charities, confined almost exclusively to boys committed by the courts for misdemeanors and sometimes felonies. [...] The courts, as guardians of public morals, have made this institution, as far as the children of Protestant parents are concerned, the reformatory agency of the city of New York.[54]

They added, "It seems to have been accepted as true that among boys of very tender years there is no perceptible difference between the so-called delinquent class and the so-called dependent class; yet the sentimental demand for the separation of the 'sheep' from the 'goats' has prevailed." The ruling barred from the The Children's Village "all children under six years of age and all others who have not been committed by the Courts."[55]

The State's penal code provided that "a child under the age of seven years is not capable of committing crime" and section nineteen of the same code read, "a child of the age of seven years and under the age of twelve years is presumed to be incapable of crime, but the presumption may be removed by proof that he had sufficient capacity to understand the act or neglect charged against him and to know its wrongfulness." Asylum Superintendent Charles Dewey Hilles expressed his thoughts on this statute: "The criticism of the existing provisions of the law on the subject is that only those below the age of seven are entirely exempt from the operations of laws applicable to adult offenders. For children seven and over 'the presumption may be removed' and in practice it too often is removed."

Asylum Boys in the Civil War

Many hundreds of the NYJA children answered Lincoln's call and served in the Civil War. The Asylum estimated that about two thousand enlisted, including at least 350 boys they sent west from 1853 to 1865.[56]

One of the Asylum's western placing agents, George H. Allan, once visited President Abraham Lincoln in Illinois:

> Having had a half hour's conversation with that gentleman, mostly in relation to the Asylum and its work among the poor and friendless children of New York City, I remarked, on rising to take leave, that the Directors were endeavoring to implant right ideas of thought and action in the minds of the boys, adding my belief that a few words

Mr. Allan had a deep interest in the NYJA boys who served in the war (as well as all others he placed in homes), as evidenced by the following advertisement he placed in Illinois newspapers in January 1864 after he resigned from his job as Western Agent due to illness:

> MR. GEORGE H. ALLAN, formerly Western Agent of the New York Juvenile Asylum, having recovered from his long and severe illness, is desirous of receiving letters from all the children he has settled in the West. Also, from all the boys who are now in the army. He promises a reply to all who write to him before January 15th, 1864, and would be glad to receive a likeness from any of the children. Direct to 71 West Thirteenth street, New York. Cut this out and keep for reference.[58]

Later that year, in Allan's final report as Western Indenturing Agent, he wrote several paragraphs about the boys of the NYJA who served in the Civil War under the title "BOYS IN THE ARMY":

> Three hundred and fifty of the boys settled in the West are now in the Army. They have nobly responded to the call of their country and have done valiant service in the field. In addition to these a still larger number of the former pupils of the Asylum, who have not gone West, have also engaged in this glorious work. As there is no reason to doubt their having responded in the same proportion as those settle in the West, I think I do not over estimate in saying that TWO THOUSAND of our boys are now or have been in the Army. Two full regiments of young heroes, full of life and vigor, have represented your Institution in the great struggle for freedom and national integrity, and the records of their devotion and patriotism are abundant and highly creditable. These boys are scattered through all parts of the Army, East and West, and probably not a battle of any magnitude is fought

Lincoln's words "emblazoned on the wall of the auditorium at The Children's Village." (*NYJA Annual Report, 1921*)

of friendly counsel directly from him to them would not only please them, but undoubtedly do them good. As he shook my hand in parting, he said, 'Tell the boys of the Juvenile Asylum that they must follow truth, justice, and humanity, if they wish to become useful and honorable men." These few words, embodying a noble sentiment, have been treasured in the minds of hundreds of our boys, and are to them full of encouragement for the future. The advice, good in itself, is rendered all the more forcible by the daily life and practice of the man who gave it, who is now setting so noble an example of 'truth, justice, and humanity' to our nation and the world. The above words have been suitably inscribed on a large tablet, and hung in the main school room of the Asylum, where they will doubtless be the means of good for years to come.[57]

in any part of the country in which some of them are not engaged. Some have laid down their lives in the service and many others have been wounded. Of the boys in Western Regiments, though they are comparatively young, quite a number are now Lieutenants and Sergeants, and one at least has attained the rank of Captain.

During my recent tour in the West I have met some of their officers and have heard many pleasing accounts of their bravery upon the battle field. I will narrate but two. D. F. [likely Dennis Farrell], of the 123d Ills., after doing good service at the battle of Stone River, was struck by three bullets, in the head, arm and thigh. Faint and bleeding he was laid by his comrades under a tree. Soon his Captain came to him, and stooping over him was attending to his wants, when a Rebel sharpshooter fired at the Captain. The bullet, however, took effect upon the wounded boy. Maddened with pain, he grasped a musket and gave the cowardly foe another volley, and then sank back exhausted. He recovered, however, by care and skillful nursing, and is now in his old place in the ranks. T. S. [Thomas Shannessy], of Co. D, 41st Ills., was ordered, together with 27 men, to charge a redoubt at the siege of Jackson, Miss. As they went forward, the Rebels poured in a terrible fire upon them, and soon the color bearer fell dead. Another took his place and soon shared his fate. Six color bearers were thus shot down in succession when T. S. was ordered to raise the flag from the mud, into which it had fallen when shot from the staff. Hastily affixing the colors to his musket, he had proceeded but a few steps, when a cannon ball shivered the gun in his hand, knocked him over, and again trailed the flag in the dirt. Springing up, he seized another musket, attached the standard, and this time carried the Star-Spangled Banner over the ramparts of the enemy, amid the cheers of his comrades. Of twenty-seven men that started with him, but nine remained unhurt. The boys often related instances of bravery in the Asylum boys, but I must not take time to repeat them here.

Eight of our boys were members of the 25th Illinois. They served through their three years, and all returned safe and well, though the regiment was much reduced by casualty and illness. Nine of our boys also served their full term of three years in the 10th Illinois. Their company numbered originally 101 men. Of these but 47 returned in safety. *All* of our boys (nine in number) were among these 47 men, and all returned healthy, hearty and robust; the fact speaking volumes for their endurance and soldierly qualities. Two of them had been severely wounded. I was present at a festival given in honor of this company on its return from the war. The flag presented by the ladies three years before was returned to the fair donors torn, dirty and battle scarred by service in sixteen engagements, but it was to my eye radiant with honor and glory, and I joined with a hearty good will in the cheers which were given for its noble defenders. Four of these boys, now men, have visited their friends in New York and addressed the children at the Asylum.

Some months since, wishing to encourage our boys in the field, I prepared a friendly letter of advice and sympathy, which was printed and a copy sent to each. Many responses to this letter have been received, and they are full of interest. They give accounts of their marches, battles and camp experiences, and though from five to eight years have elapsed since most of them left us, they always have a message of gratitude and affection for the Directors and teachers. They are also very friendly towards each other, and numbers of them, belonging to different regiments not unfrequently spend their holidays together, arranging little meetings among themselves, like the alumni of our colleges. I am now preparing a list which shall contain the names of all our boys in Western regiments so far as known, with their regiments and companies, a copy of which, in hands of each boy, will aid him in finding his old schoolmates. Some of the boys are now sending their money to the Asylum Treasurer, to be held in trust for them till the war is over, and for their relatives in case of their decease. The amount thus deposited is quite large.

New York, December 31, 1864.[59]

Asylum records indicate that one boy's life was saved when a bullet struck the Bible he carried during the Battle of Kennesaw Mountain.[60]

An article written for Memorial Day celebrations in 1906 gives many details about the NYJA boys who served:

NEW YORK, May 21. (Special Correspondence)—When on Memorial Day in New York city the veterans of the Grand Army march to the tomb of their buried leader where he lies in state of the bank of the Hudson, one of the bands that regularly joins in the procession is the Boys' band from the New York Juvenile asylum at Chauncey, New York. Forty strong, in dashing uniform of gray, it moves with martial importance, for it has traditions to bear, and it plays a really inspiring music to which the old warriors lift their feet with as much enthusiasm as ever.

About a hundred of these abandoned or erring waifs joined the army, not alone from the New York headquarters of the asylum, but from homes in the west where they had been placed with prosperous farmers, fiercely sympathizing foster-fathers who aided and abetted them in most instances to go out and fight.

A county judge in the west [Ottawa, Illinois] today, Michael H. [Hanifen], historian of a Grand Army post in Illinois, recollects that the words of Lincoln gave him his first

Judge Michael L. Hanifen who was sent west from the NYJA when a young boy and later served in the Civil War. (*Find-A-Grave Memorial 64643277*)

definite impulse in the right direction, though, having been sent to the asylum for stealing a push-cart of apples, he writes, too, that "the apple caused the fall of Adam and the rise of Mike." He joined Battery B. of the First New Jersey artillery, a division that saw some spirited action, and Mike, his comrades tell, "stuck to his gun like a friend and a brother."

The Illinois regiments, from the home state of Abraham Lincoln, won the greatest number of recruits from the Juvenile asylum. Several, indentured in the west, finding themselves too young for the regular service, enlisted as drummer boys and drummed Illinois regiments to victory. Two had become great friends and were living on neighboring farms joined the Eighth Illinois, when it mustered in at Cairo, Ill., on a hot day in July, 1861. The two comrades fought side by side at the siege of Fort Donelson, and fell there, giving their lives to the precarious victory of Grant, which made possible the more significant victories of Shiloh and Vicksburg, that gave Grant's greatness an opportunity. In other words, the young heirs of the asylum's care today would not be drumming veterans to a Grant's tomb on Memorial Day had their gallant young forerunners died in vain before Fort Donelson.

Several Asylum boys fought with the Ninth Illinois at bloody Shiloh, and were among the regiment's 387 killed on the first day of battle, the terrible 6th of April, when the field was sown with dead in a strip some four miles long and two miles wide. There were asylum boys in Nelson's division when it came bringing first reinforcements to the hard-pressed Union soldiers at Shiloh, whose "glittering bayonets, moving in perfect order, brought hope to the Federals."

One lad who lived in Champaign county, Illinois, with a good-hearted farmer whom he delighted to worry with malicious and mischievous tricks, was hanging over the fence one day plotting new vexations when he saw the famous Lead Mine regiment of Illinois volunteers go by through the dust of Champaign City. There were no more chores in the farm-yard for him. He was off and away and joined the regiment on the day it left Cairo with General Grant to bivouac on the Tennessee. There were two other asylum boys in the same regiment, and all three did brave service in the severest engagements of the Tennessee company. The regiment received its baptism of fire at Fort Donelson when it went to the relief of the Forty-sixth Illinois. It gallantly supported Sherman at Shiloh and Grant at the terrible artillery duel of Vicksburg, where it held the position directly in front of Fort Hill, regarded as the key to the enemy's fortress. It took part in the assault on the enemy's works, and was selected to be the storming party when a breach was made by the explosion of a mine. The match was applied, the regiment rushed in, and a frightful conflict ensued, in which the Lead Mines lost 83 fighters. When the city surrendered, they were given the advance, as the conquering army marched in to take possession, and in further recognition of their valor the flag of the Lead Mine regiment was raised upon the court house to denote the Federal possession.

An asylum boy was first lieutenant in Logan's crack regiment. Others enlisted in the Stanton legion, and some in Rev. Captain [Andrew Calvin] Todd's famous Missouri regiment. One was with Sigel in the fierce little skirmish at Centreville, and another was a bearer of dispatches to General Grant, and had been with General Lyon, "The heroic Lyon," when he fell at Wilson's Creek the year before. Some were with the Thirteenth Illinois when it was first at Chickasaw bayou; two joined the Lincoln rifles, and one was with Clark at the capture of Ponchatoula in Louisiana.

When Corcoran's regiment, the Sixty-ninth, returned to New York, bringing back its banners perforated with the bullets of Bull Run, and New Yorkers gave it a vast, prolonged ovation, one little asylum lad, carried off his feet by enthusiasm, broke away from the house of reception where he was temporarily detained, and enlisted as a drummer boy. A number of others joined the famous Irish brigade and followed its fortunes through Malvern Hill, Antietam, Fredericksburg, Chancellorsville and Gettysburg, dropping off, one here and one there to swell the grand total of 1,352 killed and wounded, almost half the regiment's strength.

The asylum boys of the early sixties left no records of failure behind them. Their names will fill a hundred honorable places in the immortal muster roll of the Grand Army of the Republic. The asylum boys of today who are marching in their places have, of course, no opportunity to go out with a gun and fight "fer Lincoln;" but even to their young philosophies it becomes evident that there are other battles to be fought, battles which it may be said are going on all the more bravely in memory of the asylum boys who won theirs 40 years ago.[61]

Reverend Andrew C. [Calvin] Todd of Elkhorn, Illinois, who took in a NYJA boy, recruited a company (mostly from his congregation) and served as their captain in Company F, 10th Missouri Volunteer Infantry. The Company consisted of eight or ten boys from the NYJA. and was known as the "Psalm singing company" that went to battle from Missouri "chanting the beautiful words of the 23d Psalm."[62]

One of the NYJA boys who enlisted was Thomas J. Dale. He was sent west in 1855 and later served in Company D, 35th Illinois Volunteer Infantry. He wrote to the NYJA many years after the War ended, reporting on his later life. Asylum officials printed the letter in one of their annual reports with the preface, "What the ultimate fate is of these young colonists from the streets of New York, is as interesting as their life as apprentices. The following letter is a specimen, not of the brilliant careers which are of particular value as texts with which to lecture children on the necessity of industry and good behavior, but of the average hard-working life of a man who was given a fair show and nothing more":

I was brought out to Illinois by the Asylum thirty-seven years ago. I was apprenticed to Mr. Dennis Rouse, of Danville and remained with him six years, until 1861, when I enlisted in the Thirty-fifth Illinois Infantry and served my country as a soldier through the war, a period was spent at Andersonville as a prisoner of war. After the war I went to Kansas and took possession of a quarter section which I afterward sold, and invested the proceeds in a drug store; but that venture was not a financial success, although I gained a knowledge of business which has since proved beneficial. I always desired to obtain a good education and after my failure in the drug business I attended the Kansas State Agricultural College. As I had no money I paid my expenses by manual labor and I found it hard to prosecute my studies successfully under such disadvantages. After leaving college I returned to Illinois and taught school for several years. Two years ago I received the nomination for county treasurer for Vermilion county, and was elected for a term of four years by a majority of nearly fourteen hundred. I was required to give bond for $600,000 and my bond was signed by the most substantial citizens of the county. My salary is $1,500 per annum.[63]

CHAPTER FOUR

Life in the Asylum

Education

Children admitted to the House of Reception were immediately evaluated to determine their level of education and were assigned to a grade (in later years a class) prior to their transfer to the Asylum proper. In 1874 it was explained that the Asylum children "were divided into eight grades, with a separate room and teacher for each class."[1]

Duties of the teachers called for the following: "The Teacher shall have charge of the pupils during the hours appropriated for study and shall be responsible for their conduct while under his direction. [...] He shall also impart to them, from time to time, as well upon the week days as on the Sabbath, suitable moral instruction, with a view to inspire them with correct principles of action and improve their habits."[2]

The teachers operated under the following "mode of government":

> All pupils when received shall be placed, as soon thereafter as the Superintendent shall direct, in the Probationary grade, and afterwards divided according to character and conduct, into four grades. The most exemplary being placed in the first grade: those who are less worthy, in the second; those who stand still lower, in the third: and the least tractable, in the fourth. Any pupil who may be proved guilty of profaneness, lying, stealing, attempting to escape from the Asylum, or any other grossly bad conduct may be expelled from the grades, for a longer or shorter period, according to the aggravation of the offence. Pupils under expulsion shall not be allowed any play or conversation, their food shall be bread and water, and when not at work or in school, they shall be confined in solitude. Pupils in the fourth grade shall be deprived of play and conversation. Those in the third grade may play and converse with each other, but not with the pupils in the other grades. Pupils in the second and first grades may converse and play together, and have the privilege of using the books in the library. From these two grades pupils may be selected as monitors, and for other places of confidence and honor. Pupils in the first grade may be distinguished by an appropriate badge, and be indulged with other privileges at the discretion of the Superintendent, under the general direction of the Board.[3]

The library mentioned above resulted from the bequest of one of the Asylum's founders, Benjamin F. Butler.[4]

After her visit to the Asylum in 1870, the reporter from *Scribner's Monthly* described the children while they were at school:

> It is the main school-room and chapel combined. A vase full of pretty flowers stood upon the speaker's [Dr. Samuel D. Brooks]

desk; assistant teachers were seated or standing near by. A few monitors stationed about the hall kept perfect order by means of an occasional gesture. The children all were attentive and seemed interested. On the walls hung maps, various national coats of arms, illuminated Bible-texts, and near us, on the side wall, a message sent to the children in 1860. It is printed in large letters, the American flag is draped above it, and beneath, in illuminated text, are the words, "God bless our country."

TELL THE BOYS OF THE NEW YORK JUVENILE ASYLUM THAT THEY MUST FOLLOW TRUTH, JUSTICE, AND HUMANITY, IF THEY WISH TO BECOME USEFUL AND HONORABLE MEN.

ABRAHAM LINCOLN.

When the doctor had finished, he telegraphed smilingly to a gentleman standing near. The gentlemen nodded. Straightway we saw a little tot of a boy coming down the aisle toward us. Reaching the open place in front of the platform, he bumped his head gravely against the air, and, without so much as a breath of preparation, began:

> "I'm the boy that's gay and happy,
> Wheresoe'er I chance to be;
> And I'll do my best to please you
> If you will but list to me.
> CHORUS (sung by all the children).
> So let the wide world wag as it will,
> We'll be gay and happy still;
> Gay and happy, gay and happy,
> We'll be gay and happy still.
> SPOKEN.
> If the President should sit beside me
> I'd sing my song with usual glee;
> Fools might laugh and knaves deride me,
> Still I'd gay and happy be.
> CHORUS. – Then let, etc."

We went the rounds, staying awhile in each apartment, listening to the recitations and enjoying the enlightened, progressive character of the teaching. The range of study is about the same as that in the ward schools. All the rooms are pleasant, spacious, thoroughly ventilated, and provided with comfortable seats for the pupils. Maps, charts, pretty chromos and lithographs, adorn the walls. Illuminated mottoes abound. If some walls have ears, these certainly have tongues: "SPEAK THE TRUTH," they say to the little ones; "LOVE ONE ANOTHER;" "WELL BEGUN IS HALF DONE;" "THE EYES OF THE LORD ARE IN EVERY PLACE." Again and again they insist that "NO LIE THRIVES." Sometimes they throw back a sort of echo to the child's conscience, in the wise; "I AM LATE;" "SLOTH IMPOVERISHETH;" or: "I AM EARLY;" "DILIGENCE ENRICHETH."[5]

The children's days were carefully planned in a "distribution of duties":

> The time of the pupils shall be occupied, on week days, as nearly as practicable in the following manner: School, six hours, including recesses; work, five hours; residue at meals, and in recreation. In the months of January, February, November and December, the hour for rising shall be half-past six o'clock. In March, April, September and October, six o'clock. In May, June, July and August, half-past five o'clock. The hour for bed throughout the year, shall be not later than nine o'clock. The exercises of each day shall be commenced and closed by reading a selection from the Holy Scriptures.[6]

Although their playgrounds and dormitories were separate, boys and girls attended school or recited together.[7]

It was not until a new wing was built, in 1881, that the girl's and boy's departments were completely separate, much to the gratification of Asylum directors: "Every day convinces us of the wisdom of separating the boys from the girls [...] we are free from the annoyance of boys and girls seeking to attract each other's attention in the school room and elsewhere, and passing notes to each other."[8]

Later, the Asylum devised a system of ten classes of children. In 1892, the curriculum for the ten classes (with the tenth class being the lowest level) included the following:

Tenth Class:

Language. – Reading, from chart, blackboard, and Swinton's First Reader. Spelling familiar words. Exercises in elementary sounds.

Arithmetic. – Writing numbers. Counting. Adding.

Writing. – Script letters on slates.

Lessons on form; color; the body; familiar objects.

Ninth Class:

Language. – Reading, first reader. Meaning of words and phrases, and punctuation marks. Elementary sounds. Spelling, words from lesson; phonetic spelling.

Arithmetic. – Notation, numeration, addition, subtraction. Tables of time and money. Multiplication tables.

Writing. – Copying on slates. Lessons on plain figures; drawing; human body.

Eighth Class:

Language. – Reading, second reader. Use of capitals, punctuation; lessons reproduced. Spelling – oral, written, and phonetic; defining familiar words in lesson.

Arithmetic. – Multiplication. Tables of weights and measures.

Geography. – Begun without text-book.

Writing. – Spencerian, No. 1.

Lessons in plane and solid figures; familiar objects and places; human body.

Seventh Class:

Language. – Reading, second reader; meaning of words and phrases; capitals; punctuation; lessons reproduced. Spelling – oral, written, and phonetic.

Arithmetic. – Division. Tables of weights and measures.

Geography. – Swinton's Introductory.

Writing. – Spencerian, No. 2.

Lessons on human body; familiar places, etc.

Sixth Class:

Language. – Reading, third reader. Spelling. Grammar.

Arithmetic. – Through the simple rules; mental and written; properties of numbers.

Writing. – Spencerian, No. 3.

Geography. – Swinton's Introductory; map drawing.

Lessons on human body; familiar objects, places, etc.

Fifth Class:

Language. – Third reader. Spelling. Meaning of phrases, punctuation, and words. Grammar.

Arithmetic. – Fractions, with practical examples.

Writing. – Spencerian, No. 4.

Geography. – Swinton's Introductory. Map drawing.

Lessons on familiar objects, places, etc.

Fourth Class:

Language. – Reading, fourth reader. Spelling and defining words in lesson. Grammar.

Arithmetic. – Fractions, with practical examples.

Geography. – Swinton's Elementary. Map drawing.

Writing. – Spencerian, No. 5.

Lessons on human body, familiar subjects.

Third Class:

Language. – Reading, fourth reader. Spelling. Defining words and phrases. Grammar. Dictation. Compositions on familiar objects, places, etc.

Arithmetic. – Decimal fractions. Bills.

Geography. – Swinton's Elementary. Map drawing.

Lessons on human body, places, objects, etc.

Second Class:

Language. – Reading, fourth reader. Grammar. Spelling, Swinton's Word Book – oral and written, and defining. Dictation.

Arithmetic. – Denominate numbers.

Geography. – Monteith's comprehensive. United States in detail. Map drawing.

First Class:

Language. – Fifth reader. Dictation. Spelling and defining. Grammar.

Arithmetic. – Percentage; profit and loss; commission; interest; practical examples.

Geography. – Monteith's, political and descriptive.

Writing. – Spencerian common school course, No. 6.

Lessons on topics of interest and importance.

Girls' School-room at the NYJA. (*NYJA Annual Report, 1892*)

Kindergarten class at the Asylum, circa 1895. (*NYJA Annual Report, 1896*)

The principal, Aaron P. Garrabrant, explained this curriculum and the progress of the pupils in his 1892 report:

> The course of study conforms somewhat with that of the public schools of the city. Although rudimentary in its extent, it is adapted to the requirements of our pupils, very few of whom will ever enjoy the advantages of the high school, or college; and if they master these studies they will be fitted to perform the ordinary duties of life.
>
> The ability to write a good letter is a desirable acquisition. Our pupils write to their friends, and thus an opportunity to give practical instruction in letter-writing is afforded. The pupil first writes his letter upon a slate. The teacher then points out all errors, which the pupil corrects, and then copies the letter with pen and ink on paper.
>
> Examinations for promotion are made tri-monthly. If a pupil makes unusual progress he is advanced sooner. In this way, large boys who are backward are encouraged to greater application. This is also necessary in the case of a pupil who has been educated in a school of a foreign country, but who is unfamiliar with our language and methods of instruction.
>
> Regular instruction has been given in vocal music, twice a week, to all the children in the institution, and to the boys' and girls' choirs. A new band had been organized, and is making good progress in instrumental music.
>
> The older and larger children perform some kind of manual labor daily, either in the shops, dining-rooms, or wards, and thus are taught habits of industry.
>
> A majority of our pupils are ignorant in matters of mind and heart, and have never acquired the ability to apply themselves steadily to one thing. They remain with us not longer than two years. If an instructor makes an impression upon such pupils, under such circumstances, there must be a purpose to elevate the mental and moral condition of the pupil, and the work must be done patiently.[9]

Teachers at the Asylum were often held in high regard by the pupils. Peter S. Hanlon, who was sent west on one of the Asylum's orphan trains, wrote about the influence one of the teachers had on him during his stay:

> I was finally taken to the Juvenile Asylum, and a hard, rough-scuff fellow I was. I was not contented there till one evening a lady teacher called me to her, and inquired into my circumstances. I told her everything, and she talked so kindly that it made a new boy of me. I shall never forget her kindness as long as I live.[10]

Employment

Most of the children were employed at the Asylum "in gardening, tailoring, shoe-making, the plaiting of straw and palm leaf, the manufacture of brass nails, and such other kinds of labor as may be approved by the Board of Directors." The girls were often employed in "cooking, washing, ironing, scouring, sewing, knitting, and such other kinds of work as may be suitable to their sex, and directed by the Board."[11] Asylum officials explained how the children were paid for their work: "The working children have been paid small sums of money according to their industry, amounting to from ten to twenty dollars per month. It is believed to have been a good investment."[12]

In 1870, the boys made 5,907 articles, including jackets, pantaloons, caps, and suspenders. The girls made 4,474, including clothes, bedding, curtains, table covers, and eight carpets. The articles repaired numbered 43,912.[13]

Boys who learned to make shoes worked four hours every day, five days a week. In 1874 there were twenty-six boys that made "all the children's shoes."[14] The shoes were sold at a profit of six dollars per case, earning the Asylum between four and six dollars a day, "whilst the children enjoy the instruction and supervision of a competent and trustworthy overseer."[15] No less than 3,581 pairs of shoes were made and 13,331 pairs repaired in 1898. Asylum officials later discontinued the policy of selling articles made by the children, with emphasis instead placed on "the elementary learning of a trade."[16]

The *Scribner's Monthly* reporter who visited the Asylum in 1870 made the following observation:

> We went to the little work-shop [...] where, under the direction of a master-cobbler, the boys made the shoes of the establishment. A few little fellows on benches were busily pegging away at their work. "They do pretty well," said the boss; "but our boys never stay long enough to get a trade. It helps them ever after, though, the little cobbling they manage to learn."
>
> What is that mountain of shoes in the corner?
>
> "Those are the mended ones ready for cool weather."
>
> He showed us the patches with no little pride. Shade of St. Crispin—what patches they were! The original shoe sank into insignificance beside them.[17]

The Asylum had to purchase many supplies to keep the shoe shop in operation. They placed the following order for supplies on April 10, 1903 with Messrs. J. K. Krieg & Co., 59 Warren Street, New York City:

20 skins American calf for boys' shoes
10 skins kangaroo calf for girls' shoes
20 sides sole leather, oak, 2nd grade
10 sides inner sole lining
20 pcs. 10 ox. swill lining
Set lining markers (plain figures 1-10)
5 gross No. ½ inch stay
4 quart[s] cape North Bridgewater dressing
1 dressing can
½ doz. Small sponges
5 gross round shoe laces
50 yrds. ¼ plain calf welt
5 gallons edge blacking, one set, new method
1 doz. rough face nailing hammers
1 doz. shoe knives, short blade
½ doz. small scissors
1 can Peter's clarified leather cement
50 prs. 5 E. counters
50 prs. 6 E. counters
50 prs. 7 E. counters
50 prs. 6 Men's counters
25 prs. 7 Men's counters
25 prs. 8 Men's counters
1 box 2 oz. lasting tacks
1 box 9/3 – 14 gage swede iron shoe nails
1 box 6/8 – 14 gage swede iron shoe nails
1 box 4/8 – 11 gage standard shoe nails (slug)

Life in the Asylum

25 lbs. 6/8 patent wire clinching nails

Cut taps. First selection hemlock

1 doz. 2 oz. spools Barbour's sewing machine lining thread black and white No. 60 (3 cord)[18]

The reporter continued her tour of the Asylum with an observation of a sewing class:

> Another bright-eyed lady here, who surveyed her sewing-class proudly, with a special appreciation of the good button-hole boys. She tells all about it in a few words. There are fifty little tailors, in two divisions of twenty-five each, including two sewing-machine workers. Each division works three hours a day alternately, giving also an extra hour before school. The little tailors make all the boys' jackets and trousers, and make them well, too. "They would do better [...] if we could have them longer; but the divisions are constantly changing."[19]

In 1873 the sewing-room consisted of thirty-eight girls, where, under an instructor, they "make the girls' clothing, the boys' shirts, sheets, pillow-cases, table linen, etc." There was also a mending room where thirty girls did all the mending. The boys' clothing was made by fifty-six boys in the tailor shop.[20]

In 1879, Asylum officials declared, "All our children are at work about three hours each day, under proper supervision. They make and mend all our clothing and shoes, do our baking and laundry work, raise our vegetables, and do our house-work."[21]

The Asylum owned enough property to grow many of their own crops so many of the children assisted with the gardening. The grounds and garden were described in 1882:

> The institution grounds comprise about twenty acres, the buildings and yards occupying four acres, an equal space being covered by a grove of fine oaks, and the remaining

Shoemaking class in the "Old Juvenile Asylum." (*Library of Congress/Reproduction number LC-DIG-ggbain-01563*)

twelve acres serving for the purposes of farm and garden. Here the boys may be seen busying themselves to their own advantage, it is hoped, and that of the institution. The agricultural products of a season have been nine tons of hay, two bushels of pop corn, 9,550 ears of corn, 100 bushels of salsify, sixty of carrots, fifteen barrels of spinach, 600 early cabbages, with corresponding yield of rhubarb, radishes, peas, cucumbers, onions, parsnips, squash, etc.[22]

The children had an opportunity to show off the results of their handiwork at the Asylum's "semi-annual jollification":

> One thousand and fifty-one youngsters of both sexes in the New-York Juvenile Asylum [...] had their semi-annual jollification yesterday afternoon, between 2 and 5 o'clock, when the directors and friends of the Institution made their annual visit.
>
> The rooms in all of the apartments were handsomely decorated, and the men and women, who were received by the Superintendent, Dr. Charles E. Bruce, were delighted with everything they saw.
>
> The work of the children was exhibited,

Class in Tailoring at the NYJA. (*NYJA Annual Report, 1896*)

and it was highly praised. It consisted of writing, mathematics, darning stockings, patching clothes, the exhibition of the clothes, and shoes made by the children, and of bread and cake, none of which had been touched except by the hands of the children. The children themselves had a holiday, and numerous unusual privileges.

They also participated in a programme of music and recitations, the music being furnished by the asylum band. No member of this band could read a note of music six months ago, and now all play extremely well.

Among those present were Mayor William L. Strong, James T. Barrow, Dr. John E. Truax, Mornay Williams, Henry M. Humphrey and John Seeley Ward, Jr.

Mayor Strong made an address, in which he started with a reference to a recitation made by little Celia O'Connor, entitled "When Maria Jane Is Mayor." The Mayor declared that he was looking forward to the day when Maria Jane should be Mayor literally and that he thought New-York would be the better for it.

He praised the boys and girls highly for their work and told them that there was absolutely nothing that was not within their reach, provided they made the best of their opportunities.

Speaking directly to the directors, he declared the institution to be one of the best of the kind in the world and added that such institutions were bulwarks, in that they taught that vice was abhorrent and that crime leads only to misery.[23]

Discipline

Just nine days after its founding, the Asylum detailed its plans for disciplining and improving the inmates. The pupils would be divided into four grades according to their conduct. Each grade was granted

Life in the Asylum   67

its own privileges, such as being able to play or converse, and the members were identified by a distinctive badge. The range of privilege ran from the assessment of demerits to solitary confinement. "A regular account shall be opened with each pupil, in which he shall be charged with bad marks that may have been incurred for his faults, and credited with good marks that may be awarded him for meritorious conduct. The bad marks shall be settled for by good marks, or the infliction of such punishment as their number may require."[24]

The Superintendent was in charge of disciplining the children. "In the discipline of the children, it shall be his duty to be mild, firm, judiciously rewarding the meritorious, and punishing the guilty with promptness, justice, and impartiality."[25] The Asylum detailed the punishments:

> Our first punishment is marks of disapprobation, a certain number of which places the boy in an inferior position; the next is taking away a part of the food, as the butter, molasses, cocoa, soup, or some other article; the third, depriving him of the entire meal; the fourth, placing the boy on bread and water, and the most severe, shutting him in a dark cell and keeping him on bread and water.[26]

The Asylum tallied up the punishments inflicted during 1856: "by marks, in 17,176 instances; by whippings, in 397. Number of blows struck, 791; or an average of less than two to an offence. The offences punished by whipping were fighting, swearing, disobedience, insolence, destroying property, lying, soiling beds, escapes, etc."[27]

By 1857, the staff at the Asylum began to realize that their current system of discipline was not working. "Insofar as the system of merit and demerit marks can be relied upon, it is practiced. When this will not answer, resort is had to the rod; but only in unavoidable cases." Those "unavoidable cases" numbered 397 that year—nearly one beating per inmate.[28]

Dr. Samuel D. Brooks took the helm as Superintendent of the Asylum in 1858 and brought with him a new approach to discipline. Brooks had served as Superintendent of the State Almshouse in Monson, Massachusetts for the five years previous. His wife, Eliza, served at his side as Matron.

During Brooks' administration, a State Farm School (or Reformatory for Juveniles), connected with the Almshouse department, was organized. Brooks originated the system of classification of paupers, separating the young from the old where it did not part parent and child, "giving to curable lunatics the advantages of cheery scenery and surroundings, while the dissolute were placed in something more like work-houses."[29]

After the reporter from *Scribner's Monthly* interviewed Brooks during an 1870 visit to the Asylum, she declared of Brooks, "He expects to conquer hatred with love, and overwhelm bad tendencies with Christian firmness and charity." Brooks explained to the reporter that when he began his job as Superintendent he "found lock-up cells [...] which he demolished with his own hands. Floggings, bread-and-water fare, and forcing culprits to lift heavy weights or stand in painful positions, were among the authorized forms of punishment."[30]

But Brooks could not be in all places at all times. The minutes of the Visiting Committee, dated October 1, 1866, reveal one such instance in the yard:

> Mess. [Charles A.] Bulkley and [Edmund] Dwight reported having visited Asylum. Health good, and general condition excellent. As the new Superintendent of the yard was punishing the boys with some severity, the committee to visit this week were requested to call Doctor Brooks' attention to this & to have the teacher reminded that he is not at liberty to punish at [his] discretion and also that by a standing rule and by our charter, all punishments are to be reported to the visiting committee.[31]

By 1902, the policy for punishing children had evolved into drilling them.[32] In an unsigned letter to

The boys "on parade" at the NYJA. (*NYJA Annual Report, 1896*)

"all officers who have charge of children," dated August 7, 1903, Asylum managers ordered: "Children are not to be placed on the line standing in attention for more than one half hour at a time nor for more than two hours in one day. Children will not be placed on line for more than one day without first notifying the office. If it is necessary to punish children in more strenuous manner, the punishment will be deferred until you have consulted with me. Of course the Drill Squad slips are still in effect."[33]

In the drill squads, the children had to "march and exercise all day, without recreation. They rest and do calisthenics alternately" while food rations were reduced.[34] The assignment to the drill squad was generally for a duration of one or two days.

The Asylum's explanation of the drill squads put emphasis on improving posture, but also touched on their effectiveness in discipline:

> The nearest approach to things military is a drill, instituted for the purpose of straightening stooped figures, giving the boys a better carriage and to facilitate moving them about in groups. These drills comprise only the simpler exercises of alignment, facings, marching and counter marching by squads and companies; yet this practice in the immediate response to commands conduces to habits of prompt obedience and is therefore also a factor of some value in the support of discipline.[35]

When the father of one of the boys at the Asylum complained about the ill treatment of his son to the Commissioners of Public Charities in 1897, the Asylum acted swiftly:

> In reply to your letter of April 8, 1897, relative to the complaint of Julius Seidemann in relation to the ill treatment of his son at the New York Juvenile Asylum, let me state that upon its receipt I immediately communicated with the President of that Institution and am now advised that both Mr. Bombard, the head of the shoe shop, and his assistant,

Life in the Asylum

Mr. Yerkes, have been discharged from the employment of the Asylum, and that another man is now in charge of the shoe shop. I do not think there will be a recurrence of the trouble complained of.[36]

There were some children that could not be intimidated, of course, making them not only a threat to the Asylum's order, but to their fellow inmates as well. One such boy was Eugene K., sent west by the Asylum, who ran away from his western home and returned to New York. He had previously served two years in the New York House of Refuge. During his second commitment to the Asylum, in 1903, his name was brought to the attention of Assistant Superintendent, Edwin C. Burdick: "It has been brought to my knowledge that this boy has committed sodomy on some of the smaller boys at least three times since his return here. He was sentenced [. . .] to twenty days in the cells but this did not seem to have any effect and only the other day he repeated the offense. He does not deny having done this and seems to think he has done something to be proud of."[37]

Asylum officials added: "Where 150 boys sleep together in one room, however vigilant the night watchman and the officer occupying the adjoining sleeping apartment may be, it is practically impossible entirely to prevent evil-minded boys from corrupting some of their companions."[38]

In about 1900, the State Board of Charities made a ruling abolishing the use of corporal punishment. A few years later, Asylum President Mornay Williams gave his thoughts on the effects of the decision:

> The difficulty of management has been in recent years increased by the abolition of corporal punishment. Corporal punishment properly administered by a just and responsible official, it will be admitted, is attended with great advantages; and is regarded by some whose opinions possess weight as the very best form of punishment. It is exceedingly liable to be abused, to be inflicted unjustly, cruelly and brutally, and for this reason has been made illegal. We do not advocate restoration of it, human nature being very much the same as it always has been, and since we know that persons invested with authority can seldom be counted on not to abuse the power entrusted to them.[39]

Nevertheless, administrators at the Asylum began actively seeking a reversal of the decision as they attributed the ruling to the fairly large number (fourteen) of successful escapes in 1903. The opinion expressed above by Mornay Williams was echoed by Charles Dewey Hilles, Superintendent of the Asylum at the time: "Lax discipline, dating from the day the corporal punishment regulations were made inoperative, became a source of menacing annoyance during the year. The introduction of a drill squad has retrieved much of the lost ground and its continuance will be a substantial support to internal government."[40]

Furthermore, Hilles regarded the abolition of corporal punishment as the cause for rampant breakdown in the discipline of New York schools. In a letter to a New York City principal, he noted,

> I feel that the abolition of corporal punishment is very responsible for the fact that both truant schools are full; that a very large number of your children have been sent to the Catholic Protectory; that you have taken all the surplus room in the Westchester Temporary Home [in White Plains, New York]; that you have fifty boys in the Juvenile Asylum and that you now have more than a hundred children on the waiting list for institutions.[41]

Hilles' inference was that there was insufficient motivation for young people to stay out of the truant schools and asylums as life was not harsh enough under the new ruling.

Hilles made particular reference to the Asylum's struggle to comply with the ruling:

Charles Dewey Hilles, Superintendent of the NYJA (1902-1909). (*Library of Congress, LCDIG-ggbain-01243; Bain News Service/George Kadel, photographer*)

At times the temptation has been almost irresistible and parents of the offending boys have counseled that course. With one boy it required almost two months of incessant surveillance and anxiety, and an unlimited variety of experimental prescriptions, to cure a chronic case of misconduct. We failed in two cases, because of the restriction placed upon us, and transferred the boys to the New York House of Refuge on Randall's Island.[42]

Beginning in 1913, if children committed such offenses as "talking of running away" or "being disobedient and lazy," they were assigned to the newly established correctional cottage (Rhinelander Cottage) for several weeks where they slept under the surveillance of a night watchman.[43] Boys placed in the cottage were "assigned the more arduous and disagreeable work of handling coal, digging trenches, removing stone and performing the rough and uninviting tasks." The work continued "through both the morning and afternoon periods, recreation time and evenings being devoted to school and study."[44]

The cottage system used at The Children's Village enabled Asylum officials to initiate a system of positive incentives: gold, silver, and bronze medals awarded to the cottages demonstrating the best conduct and efficiency for the month.[45] The three medals were donated by Charles M. Jesup, Treasurer of the NYJA, and were referred to as the "Jesup medals."[46] They were designed by Tiffany & Company. The boy with the highest standing in each cottage had the distinction of wearing the badge.[47]

The military drill system was also enlarged with the objective to "inculcate in the boys the habits of obedience and discipline [...] which will help them to become more dependable workmen and better citizens."[48]

Recreation

Asylum officials recognized the fact that all work and no play was not a good policy when it came to caring for hundreds of children under one roof.

The boys' playground was described as "a great bare place, where many feet have trodden the ground almost to a solid stone. [...] Here we see turning-poles, swings, flying courses, benches, and—boys. Boys shouting, laughing, racing, swinging, turning, jumping; boys playing leap-frog, and boys falling in line at the pump!"[49] In addition, the playground featured turning bars, teeter-totters, and hop-skip-jump areas.

The girls' playground differed from that of the boys. "A few girls are playing croquet; their place is prettier than the boys', because with them grass and flowers are not impossible."[50]

A new gymnasium, built circa 1870, afforded the children with both play and exercise time:

> We were glad to see that the youngsters who had appeared saints in the chapel were monkeys in the gymnasium. They climbed, and sprang, and leaped, and spun round till we

"Girls' Croquet-Ground." (*Mary E. Dodge, "A Day with Dr. Brooks," Scribner's Monthly, November 1870, 53.*)

were dizzy. One little chap, especially, seemed boneless. He slid, head first, down the long ropes; he rolled along the floor like a wheel; he rested the back of his head on the soles of his feet, and brushed his ears with his toes. Soon a colored boy, with really a lovely face, joined him, and the two tumbled about together.[51]

In 1868 the Asylum reported, "Several have been allowed to visit their homes in the city, unattended, who, with one exception promptly returned at the expiration of the time designated to be absent."[52]

During the warmer months the children were, on occasion, allowed to go swimming in the nearby Harlem and North (Hudson) Rivers.[53] Such excursions were great fun for them, but the fun turned to tragedy for four of the boys on a warm July day in 1860. The boys were nine, eleven, thirteen, and fourteen years old. All but one boy were orphans:

> Yesterday morning some forty of the boys proceeded to a small cove just above the Fort Washington Railroad depot to bathe. They were accompanied by Gilbert H. Hills, one of the monitors in the boys' department. They had hardly all got into the water when cries were heard for help from one named Jno. [John] J. Fremer, who, it seems, had ventured out too far and was unable to swim. He had no sooner called for help than he sank. A boy named Wm. [William] H. Holly, seeing the dangerous condition of Fremer swam out in the hope of saving him. Being a remarkably good swimmer, it was not long before he was at the spot where Fremer sank: and as Holly was about to dive under for his companion, Fremer came up a little distance off and was going down for the second time when Holly seized his arm and kept him above water; he then turned to swim ashore when he was met by two other boys, one Henry Huff, and Jno. Canton, who had both started out with a view of aiding Holly in saving Fremer. Huff however not being a very good swimmer, became exhausted, and on reaching Holly seized him round the neck, to rest himself. Holly was at that time keeping Fremer's head above water; but the extra weight of Huff drew him down, and he could make no headway towards the shore. Canton also having joined the three, tried to pull Huff from Holly, when all four seized hold of one another, and in this manner, clasped as it were in each other's arms, sank and were instantly drowned—not even the slightest movement of the water being visible, after they went down, that would indicate a struggle.[54]

Holidays

Special accommodations were made for holidays at the Asylum. "On Christmas, New-Year's, and Thanks-giving days, and on the Fourth of July, the children may be allowed food of a better kind than usual, and be exempt from their ordinary occupations."[55] The local paper reported on Thanksgiving celebrations at the Asylum in 1874:

> The New-York Juvenile Asylum at One-hundred-and-seventy-sixth st. and Tenth-ave. and its House of Reception at No. 61 West Thirteenth-st., both give their inmates a din-

"Boys' Play-Ground," circa 1870. (*Mary E. Dodge, "A Day with Dr. Brooks," Scribner's Monthly, November 1870, 54*)

"The New Gmnasium," circa 1870. (*Mary E. Dodge, "A Day with Dr. Brooks," Scribner's Monthly, November 1870, 51*)

ner at 12:30 p.m. This is provided for by A. [Apollos] R. Wetmore, the President, who has furnished an ample feast to the institution each successive year since it was founded. There are at present 550 children in the Asylum, and 100 in the House of Reception. An entertainment will be given the children in the evening at each place.[56]

The Asylum described how Christmas was celebrated at the Asylum and at the House of Reception, in 1883:

> On Christmas day the children had a tree in the chapel and presents of candy, peanuts, cards, and dolls to the smaller girls, and the farm boys and others who work outdoors were presented with cardigan jackets and gloves.
>
> At the House a Christmas entertainment was given by the children on Friday evening last at which several members of the Board and others were present. Mr. [Ezra M.] Kingsley commended the children for the excellence of their singing, recitations, etc. and all the visitors were greatly pleased.[57]

Christmas and New Years were celebrated in 1884 as follows:

> The children had their Christmas dinner on Wednesday Dec. 24 consisting of chicken, mashed potatoes, pickled tomatoes, etc. On Thursday they had dessert of pie, cheese, etc. On Friday afternoon the had Christmas tree in the chapel. Messrs. [Joseph B.] Lockwood and [Leighton] Williams were present and made remarks appropriate to the occasion.
>
> Dolls, necklaces, etc. were presented to the girls, and every child received presents of candy, peanuts, Christmas cakes, apples, a cake of perfumed soap, and a Christmas card.
>
> Three Artists—two of them musicians [using tumblers], and one a ventriloquist and humorist have been engaged to give the children an entertainment in our chapel on Wednesday eve—New Years Eve—commencing promptly at 6:30 o'clock.[58]

And the Band Played On

The NYJA band provided many children with an artistic outlet. It was described in 1874: "A pleasing feature of the institution is its brass band and drum-corps, under the leadership or direction of the foreman in the shoe-shop, who is a professor of music."[59] The band master often served in dual roles at the Asylum. In 1905 bandmaster Burt J. Moffitt also held the title of "Baker."[60] The NYJA band played at various events held at the Asylum and elsewhere.

On June 2, 1899, at the invitation of the Daughters of the American Revolution, the band attended the unveiling of a tablet commemorative of the battle of Washington Heights at the Jumel Mansion, and on November 1, 1899 the band returned a visit from the Leake and Watts Asylum in Yonkers, New York, and "were handsomely entertained."[61]

In 1900, a newspaper reported that the Asylum "has a band of thirty-two pieces which is reorganized every two years."[62] The Asylum band was asked to march in the GAR [Grand Army of the Republic] Memorial Day parade in New York City in 1909, which was customary. They were "forty strong, in dashing uniform of gray." Joining them at Grant's tomb were many former wards of the Asylum who were called to Lincoln's army and served their country some forty-five years previous—both from New York City and those placed on farms out west.[63]

William Sloan, age thirteen, was a member of the band at The Children's Village, but was sent west and placed with Orville C. Cross in Riley, Kansas, in 1908. Mr. Cross and his wife gave William some chickens, two pigs, and a little mule to raise. William wrote to the The Children's Village staff: "I have joined the Amarosa Band and I play the snare drum. We just got our new uniforms. This band is

The "N. Y. Juvenile Asylum Cornet Band," circa 1894. (*NYJA Annual Report, 1895*)

engaged to play for three days at the fair. I am feeling fine and dandy, and send all my best wishes."[64]

In 1909, the band "filled fourteen engagements away from the Village, and, in addition, frequently contributed to the pleasure of the children of the Village."[65]

In 1913, the band "contributed its services without charge" to a "Field Day at the Misses Master's School; The Child Welfare Exhibit in Dobbs Ferry; an entertainment at St. Christopher's Home; Memorial Day parade in New York City; Sunday School picnic at Inwood; at open air meetings of the Dobbs Ferry churches; the Hastings Country Fair and the Firemen's picnic at Tarrytown."[66]

Kitchen and Dining

Preparing three meals a day for hundreds of children was quite a feat. There was a marked difference in the type of food served to the staff versus the children. The bill of fare served to the "officers of the house" in 1859 included the following:

Breakfast: Bread & butter, Coffee, fried potatoes, cold sliced meat or beef steak.

Tea: Bread & butter, Tea, Broiled fish, smoked beef, cheese, or apple sauce.

Dinner:

Monday – Beef or Mutton Soup, boiled turnips or onions, potatoes, and bread & butter.

Tuesday – Roast mutton, bread & butter, potatoes and carrots.

Wednesday – Roast or Boiled Beef, Beets, potatoes, Bread & butter.

Thursday – Beef steak, turnips, potatoes, and, Bread & butter.

Life in the Asylum

Boys' Dining Room. (*NYJA Annual Report, 1892*)

The dining room circa 1896. (*NYJA Annual Report, 1896*)

Friday – Stewed mutton or Fish, potatoes, turnips, Bread & butter.

Saturday – Corned beef & cabbage, turnips, potatoes, Bread & butter.

Sunday – Roast beef or poultry, turnips or onions or celery, Bread & butter.

Also: An Indian Rice or Batter pudding four (4) times a week.

The bill of fare served to the children was sparse:

Breakfast and Supper: Bread and Tea, excepting Sunday night, when the children have bread and water and ginger bread.

Monday Dinner: Beef or mutton soup.

Tuesday Dinner: Bean soup.

Wednesday Dinner: Rice and sugar.

Thursday Dinner: Ham and potatoes.

Friday Dinner: Fish and potatoes or clam soup.

Saturday Dinner: Meat stew.

Sunday Dinner: Bread, butter, and cheese.[67]

The girls' dining room was located in the basement of the west wing of the Asylum and the boys' in the basement of the north wing, but they all dined together prior to 1881, at which time a new wing was built that effectively separated the boys from the girls.[68] The account below dates to 1870:

> Here a number of long covered tables, some with girls, some with boys, closely seated on each side, and always a monitor at the end. The monitors may be black or white, little or big, no matter; at their posts they are impressible and superb. The children eat with subdued ravenousness. They have soup, meat, plain vegetables, and all the bread they want. Hands are raised if supplies are needed. They glance pleasantly at each other, but not a word is spoken.[69]

The children sat down to meals at the tap of a bell, were not allowed to converse during mealtime, rose up from the table at the tap of the bell, and marched out, "so that a meal, instead of being a time of pleasurable talk, with the interchange of small courtesies, was a necessary but somewhat disagreeable function."[70]

Interaction between the children, including siblings, was carefully regimented. No play or conversation was allowed among the children while "engaged at work, on parade, at meals, or after they have retired to their sleeping rooms."[71] No communication whatsoever was allowed between the sexes, nor were they permitted to "pass into the apartments or yards of each other, unless directed to do so by an officer." In addition, boys and girls

A scene in the bakery of the "Old Juvenile Asylum." (*Bain News Service, Publisher. Old Juvenile Asylum,* [*No Date Recorded on Caption Card*] *Photograph. https://www.loc.gov/item/2014681561/*)

played in their own playgrounds and playrooms, and slept in their own wards.

After the move to Dobbs Ferry, the children were seated ten to each of the two tables in a cottage, with the officers of the cottage seated at a third table. Meals were carried out to the cottages from the main kitchen on the premises.[72] Meals were supplemented with seasonal produce from the garden.

The reporter from *Scribner's Monthly* who visited the Asylum in 1870 continued on with her tour to the kitchen, where she observed "steam-cooking apparatus, modern improvements, big windows, clean tables, tidy cooks. We were bewildered to learn of its serving up, daily, three hundred pounds of fresh meat, a barrel of potatoes, three hundred quarts of milk, besides startling quantities of beets, beans, cabbages, and other vegetables."[73] The reporter then moved on to the bakery "where three barrels of flour are cast into the oven every day, and on Saturdays nearly an extra barrel for ginger-bread."

Ice was harvested during the winter months and used to keep food cold during warmer weather: "The ice is reported to be ten inches thick at Courtland [Van Cortlandt] Lake where we get our supply."[74]

Hygiene

Hygiene in the nineteenth century, by today's standards, was a bit lax. In 1853, the Asylum's hygiene requirements called for the children to "wash their faces and hands, and have their heads combed, at

Life in the Asylum 77

Boys' Bathing Tank: "Our artist represents them at the tank before the jets are filled." Note the bench with "numbered towels" hanging off the back as described below. (*Mary E. Dodge, "A Day with Dr. Brooks," Scribner's Monthly, November 1870, 49*)

least once a day. As often as once a week they shall wash their necks and feet, and change their shirts and socks; and, whenever the season will permit, they shall have the benefit of bathing. Personal cleanliness shall be rewarded, and the want of it punished, at the discretion of the Superintendent."[75]

An author who visited the Asylum circa 1863 described the bathing room:

> Not the least remarkable feature of the building is the *bath-room*, a large space laid off in the basement, and divided into a smaller one for the girls, who are always in a minority, and a very large one for the boys. A portion of this latter is occupied with benches, each one being responsible for a nice crash towel, cake of soap, comb, etc.; and upon a word from the director they repair in companies to two great tubs forty feet in circumference, provided with a succession of little jets playing into it, one for each boy, so that he may run no risk of infection from his neighbor. Once a week, sometimes oftener, a warm plunge-bath is taken in these huge wooden ponds, and thus in winter the boys may enjoy a somewhat restrained swimming frolic. In summer the river is substituted for the domestic arrangement.
>
> A beautiful little engine, a gift from still another kind friend, suffices for purposes of bath-heating, as well as for running the ma-

This photo was captioned "Washroom, Showing Individual Towel Rack" and indicates a different method for hanging towels from the one in the earlier illustration from 1870 where they were hung on the backs of benches. (*NYJA Annual Report, 1896*)

chinery of as complete a laundry as could well be found anywhere. A colored engineer presides over this engine, and is as familiar with every part of it as the maker of it himself. He is eminently practical, and proud of his position and the trust placed in him. He was brought up in the institution.[76]

The reporter who visited the Asylum in 1870 described the bathing practice being used at that time:

Ah, the bathing-rooms, what grand places they are! None of your paltry tin basins, but great circular wooden tanks, fifteen feet across, with warm or cold water, in which the children may plunge and swim to their hearts' content. Here, morning and evening, the little ones stand washing their hands and faces, each for the time sole proprietor of the clear, bright little stream pouring out for its benefit—a wise precaution against the spread of ophthalmia or cutaneous affections. As the number of boys is very large, their bathing-room is furnished with two tanks; the girls have but one. Every child's towel, marked with his or her number, when not in use, hangs conspicuously spread out in its own particular place on the back of one of the benches, arranged in the dressing-rooms like seats in a lecture hall. It makes one think of the famous journey to St. Ives to go through these rooms. Every boy has a towel—every towel has a number—every number has a place, and every place has a comb laid on the seat, just in front of the towel. Twice a week the laundress gathers in these standards of the grand army and puts clean ones in their places, and twice a

Life in the Asylum

week, as the rotation is managed, comes each child's turn to take a plunge in the tank—so many to a shoal, like minnows.[77]

By 1895, a different system for bathing of the children was implemented at the Asylum:

> The "rain bath" is located at the end of a large hall 60x120 feet, and the actual area of the bathing space is 18x40. The brick-paved floor of the bath is sunk two feet below the level of the floor. There are 192 nozzles, each of which distributes the water in a coarse spray. Two hundred boys can be thoroughly bathed every twenty minutes. Along the walls of the room is arranged a series of lockers, one for each boy, who has a number. In this his Sunday clothing is hung. A relay of 100 boys marches into the large room, and each halts before his locker. The attendant claps his hands and the lockers are opened. Another signal and the boys quickly disrobe. Another and they form into an orderly double line. Then they march toward the bath. An attendant on either side gives each boy a cake of soap. They enter the paved space and stand at equal distances, not directly under the nozzles but in such manner that the streams from two of them strike the body. In eight minutes the bath is over and the water is turned off. Each surrenders his bar of soap and receives a towel, returns to a post in front of his locker, and at a signal begins the work of vigorously drying himself. Then clothing put off is resumed, or if it be Sunday or a holiday, the best suit is put on. Eight hundred boys can, under this plan, be bathed in eighty minutes, although the time consumed is generally extended to two hours.[78]

The Asylum did not adopt the practice that was commonplace at other New York City institutions when children were first admitted, in which the hair of the children (both boys and girls) would be cut very close to their heads to help alleviate problems with head lice and ringworm. A visitor to the Asylum in 1870 noted, "We remember now that the girls wear their hair long or short, as they please. There is no universal cropping of heads, as in some institutions."[79]

Bedtime

The children each slept in large wards. In the early 1870's it was reported that they slept "seventy-two in a ward, with a bed for each child."[80]

A new state law, implemented in 1886, stipulated that the beds should be "two feet apart all around," which allowed the NYJA enough room for 750 beds in their existing dormitories. In order to have enough space for all the beds needed, the Asylum removed the settees from the old chapel at the Asylum (which allowed enough room for ninety-six beds), and also converted the Temperance room.[81]

Each day at the Asylum concluded with "evening exercises." The boys and girls proceeded to the chapel, which seated eleven hundred.[82] The *Scribner's Monthly* reporter described the scene in 1870:

> It was a very large room, with broad, high windows on each side, through which the evening sun shone brightly, lighting up rows upon rows of little square desks [the room doubled as a classroom]. There sat the children! More than five hundred of them [...]. The little creatures, one and all, were singing their evening hymn. Somehow, I could not see their faces on account of the music, and I couldn't hear the music on account of the faces. Committees may not feel like crying on such occasions; but every one is not a committee. The performer, a young girl, was nearly hidden from where we sat upon the raised platform. As her head bent over the keys, she seemed whispering coaxingly—"Now don't try to do anything but breathe." So it breathed a soft, rich, half-sighing accompaniment while the childish voices sang:

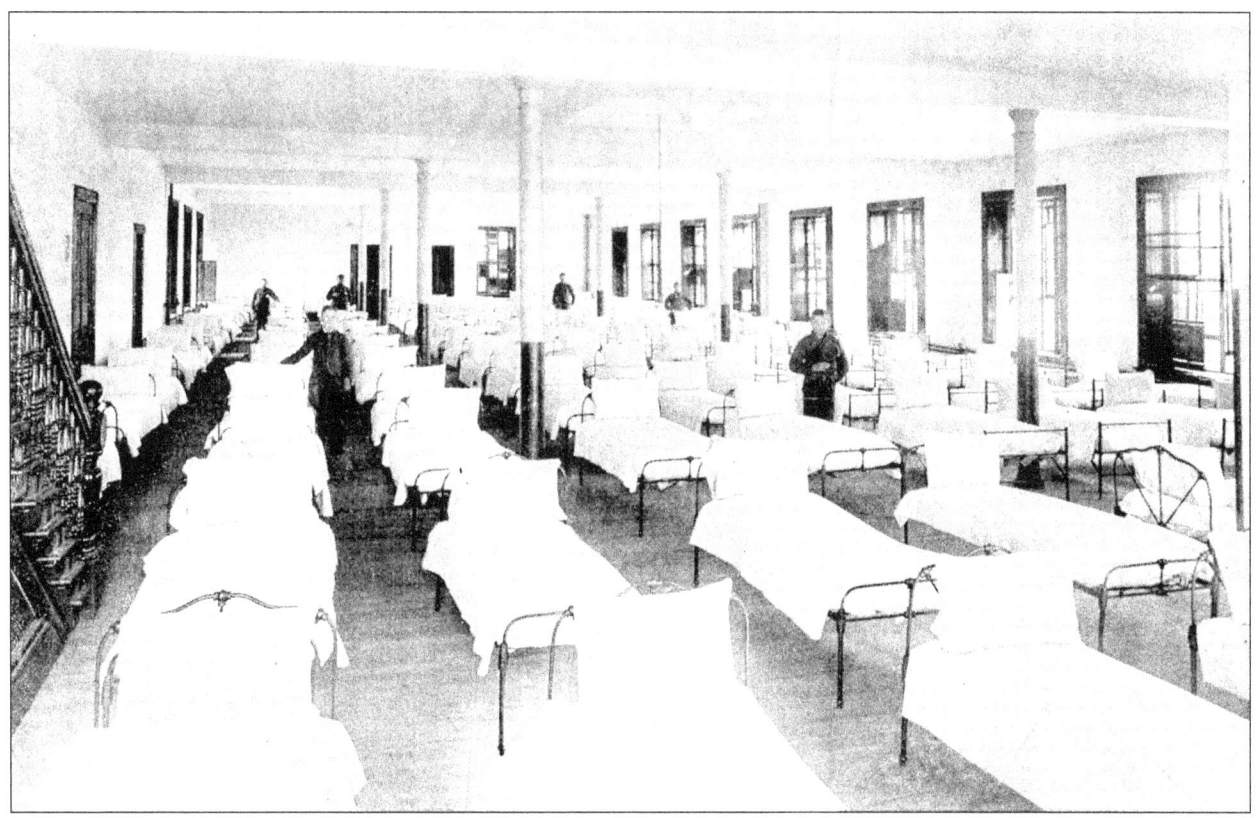

Row after row of single beds comprised a "Boys' Ward" in the Asylum. (*NYJA Annual Report, 1893*)

"On the sweet Eden shore, so peaceful and bright,

The spirits made perfect are dwelling in light:

Their white wings are wafting them gently along,

Through the beautiful regions of glory and song."

After this, a little evening speech from the Doctor [Superintendent Dr. Samuel D. Brooks]—just a few simple, fatherly words. Then, with clasped hands and closed eyes, the children said the Lord's Prayer in concert, and then stood up in their places, and looked straight at the Doctor. "Good night!" said he, cheerily. "Good night, sir!" they answered as heartily, and in perfect order quietly filed out of their places, and so went off to bed.[83]

The same reporter described the scene at bedtime in the girls' dormitory:

It was but a step from the family parlor. Miss Sanford [Emily Sandford] and I went in. The flock had indeed settled; all the children were saying their prayers. I noticed that several of them made the sign of the cross as they rose. The great room contained more than a hundred snowy cots, every one of which in a moment had an occupant. "In winter some of our girls have a curious way of arranging their bedding for the night," said the matron; "they call it 'making a nest;' would you like to see it?" "Of course I would." Soon, two girls, giggling very much, and very proud at being asked to 'show the lady,' were busily converting their beds into nests. It is a curious process. They shake the mattress and shove the straw about till a hollow is formed just large enough for the body. In this, with the covers twirled about them, they curl themselves for sleeping. One brown-eyed little girl pulled my face down close to whisper: "My

Life in the Asylum

mother hasn't been to see me at all. She's gone away out of where we used to be, and I don't know where to think she is." Poor little thing! Lonely there among a hundred. Meanwhile the children were softly bidding each other "good night!" or slyly reaching to clasp hands from one bed to another. All at once, as if blowing out a candle, the matron made a signal, and out went the voices. You could have heard a pin fall. "Now, children, it is time for us to leave. If you wish you may chant before you go to sleep." Instantly every pair of hands was crossed, every child lay motionless. We moved toward the door and listened. It was beautiful. More than a hundred childish voices chanting the Lord's Prayer!

As the reporter left, she noticed that "all the windows were open, letting in the pleasant summer breeze and the ruddy remnants of the sunset."[84]

After spending the night, the reporter awoke to a rather strange noise:

Mercy! What was the matter! [. . .] It was not thunder nor rain, nor a whirlwind, nor the roar of wild animals, nor a general collapse of the building. It was all of these sounds combined. [. . .] I sprang to the window. [. . .] Was it only the boys of the institution going to their play-ground? [. . .] I again looked down upon the flagged foot-path; yes, the long procession still was pouring out of the building—an endless string of bare-footed boys walking two by two, talking, shouting, laughing as they went. That was all. But of all the noises that ever I heard, the din of those boys was the most bewildering. What wonder—with nearly a thousand bare feet pattering on the flagging, to say nothing of all the voices. The tramping in cold weather, when stout shoes are worn, may be louder; but certainly it is not so strange.[85]

CHAPTER FIVE

Life in The Children's Village

Education

After the NYJA moved its operations to Dobbs Ferry, New York, it began to focus on vocational training. The City of New York was appropriating funds for the city's various schools and institutions. In 1909, the allowance was increased for "institutions maintained on the cottage home plan where not more than thirty children were inmates of a cottage," with special allowances given to institutions that provided vocational training. The Asylum explained its new focus on vocational training in its 1909 annual report, describing it as "the preliminary instruction in some trade or occupation which may be the source of livelihood to the student in his future life. It is not intended to cover merely common work, such as ordinary day labor or mere drudgery, but skilled employments, such as typewriting, telegraphy, electrical work, scientific gardening, tailoring, carpentry, etc."[1]

By 1910, boys twelve and older were receiving vocational training in sloyd (handicraft-based education), carpentry, telegraphy, floriculture, applied electricity, tailoring, tinning and plumbing, painting, printing, and baking. The class in mechanical drawing and sloyd gave daily employment to sixty boys, with "specimens of their work" displayed in an exhibit room in Wetmore Hall.[2] However, the exhibit room was converted to the band room and barber shop by 1911, with the band master "happily combining the two professions of barber and musician." Under his tutelage and supervision, the band made progress, and "classes of colored and Italian boys now cut the hair for the entire school."[3]

In 1913, the City's allowance per boy receiving vocational training at the Asylum was seven cents per day, applicable to children over twelve years of age.[4]

Intelligence Quotient Testing

Beginning in 1912, The Children's Village was swept up by an IQ test being promoted in the United States by Stanford University's Lewis Therman and Henry Goddard of the Vineland Training School for the Feeble-Minded in New Jersey, which was rapidly becoming popular among institutions for delinquent and dependent children. The IQ testing movement was in response to a revival of hereditarianism as the explanation for social ills in one sense and the promotion of eugenics for the solution on the other.

> It is always expected that a certain percentage of the children brought before the courts for moral delinquency will prove to be not only the victims of social evils in the way of improper housing and insufficient food and clothing, but also afflicted with certain mental or physical deficiencies, rendering special care necessary. Not a few of the children who come before the Children's Court may be classed, if not as feebleminded, at least, as of such arrested development and mental idiosyncrasy, as to require a different style of instruction from that given in the ordinary

Boys "at school" at The Children's Village. (*NYJA Annual Report, 1921*)

The boys partaking in vocational training while constructing a new cottage at The Children's Village. (*NYJA Annual Report, 1910*)

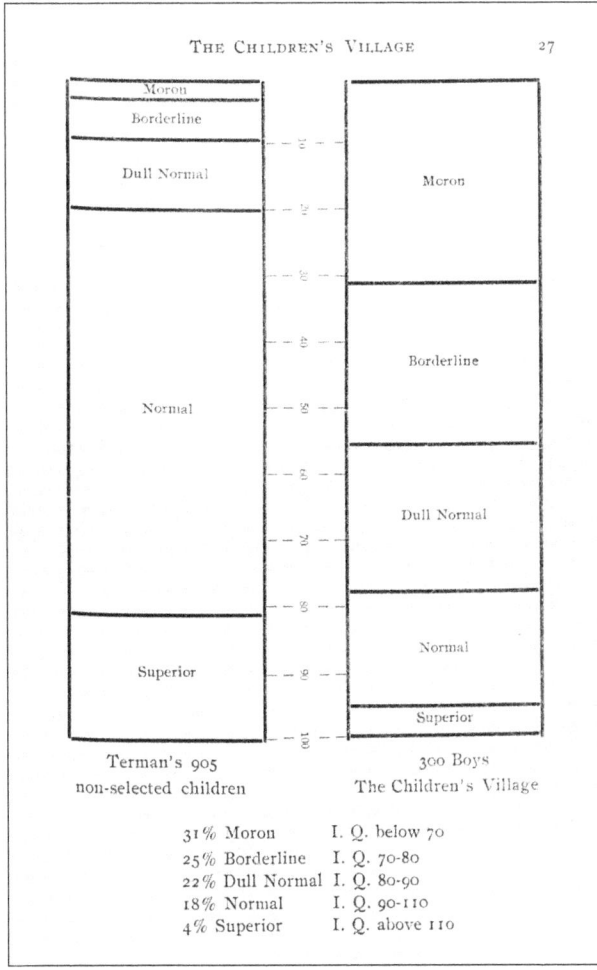

IQ test results for The Children's Village. (*NYJA Annual Report, 1921*)

strict the propagation of the feeble-minded variety of the human race."[6]

The New York State Commission to Investigate Provision for the Mentally Deficient spelled out the link between delinquency, IQ, and heredity in its report to the Legislature:

> Feeble-mindedness is a grave social menace. To it can be attributed a very definite proportion of the vice, crime, and degeneracy that tend to destroy the peace and prosperity of our communal life. Not only is it a fundamental cause of misery, but it possesses the quality of hereditary transmission, thus insuring the continuance of misery through the generations to come.[7]

Mental deficiency was being linked to delinquent children incarcerated in a variety of institutions. What was not taken into account was the fact that the vast majority were immigrants or the children of immigrants, unable to speak English. The result, intended or not, was a systematic racism associated with the movement. By 1914, it had become standard practice to give all incoming children the IQ test.

As early as 1901, "backward" pupils were placed into a special class at the NYJA. "This class," it was reported, "is not distinct by name from the others, though in reality it is peculiar."[8]

Even so, the men in charge of the NYJA did not wholeheartedly endorse the new eugenics movement:

> It may be noted that there are numerous subjects and problems very closely related to the work of an institution of this kind, and perhaps this is not the place in which to take up the discussion of them; but a survey of the boys and a little contact with them and their parents bring to mind many features of the immigration question, the eugenics propaganda and the scientific study of the causes and remedies of juvenile delinquency.[9]

classes. [...] To meet this difficulty in the case of a number of children, perhaps fourteen or fifteen, in the entire Asylum, a lady, a graduate of the school for training of teachers at Vineland, New Jersey, has been engaged.[5]

Hastings Hornell Hart was the former head of the ICHAS that helped facilitate the placement and supervision of the NYJA's children in the West. As president of the National Conference of Charities and Correction, he wrote in *The Extinction of the Defective Delinquent: A Working Program*, "In order to restrict and ultimately to put an end to the production of defective delinquents, it is necessary to re-

Sheep grazing in front of Wetmore Hall at The Children's Village. (*NYJA Annual Report, 1913*)

The "Boy's Handiwork" was displayed in this spare room (later converted to a band room and barber shop) at Wetmore Hall at The Children's Village. (*NYJA Annual Report, 1913*)

Cottage Living

Most of the staff at The Children's Village were expected to live in the cottages with the inmates. Each cottage, in addition to twenty boys, had a matron (or a matron and master) as well as two other employees, often teachers.

(at top) Boys' dining room in one of the cottages at The Children's Village. (*NYJA Annual Report, 1910*) **(above)** This view of The Children's Village appeared in a 1914 pamphlet. (*Courtesy of the author*)

> The cottage matron will have full charge of the house, supervising the dining room, the mending and housework. The food will be cooked elsewhere and delivered. She would not have other duties than those in her own cottage and would be off duty one day every two weeks and have two weeks annual vacation. The salary is $25. Two officers sleep up stairs and eat in the cottage.[10]

It was expected that the two teachers and matron would use a common bathroom and would have a small table in the center of the dining room.[11] The teachers generally consisted of unmarried women. The male masters of each cottage were tasked with outdoor duties such as vocational education and maintenance.

The former residence of George Palliser was remodeled to take the place of the old House of Reception and was called the Reception Cottage. It was located near the entrance to the property. Two rooms in the house were reserved for the meetings

Life in The Children's Village

The boys' fire brigade posed for this photo at The Children's Village circa 1912. (*NYJA Annual Report, 1913*)

of the board of directors. Another building on the property purchased from the Palliser estate served as the hospital.[12] Superintendent Mornay Williams described the functions of the Reception Cottage:

> A Reception Cottage safeguards the Village from contagion or whatever might be introduced by means of the unclean clothing or person of new boys who are received from day to day. Without exception the new arrival must spend his first fortnight at this cottage and about the grounds reserved for this group of boys who are biding the time of their quarantine. Upon his reception here a boy is given a thorough cleansing in the shower bath, his hair is clipped and his clothing either returned to his parents or destroyed. New apparel made by the trades classes of the School is issued to him. A physical examination is given by the nurse and physician and record taken of his height, chest expansion, waist measure, weight, scars, birth-marks, deformities, sense defects, etc., with especial attention to enlarged tonsils or adenoids and skin, scalp, or eye troubles. His mouth is inspected by the dentist and the unsound teeth either extracted or charted for fillings, and in turn given attention from time to time. He is provided with towel, tooth brush and comb and informed that these are his personal effects not to be confused with those of another boy.[13]

Agriculture

Henry J. Couper, a graduate of Cornell Agricultural College, was put in charge of farming operations at The Children's Village and tended to the crops and livestock.[14] Some twenty acres were plowed for garden purposes. Couper overseen the boys working in the gardens. He and his wife were also in charge of Bradish Cottage.[15]

Other crops included peas, beans, one acre of

88   *Chapter Five*

Asylum boys tending "Individual Gardens" at Andrew H. Green Cottage, Dobbs Ferry, New York. (*NYJA Annual Report, 1910*)

"Husking Bee" at The Children's Village. (*NYJA Annual Report, 1906*)

popcorn (for popping at open fires in the winter), and eight acres of "green corn." Potatoes, squash, pumpkins, and turnips were also grown and stored in the vegetable cellar. The children took great pride in their gardening work: "One boy owned a whole strawberry patch. The strawberry king was recently heard opening negotiations with a companion to 'swoop a row of me strabs fer two of your tomatoes and a coupe bean plants.' The exchange was affected with a trowel and exceeding care, and the transferred crops are thriving nicely."[16] Another boy cited his garden "with all things planted in" as something he had never experienced before:

> A house mother, one Sunday evening, was giving a little sermon-talk to the boys as they sat around her in the library. At the end she said, "And so boys, unless you feel sorry when you have done wrong, and make up your mind firmly to never do it again, you will never grow to be any better."
>
> "Hot air," came in familiar accents from a corner where the newest arrival sat listening closely. He was of the sharpest of the street gamins, and his reform had to come by degrees. So the house mother only said quietly, "What do you mean by 'hot air,' Sammy?"
>
> "I don't care; I done wrong and I ain't sorry."
>
> "What did you do that was wrong, Sammy?"
>
> "Played hookey, and I'm glad. And d'ye want to know why? Cause the cop catched me, and the Kids' Court got a hold of me, and I got sent up here, and now I have a garden with all things planted in, and I haint never seen no grass before."[17]

In preparation for the growing season in 1903, the Asylum placed the following order with Messrs. S. E. Woodruff & Sons, 82 Dey Street, New York City: "12 qts. onion sets, 8 oz. onion seed, 3 lbs. early beet seed, 3 lbs. radish seed, 4 oz. carrot seed, 500 lbs. fertilizer."[18]

Radishes were a great favorite, as one child proclaimed, because "we can eat 'em right up."[19] It was not uncommon for the children to exhibit the vegetables they grew at the local fair. Thirteen exhibits of vegetables grown in the gardens at the Village were shown at the Hastings Country Fair in 1912.[20]

A typical day for the boys at the Village was divided evenly, with the morning spent on schoolwork and the afternoon in one of the shops (baking, painting, printing, tailoring, or carpentry), or doing farm work. No conscious attempt was made to generate income from these activities.

Recreation

The athletic field was most popular during the baseball season when the boys were often joined by The Children's Village officers. As many as eight games could be played at the same time. Teams were formed in each of the cottages in The Children's Village and they played against each other.

> A friendly rivalry exists between the nines of the various cottages, and a handsome silver cup, donated by Colonel F. Q. Brown, is presented to the cottage which wins the most games during the season and held by it until the following season. [...] Many games were played with teams from neighboring villages and the Asylum nine was victorious in all but one.[21]

In a letter dated June 6, 1903 from Edwin C. Burdick, Assistant Superintendent of the Asylum, to Halsey Davison, 216 W. 105th Street, New York City, who likely ran a similar institution. Burdick accepted Davison's invitation for a match:

Dear Sir: -

Mr. George Hamilton Dean has telephoned me saying that you will be glad to bring your boys up here on Saturday, June 13th, to play us a game of ball and asking me to let you know if that date will be convenient for us.

I should be very glad to have you and your team come here, and we will do our best to give you a good time and a good beating.

Very truly yours,
Edwin C. Burdick. Asst. Supt.[22]

The children were honored when New York Giants' pitcher Christy Mathewson visited The Children's Village in 1914:

> Mathewson umpired a kid game while visiting the school and was frankly told he was "rotten." Then he told the boys some things about pitching and was hailed as a great speaker. Following the advice given them by the Giant pitcher the youngsters are trying for control, not for curves. Place the ball where you want it, then out-guess the batter, Matty said is the secret of pitching.[23]

Holidays were observed throughout the year. In 1906, Henry E. Gregory delivered an address on Lincoln's birthday, Mr. Mornay Williams on Washington's birthday, and Dr. Joseph Hasbrouck on Memorial Day. The Fourth of July was "one long round of athletic events, band concert, patriotic singing and fire-works."[24]

A Beautiful Title

After inspection by the State Board of Charities in September 1907, The Children's Village was awarded a "first class" judgment on the basis of its physical set-up—the only such judgment made in that year.[25]

The *New York Times* sent a reporter to the Village and subsequently ran a full-page spread. The reporter observed, "Something has been accomplished by calling this place on the hill the The Children's Village. It is a beautiful title, exquisitely carried out in the picturesque detail of design in architecture, in landscape, in immaculate cleanliness, in the touches of flowers, of books, of house games, of industrial occupation." As he walked the grounds he noticed

The boys partaking in Tug of War contest on July 4, 1906 on the hill they called "Round Top," which featured an interesting pagoda-shaped tower. (*NYJA Annual Report, 1906*)

the Queen Anne cottages "with their spick and span white curtains, demurely impressive of respectability within" and was soon approached by a "rosy cheeked cherub, in a little blue uniform that makes him look a man in earnest [...] trotting hurriedly along with a mailbag." A conversation ensued:

> "You are the mail man?" asks the scribe.
> "Yes, Sir. I fetch the letters at the station three times a day; also, I am the office boy, in the office," he adds proudly.
> "How did you get here?"
> "Me mother died, and I was committed," he says gravely.
> "Are you happy?"
> "Sure."
> "Do they let you play baseball?"
> "Yep. The cottages all have their own teams, and they play one against the other."

After their conversation ended, the reporter reflected on his chance meeting:

> Truth to tell, the mail carrier didn't seem to be one of the lost children. He had found himself, adjusted his little problems of life to the one golden rule of cheerfulness. [His] was a type of consciousness and bravery that

One of the Asylum boys tends to his flock of sheep on a hill known as Round Top at The Children's Village. Note the pagoda-shaped tower in the background. (*NYJA Annual Report, 1905*)

combine a wondrous strength in spite of the disadvantage of being lost. Perhaps this was due somewhat to the helpful ethics of this community, in which he was growing up to be a very brave little man, indeed.[26]

The reporter's walk would have taken him past the sizable lake on the grounds, which provided three hundred tons of ice in the prior year stored for use during the summer months. In the winter, the lake provided the children with a place to skate and play.[27]

At the peak of a hill known as Round Top he would have observed a flock of sheep grazing at the base of a green pagoda-shaped bell tower. Fourteen lambs were born in the spring that year, and their wool was harvested and sold for $57.20. The entire flock was purchased in 1905 for just $50.96. In 1910, the sale of three hundred pounds of "home-grown wool" netted sixty-three dollars.[28]

Two boys were appointed shepherds; one "demonstrated that he appreciated the honor, but that he viewed it, at first, only through the eyes of the bookish amateur, by a request to be provided with a crook." The second lad, while not so "erudite, found his enthusiasm grow and when the time came for him to leave the Asylum and his parents applied for his discharge, the Committee on Admissions, Indentures and Discharges was considerably surprised to receive a hesitating request from the boy's mother, that they should postpone the granting of her application for a time, because Willie was "so anxious to see the lambs grow up." The request was granted, and Willie stayed through the summer "to watch the growth of the lambs, quite unconscious that the larger growth had been in himself."[29]

In 1908, Superintendent Hilles reported the construction of nine more dormitory-style cottages on the ridge south of the athletic field, built to hold twenty children each. The boys slept "no more than ten to a room" in these cottages.[30] Promotions were made from the dormitory cottages to the more pri-

Kingsley Cottage—one of the single-room "honor" cottages at The Children's Village. (*NYJA Annual Report, 1904*)

vate single-room "honor" cottages based on exemplary conduct.[31] By January 1909, the structures were nearing completion. With these additional cottages, the Village was expected to increase its capacity to five hundred children, scattered in thirty-three buildings.[32]

In the summer of 1909 a "tree-plague" killed all the chestnut and hickory trees "whose nuts supplied such pleasure to the boys."[33] The board purchased a saw mill, and beginning in 1911, the boys took great pride in building a cottage each year, using lumber sawn from the dead trees found on the property.[34]

A Visit from President Taft

The children were honored when President William Howard Taft visited The Children's Village on November 16, 1912, while on a nationwide tour.[35] He was accompanied by Charles Dewey Hilles, former NYJA Superintendent (1902-1909) who was serving as Taft's secretary. Taft reached the Village at 1:00 p.m. as the band played "Hail to the Chief."[36]

The hall was massed with American flags, and the boys sang patriotic airs, and at a given signal, seated themselves with military precision, their blue uniforms and brass buttons, heightening the illusion.

President Taft, ponderous and smiling, glanced down [at] his juvenile audience, with a softened smile. Then he got upon his feet slowly, and talked to them. It wasn't an address he gave, it was just a little confidential talk. He told them that everybody worth while wanted them to make good, and that to do that, they had to be satisfied with themselves "inside."

"It's not hot air I'm giving you boys," he said, and smiled at the appreciative titter that followed the remark. "I want you to go out of here, and forget that you have started under a handicap. Everybody likes a fellow that has to beat a handicap, you know. He has to run harder and keep his wind better. Now you boys do that, and you'll be successes. And I'll be proud of you."

Life in The Children's Village

The boys all applauded loudly and then sang the national anthem, standing. When the president rolled away, they watched him, with bared heads until the car turned a curve. Then with a shout that broke the dignified strain, they swarmed out onto the great playground and commenced turning somersaults and being just plain boys.[37]

Taft left the children with some words of encouragement that day: "The world is not against you—that is, that part of the world that is worth having is not against you. They want you to succeed."[38]

PART II
Orphan Trains of the New York Juvenile Asylum

CHAPTER SIX

History of the Orphan Trains

Orphan Trains to Illinois

In October 1855 Reverend Mr. Enoch Kingsbury, likely responding to the NYJA's advertisement requesting homes in the country for its children, approached the Asylum with a plan to relieve it of some of the children. Kingsbury was a child saver of sorts who hailed from Danville, Vermilion County, Illinois. On July 4, 1855, Kingsbury had established the Vermilion County Juvenile Aid Society for the purpose of bringing homeless and destitute children from New York City to find homes for them in Danville and other locations in Illinois and western Indiana:

> PRACTICAL BENEVOLENCE.—A society has been organized in Danville, Vermillion County, Ill., to aid the poor, and especially the young and orphans, in emigrating from the cities to that rich, beautiful, healthy region, where food and fuel and house-room are cheap and labor plenty and well paid. Danville has a population of 1,200, and is located upon the edge of the Grand Prairie, 12 miles west of Wabash, and 14 from Covington, Indiana, on the Wabash and Erie Canal. The directors of the society will take charge of persons consigned to them, and provide them with good situations where they will soon become useful members of society. The Rev. Enoch Kingsbury is Secretary of the society.[1]

Kingsbury contacted the NYJA for the purpose of obtaining both children and adults to find homes and work in the West. He asked the Asylum's Committee on Admissions, Indentures and Discharges "to send a family to Danville as laborers and remitting of Fifty dollars to pay their expense, also asking to send out in the charge of same family 15 or 20 children."[2] The Asylum's officials consented and sent Kingsbury off to Danville with twenty children. The NYJA's successful collaboration with the Children's Aid Society to send children west in 1854 likely factored into this decision.

At the Committee's October 30, 1855 meeting it agreed to cover the expense of sending more children with Kingsbury: "Resolved that the chairman be authorized to arrange with the Finance Committee and the Treasurer for the advance of money to pay the expenses to Illinois of such children as it may be deemed expedient to send for disposal to Rev. Mr. Kingsbury of Danville, Ill."[3]

At its November 15 meeting, the Committee read a letter from Kingsbury announcing the arrival of the twenty children in Danville, and agreed to send even more children to him: "Resolved that the Committee send 20 boys and as near 20 girls as is practible to Rev. E. Kingsbury of Danville, Ill. And the committee engage Mr. Spencer to go out with the children."[4] Mr. [P. A.] Spencer read a report about the "boys sent West" at the Committee's December 12 meeting.

The Asylum's leadership wrote about its arrangement with Kingsbury and other associations

Reverend Mr. Enoch Kingsbury. (*Courtesy of Danville, Illinois Public Library*)

in "farming neighborhoods" in Illinois as well as a similar arrangement with someone in Maryland in NYJA's 1856 annual report, but did not mention any individuals by name:

> On the 1st January, 1855, there were 1,982 children in the Asylum, and constant additions were made to the number. The extent of our accommodations forbade their increase, whilst their character occasioned serious apprehension as to the health of those already in the family. Strenuous exertions were therefore made to find places for such as we dared to put away after a very brief probation. For some months, however the diminution of our numbers was scarcely perceptible. But during the fall, a kind Providence opened the way for our relief. Both from Maryland and Illinois calls were now made upon us for children, and very soon our anxieties were not to find homes for the children, but children for the homes.
>
> A peculiarly gratifying circumstance, in connection with the demand from Illinois, was the voluntary formation in several farming neighborhoods, of Associations, whose special object it was made to watch over the children that might be intrusted to any of their members or friends [...]. We must give still further credit to the large hearts of our Western friends; they not only pay the expenses of the children on their journey, but send an agent to accompany and protect them. With such arrangements, doubtless every contributor to our treasury, and every well-wisher to the young in our midst, will acquiesce in the decision of the Board, hereafter to decline indenturing children except under peculiar circumstances, in the vicinity of our large seaport towns, especially as the demands from the West are beyond our power to supply.[5]

The Asylum sent three large companies of children to Maryland in August, October, and November 1855, but the name of the individual or organization there that made the "call" to NYJA to do so remains a mystery.[6]

At least one of the farming neighborhoods expressing an interest in indenturing children was in Bellefame, Tazewell County, Illinois. Cyrus B. Chase was heading efforts to indenture children there as early as 1856 as shown by minutes of the Indenturing Committee: "On motion resolved that C. B. Chase of Belfame, Taywell Co., Illinois be authorized to indenture the following children to responsible parties in Illinois on the proper reference, consent of the parents having been obtained as per list of Oct. 10."[7]

Just two days later, at a November 1 meeting, the Committee alluded to Chase having taken a previous company west: "Mr. C. B. Chase was present by invitation and gave satisfactory information as to children previously indentured by him also regarding those whom he is now about to take to the West."[8]

Chase was listed as postmaster of Bellefame in the 1858-1859 *Illinois State Gazetteer and Business Directory*.⁹ Bellefame (also spelled Bellfane) was a whistle stop on the railroad and was located in Malone Township, with the post office located in the train depot.

Chase may have been the man who took a company of children west from the Asylum on March 7, 1855, as reported in a Cleveland, Ohio newspaper:

> On Saturday a man from Peoria, passed through this city, on his way home, having with him eight boys and one girl from the New York Juvenile Orphan Asylum. He was sent East by several farmers near Peoria, who desire to adopt these children. They are all bright-eyed, intelligent looking "young ones," and schooled upon the farms of the West will make useful and honorable citizens. ¹⁰

Meanwhile, Kingsbury's Society in Danville was being favorably described in newspapers nationwide. On September 20, 1855, the *New-York Tribune* reported,

> A society has been organized in Danville, Vermillion County, Illinois, to aid the poor, and especially the young and orphans, in emigrating from the cities to that rich, beautiful, healthy region, where food, fuel and house room are cheap and labor plenty and well paid. [...] The railroad fare from here is about $25. [...] It is a pity that enough of those who will starve next Winter here for want of work could not be sent to Illinois to fill all the demand for laborers both in doors and out.¹¹

The first company sent west with Kingsbury to Danville appears to be the one that left October 29, 1855.¹² He took a few hundred children west by 1857.

The Asylum had been indenturing individual children all over New York and adjoining states for several years prior to Kingsbury coming on the scene, in addition to the company they sent to Dowagiac, Michigan in 1854. A March 1856 newspaper article chronicled Kingsbury's trip west with a company of children from the NYJA:

> The minors German and Irish chiefly, will be bound to suitable persons,—boys under 14 years and girls under 12 years till they arrive at said respective ages, and those over 14 with their consent, the girls till they arrive at 18 years, the boys till 21 years, will be bound out to farmers, mechanics, &c. The person receiving them binds himself in return to educate them in the common branches, and to give them on their becoming of age the sum of $125 [girls received $50] and a new suit of clothes [each was given a Bible as well]. The children are sent out under the direction of the New York Juvenile Asylum, who get no compensation for the labors of its agents, except $10 for minors and $15 for adults from the persons receiving them.¹³

The article noted that Kingsbury had, "since November last taken to his county 98 persons, and obtained for them good places." This statement was substantiated by the Asylum in a letter to the editor of the *New York Observer*:

> Since the 1st of November last, 98 children, with 21 adults, comfortably clothed, with ample provisions, and every precaution taken to ensure comfort and safety, have been sent out to a society formed by the Rev. Mr. Kingsbury, in Vermillion County, Ill., and comfortable homes provided for all. Early in the spring it is proposed to send out to the same association as large a number; and from the interest taken in the West on this subject, it is expected that other associations will be formed, whose members bind themselves to investigate and report the characters of those who require the children, and watch over and

see that those indentured in their vicinity are properly instructed and cared for.[14]

The adults were described as "principally Irish, and unable to obtain work in New York." The article explained that they "will be found work in the country, and bind themselves in return to pay back the expense of their transportation west."[15]

The group was escorted west by Alexander C. Pearcy, Superintendent of the Asylum's House of Reception. Four days after their departure, NYJA President Apollos R. Wetmore followed:

> The President, A. R. Wetmore, Esq. [...] by careful inquiry during an extensive journey through Ohio, Indiana and Illinois, has satisfied the Board that we can in no way so well advance the interests of the children committed to our care, as by removing them from the corrupting influences of the city, and placing them with virtuous families in the country. He thus writes:
>
> "On the 30th June I took the cars of the Erie R. R. at six A. M. for Dunkirk, passed through Ohio and Indiana, and arrived at Danville on the evening of July 3rd. The next day had been set apart for the gathering of the farmers, with the children brought out from the Juvenile Asylum, by the agent of the local association [Reverend Mr. Enoch Kingsbury]. The meeting was in the Court House; so great was the interest that only a small portion of the people could be accommodated. After reading the reports I addressed the meeting, explaining the plans of our Institution, and the condition of the thousands in our city who could be saved if transferred to the happy homes on their broad prairies. A deeper interest was excited in behalf of these children as they listened to these accounts of their experience in our crowded city, and beheld the contrast in the neat attire and happy faces of some sixty, seated on the right and left of the platform.
>
> We then formed our children in to a procession; those of the village with a large number of men and women following to a grove, where a well-spread table, with water from a spring, supplied the wants of all. The farmers returned with the children to the Court House; we examined all with great care, and found but one child who desired to make a change, which was arranged without difficulty.
>
> The next day I visited several of the children at their homes, and found them surrounded with every comfort, contented and happy. In all my journey I found the great want of the country, in the house and field, was help. Any number of children of suitable age can be disposed of in the great West."[16]

The Asylum's Committee on Admissions, Indentures and Discharges voted to end its agreement with Reverend Mr. Kingsbury at the June 2, 1857 meeting, stating only that his "application was declined for want of children," and the clerk was directed to "obtain from him full matters of the children [who] are of his account." The Asylum later decided to retain Kingsbury as one of several county agents in Illinois—a position he held until at least 1860.[17]

The Asylum did, in fact, begin sending companies of children to Illinois independently just two weeks after declining to send more west with Kingsbury. At the June 26, 1857 meeting of the Asylum's Indenturing Committee, it was noted: "Several children, say as many as time would admit of about leaving for the West with Mr. [Alexander C.] Pearcy were examined by the Committee and the needful advice given them." Alexander C. Pearcy served as clerk for the Committee at the time and was also Superintendent of the House of Reception.

One notable departure from Kingsbury's plan was that the Asylum did not send any adults west— just children. The Asylum did, however, continue Kingsbury's tradition of indenture agreements as well as another tradition as described in an 1856 newspaper article. "One of the stipulations is, that

"A Reunion in The West. From a Photograph." The accompanying article indicated that "thirty-four gatherings of the wards had been held by the agent during a single year at various points in the West. Such reunions were a tradition first implemented by Reverend Mr. Enoch Kingsbury. (*Mary E. Dodge, "A Day with Dr. Brooks," Scribner's Monthly, November 1870*)

Reverend Mr. Enoch A. Kingsbury. (*Courtesy of Danville, Illinois Public Library*)

the children are all to be brought together at the County seat, on the 6th of July of each year, to enjoy a public dinner."[18] Asylum officials declared, "As they went forth in companies, with joy and hope, they were promised that some member of the Board would meet them at their annual celebration, on the Fourth of July."[19]

The reunions were a source of much joy for the children. One of the Asylum's indenturing agents, George H. Allan, recalled them in 1862:

> We have held six pic-nic parties at different points in the above counties [Lee, Ogle, DeKalb, and Whiteside]; thus affording the children a holiday among their old schoolmates. All were eagerly greeted as they arrived, brought in from the country by their friends. Brothers and sisters here met after their separation of weeks or months; juvenile games were played, and all these occasions were replete with interest.[20]

By December 31, 1864, forty-three such reunions or social gatherings of the children had taken place in Illinois.[21]

H. D. Perry, NYJA Indenturing Agent, recalled a visit he had with Reverend Mr. Kingsbury in the Asylum's 1868 annual report:

> On a recent visit at Danville, Vermillion county, Illinois, where in 1855 a large number of your children were settled under the supervision of Rev. E. Kingsbury, I learned some interesting facts connected with the earlier operations of the Juvenile Asylum, which are worthy of record.
>
> From Rev. Mr. K. I obtained the book which contains the constitution, and records of "The Vermilion County Juvenile Aid Society" which society was organized by the citizens of Danville, at a meeting held at the Court House, July 4th, 1855, having for its object, as

History of the Orphan Trains

stated in the second article of its constitution,

"To aid the poor and especially the young in emigrating from the large cities to this county, and to provide for them suitable places and employments, so that they may become useful and respectable citizens."

Thirty citizens subscribed to this constitution, at the head of which appears the name of Mr. Kingsbury, who was chosen Secretary of the Society. He informs me that at the time the society was formed he had no acquaintance with the benevolent institutions of New York City, formed for the benefit of destitute children; except what he obtained from an article in the *New-York Tribune* upon the New York Juvenile Asylum, and from conversing with a merchant who had visited the Asylum.

It was while Secretary of "The Vermilion County Juvenile Aid Society" that he had rendered such valuable services to your indenturing work, and for which he should be held in grateful remembrance by the Directors of the Asylum.

If I am correctly informed, it was the opening door to the better method of caring for its children, which the Asylum adopted two years later, and has continued to the present time.[22]

Western Indenturing Agent

By 1859, it was becoming apparent that a full-time western indenturing agent would need to be hired to handle all of the work involved with sending the companies of children west. The minutes of the March 24, 1859 meeting of the Committee on Admissions, Indentures and Discharges state:

A communication was received from Mr. [Rensselaer N.] Havens, and the following extracts there from were directed to be transcribed on the minutes.

"In communicating my views to the committee last week, I fear that Mr. [John A.] Bryan did not fully understand me. It was very true that I suggested a permanent arrangement, by which there should always be a class of children, numbering from 40 to 50, in direct training with a view to emigration. And this ought to be. The Supt. should be in daily personal intercourse with them, with a view to a thorough eradication of their old habits, and preparation for a new life.

How this may best be done, I am not just now prepared to say. It should however be done, and the system be at once and permanently engrafted upon the Asylum management. But the present distress, the overcrowded state of the Asylum, and the constant influx of children, require the immediate dispatch of another company to the West. They are sleeping 3 or 4 in a bed at the Asylum.

In connexion with my previous suggestions allow another. It has become (to my mind at any rate) quite evident, that we must dispatch a company to the West every 6 if not every 4 weeks. Mr. [Alexander C.] Pearcy admits every two months: but this will not give us the constant discharge necessary to enable us to enlarge our business proportionate to the wants of the city. But with the demands of the new H. of R. [House of Reception] its Superintendent should be kept at home. The character of our city work, requires a responsible man on hand all the time. And whatever kind of a clerk we have, there is always employment for him.

So then it appears to me, we are driven to the necessity of the employment of an agent to accompany children to the West, to look after special cases etc., etc. In short there will be work enough for him."[23]

The Committee acted on the advice of Havens at its March 31, 1859 meeting:

The Secretary reported that the chairman had made an arrangement with the President

WANTED—In a Benevolent Institution in this city, a Gentleman unincumbered with a family, to act as SPECIAL AGENT for the INDENTURING of CHILDREN, and to discharge other duties in connection therewith. To a well-educated, Christian layman, who is a good disciplinarian, and one whose heart would be in the work, a liberal salary will be paid and permanent employment given. Address Box No. 2,551 Post-Office.

The Asylum ran this circa May 1859 ad for a "Special Agent" to assist with indenturing the children. (*NYJA Records; Rare Book and Manuscript Library, Columbia University Library*)

by which that gentleman would notify the Supt. of the Asylum to select 50 children to be sent west, at an early day; also to form a class of 50 other children, to be instructed with special reference to preparing them for apprenticeship, and to keep this class permanently organized, filling vacancies as children are withdrawn from it, and also to endevour to find some suitable and proper person to relieve the Supt. of the House of Reception from the necessity of leaving his duties here to accompany children to the West.[24]

At its April 28, 1859 meeting, the Committee pressed forward with plans to hire a western indenturing agent:

> Resolved. That the Indenturing Committee do recommend to the Board appointment at as early a day as possible, of some suitable and proper person to act as Special agent in relation to apprentices and candidates for apprenticeship, and in aiding this Committee in respect to the admission and discharge of children.[25]

One of the applicants for the job was George H. Allan. The minutes for the June 16, 1859 meeting indicate that he was hired at the rate of $400.00 per year, plus expenses.[26] It was just in time as the minutes for July 19, 1859 reveal: "The Chairman of the Visiting Committee appeared before this Committee and stated that the Asylum was full."

On August 11, 1859 the Committee ordered "that the Chairman be authorized to have a hand bill printed for circulation advertising children for apprenticeship in the West."[27]

County agents (see Appendix E) were also secured in Illinois to help the western agent with finding homes, accepting applications for children, and conducting other duties associated with indenturing the children. Asylum officials recognized the agents in their 1859 annual report: "These local agents have, in some cases, performed very arduous labors for several years past, without compensation, and we take much pleasure in being able here to record our warmest thanks for their generous efforts to advance our work."[28]

Western Indentures

The Asylum required each "employer" who took in a child to sign an apprentice's indenture, including those children indentured in the Midwest. As children were indentured until a set age, ascertaining the correct age of each child for the term of indenture was quite important, yet very difficult at times. In some cases the directors of the NYJA, or the court magistrates who committed children to the Asylum, simply had to take the word of the child as to age. Western indenturing agent Ebenezer Wright raised his concern about the issue in 1897. Aaron P. Garrabrant, First Assistant to the Superintendent, replied:

> The ages sent you are taken from the records of the Asylum, and are presumably correct. He also respectfully suggests that you might raise that question at the time the indentures are signed. Many of these children are committed by a magistrate and their official age is sent with the commitment papers.[29]

It was common practice for managers of such institutions as the NYJA to use July 4 as a default month and day of birth when the actual date was not known.[30]

Aged 12 Yrs Mch 12/59

NEW YORK JUVENILE ASYLUM.

APPRENTICE'S INDENTURE.

This Indenture, made between "THE NEW YORK JUVENILE ASYLUM," of the first part, and _George B. Coffin_ of _Tolono_ in the County of _Champaign_ and State of _Illinois_ party of the second part, **Witnesseth**, That the said party of the first part, in accordance with the "Act to incorporate the New York Juvenile Asylum," passed June 30th, 1851, HAS bound out, and by these presents DOES bind out, unto the said party of the second part, _Bridget Hughes_, a _Girl_, aged (as nearly as can be ascertained) _12_ years on the _12th_ day of _March_ 18_59_, to serve the said party of the second part as an apprentice, from the day of the date hereof for and until the expiration of _5 Yrs & Mos_ years hence next ensuing. And the said party of the second part covenants and agrees with the said party of the first part, that during the said term the said party of the second part will provide the said _Bridget Hughes_ both in sickness and health, with proper medical treatment, sufficient food, lodging, apparel and washing, suitable for an apprentice; that the said party will cause _her_ to be instructed in the art of _Housewifery_ and in reading, writing, and arithmetic, at least as far as and including compound interest; that the said party will carefully watch over and guard the morals of the said apprentice, and prevent _her_ from frequenting taverns, porter-houses, play-houses, or gaming-houses of any kind, and that at the end of the said term the said party will give the said apprentice a new Bible, a complete suit of new clothes, besides those in wear, and pay _her_ _Fifty_ dollars, and in all respects will comply with the requirements of the Charter of the "NEW YORK JUVENILE ASYLUM," and especially of the sections thereof hereunto annexed and made part of this agreement.

IN WITNESS WHEREOF, the said party of the first part has caused its corporate seal to be hereunto affixed, and these presents to be signed by its President, and by the Chairman of its Indenturing Committee. And the said party of the second part has hereunto set _his_ hand and seal the _14th_ day of _September_ in the year of our Lord one thousand eight hundred and _fifty nine_.

A. N. Wetmore, President.

R. N. Havens
Chairman of Indenturing Committee.

George B. Coffin

Signed, sealed and delivered
in presence of _Geo. H. Allan_

Apprentice's Indenture for Bridget Hughes to George B. Coffin of Champaign County, Illinois, dated September 14, 1859 and signed by newly hired Western Placing Agent, George H. Allan.

APPRENTICE'S AGREEMENT.

I, _Bridget Hughes_ the person described in the foregoing instrument of indenture, do of my own free will, put myself apprentice to _Geo. B. Coffin_ for the period and on the terms described in the foregoing instrument and the sections of the Charter of the "NEW YORK JUVENILE ASYLUM," thereunto annexed, and do agree with _Geo. B. Coffin_ the party of the second part to the foregoing Indenture, to well and truly serve _him_, obey _his_ lawful commands, do no damage to the said party of the second part, nor see it done by others, without preventing the same, as far as I lawfully may, nor will I waste the said party's goods, nor lend them unlawfully to any, nor will I absent myself day or night from the said party's service without the said party's leave, nor frequent porter-houses, taverns, play-houses, or gaming-houses, but will in all things behave myself as a faithful apprentice.

IN WITNESS WHEREOF, I have hereunto set my hand and seal this _14th_ day of _September_ in the year of our Lord one thousand eight hundred and _fifty-nine_.

Signed, sealed and delivered in presence of

her
Bridget X Hughes
mark

Apprentice's Agreement for Bridget Hughes to George B. Coffin dated September 14, 1859. Bridget, unable to write, made her mark instead. See prior page for her indenture record. (*Champaign County Historical Society/Urbana Free Library/Call Number Apprentices Indenture Record 5*)

The validity of the indentures was tested in at least one case. Mrs. Meltz, a "German woman," left two of her daughters at the Asylum circa 1872. They were both sent to Illinois and indentured. By 1875, Mrs. Meltz apparently had a change of heart, and traveled to Illinois with the intention of bringing the girls back with her. After a failed attempt to grab her daughter Albertina "clandestinely while she was going to school," she filed a writ of habeas corpus. Albertina had been placed with Mr. and Mrs. Patterson in Decatur.[31]

The case was tried in December 1875, and after much debate between the two attorneys in the case, who each insisted Albertina preferred to remain in Illinois instead of returning to New York with her mother, the judge spoke privately with Albertina and made the decision to return her to Mrs. Patterson.

Changes to the verbiage on the indenture forms occurred, but were infrequent. At the June 13, 1864 meeting of the Asylum's Indenturing Committee, the following changes were made:

> Ordered That the Illinois Indentures be amended by inserting after the words "cause him (or her) to be instructed in the art of" - - - - the words "and will send him (or her) to school four months each year until he (or she) shall be taught to read and write" etc.; and after the words "morals of the said apprentice," the words, "cause him (or her) to observe the Sabbath and frequently attend places of public religious instruction." Also to leave blank space for the amount to be paid to the apprentice at the expiration of his term of indenture.[32]

In 1887 the Asylum wrote to all the children under indenture in the West and asked what they thought of lowering the age from twenty-one to eighteen for the boys so as to match the age of the girls—to which a very astute fifteen-year-old boy named George H. Miller replied: "When the boys come West they do not know any more about work than a cow knows about Sunday, and it takes them several years to learn all about farming, and not one in a dozen at eighteen knows that is best for him, nor how to appreciate a good home. At that age they are apt to have the big head, and if they were left to themselves, many of them would become tramps. I could say more, but I think you will grasp my ideas." As it turned out, the Asylum was of a like opinion and did not alter the age, nor did they ever question doing so again.[33]

The number of children who remained with their "employer" for the full term of their indentures was disappointing at best. Western Indenturing Agent Ebenezer Wright estimated the number at just 25 to 50 percent.[34] He explained to a reporter in Decatur, Illinois, in 1896:

> When a girl or a boy gets to be 14 to 16 they become restless. They get impatient of restraint, even though it may be just. They think they should have their own way more and the people they are living with can do nothing with them. Then we take them away and find homes for them somewhere else. The mere fact of making the change does them good. They learn that everything is not to be just as they would have it.[35]

The Asylum's records reveal that three girls held the record for the greatest number of homes they were placed in or indentured to. Girls named Lena and Mary tied at fifteen homes each. A girl named Louisa came in third at twelve homes.[36]

If the child was found suitable after the trial period and indentures were signed, the Western Agent was tasked with collecting train fare from New York for sending out the newly indentured child. The collection of such fares often proved difficult: "Until recently [1859], owing to the scarcity of money, we have been obliged, in many cases, to take notes or produce in payment. But our Agent experienced so much difficulty in giving attention to the conversion of these into money, that we felt it to be our duty to adopt the cash principle."[37] Collecting the fares continued to be a problem, as reported by the Asylum's western indenturing agent in 1868: "A letter was rec'd from Mr. Wright Western Agent calling attention to difficulties in the way of collecting fares: also to the length of time during which children are left on trial previous to indenture. Action on these points were deferred until another meeting."[38]

Regardless, the collection of fares continued. At its February 15, 1869 meeting the Committee ruled "that the Indenturing Agent collect the sum of twenty dollars ($20) for each child indentured in the State of Illinois to meet the expenses of transportation from the City."[39]

By 1887 (and likely earlier) the Asylum relented and dropped its policy of collecting the fares. An article related to a distribution in Monmouth, Illinois, in 1887 reported, "All expenses for transportation will be assumed by the Asylum, and the children will be placed on trial free of charge."[40] The Children's Aid Society, which was sending children west and placing them out in many of the same communities as the NYJA, did not ask for reimbursement for travelling costs from foster parents nor require indenture papers to be signed. The CAS procedure, coupled with the trouble in collecting the fares, likely figured in the Asylum's decision to stop collecting them.

An Act of Legislature

The minutes of the Asylum's Indenturing Committee for its September 6, 1860 meeting include the following statement: "Referred to often expressed opinion of Illinois lawyers that a special act of the Legislature is needed to make valid the indentures executed in that State. No action taken. Matter to be brought up again soon."[41]

The Committee later decided to take the advice of the lawyers. On November 15, 1860 the members voted to "print a memorial to the Legislature of the State of Illinois for signature by the citizens of that state to whom children have been indentured by this corporation, asking for the passage of a law giving full validity to our Indentures within said state."[42] At their January 10, 1861 meeting they noted:

> Mr. [John A.] Bryan read a letter from Mr. Allen [George H. Allan] who is now at Springfield for the purpose of securing the passage of a law, by the present Legislature of Illinois making valid the Indentures between the New York Juvenile Asylum & parties in Illinois. Gov. Yates advises Mr. Allen to remain at Springfield until the bill comes up in the Legislature & Mr. Allen wants instructions from the Committee.[43]

On January 12, 1861, Judge James M. Rodgers presented a petition to the legislature "from divers citizens of Clinton, Washington, and other counties, asking for the legalization of the acts of [the] agent of the New York Juvenile Asylum in binding children in this State."[44] The Act was approved the next month:

> AN ACT confirming the indentures of certain apprentices therein named.
>
> 1. Be it enacted by the People of the State of Illinois, represented in the General Assembly, Indentures for the apprenticeship of any minor heretofore or hereafter made and executed between the New York Juvenile Asylum, a corporation created by act of the Legislature of the State of New York, passed June 30, 1851, and any citizen of this State, in substance and form as provided by its act of incorporation, are hereby declared to be valid and binding: Provided, that all such indentures, hereafter made, the said corporation shall have inserted therein the covenants for the benefit of the apprentice which are required to be inserted in indentures of apprentices by the laws of this State.
>
> 2. This act shall take effect immediately.
>
> Approved February 18, 1861.[45]

George H. Allan reported on the passing of the Act:

> By direction of the Committee on Indenturing, I visited Springfield during the session of the Illinois Legislature, for the purpose of attending to the passage of an act legalizing our indentures in that State. A large number [125] of the employers of the children having jointly with us petitioned for the act, it passed unanimously in the Senate, and nearly so in the House.
>
> I acknowledge with gratitude the kindness of the Hon. Messrs. [James M.] Rodgers and [William H.] Underwood of the Senate, and of the Hon. Messrs. Brown, Kellogg, Maley and others of the House, all of whom interested themselves in the Bill. Governor Yates also received me kindly, interested himself in the matter, and at the proper time approved the Bill.[46]

Two of the Illinois senators who sponsored the act had a very personal connection to the children they sought to protect with it. They had themselves taken in children from the Asylum from a company sent west in 1860. Judge James M. Rodgers, of Carlyle, took a boy named John Sullivan, and William H. [Henry] Underwood, of Belleville, took a girl named Johanna Farrell.

On April 12, 1861, just a few months after the Illinois Legislature passed the act recognizing the indentures of the NYJA, Confederate forces fired upon Fort Sumter in South Carolina, which led to America's Civil War. The orphan trains of the NYJA continued going west throughout the duration of the war, which ended in 1865.

Western Agency Established

By 1867 it became apparent to the members of the board (Superintendent Dr. Samuel D. Brooks in particular) that it would be expedient for them to establish a permanent agency house in Illinois for

Senator William Henry Underwood. He was one of two men that took in children from the NYJA and were later instrumental in passing an Act in the Illinois Legislature validating NYJA indentures. (*Find-A-Grave Memorial 70895083*)

conducting the business of indenturing children.[47]

The matter was put before the Indenturing Committee which rejected the idea at its February 4, 1867 meeting:

> The question of the expediency of establishing a depot in Illinois referred to this Committee by the Board of Directors, was considered, and correspondence with Mr. [H. D.] Perry on the subject was read, and the following Resolutions recommended to the Board.
>
> Resolved that it is inexpedient at this present time to establish a "House" or "Depot" in Illinois as a part of the permanent machinery of the N. Y. Juvenile Asylum, but it is desirable that hereafter all correspondence

appertaining to Indenture in Illinois, including the semi-annual Report from employers required by the Charter, shall be directed to the Indenturing Agent at his head-quarters, for his perusal, and early transmission to the House of Reception.[48]

H. D. Perry resigned, and on May 13, 1867 the Committee decided to appoint Ebenezer Wright as "Indenturing Agent to reside in Illinois at a salary of $1000.00 per annum and traveling expenses."[49]

Wright was well-known at the Asylum as he had replaced Alexander C. Pearcy as Superintendent of the Asylum's House of Reception on May 1, 1860.[50] Previous to that post he worked alongside the Asylum's Superintendent, Dr. Samuel D. Brooks, at the State Reform School in Monson, Massachusetts.[51] Wright, born in Ludlow, Massachusetts in 1830, was the son of Rev. Ebenezer Burt Wright (of the First Congregational Church) and Harriet Goodell.[52]

In August 1867, the Committee decided to forge ahead with establishing the western residence:

After a full discussion of the Indenturing work at the West, and of communications from Mr. [Ebenezer] Wright and Mrs. Wight [Assistant to Ebenezer Wright] in regard to it, the following resolution was on motion adopted. Resolved, that for the purpose of increasing the usefulness of the Indenturing work, this Committee recommend the Board to authorize Mr. Wright to lease the house at Kenwood near Chicago, referred to in his letter at the rate of $600 per annum, to May 1, 1868—with the privilege of retaining it for three years thereafter at the same rate; and to purchase the furniture for the sum of $1,000.[53]

The subject was again brought up at the November 25, 1867 meeting:

The Chairman reported that he had authorized Mr. E. Wright to hire a house in the neighborhood of Chicago at the rate of $400. per annum to May 1, 1868. The Committee then had an interview with Mr. E. Wright and after discussion of the plan for the Western Agency referred the details of furnishing the house to the Chairman with power.[54]

A reporter later explained the establishment of the Western Agency: "Formerly the agent who attended to the indenturing of asylum children to western farmers or other employers, and who was expected to find good Christian homes for scores of girls and boys, had no local habitation or post-office address. His 'head-quarters' were on the railway or in the saddle, and of course under these circumstances it was impossible for him to fully meet the demands of such a work." The reporter credited then Superintendent Dr. Samuel D. Brooks with the idea: "Through the suggestion of Dr. Brooks a western agency is now firmly established at Chicago, and under its admirable organization an incalculable amount of good is being accomplished."[55]

At some point the plan to locate the Western Agency in Kenwood was abandoned for a location in North Chicago—about eight or nine miles north of Kenwood, in Lakeview Township. Ebenezer Wright provided details about the Agency House in 1868:

The house leased [from George R. Clark] for our headquarters is situated in North Chicago near the city limits, two & a half miles from the river, in a pleasant & healthy locality, on [611] Fullerton avenue [now Cleveland Street], second door West from Hurlbut St. & is reached by the North Clark St. (3rd door from Clark St.) horse cars (City Limits line) which pass within one hundred yards. It is a two story house, having ten rooms, besides pantries, closets, wood shed etc. conveniently arranged for our purposes. The lease expires the first of May. Until then the rent is $33.33 per month, at the rate of $400. Per annum. The expense for furnishing it amounted to $825.86. This provision not only contributes very much to our comfort, but greatly facili-

North front of the Illinois Central (Union) Depot in Chicago. Asylum Agent Ebenezer Wright conducted much of his travel out of this depot and the Massasoit House Hotel (part of which can be seen on the far right) from circa 1868 to 1872. Other railroads that used the station prior to 1871 were the Chicago & Alton Railroad, the Baltimore and Ohio Railroad, the Galena & Chicago Union and the Cleveland, Cincinnati, Chicago & St. Louis Railway from 1886 to 1893. (*Frank Leslie's Illustrated Newspaper, August 30, 1856, 13*)

tates our work & diminishing its embarrassments & difficulties, so that our satisfaction in it is increased many fold.[56]

During this time, Wright was conducting business related to indenturing children out of the Massasoit House Hotel located alongside the old Illinois Central Depot at the foot of East Lake Street, in Chicago.

The three-year extension of the lease expired in the same year of the Great Chicago Fire, which occurred in October 1871 and nearly reached the Western Agency house before it was extinguished. Following the fire, the Asylum opted to relocate its Western Agency to Normal (near Bloomington), McLean County, Illinois: "The chairman presented letters from Mr. Wright, the Western Agent, relating to the great fire in Chicago, and asking permission to remove the Agency to Bloomington. The chairman in the emergency, had telegraphed the desired authority to remove the Agency, and on motion his action was approved and confirmed by the Committee."[57]

The matter was still being discussed at the Committee's March 17, 1872 meeting: "A letter from the Western Agent dated Mch. 16 asking instructions regarding future location of Agency was read and referred to the Chairman to reply to."[58]

By May 17, 1872 the Bloomington, Illinois newspaper was reporting, "The western agency of the New York Juvenile Asylum is now located at Normal. Mr. E. Wright, the western agent, can be addressed through the Bloomington postoffice."[59] The precise location of the Agency House was on Willow Street in Normal, just north of the Illinois State Normal University. At that time, the cities of Normal and Bloomington were only separated by about one mile, with one street (Division Street) between the two. The Agency House was described as "a large dwelling, with an acre and a half of land."[60]

The Asylum's Western Agency remained in Normal, Illinois, until the first few months of 1890, when operations were once again established in Chicago—this time at 543 West 61st Street, in Englewood, a neighborhood on Chicago's southwest side.[61]

The main Englewood train station was located at a crucial junction for three railroads—the Chicago, Rock Island and Pacific Railroad, the New York Central Railroad, and the Pennsylvania Railroad. Englewood Station also served passenger trains of the New York, Chicago and St. Louis Railroad (the Nickel Plate), which operated over the New York Central via trackage rights.

Greener Pastures

By 1897, the Asylum was debating whether or not to keep the Western Agency open any longer, and at the same time was entertaining the idea of placing children in southern states. At the February 23, 1897 meeting of the Committee on Admissions, Indentures and Discharges it was noted, "The Chairman appointed Messrs. [Henry M.] Humphrey, [James T.] Barrow and [Franklin W.] Moulton a Committee to examine the question of continuing the Western Agency, and also to inquire the expediency of a southern State for indenturing children there."[62]

They explained their reason for focusing on a state other than Illinois for indenturing children:

> The State of Illinois is itself beginning to suffer from the same influence of the city that the State of New York has suffered from; it is losing its place as one of the States where a large percentage of its people own their own homes, and becoming a State where large numbers of persons are tenants only of the residences they occupy. The mortgage indebtedness of the State is increasing instead of decreasing, and the conditions of congested life, which bear heaviest on the poor, are becoming apparent in that State as in the State of New York. Hence has arisen the necessity of seeking another placing-out field, which the Directors have found in the State of Iowa.[63]

At the May 17 meeting they continued to discuss the issue, with their focus now on expanding placing-out to either Iowa or Kansas:

> Mr. [Henry M.] Humphrey reported for Sub Committee in regard to continuing the Western Agency, that full details have been obtained, but the Committee are not ready to report until they can investigate placing out in the other States and request that an appropriation be made to pay expenses of investigating the States of Kansas and Iowa through Mr. Wright and otherwise, total not to exceed $250.00, which recommendation was adopted.[64]

The Asylum had tossed around the idea of indenturing some of the children in Iowa as far back as 1888. The Asylum solicited input regarding the possibility from children previously indentured in the West when it sent the annual questionnaire to them that year; however, no action was subsequently taken.⁶⁵

This time around the Committee made a decision, as the minutes of its August 8, 1898 meeting reveal: "Communications from the Indenturing Agent [Ebenezer Wright] to Messrs. [Alfred E.] Marling and Moulton were read [regarding?] the placing out of children in Iowa, and it was resolved that if suitable homes could be found in Iowa Mr. Wright's suggestion should be followed in the case of certain children."⁶⁶ The minutes do not elaborate on what was meant by "certain children."

In 1898, Mornay Williams, president of the Asylum's board of directors, reaffirmed its policy of sending children to new homes in the country:

> The best way to help the lad is to find him a new home. Generally that home should be in the rural districts. What the street boy needs is the country. The country youth longs for the city with its incessant and varied activities, and if he has had the proper home training he is more likely to succeed there than the city bred youth; but the street boy needs the open air, the warm breath of nature on his cheek, the calm patience of her slow processes, the subtle teaching of the wild and tamed animals, and by them he grows into a well-rounded manhood.⁶⁷

Since the very beginning of the Asylum's orphan trains, occasional placements had been made in several other states adjacent to Illinois, namely Missouri, Wisconsin, and Indiana. Such placements were generally in communities located close to the Illinois border.

Western Agency of the NYJA at 543 West 61st Street in Englewood, Illinois. (*NYJA Annual Report, 1893*)

CHAPTER SEVEN

All Aboard the Orphan Train!

Candidates for the West

The Asylum's managers described the children surrendered for the express purpose of being sent west as "well brought up, but whose parents have suffered reverses, or whose parents are dead." George H. Allan, Western Agent for the Asylum, explained that the pool of candidates for the West during his tenure consisted "mainly of orphans, deserted children, and the offspring of parents too intemperate or too profligate to care or provide for them."

A sampling of three cases of children surrendered for the express purpose of being sent west in the early 1870s:

Case 1: A boy named Arthur

"The woman who brought this boy, says it was her servant's child. Its mother dying when the child was but 3 days old—Mrs. _____ took him to bring up. Having a large family of her own—she wishes to fully commit this boy to the Asylum on acc't of his disobedience & pilfering—to be placed in a Western home. Boy is smart & intelligent.

Case 2: A girl named Mary

"The Grandmother states that Mary's father has been gone for three years. Went as Steward of a Steamer Santiago de Cuba—running at that time to Europe, since which time nothing has been heard from him. The mother went off two years ago, abandoning the child & throwing its support upon the Grandmother. Is supposed to be living somewhere in Brooklyn with another man. The child is taken, by us, with consent of Grandmother—to send west."

Case 3: Two brothers

"Mrs. _____'s husband was brother to the boys' mother. She reports the father as worthless—says he has had them in a Mission—that he has entirely neglected them since the death of their mother, two years ago. Mrs. _____ desires the Committee to send these boys west. She says, the father wishes to have them kept somewhere, until they are large enough to get earnings to supply him with liquor."[1]

Occasionally a special request would come in from a court official regarding children being sent west. One such letter, dated January 18, 1877, was sent to the Superintendent of the NYJA by Police Justice Henry Murray of the Second District Police Court:

Dear Sir,

The circumstances in the case of Mary A. Siebert and her brother Edward appeal so affectingly to our sympathies that, although the boy is within the minimum of age for commitment to your institution, I respectfully suggest and request (if it be within the limits of practicability) that you extend your protecting care to both the hapless orphans, in preference to sending them upon divergent paths at this early period of their lives.[2]

The Asylum granted Justice Murray his wish and sent Edward and Mary west together in the April 2, 1877 company. Both were placed in the same home in Annawan, Illinois.[3]

Asylum managers expressed their desire to exercise great care when making their selection of children for the West, stating it was "a sin against light and knowledge, against good conscience and the universal and irrepealable law of doing to others as we would that they should do to us, to scatter abroad the seeds of city vice and wickedness in virgin soils where they cannot fail to produce harvests of misery, pollution and death."[4]

The records show that for the five companies sent west in 1899, twenty-seven children were committed to the Asylum through the NYSPCC; ten were committed for larceny, thirty-one for truancy and disobedience, and fifty-two for destitution.[5]

In 1903 the Asylum's indenturing agent discovered some interesting facts about the history of the children sent west that year, and its bearing on how they fared:

> It may be interesting to note that the record of wards prior to the commitment to the Asylum does not seem to indicate what may be expected of them in the West. Of those who have, to all appearances, settled down contentedly in the homes first provided for them, three were committed for being ungovernable, and one for petit larceny; while those who have been placed four or five times were committed for destitution and no proper guardianship. The three who absconded, however, were sent to the Asylum for vagrancy, petit larceny and ungovernableness.[6]

Investigation of Children

A more stringent procedure involving the gathering of background information on each child sent west was implemented by the Indenturing Committee at its March 8, 1867 meeting:

> Resolved, that hereafter, the Superintendent of the Asylum collect all the facts that can be ascertained relative to the parentage, family connections, and personal history of every child returned by him as a suitable candidate for deportation to the West; especially of orphan and deserted children, particularly ascertaining, as nearly as possible, the names of the parents, their residence, church connections, the age and birth place of the children, the names and age of their brothers and sisters; and when it becomes necessary in order to identify the origin of the children, the names of their Uncles and Aunts; the previous occupation of the children; and the school where they have attended; and any other facts that may be of interest to them when arrived at maturity. And that the Superintendent communicate these facts to the Indenturing Committee when the children are sent down for examination.[7]

In later years, the western indenturing agent based in Illinois was also kept apprised of the name, age, and a brief history of each child selected for each company to be sent west.

Preparing for the Journey

Before each company of children left the Asylum on what is now called an orphan train, the Asylum's Indenturing Committee instructed the Asylum's Superintendent to prepare a list of candidates to go west: "The Superintendent of the Asylum is required to select out, from time to time, among the children under his care, all such as are fit for indenture, and these are appropriately drilled and instructed with

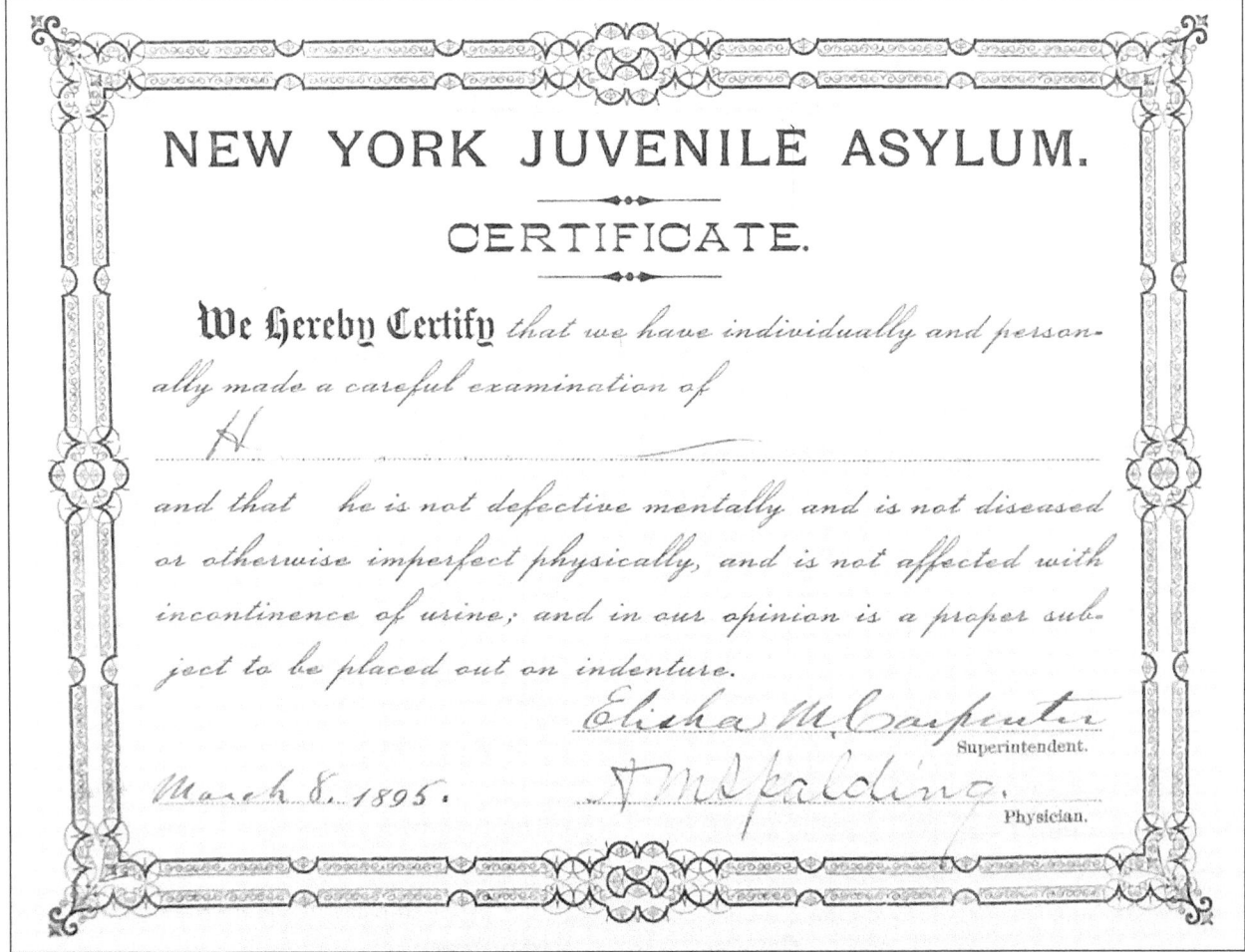

Certificates such as this would be filled out by the resident physician at the Asylum prior to each child being placed out for indenture. (*New York Juvenile Asylum records; Rare Book and Manuscript Library, Columbia University Library. Case Registers—House of Reception.*)

special reference to their speedy deportation."[8] The Superintendent consulted with the school teachers at the Asylum as to the child's performance as part of the process of selecting children to go west: "[...] and no child will be included in the company unless recommended by his teacher as likely to do well with proper care."[9]

At its November 9, 1891 meeting, the Indenturing Committee reinforced the need to at least notify, or at best, obtain written permission from relatives prior to sending children west: "Resolved that in every case it shall be stated to the Committee the date that the relatives are notified and whether by mail or messenger."[10]

Unless the children were voluntarily surrendered for the express purpose of being sent west, proper consent in writing from parents or guardians had to be obtained, "unless, by reason of their imprisonment for crime, their gross habitual drunkenness, their confirmed vagrancy, their utter degradation, their death, or their unmistakeable intention to abandon the child, it shall be found that such consent cannot be obtained."[11]

One relative of a little girl named Sarah who was chosen as a candidate for western indenture in 1875 wrote to the Asylum after receiving its letter asking for permission:

All Aboard the Orphan Train!

Dear Sir,

I will now tell you something about Sarah. At Washington's birthday her mother died and left a family of seven. I took six of them and Sarah said she wanted to [go] west. Her father is a bad man. He drinks very hard. He put them all out of the house one night. It was snowing very hard. He says that Sarah can go west if she wants to so please send her west the next company that goes.

I have her sisters with me in Connecticut so I will not be able to see her before she does, but I hope she will be a good girl and get a good home. I hope she will always think of the last words her mother said, "Honor thy father and thy mother. And love thy neighbor as thy self."

I will now finish by saying I hope she will always be a lover of the Lord.[12]

After about one month, the company of children selected was transferred to the House of Reception in preparation for the journey west:

Here our Indenturing Agent [This was handled by the Superintendent of the House of Reception until a permanent Indenturing Agent was later established in Illinois] [...] makes the acquaintance of each of them, inquires into their antecedents, consults their wishes and hears what their friends have to say. He enters all needful particulars concerning each child, in a memorandum book [...]. No child is permitted to go, however, without first being brought before the Committee, and examined as to its character, fitness, and willingness; and, in all cases, there must be a written certificate from a Physician connected with the Institution, that the health of the child is such that it is a proper subject for apprenticeship.[13]

Parents were given the opportunity to go to the House of Reception to say goodbye to their children prior to their departure for the west. Mary Westmen, the mother of Emma Jane "Jennie" and Thomas Oscar "Oscar" Westmen, intended to bid them farewell at the House of Reception on 13th street prior to their departure for Danville, Illinois on Monday, December 2, 1867, but she was devasted when she arrived too late to do so on the day they left. She was later very relieved to hear the two children were faring well at their new homes in Illinois:

New York City February 3d, 1868

Dear Oscar
It is with pleasure I write to you I am very glad to hear you have got a nice place I have had a letter from your sister you don't know how delighted I was to hear from you but dear Oscar you can't imagine how lonesome I am without you and Jennie my dear and how bad I felt when I went down to 13th street to see you and to find you gone. Oh dear little did I think I was raising you to go so far away from me. My heart is nearly broke dear child you are my first thought in the morning and the last ones at night. I feel as if I shall never see your dear face again but trust in God that we shall all three live together again. I hope you will be a good boy to your new parents and they will be good to you. Dear Oscar if I could only live near where I could see you how happy I would be knowing you are comfortably situated. Jennie wrote to me that she had such nice parents and she had lots of friends and had lots of nice presents for her holidays. I want you to write to me and let me know about yourself and the place. I am with Mrs. McTaggart now and have been since New Years. I was very lonesome at New Years without you and Jennie but as it is we must trust in God for our Future happiness. Dear Oscar you must pray to your Heavenly Father to help you through your life and never forget your own Father and dear affectionate Mother who has loved you and cared for you

in sickness and health and troubles. O [*sic*] Dear child do everything that is right in the sight of God and man and allways [*sic*] speak the truth and you will prosper dear Oscar study all you can at your leisure hours dear child you are ever in my mind. I hope you can go and see your sister once in a while for that itself will be a great blessing and comfort to me for you to see one another.

Mrs. McTaggarts family are all very anxious to hear from you and Jennie if you can't write get one of your new parents to write for you and tell me all the particulars. Mary Franky and all send their love to you and Mrs McTaggart sends her love to you and she hopes you have got a nice home and are with nice people and she hopes they will be good and kind to you for her sake for your mother grieves all the time about you pray night and morning for yourself and sister and dear loving mother and pray he may spare your health that you may be a comfort to me. My dear child the days are long and the nights are longer without you but the time will soon come around that you will be able to help take care of me in my old days when I shant be able to take care of myself. Write soon. From your ever loving mother.

A kiss to you on paper[14]

Prior to Departure

When the list was completed and final selections had been made, the children were "transmitted to the House of Reception in companies of forty or fifty, consisting of both sexes, and are marshalled, outfitted, and accompanied upon their journey of day and night travel by the indenturing clerk, who chooses each home with a view to the well-being of the child."[15]

It was tradition (at least in the earlier years) for the children selected to go west to appear together at a selected church on the Sunday prior to their departure. In 1860, a New York City newspaper reported on the Asylum: "The congregation of Madison Square church were deeply interested last Sabbath by the singing and recitation of the thirty-six children selected to go West from this institution."[16]

Notices were placed in Illinois newspapers and handbills displayed in the post office for several weeks prior to the arrival of a company of children. The following notice ran in the *Central Illinois Gazette* on July 13, 1859:

To Farmers

The New York Juvenile Asylum is desirous of securing homes in this vicinity, for 40 or 50 children, with farmers and mechanics. These children are from 7 to 14 years of age, and have been in the institution long enough to give good assurance of their future good conduct. Nearly all of them can read, write and cipher, and are healthy and well clothed. Two thirds are boys and the remainder girls. They will be indentured, to those taking them, the girls receiving $50 at 18 and the boys $100 at 21 with a fair English education. The expense of bringing them out, (from $15 to $18) will be borne by those to whom they are indentured. Should there be a sufficient number of applications arrangements will be made to have the children in West Urbana [now Champaign, Illinois] on the 26th of August, 1859. Application to be made immediately to J. W. Scroggs or if preferred, at the institution, 71 West 13th St. New York City.[17]

Many of the children were excited about being sent west, but some were affected very deeply by the prospect, and they tended to be the children who knew they had one or both parents living. Officials at the Asylum tried to minimize these separations:

The hardships attending the separation of children from their relatives is sometimes more apparent than real. But when the par-

ASYLUM CHILDREN!

A Company of Children, mostly Boys, from the New York Juvenile Asylum, will arrive in

GIBSON, AT THE BURWELL HOUSE,

THURSDAY MORNING, Nov. 21, 1889,

And Remain Until Evening. They are from 7 to 15 Years of age.

Homes are wanted for these children with farmers, where they will receive kind treatment and enjoy fair advantages. They have been in the asylum from one to two years, and have received instruction and training preparatory to a term of apprenticeship, and being mostly of respectable parentage, they are desirable children and worthy of good homes.

They may be taken at first upon trial for three months, and afterward, if all parties are satisfied, under indentures,—girls until 18, and boys until 21 years of age.

The indenture provides for four months schooling each year, until the child has advanced through compound interest, and at the expiration of the term of apprenticeship, two new suits of clothes, and the payment to the girls of fifty, and to the boys of one hundred and fifty dollars.

All expenses for transportation will be assumed by the Asylum, and the children will be placed on trial and indentured free of charge.

Those who desire to take children on trial are requested to meet them at the hotel at the time above specified.

E. WRIGHT, Agent.

PLEASE EXTEND THIS INFORMATION.

A handbill announcing the arrival of a company of children in Gibson, Illinois, in 1889. (*Courtesy of the author*)

Samuel D. Brooks, M.D. He served as both Superintendent and Physician at the NYJA from 1858-1871 and was responsible for examining the children prior to riding an orphan train. (*Mary E. Dodge, "A Day with Dr. Brooks," Scribner's Monthly, November 1870, 37*)

ents or other relatives are convinced by the clearest and best testimony that the children are favorably situated, and are happy and contented in Western rural homes, they generally soon become reconciled to the new circumstances.[18]

Word would often get out, or a notice would appear in the newspaper, regarding the plans for another company of children to be sent west. There are several instances noted in the Asylum's records of children showing up at the House of Reception from the streets of New York City and asking to go along. Several were allowed to join the company about to depart, never having been officially admitted to the NYJA.

In 1876, prior to leaving for Dixon, Illinois, a company of children was gathered at the House of Reception at 61 West Thirteenth Street for "two or three days before their departure" where "they received visits from friends and relatives, had their pictures taken, and were fitted out with an extra suit of new clothes [...]. On Sunday afternoon they were all assembled in the chapel and listened to short addresses by various gentlemen who were interested in the Asylum. Among those who spoke was Apollos R. Wetmore, who was "now in his eightieth year, who has been acting President of the asylum from the time of its inception, 24 years ago." After Wetmore spoke, the children "sang a number of hymns from the Moody and Sankey collection."[19]

In 1877, and again in 1878, Robert Carter, a New York City publisher with Robert Carter & Brothers, was thanked by the Asylum for "his frequent addresses to the children going West, together with his liberal donation of books to take with them." In 1878, Carter made a gift of one hundred volumes from the A.L.O.E. (a lady of England) series.[20] A.L.O.E. was the pen name of author Charlotte Maria Tucker of England. Tucker once explained in a letter to her publisher, "My position in life renders me independent of any exertions of my own; I pray for God's blessing upon my attempts to instruct His lambs in the things which concern their everlasting welfare."[21] Tucker's portrayal of the poor in her books was likely drawn from her experience as a workhouse visitor in Marylebone, England. She often donated proceeds from her writings to missionary or charity work.

The children leaving New York were often presented with a small bible prior to their departure, and in the winter, were also given a new blanket to take along.[22] The earliest reference to this practice is in the minutes of the Indenturing Committee for March 12, 1856: "Resolved that a neat engraving of the asylum be prepared to accompany each Bible given to children on leaving the institution."

It was typical for the children to be sent west in new gray uniforms of the type worn at the Asylum.[23] A newspaper reporter described their clothing after witnessing a distribution of children at Decatur, Illinois in 1880: "They were all dressed alike in course gray suits, except the girls, who were attired

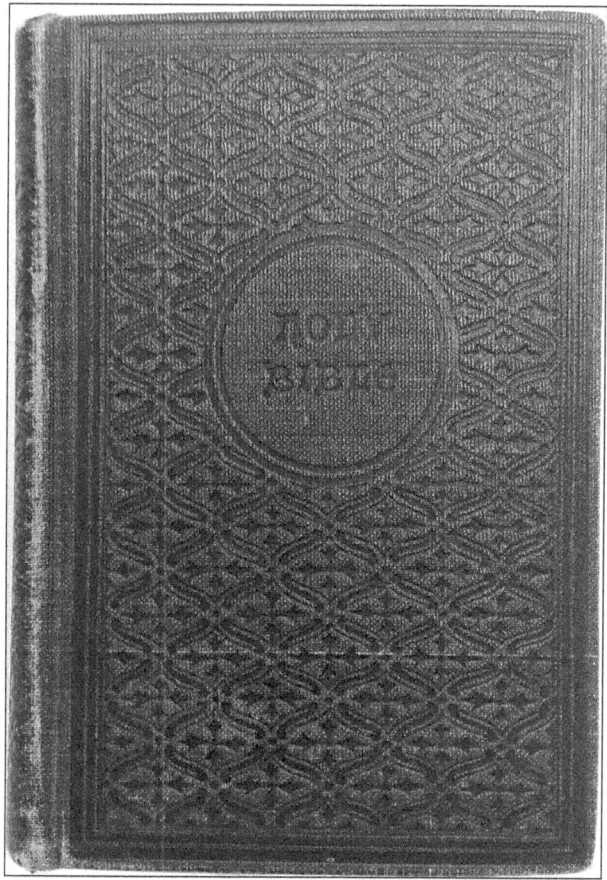

This bible was presented to Frank Thiel by the NYJA when he was sent west on June 3, 1901. See presentation plate from inside the bible on right. (*Kevin Fryer*)

Presentation plate for bible given to Frank Thiel by the NYJA when he was sent west on June 3, 1901. See bible cover on the left. (*Kevin Fryer*)

in dresses of varied colors."[24] Another description of the girls' clothing was given by a reporter visiting the NYJA in 1870, "Pink and lilac calico dresses for Sunday wear abound; so do high-necked gingham aprons."[25] A description of the children's clothing appeared in the Asylum's annual report for the year 1859:

> The clothing is selected with reference to neatness, durability and economy—that for boys' winter wear being a grey satinet jacket and trousers, and blue striped twilled cotton for shirts.
>
> The cost of an entire winter suit, comprising jacket, pants, shirt, cap, shoes, and socks is about $6. The summer clothing consists, for boys, of blue Kentucky jeans and denims for jackets and trousers, and an entire suit costs about $4. The girls usually wear out of style calicoes and ginghams, linsey Woolsey petticoats, unbleached muslin chemises, and, in winter, Canton flannel drawers, all which, with hood, shoes and stockings, cost about $3.[26]

Beginning of the Journey

The NYJA almost exclusively utilized the services of the Erie Railroad in Jersey City, New Jersey, for these trips west, until the Asylum closed its Western Agency. A newspaper report in 1856 described the process at that time:

> BOYS FOR THE COUNTRY.—The officers of the New York Juvenile Asylum will send out today by the Erie Railroad, about seventy-five children and twenty-five adults or one hundred in all, bound for Illinois, where they will become agriculturists, or engage in other useful employments.
>
> They will leave the House of Reception in 13th street between two and three o'clock in the afternoon, and walk down Broadway to Chambers street, and thence to the Railroad depot in Jersey City. Two cars will be appropriated to them. The number of children and youth annually sent out from this city to the Western States, through the agency of philan-

thropic institutions, is becoming quite large. Most of them will in this manner become useful citizens, while, if neglected, they would almost inevitably go to ruin.[27]

Upon their arrival at Erie Railroad's Pavonia Ferry terminal at the foot of Chambers Street in lower Manhattan, the children would board one of Erie's ferry boats to cross the Hudson River (North River) to Erie's Jersey City depot.

It was customary for the smaller companies to enter the train car ahead of the rest of the passengers. They would sit on one end, and when they had everything in order, railroad officials would let the rest of the passengers in the car. The railways often provided a separate day coach for the larger companies of children sent west. The NYJA companies nearly always departed at 5:00 p.m. on Monday afternoons on one of Erie's express trains.

The railroads provided discounted rates for the transportation of the children. As early as 1858, it was noted that the NYJA was receiving reduced rates: "The Railroad Companies very liberally, transport them at two thirds the usual fare, upon the express trains."[28] It was common in later years for them to offer "one quarter fare for all under

(at top) The Susquehanna ferry boat docked at the Erie Railway depot in Jersey City, New Jersey, ca. 1868. (*Mariner's Museum*). **(above)** Close-up of the depot's roof from photo at top of this page, showing the words "Erie Railway."

twelve years, and one half for older ones"[29] to children riding the trains of the CAS, and the NYJA undoubtedly had a similar arrangement.

Railroads were still providing special passes to the Asylum for the distribution of children in Illinois and Iowa as late as 1903. Asylum Superintendent Charles Dewey Hilles alluded to this procedure in a letter to the Western Indenturing Agent, James W. Shields: "I enclose 1903 passes over the Iowa Central and the Minneapolis & St. Louis Railroads."[30] Depending on the class of the ticket, the cost of the

All Aboard the Orphan Train!

This Chicago, Milwaukee & St. Paul Railway pass was presented to Children's Aid Society Placing Agent Rev. H. [Herman] D. Clarke for the year 1904. Indenturing agents of the NYJA were also given such passes, which allowed for reduced fares for both agents and the children. (*Courtesy of Reverend Mr. Clarke's descendants*)

Children sent west from the NYJA passed through this Erie Railroad depot in Jersey City between December 4, 1887 and the end of the orphan train movement. Circa 1910 photo. (*Pavonia Terminal—Wikipedia.org*)

trip from Jersey City to Chicago was between nine and twelve dollars at the time.

It was common for the children to sing songs after boarding the train in Jersey City. A newspaper article reported on some songs one company of children sang as they were about to depart from the Erie Railroad depot in 1858: "We were deeply interested in looking upon their bright and happy faces, their comfortable and neat attire, and listened with emotion to their songs of praise for the 'Home Sweet Home' that had sheltered them, and the glee with which they sang, 'Illinois is large enough to give us each a farm.'"[31]

Another description appeared in the Asylum's annual report in 1859:

> Here, again, some of the same exercises are repeated, to the gratification of crowds of passengers; and, while they move away, on their journey, with tears of joy and beating hearts, they carry with them the prayers of many who attend to see them off, that their Father in Heaven may preserve them from danger and watch over and guide them in all their future lives.[32]

The singing continued during their journey, "and the Indenturing Agent is frequently urged by passengers, while the cars are in motion, and by the citizens of the large towns where the train stops, to allow them to sing and repeat some of the lessons they have learned."[33]

These companies of children often caught the attention of fellow passengers. It was common for people to give the children nickels and dimes on the trip, or offer to braid the hair of the girls.[34]

Journey to the West

Very few accounts exist of the journeys of these companies of children sent west. After perusing hundreds of newspapers online, this writer discovered a letter sent by a traveler from Canada to the editor of a New York newspaper that gives a glimpse of what the children experienced.

Toronto, C. W., September 21, 1861.

I left your city by the Erie rail road on Monday evening. On stepping into a car at the Long Dock [riverfront location of Erie's depot in Jersey City], I found it about one-half occupied by children—thirty-four graduates of the juvenile asylum of your city, who were seeking their new homes in the West, under the guidance of one of the agents of the Society. They were a fine set of boys and girls, and appeared as if they might make their way in the world, having only the advantage of a fair start, which they will doubtless obtain through the care of the association which has assumed their direction. As we left the depot they gave three cheers for the West, and with their cheerful songs, and merry conversation they enlivened the way and tended materially to dissipate the tedium of travel.

To be seen to full advantage, the Erie rail road should be travelled by day, and by sections; but even under the disadvantage of a hasty transit, the greater part by night, there is much of interest, especially if, as was the case with me, the traveler has the aid of the moon to lighten up the view, and beautify the magnificent scenery of the route. Hour after hour I gazed upon the floating beauties of the landscape; now admiring the strong contrasts of light and shade, as passing through some mountain gorge, and then watching the silver play of the moon-beams on the rippling waters of the Ramapo, until at last exhausted nature gave way, and I slept almost as soundly as my young companions, who had long before subsided into silence, and were perhaps dreaming of future happy homes and successful fortunes, the fruits of their own exertion, in the Western land to which they were bound, and where the strong hand and willing heart usually command success.

At about six o'clock in the morning we reached Hornellsville, 331 miles from Jersey City, and the junction of the Buffalo division of the road [. . .]. All seekers after the picturesque should make it a point to pass over this road and view the falls of the upper Genesee, at Portage, where the rails are carried high over the bed of the river on a bridge which is a masterpiece of engineering ability, and the water may be seen descending in a series of cascades hundreds of feet below the railroad track. We reached Buffalo in the midst of a rain storm [. . .]. Yours, truly, J. G. C.[35]

Erie's tracks extended 460 miles west from the Hudson River at Jersey City to Dunkirk, New York, at Lake Erie. From Dunkirk the trains had to utilize the tracks of the Lake Shore and Michigan Southern Railroad to complete their connection to Chicago, Illinois. When Alexander C. Pearcy, Superintendent of the Asylum's House of Reception, recalled his trip with a company of children to Havana, Illinois, in 1858, he acknowledged the agents of the Erie, Lake Shore and Rock Island Railroads for "having saloon cars locked and waiting for us at each change, and obliging hands to render us all needful aid."[36]

The trains continued west into Ohio. Until at least 1864 it was common for the train to break up the trip with a stop at Cleveland, where the children were taken to a nearby hotel to spend the night.[37] The children were generally well behaved on these trips, but the records reveal that one boy was "dismissed due to bad conduct" during an 1862 stop in Cleveland.[38]

The train would stop briefly at large train stations along the tracks. The children undoubtedly noted how the sleepy little towns they passed through stood in stark contrast to New York City.

After 1885, Erie's tracks terminated at Dearborn Station (Polk Street Station) in Chicago. It was owned by the Chicago & Western Indiana Railroad, which in turn was owned by the companies operating over its line. Dearborn Station, built in the Romanesque Revival style, faced Polk Street.

The orphan trains of the New York Juvenile Asylum stopped at this station until the Asylum moved its Western Agency to Englewood, Illinois, in 1890.

The various railroads utilized by the NYJA to transport the children played an important role. In

This old post card depicts Dearborn (Polk Street) Station in Chicago. The western tracks of the Erie Railroad terminated at this station. The orphan trains of the New York Juvenile Asylum arrived here from New York from May 1885 until early in 1890. (*Courtesy of the author*)

his 1864 final report, George H. Allan, retiring Western Agent for the NYJA, thanked people at the railroads utilized by the Asylum as of that time: "I wish also to remember with gratitude the valuable aid and assistance rendered by good friends at the West, prominent among whom may be mentioned: W. R. Arthur, Esq., of the Illinois Central, E. H. Williams, Esq., of the Galena, and C. G. Hammond, Esq., of the Burlington and Quincy Railroads, whose courtesy and liberality have aided me materially in my labors among children."[39] In 1868, H. D. Perry, successor to Allan, called out the Chicago & North Western; Chicago, Burlington and Quincy; Chicago, Alton and St. Louis; and the Illinois Central Railroads.[40]

Arrival at Their Western Destination

Perry described what these journeys west were like in 1868:

> It gives me pleasure to testify to the general good conduct of the children during these long and wearisome journeys, whereat strangers have often expressed their admiration, sometimes by special inquiries as to the methods of education and discipline used in the Asylum; sometimes by complimentary addresses to the children, and sometimes in other ways, quite as expressive to hungry little ones. At times the children have arrived at their place of destination in inclement weather, when they must remain at the hotel for several days, and on such occasions I have known fathers to bring their children to spend a winter's evening, with a group of Asylum children, that they might be led to imitate, in their conduct to each other, the harmony, cheerfulness and general good behavior of the children of your Institution. A careful study and observation of the habits and conduct of the children of the Asylum, for nearly five years, has impressed me with profound respect for the work done for children, by the instruction and discipline which they receive while in the Asylum.[41]

Due to advertisements for several weeks prior to their arrival, large crowds often met the companies of children when they reached their destination. The local newspaper reported on one such scene at a distribution (the term used for placement of the children with their new foster parents) in Joliet, Illinois, in 1879: "The people, who had been previously informed of their coming, preceded their arrival and by 10 o'clock the street from the [St. Nicholas] hotel for nearly a square was blockaded with teams from the country."[42]

It was not uncommon for prospective foster parents to travel to the distribution point from great distances. At a distribution in Decatur, Illinois, in 1884, "People flocked to town from a radius of twenty miles, and the supply did not equal the demand."[43]

A precious few firsthand accounts of the distributions of children from the NYJA have survived—most all of them are forever lost in the attic history. One account by a boy named John Dunlap, sent west in 1896, demonstrates that the distribution process was not always a pleasant one, at least for some of the children:

Lewis J Simmons 14. Aug. 28. 1872
Menta Paddock

APPLICATION FOR A _boy_ — AGED will be 14 the 29 day of ~~~
Sent Indenture
Nov. 18, 1872

Date of Application, _____

Name in full of applicant (If a married lady, the husband's name).
Answer: Samuel Underhill

Residence (Township and County)
Answer: Tompkins - Warren Co.

Post Office (Name of Post Office and County)?
Answer: Young America

Name of nearest Railway Station, and distance and direction from it?
Answer: Young America distance 2 miles South East

How long a resident of this State?
Answer: 2 years

From what State or Country formerly?
Answer: New York

Occupation?
Answer: Farmer

Real Estate owned?
Answer: 40 acres

What members of the family are connected with a Church and what is its denomination?
Answer: all Methodist E. Church

Are the family regular Church attendants?
Answer: yes

Distance from Church?
Answer: two miles

Distance from Day School?
Answer: half mile

How many own children?
Answer: one

Number and ages of sons?
Answer: 1 - 19 years old

Number and ages of daughters?
Answer: none

Farmer Samuel Underhill of Young America, Illinois, filled out this application for a boy (he took Lewis J. Simmons), in 1872. (*NYJA Records; Rare Book and Manuscript Library, Columbia University Library*)

Caption on bottom of original photo: "The children above photographed left the New York Juvenile Asylum June 27, 1864, to be located in homes in western Illinois. In an interval in their journey the picture was taken that each child might receive one, and thus have an interesting memorial of his companions and of the time so important in his history. It is to be hoped that each child, so often as he sees this picture of himself and his companions will resolve ever to be an honor to the Asylum and to his companions, and an honor to his friends and to those who may become his friends. Each is hereby reminded that the best wishes of many are with him, to encourage him to do well. New York Juvenile Asylum, 175th St. and 10th Ave., New York City (H. D. Perry, Indenturing Agent)." From left to right, first row: Daniel O'Brien (he's got his mouth open), Emil White (called "Lafe"), George Beck, Charles Beck, William Groharing. Second row: Theresa Hoover, Alexander Hoover, Richard Groharing, John Flynn. Third row: William McPherson, Daniel Summerton, James Summerton, James Wicks, Thomas Cochran. Indenturing Agent H. D. Perry in back. (*Thomson Review*, March 10, 1932. "Thomson's Orphans of 1864")

The woman agent of the Juvenile Asylum was waiting for us at the depot. She took us up to the principal hotel in the town. After we had our supper we were bathed and then taken up to the parlor and seated around on chairs. The folding doors were then opened and in trooped a number of farmers and their wives, who had driven in from thirty miles around. They expressed dissatisfaction and disgust because we were so small. They expected they were going to get fully developed men and women to work for them for nothing. They walked around, and pounded and thumped us as I afterward saw them pounding cattle on market day. A farmer named Ellis secured me. He was a tough master, but his wife was tougher. I had to work as hard in winter as in summer. I had to do all the work of a hired man, although I was only fourteen years of age at the time.[44]

A reporter was present at a distribution of NYJA children in Burlington, Iowa, in 1898, and made the following observation:

They laughed and chatted, and "kidded" each other, never paying the slightest attention to the crowd standing around who were discussing their merits and de-merits like they would so many cattle they intended to purchase.

Invariably when the boys were asked whether they would rather live in the city or in the country they answered in the affirmative in the former, although they seemed perfectly willing to go any place. While they were scrupulously polite and modest when answering questions put to them by older people, a slang word or phrase as the absence of the "th" sound was discernable when talking among themselves. Two of the little fellows were giving vent to their exuberance in a wrestling match when the youngster who went down first called out to the one, who had accidentally kicked him in the head, "Say Billy, 'taint fair to kick a man in de nut like dat," but as far as could be seen there was no viciousness in their natures nor did they utter one improper word while scuffling.

"I want that boy because he has his hair combed," said one lady, pointing to a lad who stood to one side and took no part in his companions' conversation. "I'm sure he is a good little boy, and don't appear half so rough as the rest." She filled out the necessary papers and took the child away.

The most mischievous boy in the crowd, a little brown-eyed round faced urchin, was picked out by a young couple from Carthage. "He will be able to do all the chores in a short time," said the young man as he led his charge out of the room.[45]

And off the scores of children went, with total strangers, taking an incredible leap of faith—not knowing what the future held in store for them.

The third and final known account comes from Elbert Hubbard. When a boy of eleven he read in the Bloomington, Illinois, *Weekly Pantagraph* that a company of twenty-five children from the NYJA was going to arrive the following week in Bloomington. He lived with his parents in Hudson, McLean County, Illinois—some ten miles distant from Bloomington. Elbert had had three brothers, but all died very young. He suggested to his parents that he could go to Bloomington and pick out a brother for himself. His father was hesitant, pointing out instances he'd heard of where orphan boys had "set fire to haystacks, turned the cows in the corn, stolen chickens, and cooked them on wire fences by making a fire beneath." His sister saved the day by chiming in to name three boys who not only worked well, but "had joined the Baptist church and been baptized by cutting a hole in the ice in the creek, a few months before." Elbert was granted the permission he needed to go to Bloomington and "pick out a brother."

I walked into the office, looked around, and asked for the orphans.

"Parlor, upstairs," said the clerk.

I climbed the stairs, two steps at a time and entered the parlor. It was not yet nine o'clock in the morning, but there the children were, seated all around the walls of the room. Several men and women were standing around, looking at the children and talking.

"How old are you, sonny?" said an old man to me.

"Leven, going on twelve," I answered.

"Can you work?"

"I guess so," I answered. He called his wife over and they both looked at me earnestly. Then the old man said to one of the widow women in black: "We think we will take this one."

"I'm already took; you'll not get me," I roared. "I'm here to pick out a brother. I want a boy that can work, and who can play ball!"

This centered the attention on me. Most everybody laughed. The boys were dressed in gray and the girls in red. They all seemed quite content—not near as miserable as I thought orphans should be.

I walked twice around the room looking at these orphans. None of them seemed to answer—all were too yellow, and several of them made fun of me. I was in my bare feet and they wore shoes and stockings. All at once I saw in the corner a boy with tow-head and freckles. He was so homely he was attractive.

I walked over to him and asked, "Can you work and play ball?—I want a brother!" I had suddenly noticed that he was a hunchback. He just looked at me and gulped, scared like.

"Is your name—your name Mudsock?" he whispered.

"No, I'm Bert Hubbard," I said.

"Are you a relation of Si Mudsock?"

"Nobody around us by that name," I answered.

"Then, I'll go with you and be your brudder," he answered. He stood up. He only came to my shoulders. "I'm fifteen," he said as if in apology. "I'm not sick—I had spinal complaint—but I'm all over it now. I'm strong—can work and I can play ball."

I took him by the hand and led him to the widow and said, "If you please, Missus, I'll take this one."[46]

It seems the boy was previously indentured to an abusive foster father by the name of Mudsock (likely a fictitious name) and he was fearful of anyone that may be connected to him.

⸙ CHAPTER EIGHT ⸙

Challenges and Successes

Placement Challenges

Finding good homes for each company of children sent west was not without its challenges. Western Indenturing Agent Ebenezer Wright, in his second year on the job, explained the "poor success" with placing out a company of children in Illinois in 1869 as due to "the all engrossing season of harvesting, & the prevalent distrust of New York children in those portions of the state to which the company was taken." He extrapolated:

> My experience at Aledo in connection with the June Company is worthy of mention. I took 19 children to that point on the 10th of June & only placed two girls & six boys in two days. The Agent of the C. A. [Children's Aid] Society arrived at the same point on the 3rd of July following with 21 boys & 2 girls & placed them all the same day. Upon inquiry I learned these reasons why their children were taken more readily than ours: first, employers were not bound to keep them longer than was mutually agreeable; second, the boys were larger & able to make themselves immediately useful; Third, the operation was attended with less expense & trouble. The farmers thought they were getting more desirable boys without incurring any responsibility—or risk, & at half the cost. Seven children of the last company were taken to Ottawa where three years ago the C. A. Society distributed a large company. I was advised by clergymen there that I would not be likely to succeed on account of the prejudices against New York boys since that company had been left there & it turned out as they predicted. Only two boys & two girls out of the seven were taken.[1]

The motives people had for taking in a child were often suspect. Mr. Wright, and the other western indenturing agents, carefully quizzed each applicant and secured good character references for the applicants, which generally included the minister at the church they attended and a prominent businessman or two. Mr. Wright was fully aware that most people just wanted an extra set of hands to assist them with their daily work:

> I suppose that many of these people who come for children, in fact the most of them, come with the idea of getting the children for their services. That is proper. In the asylum we can teach the children obedience and order, but not much more. They must be taught to work, to maintain themselves. There is no better way for them to learn that. We put them in these homes and even if they do work they also learn how to support themselves.[2]

When Wright received a letter from a man in 1870 asking for a girl to replace a boy he had taken, Wright replied to the man with a different proposal, acknowledging the fact that the couple basically just wanted a housekeeper:

> Dear Sir,
>
> Yours of the 28th ult. With indenture enclosed is to hand. Mrs. Everett asks for a girl. It is doubtful about my being able to let you have a girl. Girls are scarce & the demand is much greater than the supply.
>
> I can let you have another boy & one that will help in the house. I have one now a German about 12 yrs. old, who seems to be a good boy. He has been with me some two or three months, out of health, but is well now. I think he would be quite handy & useful about the house if that is what you want him for. Shall I send him to you[?].
>
> Yours Truly,
> E. Wright[3]

A Matter of Religion

Other factors could affect the success of each distribution of children. For instance, a company of children left New York in September 1875, bound for Joliet and Peru in LaSalle County, Illinois. The distribution took place on September 9 with Ebenezer Wright in charge. Several Catholics (some being farmers) had applied for some of the children. Leading the group of Catholics were Fathers Smith and Gray, prominent Catholic clergymen in the vicinity. Three of the four Catholic children in the company were placed with Catholic foster parents, and just as the fourth Catholic child was about to be placed with one John C. Hennessy, the group of Catholics headed by Fathers Smith and Gray forcibly took possession of six or eight of the children including Louis and August Simon, Alexander Lindsay, and two sisters, Nannie and Gertrude Wells. The Catholics took the children to St. Mary's Academy. Apparently, they were upset because their applications were rejected (for reasons not given) by Mr. Wright. Wright telegraphed the Asylum in New York for instructions on how to proceed.

On September 14, *The Pantagraph* in Bloomington, Illinois, published Mr. Wright's letter to the editor regarding the fiasco. He ended it with "The action of the Catholics at Peru was hasty and inconsiderate, and it is they, and not myself, who have been placed in a dilemma thereby."[4]

Not all of the children were returned to Mr. Wright, as the records indicate that only the Wells sisters were returned on October 1 and November 6, and the Lindsay boy on October 1. All three were returned to the Western Agency. Louis Simon was reported as being in a hotel in Joliet as of September 30.[5]

For many years prior, members of the Catholic community had been objecting to Catholic children being placed in Protestant homes in the West. This concern was probably a significant factor in the establishment of the Catholic Protectory in New York City in 1863. Especially during the early years, admissions of Catholic children to the NYJA far exceeded those of Protestants. For instance, in 1854, admitted children included 576 identified as Roman Catholics, and only 292 identified as Protestants.[6]

Ironically, in 1875—the year the debacle in Peru, Illinois took place—the New York Legislature passed the Children's Law (Chapter 173, Laws 1875), by which it was "forbidden to send able-bodied, intelligent children, between the ages of three and sixteen years, to a poor-house or almshouse, and the various court magistrates, superintendents or overseers of the poor, or other authorities, were empowered to provide for such children 'in families, orphan asylums or other appropriate institutions,' and the boards of supervisors were required to take such action as was necessary to carry out the law." The following clause was added: "In placing any such child in any such institution, it shall be the duty of the officer, justice or person placing it there, to commit such child to an orphan asylum, charitable or other reformatory institution that is governed or controlled by officers or persons of the *same religious faith* [emphasis added] as the parents of such child, so far as practicable."⁷

The NYJA later publicly emphasized its desire to place children with foster parents of the same faith as reported in an Ottawa, Illinois, newspaper regarding a distribution of children there in 1885:

> The lady in charge, Miss M. Cronin [Mary Cronein], was very particular to whom the children were to be given. Farmers who were abundantly able to provide for the little ones and give them a good home and kind treatment were preferred, and when any were given to parties in the city it was only by way of exception. [...] Children of Catholic parents would only be given to Catholics, and those of Protestant parentage to Protestants. This is an inflexible rule.⁸

On May 5, 1897, Governor Brown of New York held a hearing on Senator Brown's bill declaring that no destitute or orphan children should be placed in families, except under rules and regulations that the State Board of Charities established. The bill also contained a clause providing that "every such child must be put in an institution of his or her religious faith." The clause was cause for concern by the New York and the Brooklyn Children's Aid Societies as well as the NYJA—all of them Protestant organizations. The New York Children's Aid Society sent a delegation to the hearing consisting of D. Willis James, William C. Osborn, Evert J. Wendell and Charles Loring Brace, Jr. Charles Wallace represented the Brooklyn Children's Aid Society. Those representing the NYJA included its President, Mornay Williams, and Henry E. Gregory, Vice Chairman of the Admissions, Indentures and Discharges Committee.

The Children's Aid Society argued that it had sent some ninety thousand children to "homes in the country" since the Society was established, and they had "grown up good children." For the CAS, the bill "struck at the continuance of the system."

CAS representatives further explained that at the Brace Farm School in Kensico, New York, the children were "trained to farming," adding that since many were "Hebrews [Jews]" and some were Catholics it would be impossible to find homes for them if "a religious test was made." They proclaimed that no Jewish farmers could be found to take the Jewish children—that it was "American farmers who would take the boys"—and no attempt was being made to proselytize them.

Mornay Williams opposed the bill because of the difficulties he envisioned with carrying out its provisions. He explained that large numbers of Russian and Polish Jews came into the Asylum's care, but the Jews "were not an agricultural people." He declared, "We could not find homes of exactly the same religious faith for these children [. . .] and therefore we should have to abandon the work. Other States make no such condition. Why should this State?"

Attending in support of the bill was John T. McDonough, a representative of the Roman Catholics. "Why should fifty thousand children be sent out of this State without record as to their religious faith?" he asked. He maintained that religious freedom demanded that Catholic children should be put in care of Catholics and Protestants with Protestants, and added that children of the State of New York "ought to be retained in it." After the matter was discussed at length, the State Board of Charities adopted this resolution:

> Resolved, That the State Board of Charities unanimously approves the spirit of the original Senate bill No. 1,709, an act regulating the placing out of children, but it is not unanimous in approval of the mandatory provision of the bill in Section 2 thereof (compelling the placing out of children in homes of their own religious faith), but a majority of the Board decline to oppose the approval of the bill by the Governor.⁹

In 1903, the NYJA told a Catholic applicant interested in placing a child in the Asylum that the Catholic Protectory was a viable alternative when explaining the Asylum's policy on admitting children in general, and Catholic children in particular:

> Children can be admitted here in three ways. They can be surrendered by their parents or guardians, who will sign an agreement to pay us $2.00 [per week] during the time that the child stays here. They may be taken to the Department of Charities and be committed here from there, or they may be taken to the nearest magistrate and be committed by him upon the technical charge of ungovernableness. If the boy is destitute he must be taken to the Department of Charities and committed from there [...]. The fact that the boy is a Roman Catholic is no bar to his admission here, but this institution is entirely Protestant and we do not have priests here. There is a Catholic institution, the N. Y. Catholic Protectory with offices at 415 Broome Street, N. Y. City which is similar to this.[10]

A Matter of Nationality

A child's religious affiliation was not the only source of contention the NYJA dealt with when indenturing its children. The children of immigrants, born "to races or nationalities whose representatives are not welcomed in the rural communities of the West," also posed a particular problem for the directors of the Asylum and its western indenturing agents.[11] Compounding the difficulties was the fact that the parents of Italian and Russian children were especially reluctant to give them up for western placement: "These parents, generally ignorant foreigners, are ready enough to part with the custody of their children for eighteen months or two years and to escape the necessity of supporting them; but they strenuously object to having them removed to Illinois for permanent residence."[12]

The nationalities of children sent west from the Asylum in the year 1900, in a total of four companies, consisted of the following: American (25); German (15); Hebrew (14); Irish (10); Italian (3); English (3); Bohemian (2); French (1); and Scotch (1). The Western Agent for the Asylum added: "The large percentage of American and German children remains about the same from year to year. In the applications that come to the office for children, nine-tenths of them want either German or American, so that the large number of these two nationalities is especially gratifying."[13]

A Matter of Race

The race of children sent west was predominantly Caucasian, but a few African American children were also sent. The records reveal that a total of just seven African American children were sent west on orphan trains from the Asylum.[14] The vast majority of them were placed "in the neighborhood" (New York City).

The Superintendent of the House of Reception accompanied a company of thirty children to Tazewell County, Illinois, in 1857 and noted there was one "colored boy" among some thirty children that came in just after breakfast to watch the distribution take place, "part of whom had found homes in that vicinity more than a year ago [. . .]. On one side stood a poor colored boy who had many a time raked up his only meal for the day from the refuse of Washington Market [a produce market in New York City], now sleek and well dressed, showing every tooth in his head as he shook my hand and asked me to take a ride behind his mare, that had been given him for learning to plow so well last Summer."[15]

Apparently, it became harder and harder to place children of color in the West during the ensuing years. Asylum records reveal that a girl sent west in 1893 was rejected when they reached Illinois for being "small and suspicious of being tainted with colored blood." She was promptly returned to New York.[16]

Girls were easier to place than boys: "Girls are more sought after, and we experience some difficulty in supplying the demand for them."[17]

This scene was captioned "Children Received at House of Reception, By Mr. E. G. Bates." William F. Gardner is in back center. He rode an NYJA orphan train to Illinois in 1869. The African American boy to his left was his friend, George Washington Jefferson, aka "Bones." (*Mary E. Dodge, "A Day with Dr. Brooks," Scribner's Monthly, November 1870, 42*)

Regardless of their nationality, race, sex or religion, children who grew up in the streets of New York City took some time to get acclimated to life on the farm. Most did fairly well, but others had a real struggle.

Follow-Up Visits and Communication

The Asylum's western indenturing agents made infrequent visits to the homes where the children were placed. Most visits were made for the purpose of settling disputes, removing a child, or placing a child in a new home. As time passed the NYJA adopted a policy of more frequent visits to check on the welfare of the children, but for the first several decades of western placement such visits were very infrequent. Instead, the employers were asked to answer a series of questions in a questionnaire the Asylum mailed approximately every six months.

Compliance with filling out and returning such questionnaires was a problem for the Asylum from the very onset. As early as 1855 officials reported:

> It is much to be regretted that masters are slow in performing that part of their contract, which requires them, at least twice in a year, to report to the Board of Directors the conduct and behavior of the apprentice or child, and the fact whether he is under the care of the person to whom he was originally bound. To insure more prompt returns, the Committee on Correspondence have, through the Superintendent of the Asylum, addressed a circular to each master, requesting him to answer the questions proposed with at least a simple yes or no, as the case might require,

Challenges and Successes

and return the paper thus filled out to the Superintendent. In many cases we have had answers, some of them exceedingly satisfactory, but we are sorry to state that hardly a majority have yet responded to our call.[18]

In their 1859 annual report, Asylum officials reflected back on the situation: "We did not receive regular and systematic replies from more than one half of the persons addressed."[19]

When questionnaires were returned, the replies were not always positive: "Lizzie is here yet & well. Attends church & Sunday school regularly. She is not such a girl as we like at all. She is more trouble than all my family; it is only through charity we keep her."[20] Another employer wrote:

> There is no truth in him. He wets the bed every few nights (other specifications are too indecent to mention here). I think we have put up with it long enough. He gets worse instead of better. Please write as soon as you get this & let me know when you want him delivered for I don't want to keep him any longer."[21]

One of the more positive replies to the questionnaires included one from the widow of a man a boy was indentured to in Lincoln, Illinois: "My husband has gone to his Heavenly Father I trust, but I still keep Frank. He does my little chores & goes to school & gets along well in his studies. The [school] master gives a good account of him. His health has never been very good."[22]

Some replies were mixed, such as one from an employer in Metamora, Illinois regarding the boy indentured to him:

> Peter is still with me & enjoying good health. Attends church & Sabbath School regularly. Has attended district school a little more than six months. He is a tolerable good boy but has some unpleasant traits of character. If he is a good boy I will do a good part by him. There is an outside influence against your children I am sorry to say.[23]

Due to the low response rate to the questionnaires it became imperative to arrange for in-person meetings, but such meetings did not begin occurring until the early 1860s. Prior to that time the Asylum often enlisted the help of people in the community in the continued oversight of the children:

> We endeavor, wherever we locate a company of children, to enlist the sympathies of clergymen, school teachers, and other philanthropic individuals. Our Agent places in their hands copies of our Annual Reports, and requests them to exercise for us a watch and care over the children, and communicate to us any information concerning them which may be deemed of interest; and we have found their cooperation an important help in the execution of this department of our work.[24]

George H. Allan, western indenturing agent for the Asylum, described the process he was using in 1864:

> In my visitations, the usual plan has been to prepare a circular, inviting the children to meet the Agent at the hotel at some designated point on a certain day. Frequently, several of these are arranged for at different points on the same handbill, and a copy mailed to each child. Sometimes when the gatherings are comparatively near each other, the boys attend several on successive days, thus meeting a new class of their old schoolmates at each place. The children generally appeared robust and healthy, well dressed, and very much improved. Juvenile games are played, stories related, songs are sung, and occasionally addresses are made by friends present.
>
> Opportunity is also taken to confer privately with every child, to ascertain whether

NEW YORK JUVENILE ASYLUM.

New York, June 12th 1855

To Master George Ryer:

Not having received a letter from you ~~for the past~~ ~~months,~~ the Board of Directors wish you to write and inform them how you are doing, and what are your prospects. They hope to hear that you are well, contented, and happy. In order to guide you in giving the kind of information desired, they have framed the following questions, which they wish you to answer in your letter:

1st. Is your health good?

2d. Are you comfortably provided with food, clothing, and lodging?

3d. Do you attend Sabbath School and Public Worship on the Sabbath?

4th. Have you improved in reading, writing and arithmetic?

5th. Are you improving in a knowledge of your business, so as to be useful to your employer?

We desire a brief answer to each of these questions, with any other information concerning yourself you may think it important the Directors should know. Though you are separated from us, we still feel a deep interest in your welfare. You may ever confide in the Directors as your sincere friends.

By order and in behalf of the Directors,

John D. Russ
Superint'd't

The NYJA sent letters such as this one to each child indentured as part of its concern over the child's welfare after leaving the Asylum. This letter, sent to George Ryer in care of his employer, Allanson Cook, Esq. of Bridgehampton, New York, dated June 12, 1855, was signed by Asylum Superintendent John D. Russ. (*Courtesy of the author*)

his relations with his employer continue harmonious and pleasant. If any child makes a complaint on account of overwork, insufficient food or clothing, or deprivation of school privileges, the employer is immediately seen, the case investigated, and action taken if necessary.

After some slight refreshment, the children leave at an early hour for their good homes, happy and contented.[25]

The indenturing agents were often held in high regard by the Asylum children. One boy learned that the agent who placed him in his Illinois home was going to be in a city in his area with another company of children in 1861. He travelled twenty miles on horseback just to see the agent again.[26] Another boy rode seven miles by horseback to see an agent in 1864.[27]

In a report dated December 31, 1871, Asylum indenturing agent Ebenezer Wright expressed his desire for more frequent visits with the children in their western homes:

The number of children under the charge of the Agency has become so large, and they are scattered over so wide an area that it has become a laborious and expensive task to reach them all. But long continued experience serves only to convince me that the importance of systematic and frequent visitation can hardly be over stated. Every child ought to be visited semi-annually instead of bi-ennially, as our present scale of operations contemplates.[28]

Wright's sons often accompanied him during visits to the homes of the hundreds of children he had under his care at any given time. His son, Charles S. Wright, explained during an interview with a reporter in Edwardsville, Illinois, in 1896:

While there is much responsibility connected with the work, there is also a great deal of pleasure in securing good homes for the homeless. My father has represented the asylum for 29 years and during that time has placed 7,000 orphan children in this state. At present we have upwards of 600 charges under age in Illinois, and they require constant attention. The months of June, July and August are devoted to our annual visits and we see the children at their homes just as they are. We call unexpectedly and are always welcomed by the children.[29]

By 1900, the Asylum's Western Agent, James W. Shields, was reporting that he traveled 29,112 miles on railroads from March 1 to December 31 while conducting his work of visiting and placing children in homes.[30]

Another method the Asylum utilized to stay in touch with the children was its practice of distributing copies of the Asylum's annual reports to them. Beginning in 1899 the reports were printed by the printing class at the Asylum.[31] Other publications were sent to the children as funds would allow. In 1892, hundreds of copies of the Youth's Companion were sent. Several thousand dollars was bequeathed to the Asylum in 1893 for the express purpose of sending out a book published by the American Tract Society to each child.

The Asylum kept track of the children via its Western Agency until their indentures expired. The children themselves often endeavored to keep in touch with the Asylum after the expiration of their indentures—reporting their marriages, births of children, and vocational accomplishments. On occasion, they wrote to the Asylum for their history, exact age, or information that could help them reunite with family members.

It was not unusual for the children sent west to keep in touch with their teachers in the Asylum. One such letter survives (see page 138), written from teacher Grace O. Palmer to Matilda "Tillie" Kimmel who was sent west on March 16, 1896.

Letters from the children and their employers selected for the Asylum's annual reports provide a glimpse into the day-to-day life of the children and

"Printing Office" at the NYJA. The children in this class did all of the printing for the Asylum, including the Annual Reports, blank indenture forms for the Western Agency, and considerable work for the House of Reception. (*NYJA Annual Report, 1900*)

interactions with their employers. Such letters were undoubtedly carefully chosen for publication as they contain very few accounts of discontent on the part of the child or mistreatment by foster parents. For the first twenty years of the annual reports, only the initials of the children, their foster parents, and the initials of the city, county, and state they lived in were used. Through careful comparison with the original records of the Asylum, this writer has managed to identify the vast majority of the children and foster parents associated with each letter.

The following letter from Pauline Held, sent west in 1883, appeared in the 1888 annual report. Pauline answered several questions posed to the children, including their opinion on changing the length of indenture and whether to begin placing children in Iowa:

> I now take the pleasure of answering your most welcome letter, and telling you that I am very much pleased to get the Reports of the Asylum. And I am also thankful to you and the Asylum for your kind care, and for sending me the *Christian Weekly*. I am thankful to say that I like my home and employers. I go to school and to Sunday-school and church. I have the picture of my Sunday-school teacher and classmates. I was sixteen last month and I intend to stay with my employers until I am of age, and I would advise all of the children to do the same, boys and girls. They will be much better, they will find, and they will make much more in the long run.
>
> I do not think it would be advisable to free the boys at eighteen, any more than it would be to free the girls at fifteen, because they are not old enough to take care of themselves, and then I think they ought to stay with their employers and help them as long as they can, because their employers have done so much for them, and they are just old enough at eighteen to be some help.

Challenges and Successes

Letter from NYJA teacher Grace O. Palmer to Matilda "Tillie" Kimmel who was sent west in 1896: "17 East 124 Street, New York City. June 30, 1897. My dear Tillie—Surely you know how earnestly I wish you all that is good in life; and yet I want to tell you how sincerely I wish you now, more than ever before—'Health wealth and happiness.' By this mail I send you a little remembrance. I wish it were more. If it had not taken so long to have the engraving done—I would have sent them sooner. I trust they will reach you safely. With kind regards to your husband to be—and loving remembrances to those who have done so much for you. - I am Grace O. Palmer." (*Courtesy of Linda Mins, Nancy & Jerry Cotton*)

I agree with you about including Iowa, because there are not places in Illinois for all of the children that come out West. You ask me to express my opinion why so many of the children get dissatisfied at the age of fifteen to eighteen. I think the reason is because they think they are old enough to take care of themselves, but they are badly mistaken. They are just old enough to go to ruin, but they are not wise enough to know it.

Another reason is that, in so many cases, outsiders come in and talk with the children, and tell them that they could do so much better some place else, just to lead them astray, and then they become stubborn, and their employers have to be firm with them, and they think them mean, and become dissatisfied and make trouble, and no one is to blame but themselves.

I would advise all the children to keep their places as long as they can, and if they do right God will be with them if no one else is.

It would be a good thing to have two or three agents go around to all the homes of the children once a year, and not tell either party they are coming, and bounce on them unexpectedly, and get a full view of their every-day life and surroundings.

Tell all the children in the Asylum for me to come out West, and get homes and keep them.

I will now close my letter hoping all the children will keep their homes."[32]

In October 1902, the Asylum hired Charles A. Crocker of Delphi, Indiana, as "Special Visitor" to go "unannounced into the homes of the wards, investigating the conditions and environments, offering counsel and encouragement and making a full written report of each home and the situation of each ward." Crocker concluded his visits in February of 1904. His findings were bound in a book by the Asylum, which has sadly been lost.[33]

Seeking Relatives

Sometimes siblings left in New York attempted to reconnect with long-lost brothers or sisters previously sent west. Harry Brooks was one such person. He found out the name of an attorney suing his sister's employer in Illinois, and the local newspaper ran his letter:

Some time ago I. A. Buckingham received a letter from Harry Brooks making inquiry about his sister. The attorney does not know where she is and the Herald publishes the letter for general information. Any one who can supply the information can leave the same at this office or notify Mr. Buckingham. The letter reads as follows and is self explanatory:

New York, March 7, 1900. Mr. Buckingham: Dear Sir—I am inquiring for my sister, Adeline Cooper, who was sent out west by the New York Juvenile Asylum. Their records show that she was last working with a Mr. L. Lancaster of Niantic, Illinois. And that she is suing him through you. So I thought that you would most likely have her present address. I am very anxious to find her, as she is my only living relative in the world. I will thankfully receive any information concerning her. I never knew my mother or father as they died when I was a babe and my sister was taken away from the lady who was keeping us by the Society and sent out west. She was about 10 years old then, I think. So you can imagine how overjoyed I will be to hear from her again. I remain in suspense. Yours, etc., Master Harry Brooks, No. 24 West Thirty-Third St., New York.[34]

Conversely, many of the children who remained in the West after their indentures expired placed advertisements in the New York papers looking for long-lost family members. Such was the case with William Wallace who was sent west in 1866. In the advertisement he placed in the *New York Sun*, he reveals an issue many orphan train rider descendants deal with when trying to research their family history—the fact that he took on the last name of his foster parents without being legally adopted:[35]

Who Can Help this Inquirer?

TO THE EDITOR OF THE SUN—*Sir*: I have a mother somewhere, and would like to know where she is. When last seen she was in New York city. I was in the New York Juvenile Asylum. My original name was William Wallace. I was carried from New York to Illinois and bound out to a man of the name of Lindsley and I still retain his name. We left New York on May 24, 1866 and I think I was about nine or ten years old. My mother's name was Eliza Wallace. I don't know her maiden name. I think some one in the city knows or can give some information of her, which would be thankfully received. J. W. LINDSLEY. GREENVILLE, Hunt county, Texas. Oct. 15.

Another example is John Harrington:

Separated From Kin 19 Years.

Challenges and Successes

John Harrington, who is now 27 years of age, told the police today that he had not seen his parents and three sisters for 19 years, and he was anxious to again join his family. In the story that Harrington related to Lieut. Richard Flynn, at police headquarters, he said he lived with his folks at 27 Bedford street, in Old Greenwich village, till he was 8 years of age, when his father placed him in the New York Juvenile Asylum.

From there he was sent to a farmer in Bernardsville, Ill. The farmer, he says, intercepted letters from his sisters and beat him. Later on he escaped and was placed with another farmer, who treated him well.

Harrington finally got a place on the Rock Island road, and is now a fireman. He is staying at 315 East Fifty sixth street and had searched Greenwich village without getting any trace of his folks.[36]

There were no subsequent articles regarding John's search for his family, so it is not known if he was successful in reuniting with them.

Removals

In 1860, the Asylum boasted that out of eighty-three children sent to Washington County, Illinois, only three were reported as "decidedly bad [...]. The larger girls are most uncertain; next the larger boys; then the little girls; the smaller boys hardly ever turning out badly."[37]

Ebenezer Wright commented on the difficulties incurred with placing and replacing children in the first year he began his job (1868):

> The Western Agency has always suffered more or less embarrassment for want of means adequate to its needs. It is easy to find homes for a company of children just from the Asylum. This, so far from being the main work of the Agency, as is generally thought, is its lightest and pleasantest task. The strain comes after the first few months have passed and the novelty has worn off; when the real dispositions and characters of the children are fully awakened, and the employer begins to be weighed down by the labor and responsibility he has incurred. Then come appeals for advice, complaints, and petitions for a release from their contracts [...]. Incompatibility of temperaments, too much lenity at the outset, want of the governing faculty, are among the commonest sources of trouble. In these cases children often have to be removed and other homes procured for them. The whole time of one agent, who should possess rare good judgment, tact and experience, ought to be given to this kind of work.[38]

A page titled "Extracts from Charter" was included with each indenture signed by the masters and children. The page included the sections of the Asylum's Charter pertaining to the indenture of children. Section 19 addressed how to handle a situation that arose in which there was dissatisfaction on the part of the child or master:

> No person receiving an apprentice under the provisions of this act, shall be at liberty to assign or transfer the indenture of apprenticeship or to let out or hire for any period the services of such apprentice, without the consent, in writing, of the directors of this corporation. In case the master of such apprentice shall be dissatisfied with his or her conduct or behaviour, or for any other cause, may desire to be relieved from said contract, upon applications, the said directors may, in their discretion, cancel the said indenture of apprenticeship; and resume the charge and management of the child so apprenticed, and shall have the same power and authority in regard to it, as before the said indenture was made.[39]

When Wright received word from a disgruntled

employer he'd often write a letter of encouragement to the child to try to quell the difficulties. He wrote one such letter in 1868:

My dear Charlie,

Mr. Gaston's letter in answer to my circular of inquiry concerning your conduct is not so favorable as I desire such reports to be, & as most of the others are, but I hope for better things in future. Strive to be perfectly obedient & to win the respect & affection of Mr. & Mrs. Gaston & of all. It is not only wrong but very unwise & very much against your best interests to behave as you have.

Resolve soon to do right henceforth. It is not too late to retrieve your character & acquire a good name. Try & make friends of all good people. I will send you the last Asylum Report. Read the letters from employers & see how many of the boys & girls are growing satisfaction & doing honor to all their friends. Try to be a good obedient, faithful boy.

Very truly yours,
E. Wright[40]

When such letters failed to correct the situation and removing a child from a home became necessary, the agent asked the foster parents to be patient as he made arrangements to pick up the child just prior to the next company of children being sent out from New York (unless it was a more urgent matter), and simply added the child to that company for placement with another individual in Illinois.

One couple, after taking in a little girl, wrote to Wright requesting her removal and gave the reasons why:

When our little girl first came to us we felt sorry for her and tried to make everything as pleasant as possible for her, but soon her real self appeared, and she got so bad we could hardly live with her. A smart spanking would do her good, but she would make such an outcry that the town would think we were murdering her. She goes in the best society, with daughters of bankers, merchants and professional men, and we have spent many dollars upon her and by coaxing, hiring and punishing, have tried to straighten her out, but I confess we have failed. I taught school for eight years and thought I knew how to win and govern, but I give it up and must ask to have her removed.[41]

In cases of repeated disruptive behavior, or of criminal activity, a child was usually sent back to the Asylum or to the New York House of Refuge in New York City. One such girl, having been removed from numerous homes in Illinois for various reasons, was finally sent to the New York House of Refuge after being discovered in her foster brother's room (he was sick in bed at the time) "in a position to entice any man," and furthermore was previously "caught fooling with the dogs."

Wright spoke of another problem he was facing in his work:

That we have not met with our usual success in disposing of this company is no doubt attributable to the fact that companies placed at these points several years previously have on the whole not done well. I am not disappointed at the result, my experience with my first company in June 1867 in Warren & McDonough counties, where companies were settled several years before, having taught me not to expect a very enthusiastic reception at such points. When many children placed within easy reach of one another they will conspire together & encourage one another to do what they would not attempt separately; & one or two bad children will exert a demoralizing influence upon all the others.[42]

In a letter addressed to his brother, dated

March 27, 1868, Wright was very candid about his frustrations:

> I have worked hard this month but can hardly keep up with the demands of the work. There are thirty to forty bad cases that I cannot get rid of. I have to keep changing them from place to place with no prospect of any relief. It is a great mistake to send such children out here. Some less expensive & troublesome way of disposing of them is desirable. [...] I have travelled this month by railroad 1,800 miles; have written 130 business letters; sent about 100 circulars to employers & children.[43]

At any given time, there were a number of these "bad cases" being temporarily housed at the Western Agency until new homes could be found for them. Others were often housed at the agency due to illness.

Wright's predecessor, H. D. Perry, reflected on the placing-out process and the need to remove children from unsuitable homes, in his final report as Western Indenturing Agent, in 1868:

> The end sought in this as in every other part of the Asylum work is to secure to the children education, habits of industry, kindness of disposition, with good moral and religious characters, and when these ends were not likely to be obtained in one home, your agent has removed the child to another, and the results are a sufficient justification of this course. Removals then are necessary, but not necessarily an evil.[44]

Perry also wrote that the average time the children indentured in the West were wards of the Asylum "exceeds six years."

Abuse and Tragedies

The NYJA addressed the consequences of any abuses that may occur while a child was under indenture to his or her master in Section 20 of their Charter:

> If any master shall be guilty of any cruelty, misusage, refusal or neglect to furnish necessary provisions or clothing, or any other violation of the terms of indenture or contract towards any such child so bound to service, such child may make complaint thereof to the board of directors of this corporation, or to two justices of the peace of the county in which such child is so bound to service, or to the mayor, recorder, or alderman of any city in which such child is bound to service, or to any two of them, who shall summon the parties before them, and examine into, hear and determine the said complaint; and, if upon such examination the said complaint shall appear well founded, they shall, by certificate under their hands, discharge such child from his obligations of service, and restore him or her to the charge and management of this corporation in the same manner, and with like powers, as before the indenture of such child.[45]

Some of the children sent west on the orphan trains were abused, unfortunately.

One of the earliest recorded cases of abuse was that of little Martha Potter, sent west with Reverend Mr. Enoch Kingsbury in March of 1856 and indentured to Daniel R. Sandford of Paris, Illinois. Martha was about twelve years old at the time. By November 1857 a man name Elijah Bacon reported to the NYJA that Martha had been "most cruelly ill used by both Master & Mistress" from whom she ran away and took refuge with Mr. Bacon. Bacon gave her back to Mr. Sandford "under the promise that she should not again be so beaten." Sandford's promise didn't last long as they no sooner reached the Sandford residence when Martha was "more severely flogged and in other respects ill used." A neighbor later made an unsuccessful attempt to rescue her from her abusive home:

> A neighbour [sic] commiserating her sufferings assisted to get her away in his waggon [sic], but was followed by Mr. S. who upon coming up with them did then and there most fearfully whip the said Martha while in the waggon, and was with great difficulty made to desist, after which she was again taken home by Mr. S.[46]

Mr. Bacon "afterwards missing the child instituted enquiries for her, but could obtain no farther information than that she had again run away."

Martha eventually made her way to Chicago as she is recorded as an inmate of the Home for the Friendless in that city on the 1860 Federal Census.

Cases of abuse were often reported in the local newspapers. One such instance was noted in a paper in Gibson, Illinois, in 1880:

> A brute named John Wilder was bound over Monday last, in the sum of $800, to answer the charge of inhuman cruelty to a little orphan girl he was raising. Her body was bruised and beaten until it presented a pitiful sight. The wretch deserves a term at Joliet [Prison].[47]

Neighbors would often report abuse to the western indenturing agents. In one instance agent Ebenezer Wright received word of a man abusing two Asylum children previously indentured to him. Overwhelmed with work and unable to visit the home in person, Wright wrote instead:

My dear Sir,

You have two Asylum children [...] indentured to you by H. D. Perry, Agt. N. Y. Juv. Asylum. It has been reported to me that you do not use them properly. Please let me hear from you concerning them. What is the occasion of such an accusation being made against you. I send letters to the children & envelopes so that they may write to me themselves & let me know whether they are satisfied or not.

Please let me hear from you immediately.

Truly yours,
E. Wright

Writing was a poor substitute for paying the man an actual visit under the circumstances. Trusting the man to fess up to any wrongdoing in a return letter was wishful thinking at best. It's not a stretch to imagine such a man standing watch over the children as they each penned their replies, carefully censoring them.

Another case involved little Johanna "Jennie" J. Dee. Jennie had trouble staying in the homes where she was placed. On June 29, 1883, she was placed in her fourth home—with J. M. Robnett, of Centralia, Illinois. Her stay in this home lasted just a little over two months. About three weeks after her arrival, Jennie was impregnated by Robnett. Jennie, whose condition was unknown to Mr. Wright, was taken from the Robnett home and placed in the home of Thomas T. Townley of Coles Station, Illinois, on September 5, 1883.

Mr. Townley returned Jennie to the Asylum's Western Agency in April 1884 in a "delicate condition." On April 21, 1884, at the age of twelve, Jennie gave birth to a baby girl weighing five pounds. Medical professionals pronounced her the "youngest mother in the state."[48]

Robnett was arrested on a charge of rape and bastardy, and his bond was set at $700.00. The case was tried by John Donovan, a former ward of the NYJA, who was indentured in Illinois in 1859. Donovan himself suffered from abuse in the first home where he was placed by the NYJA.[49] He enlisted in Company C, 56th Illinois Infantry Regiment in the Civil War while in his second home, was mustered out, and then taught school in Centralia, Illinois. He later studied law with Judge Hubbard of Kinmundy, Illinois. By 1878, Donovan was a lawyer and post-

Challenges and Successes

In its 1904 annual report the Asylum revealed, "Two men who were responsible for the 'ruin' of two girls, were successfully prosecuted, one being sentenced to a term of fifteen years in prison."[53]

Asylum records reveal the case of a man in Monticello, Illinois, beating the girl he took in so badly with a broomstick that he dislocated her thumb. A note in one boy's file says, "Used the boy like a slave." He had been indentured to a man in Ogle County, Illinois.[54]

A girl named Sarah suffered abuse in her second Illinois home, as recalled by one of her descendents:

> When Sarah lived with Henry _____, her 2nd home after the [orphan] train, at night she would have to move her dresser in front of her door to keep him from sexually abusing her. Then the wife would physically abuse her, and she hit Sarah so much with a ladle or spoon on the side of her head that she actually had hearing loss. At some point she moved from Henry's farm to his brother's farm. From there she met Albert and ran off to marry him and get away from the family, and abuse.[55]

It was not always the NYJA children who were abused. Sometimes it was the children themselves who committed violent acts against their master or the master's wife and children. One case in point is that of a seventeen-year-old boy sent to Iowa who was caught raping the four-year-old daughter of his master. He was caught in the act by the girl's mother, but managed to escape after a struggle. He was later apprehended by the authorities.[56]

A fifteen-year-old Asylum boy raped the five-year-old daughter of his master in Livingston County, Illinois. After being punished by the girl's father, the boy ran away.[57]

Another Asylum boy hit his foster mother in the head with a shovel, was indentured to a different couple for doing so, and then knocked the next woman over with a stool. Yet another boy threw his foster mother against a stove in his Randolph

John F. Donovan. He was sent west by the NYJA, served in the Civil War, became a lawyer, and was elected Mayor of Kinmundy, Illinois. (*Find-A-Grave Memorial 85309435*)

master in Kinmundy, and by 1883 he was elected mayor of Kinmundy.[50]

The case received a great deal of attention in the newspapers. The jury "failed to agree" on the first trial, which took place in June 1884, but Robnett was tried again and was convicted. Jennie Dee was placed in a total of eight homes in Illinois. Her father requested she be returned to him in New York in 1888, which was granted.[51]

In 1861, a twelve-year-old Asylum girl was raped by the son of the man she was indentured to in Champaign County, Illinois. No further notes on this case were recorded in the case files.[52]

County, Illinois home, "rendering her senseless." He fled to New York, but authorities had been notified and planned to arrest him upon his arrival there.[58]

Guns and knives were the weapons of choice of the children in several instances. In Ford County, Illinois, an Asylum boy threatened his teacher and fellow students with a "loaded pistol and large knife." Another boy attacked the man he was indentured to in Washington County, Illinois, with a butcher knife and then "ran off." Yet another drew a knife on his teacher in Perry County, Illinois, and was expelled.[59]

It was rare for the girls to be physically abusive. They used other means to take out frustrations on foster parents. There are at least two cases of girls poisoning an entire family. One girl put strychnine in the coffee, making her foster parents sick for a week, in Kankakee, Illinois.[60]

There are numerous cases noted in the Asylum's case files of boys abusing livestock. One boy "beat a horse badly in the head, killed 12 pigs, and a valuable colt." Yet another killed several turkeys "with some other boys," and a warrant was issued for their arrest. An Asylum boy killed a horse with a pitchfork in Randolph County, Illinois.[61]

Several instances of boys threatening to kill their master or his wife are noted in the records, as well as several cases of the children setting fire to barns. One such boy succeeded in burning the barn *twice* on the same farm in Ford County, Illinois.[62]

It's safe to assume that some of these children were acting out their frustrations related to being orphaned or separated from family, and other issues.

Farm accidents took the lives of some children. Many such accidents involved horses. Asylum records indicate that several boys met their end after being kicked by a horse. One boy survived but was "badly disfigured." Another boy's horse ran away, throwing the boy off. The boy broke his arm in the fall and had to have it amputated just below the elbow. Yet another boy who used a horse to run some errands in Macon County, Illinois, was late returning home. After a search, he was found with the halter tied around his wrist, having been dragged some sixty yards to his death.[63]

In 1876, Richard Hall, indentured to Mr. Stevens in Norton Township, Illinois, perished after being "terribly mangled in a horse's stall [...] his brains oozing from a deep wound in the head."[64] David L. Straight, sent to Illinois in 1867, described how he survived two brushes with death: "I have had to work, no discount on that, and endure many hardships; was nearly killed twice, first, by a black oak-tree eighteen inches in diameter falling on me, but the limbs prevented my being crushed; second, by a kick from a horse, which broke both jaws and knocked out six teeth. I could eat nothing for a week."[65]

Another boy went to gather eggs in the chicken coop and died after sliding playfully down a straw stack and driving a hay knife (concealed in the straw) into his neck. Another was killed by a bull. A few died of accidental gunshot wounds.[66]

Perhaps the most heart-wrenching story of all belongs to a fourteen-year-old boy named James. For some, after years of longing to be reunited with the family they were separated from back east, or being orphaned with no parents to comfort them at all, a particularly upsetting event in their lives was just too much for them to bear. Fourteen-year-old James Kenmore, indentured to John Karr in Peotone, Illinois, helped the Harris children "with whom he had been raised" decorate the tree on Christmas Eve in 1886. All those present received gifts with the exception of James, who "became very despondent to think that he had not been remembered." The following Friday he was found hanging by a rope from a joist over the horse manger in Mr. Karr's barn.[67]

William Weiner was another tragic case. He lost his father and was surrendered to the Asylum by his mother due to destitution. He was sent west in 1885 and indentured in Pontiac, Illinois. After his indenture ended, he went to work for Frank Howard, a farmer in Ocoya, Illinois. William was described as a "steady young man" who "bore a good reputation and saved up $1,500." On January 1, 1900, William became despondent over a "love affair." At three o'clock, Mrs. Howard, who was in the farmhouse with her three children, heard two gunshots. She found William lying across the bed, shot once in the head, and once in the heart. On the bed with him were pictures of his mother and sister in New York. He was twenty-seven years old.[68]

Runaways and Returns

It was not uncommon for a child to run away (Asylum officials also used the word "abscond") almost immediately after being placed in a home. Some did so after several weeks, months, or even years. Many of these children were never found and notes such as "ran away—whereabouts unknown," were made in the case files for the children.[69] One boy made his escape from the hotel he and the rest of his company were at upon first arriving in Illinois in September 1869. The following January his mother wrote to Ebenezer Wright at the Western Agency asking how he was doing as she had not heard from him. Wright replied:

> Your letter of inquiry concerning your son Charles is to hand. He was taken to Morris—Grundy Co., Ill. with a company of Asylum children last September and ran away from the Hotel before a place was procured for him. I made inquiry but could get no trace of him. He may be with a family in that region & will advertise in the Morris papers and see if I can find him.[70]

In 1861, two brothers were placed in homes near each other in Aurora, Illinois. Notes in their case files reveal that both ran away together "before tea time" the very same day they were placed.[71] One boy absconded after accidentally shooting his master's horse during a hunting excursion in 1863.[72]

Occasionally, after receiving a whipping from their employer, a boy would run away and make his way to the Western Agency. After thinking about what happened a few of them would express regret for leaving, perhaps realizing that they may have had the whipping coming, and asked the Western Agent to arrange for their return to their former employer. If both employer and child agreed to a reconciliation, arrangements were made. Such was the case with a boy named Robert, in 1869:

> Dear Sir,
>
> I have discovered as sufficient reason for removing Robt. from your guardianship. Probably you used unjustifiable severity in punishing him for his offense & I hope you will exercise more self control under such circumstances in future. It is Robert's desire to return & complete the term of his apprenticeship & I am informed by Mr. [Charles H.] Colegrove that you do not object to his doing so. I therefore send him back to you. If it be necessary I will submit the case to our Directors & have the old Indentures restored or new ones executed. I don't know in what shape the matter stands & wish you would write & inform me.
>
> Yours truly, E. Wright.[73]

Ebenezer Wright, clearly frustrated, shared some of his ideas on how the Asylum might deal with the problem of so many runaways with the Indenturing Committee in 1869:

> Rather than remove a child from a good home where it is desirous to remain whether or not we should yield to such objections is a question about which the agent desires instructions. These objections are made by a class of men whose opinions are worthy to be heeded. There is no question but that the prejudice against the present form of indentures is growing stronger & more general. Perhaps a less antiquated & cumbersome form of contract avoiding the objectionable phraseology & changing the terms somewhat would be

more acceptable & serve a better purpose. The phrase "bind out" is objected to by both employers & children & in numerous instances probably it moves apprentices to abscond.

A much larger compensation might be secured to the children if annual payments were substituted for the present plan & boys would be much more likely to remain in their places. Sixteen absconders are reported this month.[74]

Some of these children returned to New York on their own, a few via cattle train. One boy returned to New York and was found at the Newsboys' Lodging House, where he was apprehended by authorities.[75]

Samuel Swensky ran away from his home in Illinois, returned to New York, and made his way back to the NYJA. Edwin C. Burdick, Assistant Superintendent, immediately informed his mother of the situation: "Your son Samuel was caught here Sunday on the fence and, as he is still a ward of this institution, having run away from the home in which he was placed in the west we shall keep him here. You can visit him on the regular visiting days, the last Thursday of each month."[76]

When Zachariah Taylor ran away from his employer in Sterling, Illinois, the man ran the following notice in the local paper:

Ranaway.

From the subscriber, one mile north of Sterling, ZACHARIAH TAYLOR, a boy indentured to me by the New York Juvenile Asylum. All persons are forbid trusting said boy on my account after this date. GEORGE S. HOOVER. Sterling, April 4, 1866.[77]

Others ran away and went to work for a sympathetic neighbor of the farmer with whom they were initially placed. One boy ran away and "joined a travelling circus." Many of these runaways ended up in county almshouses. The minutes of the Indenturing Committee refer to one such case, in 1861:

Mr. [William C.] Van Meter communicated to the Committee, by letter, the intelligence that during a recent tour in Illinois he had found a girl, who had been sent West by the Asylum, in a county Almshouse & that expenses had been incurred by the Supervisors on her account to the amount of twenty-five dollars. He expressed the hope that, as the occurrence would be likely to hinder the enterprise of sending children from this city to that state, the committee would investigate the matter & set it right.[78]

In many cases, the Asylum's policy of allowing parents of the children placed in the West to correspond with them during the entire time they were under indenture was the cause of children running away. On occasion, employers even allowed well-behaving children to return to New York for brief visits with their parents and friends, then return to their foster home in Illinois.

Ebenezer Wright wrote of his concerns about parents visiting their children out west, and of one mother in particular: "Her son, Daniel, came out nearly two years ago & did well until she came on. Now his employer has reported that he can do nothing with him & asks to be relieved from his indentures. I don't know of an instance where children have continued to do well [for very] long after their mother came out."[79]

Asylum Superintendent Elisha M. Carpenter once broke from the normal policy of providing parents with the address of their child out West in the case of Ida Van Loon, in 1890. It nearly cost him his life.

Ida's mother, Sophia Van Loon aka Sophia Peters placed fifteen-year-old Ida in the Asylum for being "a liar, a thief and incorrigible." After Ida had been in the Asylum for some time, her mother tried to secure her release. Carpenter was soon told by Ida's father to not disclose the girl's whereabouts to his wife, with whom he was no longer living, because she "ran off with another man" and was

Challenges and Successes   147

not a "fit custodian for the girl." At the end of her two-year stay in the Asylum Ida was sent west to a wealthy woman who promised to educate her.

About six months elapsed when Ida's mother began repeatedly demanding that Mr. Carpenter give her Ida's address. Carpenter held his ground and refused to do so.

On Sunday afternoon, November 23, 1890, Van Loon went to the NYJA and asked to speak to Carpenter. She was told he and his son would be returning soon as they had gone to church. Van Loon concealed herself behind one of the gate posts at the entrance to the Asylum, and awaited their return. She had loaded five rounds into a Colt revolver, and just as Carpenter's carriage passed through the gate she sprang out, leveled the pistol at Carpenter, and "snapped the trigger." It did not discharge so she pulled the trigger again, repeatedly. The coachman "sprang from his seat, and young Carpenter jumped from the carriage and seized and disarmed" Van Loon. The horses ran off during all the commotion and smashed a part of the picket fence surrounding the grounds of the Asylum before being stopped by a member of the mounted police. It seems Van Loon had fashioned a 22-caliber cartridge to fit a 32-caliber pistol by wrapping the cartridges with paper, causing it to misfire.

Van Loon was hauled off to the Washington Heights police station and charged with felonious assault.[80]

In 1904, Hastings H. Hart, head of the ICHAS which took over the Western indenturing program of the NYJA, made his case to Asylum officials for discontinuing the practice of parental correspondence, at least for "unworthy" parents:

> Dr. Hart is pressing his point in favor of the abolition of the rule permitting unworthy parents to correspond with their children in the west. The recision of the right of communication would be drastic, yet many of Dr. Hart's arguments are unanswerable. Numerous instances were recited, from time to time during the year, of children made restless by friends in the east. [...] Where communication is continuous between the relative and the child, in a large majority of cases the result is unnecessary agitation and disquietude. When relatives find the child has reached the age of self-dependence, their appeals are made irresistible. Possibly a clearing house for such letters, either at the Asylum or the Chicago office, would prevent the inculcation of discontent.[81]

Hart's concerns were not unfounded. An episode that occurred in and around Cedarville, Illinois in 1883 is a good case in point:

> George Venette, of New York, arrived in the city, and paid a visit to Cedarville, where his son fifteen years of age was living with Samuel Adams. The little fellow was given to this gentleman last September by the agent of the New York Juvenile Asylum, to raise; another son eleven years of age was given to Uriah Rubendahl, of Fountain Creek, and a man named Spatz, at Brookville, had a daughter about 12 years of age. Venette obtained possession of the trio and has started East with them again. He reported that he had reformed and was able to take care of them; that their mother was in ill health and desired to see the children before she passes away. It is altogether probable the children will never see the west again.[82]

It's unknown if Hart's advice was heeded at the time, but addresses of parents were still being provided in 1910 as evidenced by a letter from thirteen-year-old Sarah Gloss, who went west in 1905 and was indentured at LaGrange, Illinois. Sarah thanked the Asylum for providing her with her mother's address:

> I am very sorry for not answering your letter sooner, for I enjoyed it very much. I will

tell you what I got for Christmas. A five dollar gold piece, a box of writing paper, hair ribbons and other useful articles, a bible, a half dollar and a picture of my brother. I am sure that you could not have placed me in a better home. They are all very kind and just to me and I am very happy. I have no pets but something nicer, a dear little baby brother. I take care of the baby and help wash the dishes. I will now close this letter, thanking you for my mother's address and wishing all good health and happiness.[83]

Some of the children, after having ran away and returned to New York, later expressed regret. Elisha M. Carpenter, General Superintendent of the NYJA, received a letter from one such boy in 1893:

Dear Sir:—I take pleasure in writing you these few lines to let you know that I am not dead yet. It is about ten years since I left the Asylum and went West; and I can say it is the best place I've been yet. There's where all the boys and girls at the Asylum ought to go. It is much better than in the city. I came back to the city in August, and I'm so sorry I came back. I really did not know how well off I was out there. And now, Mr. C., I want to ask you one question: Would it bother you much to let me go back there with the next company? I have spent all my money, and I can't get any work. No work, no money, no nothing, I just don't know what to do. I am now going around like a tramp. I am ashamed to walk through the streets. So I would be much obliged to you if you could find some way for me to get back again. If I had known this I never would have come here; and if I ever get back I will never come here again.

Hoping to hear from you soon,
Very truly yours, O. A.[84]

It was not noted whether his wish was granted, but it was not unheard of for children to return to New York for discipline, health, or other reasons, and then be sent west a second time from the Asylum—usually indentured to a different employer than they were previously.[85]

Some children returned to parents or relatives in New York, only to find them in such a state that the children wished they had stayed out West. Carpenter wrote about a girl in this situation:

Last week a girl who was sent to Illinois eleven years ago, and who had just become of age, returned to this city to live with her parents. She found them profane, intemperate people, and said she could not live with them. So she came to the Asylum and asked us to get her a special rate ticket to return to her home in Illinois. The ticket was procured, and she returned there on Monday last, not having unpacked her trunk.[86]

Happy Endings

Elisha M. Carpenter concluded his 1893 report by saying, "The names of lawyers, physicians, clergymen, school-teachers and prosperous farmers, now scattered throughout Illinois and other Western States, and not a few who have returned to the city of New York and are doing well, all of whom were sent from the Asylum to Illinois in past years, would fill volumes. We are constantly meeting with glad surprises in this direction."[87]

One of the Asylum children Carpenter was referring to as being a "glad surprise" was undoubtedly John J. Brown. After the death of their Irish immigrant parents in New York City, he and his brother William were sent to Illinois in the July 16, 1860 company. They were both indentured to William Henninger of Vandalia, in Fayette County. John graduated from Wesleyan University (class of 1881) and was principal of Vandalia's high school for six years before studying law and becoming a partner with William M. Farmer, a justice of the state

John J. Brown, sent west in 1860, later held high positions of importance in Illinois, and was nearly elected Governor. (*Historical Souvenir of Vandalia, Illinois, 1904/HathiTrust Digital Library*)

supreme court. Brown was elected to the Illinois general assembly in 1886, was appointed commissioner of the Southern Illinois Penitentiary at Chester, was secretary of the Illinois commission of the Louisiana Purchase Exposition (St. Louis World's Fair), and was a member of the centennial commission. He was also active in Republican primaries as a candidate for governor, secretary of state, and congressman at large. Brown died in Vandalia in 1932 at the age of seventy-nine.[88] His obituary described him as "an orphan who rose to some of the highest honors the state had to offer."

Those who did not become doctors and lawyers, or even prosperous farmers, left their marks nonetheless, and they are forever woven into the social fabric of America's Midwest.

For many of the children sent west, the people they were indentured to were the only family they ever really knew. Long after their indentures were concluded, some clung to any connection they had to their western family. When John Hunter was struck by a train and killed near Galva, Illinois in 1891 at "about 40 years of age," the only identification found on him was his indenture papers showing "that he had been at one time an inmate of the Juvenile Asylum of New York and was bound out in 1862 for 12½ years to George Glossop, a farmer of DeKalb county, Ill."[89]

At least two instances of fellow Asylum wards marrying each other after being sent west are noted in the records. Several other cases of Asylum children later marrying one of their foster brothers or sisters are noted. There are even a few instances of Asylum girls later marrying their employers.[90]

Some employers became so attached to the children they took in that they remembered them in their wills, leaving them gifts of large farms and livestock. One such boy, who later became a "wealthy stock-farm owner," stopped at a hotel in Long Acre Square [now Times Square] in New York City on his way to London, in 1906. He said he had not been in New York longer than a day since his boyhood, when he spent two years as "a regular boarder at the Newsboys' Lodging House":

> My first steady job was handed out to me from the Newsboys' Lodging House. [. . .] It was running errands for a banking house. But I was unappreciative, got myself mixed up with a street gang, and for constantly disturbing the peace was sent to the New York Juvenile Asylum on Washington Heights. They've moved since then, I understand, to a fine cottage settlement at Dobbs Ferry, or Chauncey. They treated me well; if it hadn't been for the help they gave me, real friendly help as from man to man, Lord knows where I'd have been. They sent me West to do the work I felt myself longing for, tinkering with the ground and seeds and live stock. I was apprenticed to a

man who owned a lot of stock, and he liked me enough to call me his son. I certainly liked him, and between us we worked that plant up to a big thing, and when he died it was all left to me. That's how I come to stand a rich man.[91]

Many received fine gifts at the expiration of their indentures, for weddings and the like. One employer promised the boy he took in "a horse and saddle" in addition to the $100.00 he had coming when the indenture expired. An employer in Tazewell County, Illinois, gave the boy indentured to him "a team of horses, wagon, new set of harnesses, and a plow, when of age, and he commenced farming on his own account."[92]

Perhaps most inspiring of all are the notations in the records of several Asylum children, after growing up and getting married, contacting the NYJA for the purpose of taking in an Asylum child themselves.

H. C. Warrens of Loda, Illinois, wrote to the Asylum in 1903 asking for a boy as well as information on his own early history, to which the Asylum replied:

> We have your recent letter and are glad to know you are doing so well. In reference to your inquiry concerning your relations, we find on investigation that you were here for fifteen months, having been committed by Mary Patterson. [...] During the whole time that you were here, you were never visited and no inquiries were made concerning you. We regret, therefore, that we are unable to give you any further information.
>
> In reference to the application for a boy, this will be submitted to the proper committee and you will be informed later.[93]

Challenges and Successes

CHAPTER NINE

Partners in Placements

Passing the Torch

Following the resignation of its western indenturing agent, Ebenezer Wright, on December 31, 1899 (he passed away just two weeks later) the Asylum closed its Western Agency: "The old headquarters for the indenturing work in Englewood, Chicago, is no longer called for, and the board resolved to close that indenturing agency with the end of the present year [1900], and to conduct the work from the New York office, employing, however, visitors in the West as heretofore."[1] Wright was remembered fondly in the Asylum's annual report:

> They have been remarkably fortunate in having had for the period of thirty-three years as their indenturing agent at Chicago, a man of exceptional qualifications for such work, Ebenezer Wright, whose sudden death in January, 1900, shortly after his resignation, should not pass unnoticed here.
>
> In a minute adopted by the Board in recognition of Mr. Wright's service, is the following: "The Directors in carrying on their placing-out work needed a man of force as well as of sound judgment and discrimination. These qualities they found in Mr. Wright. His diligence, his knowledge of the districts in which the children were placed, his attention to detail, his fidelity and steadiness, his personal interest in the welfare of the wards of the Asylum—all these have been and are highly appreciated by the Directors."

From the time that the work of distributing children in rural localities was begun, down to the end of the year 1899, the Asylum has placed-out in western homes 6,055 children. Of this number all but about 500, Mr. Wright stated, had come under his observation, and most of them had continued under his guidance through the critical adolescent years, and until they had begun their careers, most of which were successful.[2]

Wright once visited many of the former wards placed in Illinois, and the closing words of his report after the trip nicely sum up his views on what ended up being his life's work:

> To see so many now prosperous and respected members of society, hear them tell their childhood history, and see their manifestations of gratitude for their preservation from a wretched life, has been to me convincing evidence of the high relative value of such an agency as this, among the instrumentalities employed for ameliorating the condition of the unfortunate.[3]

At its February 19, 1900 meeting, the Indenturing Committee reported on the progress of closing the Agency:

Dr. [Charles E.] Bruce reported on his trip to Chicago, that the Indenturing Agency property is at present unsellable and that by his advice, Treasurer had sent to Miss [Mary] Cronein $300.00 to pay running expenses to April 1, 1900.[4]

On Dr. Bruce's recommendation, the Committee determined to allow the use of the Agency house to Mrs. Ebenezer Wright until April 1, 1900 and upon her withdrawal to entrust the care of the property to Miss Cronein at a salary of $45.00 per month. The rear building and portion of the house were to be closed and the expenses were to be paid by the Asylum.[5]

Ebenezer Wright's replacement was his former assistant, James W. Shields, who was hired "as Western Representative and Visitor at $100.00 per month from March 1 to November 1st and to have the privilege of residing in the Agency, it being understood that Miss Cronein is to have charge of the correspondence."[6]

Mary Cronein resigned effective December 1, 1900. She was granted permission to temporarily occupy one of the rooms at the Western Agency "in consideration of which she is to give assistance to the new Clerk as recommended by Mr. Shields."[7]

The fate of the Agency House was finally sealed as revealed in the minutes for December 3, 1900:

After conference with Mr. Shields the Western Agent in his recent visit to New York the Committee have concluded to continue the work at the present Agency until May 1, 1901, with directions to Mr. Shields to put the rear house on West 61st St. in order for rent at estimated figure of $10.00 per month, and also to shut off as much of the upper part of the front house as is not required. After May 1, 1901, it is proposed to rent an office in the business district of Chicago at about $200.00 per annum, and secure services of a stenographic assistant to attend to correspondence, records on a salary of $625.00 per annum.

The 61st St. property to be sold, and failing in that it is to be rented at $600.00 the estimated rental value made by Mr. Shields.[8]

The office in the "business district of Chicago" was subsequently located at 79 Dearborn Street per an advertisement in *The Farmer's Review* of Chicago, Illinois:

The New York Juvenile Asylum wants good family homes for ten boys, 12 to 15 years of age, in Iowa and Illinois. These are promising, likely boys who want to make something of themselves. Please address Western Agency N. Y. Juvenile Asylum, Room 601, 79 Dearborn St., Chicago, Ill.[9]

In 1901, the Asylum's Indenturing Committee decided to seek similar legislation in Iowa to that granted in Illinois in 1861. At its March 11, 1901 meeting the Committee "moved and seconded that the Vice Chairman of this Committee be authorized to employ counsel to draft a bill for presentation to the legislature of Iowa validating the placing of children in that State. Motion carried."[10] No evidence has been found to suggest that such legislation was either presented or passed.

The Asylum sent 111 children (106 from the Asylum and five volunteers) to Illinois and Iowa in 1901, after an average detention of just over sixteen months in the Asylum. Forty-seven of those sent were committed to the Asylum at the instance of the NYSPCC.[11]

In 1903, James W. Shields renewed his predecessor Ebenezer Wright's recommendation to transfer the headquarters of the Western Agency from Chicago to Central Iowa, "inasmuch as children are latterly being almost exclusively placed in Iowa." However, Asylum officials decided to close the Western Agency on September 1 and removed all records to New York, where "correspondence and other clerical duties" were to be attended to at the Asylum.[12]

Their decision may have been influenced by the fact that the Iowa State Legislature passed an act in

1903 regulating the placing of children from another state, requiring, among other things, from foreign (out-of-state) associations, a bond that children brought into the state would not be permitted to become public charges within five years. Mr. W. E. Bain and Mr. C. B. Hubbard of Independence, Iowa, agreed to become sureties on the Asylum's bond.[13]

On October 6, 1903 the decision was made to transfer the western indenturing work to the care of the ICHAS in Chicago, headed by Hastings H. Hart.[14] Hart was a man of national prominence in child welfare and in penal organizations. A graduate of Oberlin College, he was an ardent supporter of the placing out system: "Our experience proves that many children ought, for their own good, to be removed to a distance from their early environment in order to escape the influence of vicious relatives, or to get beyond the odium which has arisen because of the conduct of their parents."[15]

The ICHAS was founded in 1883 by Reverend Mr. Martin Van Buren Arsdale, a Methodist minister, to aid orphaned and abandoned children. Originally called the American Educational Aid Association, it sought to place homeless children in private family homes instead of institutions. Reverend Mr. Arsdale declared, "There is a home in a good family for every homeless child and woe to me if I do not find it." The Association established advisory boards throughout Illinois to handle placement and created receiving homes for children awaiting placement. Van Arsdale sought national expansion and eventually thirty-six societies were established in other states. With expansion, the name was changed to the National Children's Home Society, and in 1897 it was changed to the ICHAS.

The reason the New York Juvenile Asylum chose this particular society for its western indenturing work is unknown, but the NYJA was familiar with the ICHAS and held it in high regard based on a statement the Asylum's western indenturing agent, James W. Shields, made in the Asylum's 1901 annual report: "It has been a graceful tribute as well when the ICHAS have placed children in the same homes where our wards are or have been."[16] In ad-

Hastings H. Hart ca. 1915. Hart ran the ICHAS at the time it assisted the NYJA with placing-out children. (*Minnesota Historical Society/por 17425 r1*)

dition, one of the Society's branches was located in Englewood where the Asylum's Western Agency was located.

The Society initially assumed responsibility for placing and visiting children in Illinois, but on March 8, 1904 it, somewhat reluctantly, took on responsibility for Iowa and other states as well. Hastings Hart explained, "We were asked to look after the emergency cases only; but finally we were asked to assume the agency for Iowa and other Western States. [...] We found it easier and less expensive to secure homes in Illinois than in Iowa, for the reason that we have so many efficient agents in Illinois."[17] Hart also reported that several children were placed "in Northern Missouri, near the Iowa line" that year.[18] Hart reported that Joel E. Field, a sixteen-year employee of the ICHAS, had devoted

Partners in Placements   155

Miss Mary S. Jewell, Placing Agent for the ICHAS. (*St. Louis Post Dispatch, June 1, 1906*)

about two-thirds of his time to "the Iowa work" since about March 1, 1904. Other agents assisting were Herbert T. Root, Laura J. Donaldson, and Mary S. Jewell.[19]

The Asylum's western indenturing agent, James W. Shields, retired in September of 1904, completing the merger with the ICHAS. The Asylum was represented in the formal transfer by John Klein, Second Assistant Superintendent of the NYJA, who "had charge of the emigration work several weeks, acquitting himself in the difficult assignment with credit." The Asylum declared that "as soon as this preliminary [work] is concluded, a company of volunteers will be sent to the selected homes. Each child now a ward in the West or that may hereaf-

ter become a ward, is to be visited by a representative of the Society at least once a year, and supplied from the Asylum with the 'Youth's Companion,' an annual letter and a copy of the [annual] report."[20]

The ICHAS had been in existence for twenty years, had forty employees (including ten district superintendents and a field secretary), and maintained four receiving stations in Illinois, each with a capacity of twenty-four children.[21] The receiving stations were in Englewood, Rantoul, Shelbyville, and Du Quoin.[22]

Children placed out by the ICHAS were not indentured, as was the policy of the NYJA for so many decades. Instead, the Society's agents were given a list of eighty questions to investigate the applicants for children "by his personal observation, by inquiry of neighbors, teachers, business men, etc." Applicants who were approved signed an agreement to "give the child suitable care, training, clothing, school privileges and church privileges; to treat it as a member of the family and to return it without question, if at any time, in the judgement of the Society, it is for the interests of the child." Hastings Hart explained: "Children are placed on 90 days' trial and are not indentured: our experience being that the indenture protects neither the child, the foster-parents nor the society."[23]

In Hart's first yearly report to the NYJA, he explained some details of the work:

> These statistical figures given above present only the dry bones of the work. They can give no idea of the night journeys, the drives in winter's cold or in summer's dust and heat. They cannot present the anxious thought and the difficult endeavor to secure the best welfare of the children.
>
> Restless and homesick children have been encouraged and exhorted. Wayward girls have been watched over, sheltered and befriended, lazy, indifferent boys have been stimulated and inspired, discouraged foster parents have been advised and upheld. Stingy farmers have been forced to do justice to boys on indenture and

These twelve "destitute" boys were sent from the NYJA to the Chidlren's Home in Mineola, Long Island, New York, on March 18, 1907. (*NYJA Annual Report, 1907*)

thrifty housewives have been deprived of girls whom they sought to use as unpaid drudges.[24]

By 1906, Hart was reporting that his society "found homes for more than five hundred children" for the NYJA. He added, "Out of that number only four have had to be returned as incorrigible. In the rapidly growing towns of the Western States these children, carefully placed in reliable homes where they can have the companionship of good playmates, grow up to be respected and useful citizens."[25]

Mrs. Laura J. Donaldson was the person who made follow-up visits to homes in Iowa, Missouri, and Oklahoma on behalf of the ICHAS during this time period.[26] Some children moved to other states with their foster parents and Donaldson made occasional visits to them as well. During one such trip she arrived at a "jumping-off place" on a railroad in Texas to visit a child on a farm some fifteen miles distant, and found that several weeks of rain had left the road and rivers nearly impassable. By coincidence, she located the farmer she was going to visit in a nearby home, but he himself had not been able to return to his farm for two weeks due to the condition of the roads. He informed her it would be impossible to go out to the farm. The discouraging news had little effect on the "plucky woman," who, after being denied a horse to ride, procured four mules and a wagon, and managed to make the journey "which the old residents would never have attempted."[27]

The Asylum did not "encourage emigration to Western States in 1907," which appears to be at least in part related to the fact that the State Board of Charities had ruled that destitute children could no longer be placed in the same institution as delinquent children, as described in an earlier chapter. As a result, the Asylum sent only one child west in 1907, through the CAS. It was the first time in fifty years that the Asylum did not send companies of children west. The cost of sending the companies west in that fifty-year period was estimated at a half million dollars "of which vast sum the city had not contributed a dollar." The average age of a child sent west was eleven; therefore, the Asylum assumed "an obligation that it may not discharge for seven years."[28]

The net deficit per child in 1907, for supervision alone, was more than $10.00. Of the remaining non-delinquent children that year, one, an orphan eighteen years old, enlisted in the U.S. Navy; two were transferred to Hope Farm [School]; and ten were adopted. On March 18, twelve destitute boys were transferred to the Protestant Home at Mineola, Long Island, and two others were returned to the Department of Charities by direction of the Comptroller, in order to comply with the new rule.[29]

Another factor that may have had a bearing on the Asylum's decision to not send any children west in 1907 was the withdrawal of half-fare railroad privileges from charitable organizations that year.[30]

In 1908, Hastings H. Hart commented, "Some good people in the West have opposed the introduction of these friendless children from the large cities, but the West is richer and stronger for the children who have come out under the auspices of the New York Juvenile Asylum."[31]

Henry W. Thurston succeeded Hastings H. Hart as Superintendent of the ICHAS by 1909. Mrs. Laura J. Donaldson was Thurston's assistant, as they continued their collaboration with the NYJA.[32] The year 1909 was the last year children were placed in the West from the NYJA via the ICHAS. One child was

Partners in Placements

Robert N. Brace, Superintendent of the Emigration/Placing-out Department at the New York Children's Aid Society. (*Courtesy of the Sayre Family*)

sent that year, but it was noted the child "did not come directly from the Asylum." The ICHAS continued filing annual reports for many years afterwards regarding how the children previously sent west under their care were faring.

Renewed Collaboration

In 1908, Charles Loring Brace, Jr., president of the CAS, and the son of its founder, approached the NYJA about reestablishing a loose partnership similar to the one used, albeit briefly, back in 1854, in which the CAS took a limited number of children for the purpose of being placed out in the West.[33] The NYJA accepted the offer.

Under the arrangement, boys were first sent to the Brace Farm School in Valhalla, New York, for several months, where they were trained to be little farmers. They tended crops and farm animals as part of this training.

Once trained, they were placed on an orphan train and sent west under the auspices of the CAS. Brace continued this arrangement with the NYJA until at least 1922, and perhaps a bit later. The records of the NYJA denote which children were taken by the CAS, but all follow-up visits of the children after placement were performed by the latter.

Robert N. Brace, brother of Charles, Jr., was Superintendent of the Emigration/Placing-out Department of the CAS and handled many of the placements of the Asylum's children. For several years he wrote a chapter in the annual reports of the NYJA, giving a report of the children placed in the West, often providing the names and photos of the children. The NYJA also continued its tradition of including letters from these children and their foster parents in the annual reports.

In 1913, Brace explained the CAS's philosophy on placing children on farms in the Asylum's annual report:

> The policy of the CHILDREN'S AID SOCIETY has always been to start the boys on farms. It has been and still is our belief that there is nothing comparable to farm life in building up both physique and character. The habits of industry, economy and strict honesty learned by the growing boy on the farm stand him in good stead in later life no matter whether he continues at farming or takes up a trade or profession. That a boy is not tied down to farming by starting on a farm is shown by the careers of your boys who have come under our care. Of the older boys four have taken up railroading, two are preparing for college and others have become clerks and mechanics.[34]

The CAS placed out only one child for the Asylum in 1907, but the number increased to forty-two

Godfrey aka Godfried (left) and William McNeil, sent west on July 15, 1908. (*NYJA Annual Report, 1908*)

children in 1908, sent primarily to Nebraska and Texas.[35]

Among the children were brothers Joseph (aka Godfrey or Godfried), age thirteen, and William McNeil, age eleven. The boys were transferred from the NYJA to the Brace Farm School in Kensico, New York on July 15, 1908, where they were trained in farm related work for three months. The CAS then sent them to the home of the William Collins family on their Oak Dale Ranch in Lampasas, Texas. Godfrey later wrote: "Lampasas [...] has large Sulphur springs. Every day I feed about 100 chickens, 100 turkeys, 160 sheep, 3 pigs and 10 horses. We have three dogs and go out hunting. We had a race with a rabbit and caught a cotton tail."[36]

Robert N. Brace reported on the boys in 1910: "Godfrey and William McNeil have one of the nicest homes in Texas, with cultivated, high-class people, and each of the boys was presented last winter with a pony and a new saddle. Our agents always speak of them as two of the happiest boys in the world."[37]

After 1909, the only children sent west from the NYJA were placed out through the auspices of the CAS, until their collaboration ended.

The End of an Era

Over the course of time, attitudes about how best to care for needy children changed in America. Just twenty years after the system of sending companies of children west began, it came under close scrutiny, and at times criticism, from the philanthropic world. Peer organizations as well as the boards of state charities began to file complaints against the system and its potential abuses.

In 1874, at the National Prison Reform Conference, a delegate from Wisconsin, probably Hiram H. Giles, complained that for "the past twelve or fifteen years car loads of criminal juveniles [...] vagabonds, and gutter snipes" had been sent west, specifically to Wisconsin. Hiram H. Giles, member of Wisconsin's State Board of Charities and Reform, proclaimed: "[I]t is a misdemeanor to scatter and sow noxious weeds on the prairies and in the openings of Wisconsin, but it is 'Moral Strategy' to annually scatter three thousand obnoxious, 'iron-clad orphans,' juvenile criminals among the peaceful homes and in the quiet neighborhoods of the state."[38]

By 1882, Conference attendees were increasingly vocal in their criticism. Andrew E. Elmore, a Wisconsin resident and president of Wisconsin's State Board of Charities and Reform, stated, "I would say a word in reference to thieves, liars, vagabonds, as we call them, they bring them west and turn them loose without any after supervision, and it would be as well if you cut their jugular veins in the first place." Hiram H. Giles, added, "They are wild as Mexican mustangs, and they should be treated as such. The first thing should be to corral them and teach them to be obedient."[39]

In a rare public criticism of a fellow "apprenticing agency" (undoubtedly referring to the CAS), Ebenezer Wright called out the lax supervision he perceived to be an issue in a statement he made in connection with the National Conference of Charities and Correction, in 1885. He said that during the previous thirty years the New York Juvenile Asylum had placed out 4,285 children in Illinois:

> The beneficence of an apprenticing agency is not attested by the number of children which it disposes of. It is not quantity, but quality, that determines the real excellence of its work. It would be an easy matter for us to place a thousand children annually in homes, in the Western States, if nothing more than that were required. But, of all the outrages that have been perpetrated in the name of Christian charity, none is more reprehensible than that of leaving helpless children without recourse in such situations. That this is not an extravagant assertion could be proved from the experience of this agency during almost any single week in its history.[40]

Wright had previously expressed a very similar opinion in an 1872 report to NYJA directors:

> Not a month goes by that does not furnish cases where, but for timely attention, suffering, mischief, and irreparable evil would result. A little familiarity with the field work of this agency would convince its most obdurate opponent that to leave helpless children without recourse among strangers in a strange land is an unjustifiable procedure.[41]

The increasing social outcry against placing-out resulted in a law being passed in New York in 1898 prescribing more follow-up and supervision.[42]

Many states began passing laws that either forbade the placement of orphans within their borders from out of state, or required placement agencies to put up bonds, usually for $1,000, to ensure that the agency would immediately remove, in the words of an Iowa bond from 1907, "any child having contagious or incurable disease, or having any deformity or being of feeble mind, or of vicious character [or] any child [...] which shall become a public charge within the period of five years." Michigan had been the first to pass such a law, in 1895. The states of Indiana, Illinois, and Minnesota followed suit in 1899, with Missouri and Nebraska two years later.[43]

The wording of the Illinois law was similar to that of Iowa, stating that no child "having any deformity, or being of feeble mind, or of vicious character, shall be placed in any family home within the boundaries of the State of Illinois by any association which is incorporated under the laws of any other State."[44]

In 1900, the Asylum fought a high-profile case regarding the indenturing of children in Illinois. Giuseppe Billotti, a cheese dealer in New York City, surrendered his three children, James, Annie, and Rosie to the Asylum in 1897 for the standard two years, but the children were subsequently sent to Iroquois County, Illinois, and indentured.

When the two-year period expired, Mr. Billotti went to pick up his children and was "dumbfounded when informed at the asylum that the children were no longer there." Their indentures were still in full force in Illinois, having been signed just eighteen months earlier.

Billotti took immediate legal action. "White slavery, that's what it amounts to," declared Michael J. Scanlan, counsel for the Society of St. Vincent De Paul, who was representing the Plaintiff.[45]

Justice Lawrence of the New York Supreme Court, in the case of People vs. New York Juvenile Asylum (66 New York Supp., 158), handed down his decision on the case in October 1900:

> Under a voluntary surrender by the father of the three children mentioned in the petition to the New York Juvenile Asylum for the period of two years, within a few months after such surrender the asylum assumed to apprentice such children to certain parties in the State of Illinois: the girls until they were eigh-

Chapter Nine

teen years of age, and the boy until he should become twenty-one years of age. This is conceded by the counsel for the respondents in his brief. And the position is taken that there is no difference between the case of a child who has been voluntarily surrendered for a limited period and one who has been committed to such asylum by a police magistrate. This position is untenable. A voluntary surrender for a limited period clearly does not confer power upon the asylum to indenture the child beyond that period and during the entire time of its minority, as has been done in this case.[46]

He closed by ordering NYJA officials to produce the children in twenty days. A newspaper reported that the Asylum had the three children returned to the father, but then, "in the course of three days they spirited the boy away to Illinois once more, but fortunately failed to get the girls who will not under any consideration leave their father."

The Asylum appealed Justice Lawrence's decision to the Appellate Division of the New York Supreme Court. Affidavits from Charles S. Wright (son of indenturing agent Ebenezer Wright) and James W. Shields, western indenturing agents for the Asylum, were presented to the Court. Shields' affidavit states:

> JAMES W. SHIELDS, being duly sworn, on his oath deposes and says that he is a resident of Chicago, County of Cook in the State of Illinois. That he is by occupation Western agent of the New York Juvenile Asylum. That he visited Rosie, Annie and James Billotti in their homes with Joseph McIntosh, Charles A. Lawhead and James Hasbrouck, respectively, all residing in the Iroquois County, State of Illinois, and did then and there while at each individual home make demand first upon the guardian for the custody of the children, and each and every guardian refused to permit me to take the children or to have the indenture cancelled: second: upon each and every one of the Billotti children aforementioned [asked] that they return with me to New York City, and they did each and every one absolutely refuse to go to the aforesaid New York City, and from observation and the testimony of neighbors he believes that each of the aforesaid children have good homes, kind guardians and are taken into the homes and hearts of their guardians as one of their own children, and further this deponent sayeth not.

Letters from the Billotti girls were also presented:

> To the Supreme Court of the State of New York:
>
> I am eleven years old. Have been going to school since September 1st, 1899, and learning very fast. I am well contented and happy, and do not want to leave my home with Mr. Lawhead. I am writing this letter and saying these of my own free will and account. Respectfully, Annie Billotti. Gilman, Iroquois Co., Ill.

> To the New York State Supreme Court, New York:
>
> I desire to say that I am perfectly contented with my home and will not return to my father unless I am compelled to do so. I am well taken care of and happy. This statement is in my own handwriting and made of my own free will and accord. I am nine years old. Respectfully, Rosie Billotti.

Joseph Billotti submitted the following statement in his defense:

> That the said imprisonment and detention of said children from petitioner is illegal, because during the month of September, 1897, and shortly after the death of the mother of said children, the said children were surrendered by petitioner to the care of said asylum

in New York City, for a period of two years, which period has expired and your petitioner before said children were sent to said persons in Illinois by said asylum, protested against such action being taken, but his protests were disregarded by the officers of the said asylum.

The Appellate Court considered all the testimony and handed down its decision on January 25, 1901, ruling in favor of the Asylum:

> That in the Billotti case the New York Juvenile Association [sic] proved to the satisfaction of the court that it was impossible for them to get the children; and for that reason the lower court should not make an order that could not be obeyed as the writ of habeus corpus was never intended to be used as a means of punishment in such circumstances. [47]

The change in attitudes, coupled with the implementation of new foster care laws, proved to be the beginning of the end for America's orphan trains. Social workers believed that it was more beneficial to allow a child to remain with his or her birth parents and siblings, or with a member of the extended family, if at all possible. Their sentiments were echoed by officials, all the way up to the president of the United States.

A significant change in national policy took place after President Theodore Roosevelt arranged for a White House Conference on the Care of Dependent Children on January 25 and 26, 1909. It was just six weeks before Roosevelt retired from the presidency. The Conference was attended by more than two hundred of the most prominent figures in American child welfare and social work. NYJA President Mornay Williams was one of the invited speakers at the Conference, as was Dr. Hastings H. Hart who headed the ICHAS that helped facilitate placements and visitation of children from the Asylum in western homes after the closing of the Asylum's Western Agency.

The 1909 Conference could indeed be regarded as the birth of modern child welfare. In direct reference to the policies of children's aid societies, a report following the Conference declared:

> Home life is the highest and finest product of civilization. It is the great motive force of mind and character. Children of parents of worthy character, suffering from temporary misfortune, and children of reasonably efficient and deserving mothers who are without the support of the normal breadwinner, should, as a rule, be kept with their parents, such aid being given as may be necessary to maintain suitable homes for the rearing of children. [...] Except in unusual circumstances the home should not be broken up for reasons of poverty, but only for considerations of inefficiency or immorality.[48]

The report continued with another rejection of the placing-out policy:

> Such homes should be selected by a most careful process of investigation, carried on by skilled agents through personal investigation and with due regard to the religious faith of the child. After children are placed in homes, adequate visitation with careful consideration of the physical, mental, moral, and spiritual training and development of each child on the part of the responsible home finding agency, is essential.[49]

In a move that potentially curbed the flow of children into New York's institutions sending children west on orphan trains, the New York Legislature enacted a statute in 1910 that held parents in stricter accountability for the proper care and training of their children:

> Chapter 699 of the Laws of 1910 provides that "a parent, guardian or other person hav-

You are cordially invited to be present
at the session of the

Conference on the Care of Dependent Children

called by

President Theodore Roosevelt

to be held at eight o'clock

Monday evening, January twenty-fifth
nineteen hundred and nine

at the

New Willard Hotel

and also at the Subscription Dinner and final session of the
Conference, to be held at the same place at eight o'clock
Tuesday evening, January twenty-sixth,
nineteen hundred and nine

Please reply on enclosed cards
Admission by Ticket

SEE INSERT

Invitation to the Conference on the Care of Dependent Children called by President Theodore Roosevelt in January 1909. (*Library of Congress/ https://www.loc.gov/item/rbpe.2400200a/*)

THESE TWO SESSIONS HAVE BEEN ARRANGED BY THE COMMITTEE IN CHARGE, MESSRS HOMER FOLKS, THOMAS M. MULRY AND JAMES E. WEST, WITH THE APPROVAL OF PRESIDENT ROOSEVELT, WITH A VIEW TO AFFORDING TO AS MANY AS POSSIBLE OF THOSE DIRECTLY INTERESTED, AN OPPORTUNITY OF HEARING THE VIEWS OF SOME OF THOSE ATTENDING THE CONFERENCE ON THE SUBJECTS TO BE CONSIDERED.

AT THE SESSION MONDAY EVENING IT IS EXPECTED THAT THE SPEAKERS WILL BE AS FOLLOWS:-

HON. H. B. F. MACFARLAND
RABBI EMIL G. HIRSCH
RT. REV. D. J. McMAHON
MISS JANE ADDAMS
MR. DAVID F. TILLEY
DR. HASTINGS H. HART
DR. BOOKER T. WASHINGTON

THE SESSION TUESDAY EVENING WILL BE A SUBSCRIPTION DINNER AT $3.00 PER PLATE. AT THIS DINNER THE REPORT OF THE CONFERENCE WILL BE PRESENTED TO PRESIDENT ROOSEVELT WHO WILL REPLY THERETO. OTHER SPEAKERS ARE EXPECTED TO BE AS FOLLOWS:-

MISS LILLIAN D. WALD
MR. MORNAY WILLIAMS
HON. HERBERT A. PARSONS
REV. FRANCIS H. GAVISK
HON. HERMAN A. METZ
JUDGE BEN. B. LINDSEY
JUDGE JULIAN W. MACK

MAKE CHECKS PAYABLE TO
JOHN B. SLEMAN, JR.,
TREASURER, BANQUET COMMITTEE.

Schedule for the Conference on the Care of Dependent Children called by President Theodore Roosevelt in 1909. Two men associated with the NYJA (Mornay Williams and Dr. Hastings H. Hart), and one woman (Miss Lillian D. Wald), were invited speakers. were invited speakers. (*Library of Congress/ https://www.loc.gov/item/rbpe.2400200a/*)

ing custody of a child actually or apparently under sixteen years of age, who omits to exercise reasonable diligence in the control of such child to prevent such child from becoming guilty of juvenile delinquency as defined by statute, or from becoming adjudged by a Children's Court in need of the care and protection of the State as defined by statute, or who permits such a child to associate with vicious, immoral or criminal persons, or to grow up in idleness, or to beg or solicit alms [...] shall be guilty of a misdemeanor.[50]

The Illinois Legislature, which had wholeheartedly passed the Act in 1861 recognizing the indentures of the New York Juvenile Asylum, eventually joined the chorus of other states in their condemnation of the practice. In 1915, the Illinois Legislature launched a joint committee investigation of placing out and found the practice to be "unwarranted, illegal, and uncharitable," likening it to slavery. The committee not only condemned the placement of eastern children in Illinois, but also the placement of Illinois' resident children in other states and foreign countries.[51]

The *Chicago Tribune* questioned its morality: "The practice of indenturing children, it is obvious, invites abuse," the paper observed in an editorial, and cited a recent federal report that had found children in Wisconsin "in homes which were filthy, in which parents were incompetent, ignorant, immoral or drunken; children were found cruelly treated, overworked, neglected physically, mentally and morally and deprived of schooling. Some homes combined many of these disqualifications."[52]

It is estimated that around two hundred thousand children were placed on orphan trains in the seventy-five year span between 1854 and 1929, in what is now called America's orphan train movement. Historians believe that nearly two million Americans descend from these orphan train riders.[53] Such a mass migration of children assured that the orphan trains would forever be a part of America's social history and folklore. The practice of placing out also proved to be an important step in the evolution of child welfare in America, laying the groundwork for the present-day foster care system.

The New York Juvenile Asylum reported that the total number of children it sent west between 1854 and 1903 was 6,362.[54] The number of children it sent west in subsequent years slowly decreased until only one was sent in each of the years 1921 and 1922. The Asylum reported that there were just ten children left under its supervision in western homes as of December 31, 1921.[55]

By the time it stopped sending children west, including those sent under the arrangement with the ICHAS and the CAS, the NYJA had contributed approximately 6,620 children to America's Orphan Train Movement.[56]

In the Asylum's annual report for the year 1921 it proudly proclaimed, "Our records indicate that of five thousand boys placed in western homes after a two years training here and supervised until they reached their majority, ninety-one per cent have lived within the law and become good and respectable citizens."[57]

The CAS sent three boys on an orphan train to Sulfur Springs, Texas, on May 31, 1929 on what is generally considered America's last orphan train—effectively ending America's Orphan Train Movement.[58]

As of December 31, 1921, no less than 43,757 children had been admitted to the New York Juvenile Asylum since its incorporation.[59]

The Children's Village is still in operation to this day, nestled in the hills at Dobbs Ferry, where they continue working "in partnership with families to help society's most vulnerable children so that they become educationally proficient, economically productive, and socially responsible members of their communities."

APPENDIX A

Superintendents of the NYJA and The Children's Village

Superintendents of the NYJA/The Children's Village during America's orphan train movement:[1]

1851 to 1858—John D. Russ, M.D. (also Secretary)
1858 to 1871—Samuel D. Brooks, M.D. (also Physician)
1871 to 1896—Elisha M. Carpenter (elected April 1st)
1896—Aaron P. Garrabrant, A.M. (acting)
1897 to 1902—Charles E. Bruce, M.D.
1902 to April 15, 1909—Charles Dewey Hilles
1909 to June 1, 1924—Guy Morgan
June 1, 1924 to 1941—Col. Leon Faulkner

APPENDIX B

Presidents of the NYJA and The Children's Village

Presidents of the Board of the NYJA/The Children's Village during America's orphan train movement:[2]

1851 to 1854—Luther Bradish
1854 to 1881—Apollos R. Wetmore
1881 to 1894—Ezra M. Kingsley
1894 to 1897—Frederick W. Devoe
1897 to 1910—Mornay Williams
1910 to 1916—Charles Dewey Hilles
1916 to 1920—William S. Hawk
1920 to ____—Edmund Dwight

APPENDIX C

Directors of the NYJA and The Children's Village

Directors of the NYJA up to 1921:[3]

Last Name	First Name	Year Elected	Year Died	Year Resigned
Adams	John T.	1855	1881	
Adams	Charles D.	1872	1889	
Agnew	Andrew Gifford	1886		1900
Agnew	George B.	1915		
Allen	Horatio	1851		1855
Astor	John Jacob, Jr.	1856		1859
Baker	Josiah W.	1872		1882
Barrow	James T.	1890		1918
Bigelow	Richard	1854	1863	
Bishop	Nathan	1865		1867
Bonney	Benjamin W.	1867		1868
Bradish	Luther	Original Corporator		1858
Brown	Stewart	Original Corporator		1852
Brown	James	1852		1853
Brown	William Harman	1886		1894
Bryan	John A.	1858		1868
Bulkley	Charles A.	1857	1886	
Butler	Benjamin F., Sr.	Original Corporator		1858
Butler	Benjamin F., Jr.	1858	1884	
Butler	Willard Parker	1900		1909
Byers	John	1879	1888	
Bayes	William R.	1918		

Last Name	First Name	Year Elected	Year Died	Year Resigned
Carter	Peter D.	1874		1895
Chapin	Henry, M. D.	1896		1918
Collins	Joseph B.	Original Corporator	1867	
Collins	George C.	1865		1866
Cooper	Peter	Original Corporator	1883	
Coates	Joseph H.	1865	1888	
Crolius	Clarkson	1851	1887	
Curtis	Cyrus	1852		1852
Cushman	James S.	1906		1914
Davenport	John	1853		1854
Dana	Richard P.	1866		1882
Denny	Thomas, Sr.	1852	1874	
Denny	Thomas, Jr.	1870		1879
Devoe	Frederick W.	1889		1903
Dorman	Richard A.	1891		1902
Dowd	William	1881		1895
Duer	John	Original Corporator	1857	
Dwight	Edmund, Sr.	1853		1893
Dwight	Theodore W.	1863		1874
Dwight	Edmund	1893		
Day	Joseph P.	1920		
Edmonds	John W.	Original Corporator		1853
Ely	Charles	1852		1853
Ewing	Thomas	1906		
Field	Frank Harvey	1903		1918
Fisk	Wilbur C.	1906		
Gallaway	Robert M.	1892		1894
Garth	Horace E.	1886		1900
Geissenhainer	Frederick W., Jr.	1865		1879
Gilbert	Albert	Original Corporator	1858	
Gilman	William C., Sr.	1851	1863	
Gilman	William C., Jr.	1864		1877
Gibson	Isaac	1855	1860	
Goeller	Robert	1910	1910	
Goodrich	Samuel G., 2nd	1859		1865

Last Name	First Name	Year Elected	Year Died	Year Resigned
Gould	E. R. L.	1904	1915	
Graham	John A.	1865		1867
Green	Andrew H.	1878	1903	
Gregory	Henry E.	1895		
Griggs	Maitland F.	1910		
Gould	J. W. DuBois	1920		
Hammond	John H.	1915		1917
Hartley	Robert Milham	1853		1868
Hartley	Joseph W.	1895	1905	
Havens	Rensselaer N.	Original Corporator	1876	
Hadden	Alexander, M. D.	1896		1901
Hadden	Alexander M.	1902		
Hawk	William S.	1895		Term exp'd Jan. 1896
Hawk	William S.	Re-elected 1910		1919
Herring	Silas C.	Original Corporator		1855
Hills	Henry F.	1875		1879
Hilles	Charles Dewey	1909		
Hopper	Isaac T.	Original Corporator	1852	
Holden	Daniel J.	1879		1895
Humphrey	Henry M.	1889		1899
Hurry	Randolph	1895		
Jenner	Solomon	Original Corporator		1861
Jesup	Charles M.	1906		1920
Jesup	Richard M.	1916		1918
Johnson	John E.	1868		1874
Joy	Joseph F.	1861	1891	
Kelly	James	Original Corporator		1853
Kennedy	David S.	Original Corporator		1852
Kingsley	Ezra M.	1861		1894
Kingsley	William M.	1894		1895
King	William V.	1882		1885
Kirkbride	Franklin B.	1918		1919
Lambert	William	1893		1894
Lockwood	Joseph B.	1882	1893	
Lockwood	Roe	1856		1858

Last Name	First Name	Year Elected	Year Died	Year Resigned
Lovell	Leander N.	1872		1879
Lowery	John	1858		1861
Lunger	John B.	1913	1919	
Low	Benjamin R. C.	1920		
McNeir	George	1912		1917
Marling	Alfred E.	1892		1909
Marling	Alfred E.	Re-elected in 1918		
Miller	Walter T.	1867		1869
Minturn	Robert B.	Original Corporator		1852
Morrison	James M.	1867		1869
Moulton	Franklin W.	1896		1901
Newbold	Clayton	1856		1865
O'Conor	Charles	Original Corporator		1854
Opdycke	Leonard E.	1901		1906
Parkin	William W.	1854		1857
Partridge	Charles	Original Corporator	1885	
Peck	Charles C.	1876		1894
Plummer	John F.	1888		1890
Powel	Robert J. H.	1920		
Quincy	John W.	1858	1888	
Redfield	James S.	1853		1854
Robb	J. Hampden	1889		1892
Russ	John D., M. D.	Original Corporator		1853
Roe	Frank O.	1921		
Schwab	Gustav H.	1887		1900
Sherman	Benjamin B.	1879		1885
Sherman	William Watts	1900		1902
Slade	John M.	1877		1888
Slade	Francis Louis	1903		1917
Smith	Orison B.	1894		1902
Smith	William W.	1906	1906	
Speer	Robert E.	1902		1914
Strong	William K.	1855		1856
Strong	Theron G.	1885		1901
Stokes	Anson G. P.	1869		1872

Last Name	First Name	Year Elected	Year Died	Year Resigned
Stokes	J. G. Phelps	1902		1906
Stratton	Robert M.	Original Corporator		1852
Sutton	George D.	1868		1872
Sweetser	Joseph A.	1874	1874	
Talmadge	Henry	1872		1903
Talbert	Joseph T.	1915		1918
Taylor	William B.	1883	1899	
Tifft	Henry N.	1891		
Tillon	Francis R.	Original Corporator		1865
Townsend	Howard	1898		1905
Trow	John F.	1868	1886	
Truax	John G., M. D.	1896	1898	
Van Amringe	Guy	1906		
Van Schaick	Myndert	Original Corporator		1852
Van Wagenen	William F.	1861		1865
Vermilye	Jacob D.	1881	1892	
Verplanck	William E.	1901		
Ward	Lebbeus B.	1852		1865
Ward	John Seely	1894		1916
Warren	Charles Elliot	1917		
Wetmore	Apollos R.	Original Corporator	1881	
Wemple	Christopher Y.	Original Corporator		1859
Wendell	Evert Jansen	1900		1905
Wheelock	William E., M. D.	1883		1892
Williams	Leighton	1883		1887
Williams	Mornay	1887		1909
Winston	Frederick S.	Original Corporator		1855
Wolcott	Frederick H.	1852		1856
Worth	J. L.	1853		1856
Wood	Oliver E.	1857	1883	
Woodhouse	Lorenzo G.	1889		1900
Wyckoff	J. Edwards	1918		
Wilcox	William G.	1918		

APPENDIX D

Matrons of the NYJA, The Children's Village, and the House of Reception

Matrons up to 1921:[4]

	Asylum (Children's Village from 1905 forward)			House of Reception		
Year	Last Name	First Name	Title	Last Name	First Name	Title
1860	Unknown	Unknown	Matron	Bush	Mrs. Irena A.	Matron
1861	Appley	Mrs. Emma A.	Matron	Bush	Mrs. Irena A.	Matron
1862	Appley	Mrs. Emma A.	Matron	Curthworth	Catharine	Girl's Matron
1863	Appley	Mrs. Emma A.	Matron	Curthworth	Catharine	Girl's Matron
1864	Appley	Mrs. Emma A.	Matron	Sell	Fannie J.	Girl's Matron
1865	Appley	Mrs. Emma A.	Matron	Shaw	Amelia	Girl's Matron
1866	Appley	Mrs. Emma A.	Matron	Schultz	Miss Ruthella	Girl's Matron
1867	Appley	Mrs. Emma A.	Matron	Shaw	Amelia	Girl's Matron
1868	Appley	Mrs. Emma A.	Matron	Shaw	Amelia	Girl's Matron
1869	Appley	Mrs. Emma A.	Matron	Shaw	Amelia	Girl's Matron
1870	Appley	Mrs. Emma A.	Matron	Libbey	Mrs. Nellie M.	Matron
1871	Appley	Mrs. Emma A.	Matron	Shaw	Amelia	Girl's Matron
1872	Dunlap	Mrs. N. J.	Matron of Cultural Dept.	Unknown	Unknown	Girl's Matron*
1873	Dunlap	Mrs. N. J.	Matron of Cultural Dept.			Vacant position
1874	Dunlap	Mrs. N. J.	Matron of Cultural Dept.	Carpenter	Mrs. J. C.	Matron
1875	Dunlap	Mrs. N. J.	Title listed as "Teacher"	Carpenter	Mrs. J. C.	Matron
1880	Price	Miss S. M.	Matron of Girl's Dept.			Vacant position
1881	Price	Miss S. M.	Matron of Girl's Dept.			Vacant position
1882	Price	Miss S. M.	Matron of Girl's Dept.			Vacant position
1883	Price	Miss S. M.	Matron of Girl's Dept.			Vacant position

	Asylum (Children's Village from 1905 forward)			**House of Reception**		
Year	Last Name	First Name	Title	Last Name	First Name	Title
1884	Dick	Miss E. A.	Matron of Girl's Dept.			Vacant position
1885	Dick	Miss E. A.	Matron of Girl's Dept.			Vacant position
1886	Dick	Miss E. A.	Matron of Girl's Dept.			Vacant position
1887	Dick	Miss E. A.	Matron of Girl's Dept.	MacDonald	H. M.	Girl's Matron
1888	Dick	Miss E. A.	Matron of Girl's Dept.	MacDonald	H. M.	Girl's Matron
1889	Dick	Miss Emily	Matron of Girl's Dept.	MacDonald	H. M.	Girl's Matron
1890	La Bruce	Miss E. L.	Matron of Girl's Dept.	MacDonald	H. M.	Girl's Matron
1891	La Bruce	Miss E. L.	Matron of Girl's Dept.	MacDonald	H. M.	Girl's Matron
1892	La Bruce	Miss E. L.	Matron of Girl's Dept.	MacDonald	H. M.	Girl's Matron
1893	Weaver	Miss C. L.	Matron of Girl's Dept.	MacDonald	H. M.	Girl's Matron
1894	Miles	Miss Emma V.	Matron of Girl's Dept.	Ferdon	Miss Edna	Girl's Matron
1895	Miles	Miss Emma V.	Matron of Girl's Dept.	Ferdon	Miss Edna	Girl's Matron
1896	Miles	Miss Emma V.	Matron of Girl's Dept.	Ferdon	Miss Edna	Girl's Matron
1897	Miles	Miss Emma V.	Matron of Girl's Dept.	Ferdon	Miss Edna	Girl's Matron
1898	Miles	Miss Emma V.	Matron of Girl's Dept.	Ferdon	Miss Edna	Girl's Matron
1899	Miles	Miss Emma V.	Matron of Girl's Dept.	Ferdon	Miss Edna	Girl's Matron
1900	Miles	Miss Emma V.	Matron of Girl's Dept.	Ferdon	Miss Edna	Girl's Matron
1901	Miles	Miss Emma V.	Matron of Girl's Dept.	Ferdon	Miss Edna	Girl's Matron
1902	Miles	Miss Emma V.	Matron of Girl's Dept.	Ferguson	Miss W. K.	Matron
1903	Colburn	Miss Elizabeth T.	Matron of Girl's Dept.	Ferguson	Miss M. K.	Matron
1904	Colburn	Miss Elizabeth T.	Matron of Girl's Dept.	Ferguson	Miss M. K.	Matron
1905	Black	Mrs. Joseph	Matron Cooper Cottage	Webber	Mrs. R. T.	Matron
	Bleekman	Miss K. O.	Matron Stuart Cottage			
	Hosler	Mrs. C. O.	Matron Kingsley Cottage			
	Iles	Mrs. Belle S.	Matron Lenox Cottage			
	Johnson	Miss S. M.	Relief Matron			
	Lyle	Mrs. A. J.	Matron Green Cottage			
	Pollard	Mrs. E. L.	Matron Rose Cottage			
	Sheffold	Mrs. George	Matron Hartley Cottage			
	Van Brunt	Mrs. E. M.	Relief Matron			
	West	Miss Cornelia B.	Matron Willetts Cottage			
1906	Bleekman	Miss K. O.	Matron Stuart Cottage	Sackey	Mrs. E. A.	Matron
	Colvin	Mrs. E. F.	Matron Russ Cottage			
	Couper	Mrs. Henry J.	Matron Bradish Cottage			

	Asylum (Children's Village from 1905 forward)			House of Reception		
Year	Last Name	First Name	Title	Last Name	First Name	Title
	Davis	Mrs. Lelah	Acting Matron Willetts Cottage			
	Dick	Miss Eliza	Matron Scholes Cottage			
	Edwards	Miss Henrietta	Matron Butler Cottage			
	Ferdon	Miss Edna	Matron Dwight Cottage			
	Halsey	Miss Ada	Matron Howard Cottage			
	Hosler	Mrs. C. O.	Matron Kingsley Cottage			
	Iles	Mrs. Belle S.	Matron Lenox Cottage			
	Johnson	Miss S. M.	Relief Matron			
	Lyle	Mrs. A. J.	Matron Green Cottage			
	Pollard	Mrs. E. L.	Matron Rose Cottage			
	Sheffold	Mrs. George	Matron Hartley Cottage			
	Somers	Miss Sophia	Matron Collins Cottage			
	Stewart	Mrs. T. M.	Matron Cooper Cottage			
	Van Brunt	Mrs. E. M.	Relief Matron			
1907	Alvord	Miss Franc	Matron Howard Cottage	Sackey	Mrs. E. A.	Matron
	Bleekman	Miss K. O.	Matron Stuart Cottage			
	Colvin	Mrs. E. F.	Matron Russ Cottage			
	Couper	Mrs. Henry J.	Matron Bradish Cottage			
	Dick	Miss Eliza	Matron Scholes Cottage			
	Edwards	Miss Henrietta	Matron Butler Cottage			
	Hosler	Mrs. C. O.	Matron Kingsley Cottage			
	Iles	Mrs. Belle S.	Matron Lenox Cottage			
	Lenhart	Miss May	Matron Willetts Cottage			
	Lyle	Mrs. A. J.	Matron Green Cottage			
	Pollard	Mrs. E. L.	Matron Rose Cottage			
	Riggin	Mrs. Fannie	Matron Dwight Cottage			
	Sheffold	Mrs. George	Matron Hartley Cottage			
	Somers	Miss Sophia	Matron Collins Cottage			
	Stewart	Mrs. T. M.	Matron Cooper Cottage			
	Van Brunt	Mrs. E. M.	Relief Matron			
1908	Alvord	Miss Franc	Matron Howard Cottage	Sackey	Mrs. E. A.	Matron
	Bleekman	Miss K. O.	Matron Stuart Cottage			
	Colvin	Mrs. E. F.	Matron Russ Cottage			
	Davis	Mrs. Lelah	Matron "S" Cottage			

Asylum (Children's Village from 1905 forward)				House of Reception		
Year	Last Name	First Name	Title	Last Name	First Name	Title
	Dick	Miss Eliza	Matron Scholes Cottage			
	Edwards	Miss Henrietta	Matron Butler Cottage			
	Hosler	Mrs. C. O.	Matron Kingsley Cottage			
	Iles	Mrs. Belle S.	Matron Lenox Cottage			
	Lawyer	Mrs. Glen A.	Matron Bradish Cottage			
	Lenhart	Miss May	Matron Willetts Cottage			
	Lyle	Mrs. A. J.	Matron Green Cottage			
	Mills	Miss Ella B.	Matron "T" Cottage			
	Pollard	Mrs. E. L.	Matron Rose Cottage			
	Rector	Mrs. Walter	Relief Matron			
	Riggin	Mrs. Fannie	Matron Dwight Cottage			
	Sheffold	Mrs. George	Matron Hartley Cottage			
	Somers	Miss Sophia	Marton Collins Cottage			
	Stewart	Mrs. T. M.	Matron Cooper Cottage			
1909	Alvord	Miss Franc	Matron Howard Cottage	Sackey	Mrs. E. A.	Matron
	Bleekman	Miss K. O.	Matron Stuart Cottage			
	Colvin	Mrs. E. F.	Matron Russ Cottage			
	Davis	Miss Bessie	Matron Butler Cottage			
	Davis	Mrs. Lelah	Matron "S" Cottage			
	Dick	Miss Eliza	Matron Scholes Cottage			
	Edwards	Miss Henrietta	Matron "U" Cottage			
	Honeyman	Miss Caroline K.	Matron Willetts Cottage			
	Hosler	Mrs. C. O.	Matron Kingsley Cottage			
	Lawyer	Mrs. Glen A.	Matron Bradish Cottage			
	Lyle	Mrs. A. J.	Matron Green Cottage			
	Mills	Miss Ella B.	Matron "T" Cottage			
	Payne	Miss Charlotte	Relief Matron			
	Pollard	Mrs. E. L.	Matron Rose Cottage			
	Rector	Mrs. Walter	Matron "W" Cottage			
	Riggin	Mrs. Fannie	Matron Dwight Cottage			
	Scheurman	Miss Mary T.	Matron Lenox Cottage			
	Sheffold	Mrs. George	Matron Hartley Cottage			
	Somers	Miss Sophia	Matron Collins Cottage			
	Stewart	Mrs. T. M.	Matron Cooper Cottage			
	Sweyer	Miss Minnie	Relief Matron			

Asylum (Children's Village from 1905 forward)				House of Reception		
Year	Last Name	First Name	Title	Last Name	First Name	Title
1910	Alvord	Miss Franc	Matron Howard Cottage	Sackey	Mrs. E. A.	Matron
	Baker	Mrs. Joseph	Matron "V" Cottage			
	Bleekman	Miss K. O.	Matron Stuart Cottage			
	Colvin	Mrs. E. F.	Matron Russ Cottage			
	Cox	Mrs. Henry	Matron Bradish Cottage			
	Daly	Miss May	Relief Matron			
	Davis	Miss Bessie	Matron Butler Cottage			
	Davis	Mrs. Lelah	Matron "S" Cottage			
	Edwards	Miss Henrietta	Matron "U" Cottage			
	Honeyman	Miss Caroline K.	Matron Willetts Cottage			
	Hosler	Mrs. C. O.	Matron Kingsley Cottage			
	Lyle	Mrs. A. J.	Matron Green Cottage			
	Mills	Miss Ella B.	Matron "T" Cottage			
	Pollard	Mrs. E. L.	Matron Rose Cottage			
	Rector	Mrs. Walter	Matron "W" Cottage			
	Riggin	Mrs. Fannie	Matron Dwight Cottage			
	Rose	Mrs. H. E.	Matron "A" Cottage			
	Scheurman	Miss Mary T.	Matron Lenox Cottage			
	Sheffold	Mrs. George	Matron Hartley Cottage			
	Somers	Miss Sophia	Matron Collins Cottage			
	Stewart	Mrs. T. M.	Matron Cooper Cottage			
	Sweyer	Miss Minnie	Matron "X" Cottage			
	Van Pelt	Miss Camilla	Matron Scholes Cottage			
	Worrall	Mrs. Fred	Matron "B" Cottage			
1911	Abrams	Miss Elizabeth	Matron Dwight Cottage	Sackey	Mrs. E. A.	Matron
	Alvord	Miss Franc	Matron Howard Cottage			
	Baker	Mrs. Joseph	Matron "V" Cottage			
	Brown	Mrs. George	Matron Bradish Cottage			
	Colvin	Mrs. E. F.	Matron Russ Cottage			
	Davis	Miss Bessie	Matron Butler Cottage			
	Davis	Mrs. Lelah	Matron "S" Cottage			
	Dermitt	Miss Jane	Matron Scholes Cottage			
	Edwards	Miss Henrietta	Matron "U" Cottage			
	Geer	Mrs. Joseph	Matron "A" Cottage			
	Grant	Mrs. Theodore W.	Matron Kingsley Cottage			

Asylum (Children's Village from 1905 forward)				House of Reception		
Year	Last Name	First Name	Title	Last Name	First Name	Title
	Hanaway	Mrs. Frank	Matron "C" Cottage			
	Honeyman	Miss Caroline K.	Matron Willetts Cottage			
	Krech	Miss Lucy	Matron Lenox Cottage			
	Lyle	Mrs. A. J.	Matron Green Cottage			
	McClintock	Mrs. C. E.	Matron Cooper Cottage			
	Mills	Miss Ella B.	Matron "T" Cottage			
	Pollard	Mrs. E. L.	Matron Rose Cottage			
	Richey	Mrs. Eugene	Matron "W" Cottage			
	Sells	Miss Ione B.	Matron Stuart Cottage			
	Sheffold	Mrs. George	Matron Hartley Cottage			
	Silvester	Miss Florence	Relief Matron			
	Somers	Miss Sophia	Matron Collins Cottage			
	Van Pelt	Miss Camilla	Matron "X" Cottage			
	Worrall	Mrs. Fred	Matron "B" Cottage			
1912	Abrams	Miss Elizabeth	Relief Matron	Sackey	Mrs. E. A.	Matron
	Anderson	Mrs. Pierson A.	Matron Howard Cottage			
	Baker	Mrs. Joseph	Matron "V" Cottage			
	Bower	Mrs. Isaac N.	Matron Stuart Cottage			
	Brown	Mrs. George M.	Matron "T" Cottage			
	Colvin	Mrs. E. F.	Matron Russ Cottage			
	Davis	Miss Bessie	Matron Butler Cottage			
	Davis	Mrs. Lelah	Matron Williams Cottage			
	DeWees	Mrs. Roy H.	Matron "C" Cottage			
	Geer	Mrs. Joseph	Matron Lincoln Cottage			
	Grant	Mrs. Theodore W.	Matron Kingsley Cottage			
	Hilles	Miss Anne F.	Matron "U" Cottage			
	Honeyman	Miss Caroline K.	Matron Willetts Cottage			
	Krech	Miss Lucy	Matron Lenox Cottage			
	Lake	Mrs. William E.	Matron Dwight Cottage			
	Lyle	Mrs. A. J.	Matron Green Cottage			
	McClintock	Mrs. C. E.	Matron Cooper Cottage			
	McDonough	Mrs. George	Matron Scholes Cottage			
	Pollard	Mrs. E. L.	Matron Rose Cottage			
	Richey	Mrs. Eugene	Matron "W" Cottage			
	Sheffold	Mrs. George	Matron Hartley Cottage			

Appendix D

Asylum (Children's Village from 1905 forward)				House of Reception		
Year	Last Name	First Name	Title	Last Name	First Name	Title
	Somers	Miss Sophia	Matron Collins Cottage			
	Van Pelt	Miss Camilla	Matron "X" Cottage			
	Wilson	Mrs. James	Matron Bradish Cottage			
	Worrall	Mrs. Fred	Matron "B" Cottage			
1913	Abrams	Miss Elizabeth	Matron Brown Cottage	Sackey	Mrs. E. A.	Matron
	Baker	Mrs. Joseph	Matron Lord Cottage			
	Bower	Mrs. Isaac N.	Matron Stuart Cottage			
	Brown	Mrs. George M.	Matron Van Horn Cottage			
	Colvin	Mrs. E. F.	Matron Russ Cottage			
	Davis	Miss Bessie	Matron Butler Cottage			
	Davis	Mrs. Lelah	Matron Williams Cottage			
	Dunham	Mrs. E. W.	Matron Howard Cottage			
	Grant	Mrs. Theodore W.	Matron Kingsley Cottage			
	Hilles	Miss Anne F.	Matron Havens Cottage			
	Holt	Mrs. F. R.	Matron Dwight Cottage			
	Honeyman	Miss Caroline K.	Matron Willetts Cottage			
	Hood	Miss Katherine	Relief Matron			
	Humphries	Mrs. E. M.	Matron Scholes Cottage			
	Lyle	Mrs. Harry	Matron Lenox Cottage			
	Lyle	Mrs. A. J.	Matron Green Cottage			
	McClintock	Mrs. C. E.	Matron Cooper Cottage			
	McDonough	Mrs. George	Matron Lincoln Cottage			
	Pollard	Mrs. E. L.	Matron Rose Cottage			
	Richey	Mrs. Eugene	Matron Wolfe Cottage			
	Sheffold	Mrs. George	Matron Hartley Cottage			
	Somers	Miss Sophia	Matron Collins Cottage			
	Wilson	Mrs. James	Matron Bradish Cottage			
	Worrall	Mrs. Fred	Matron Fanshaw Cottage			
	Wright	Miss Grace	Matron Crolius Cottage			
1914	Baker	Mrs. Joseph	Matron Lord Cottage	Sackey	Mrs. E. A.	Matron
	Brown	Mrs. George M.	Matron Van Horn Cottage			
	Colvin	Mrs. E. F.	Matron Russ Cottage			
	Davis	Mrs. Lelah	Matron Williams Cottage			
	Dunham	Mrs. E. W.	Matron Howard Cottage			
	Hale	Miss Grace E.	Matron Butler Cottage			

Asylum (Children's Village from 1905 forward)				House of Reception		
Year	Last Name	First Name	Title	Last Name	First Name	Title
	Hilles	Miss Anne F.	Matron Havens Cottage			
	Holt	Mrs. F. R.	Matron Burr Cottage			
	Honeyman	Miss Caroline K.	Matron Willetts Cottage			
	Humphries	Mrs. E. M.	Matron Scholes Cottage			
	Lyle	Mrs. Harry	Matron Lenox Cottage			
	Lyle	Mrs. A. J.	Matron Green Cottage			
	McClintock	Mrs. C. E.	Matron Cooper Cottage			
	McClure	Mrs. E. W.	Matron Brown Cottage			
	Merrill	Mrs. J. M.	Matron Kingsley Cottage			
	Moore	Mrs. Orville	Matron Hartley Cottage			
	Pedersen	Mrs. Julius	Matron Stuart Cottage			
	Pollard	Mrs. E. L.	Matron Rose Cottage			
	Sheller	Mrs. John	Matron Lincoln Cottage			
	Somers	Miss Sophia	Matron Collins Cottage			
	Stockin	Mrs. Gordon	Matron Bradish Cottage			
	Virden	Mrs. Charles E.	Matron Dwight Cottage			
	Webster	Mrs. Vernon	Matron Wolfe Cottage			
	Wilson	Mrs. James	Matron Smith Cottage			
	Worrall	Mrs. Fred	Matron Fanshaw Cottage			
	Wright	Miss Grace	Matron Crolius Cottage			
1915	**			Unknown	Unknown	Matron
1916	Baker	Mrs. Joseph	Matron Lord Cottage	Sackey	Mrs. E. A.	Matron
	Brown	Mrs. George M.	Matron Van Horn Cottage			
	Colvin	Mrs. E. F.	Matron Havens Cottage			
	Davis	Mrs. Lelah	Matron Williams Cottage			
	Grant	Mrs. T. W.	Matron Kingsley Cottage			
	Guynne	Mrs. Harry	Matron Cooper Cottage			
	Hilles	Miss Anne F.	Matron Minturn Cottage			
	Holt	Mrs. F. R.	Matron Burr Cottage			
	Honeyman	Miss Caroline K.	Matron Willetts Cottage			
	Humphries	Mrs. E. M.	Matron Scholes Cottage			
	Lyle	Mrs. Harry	Matron Green Cottage			
	McClure	Mrs. E. W.	Matron Brown Cottage			
	Miller	Mrs. Lilly	Matron Collins Cottage			
	Morgan	Mrs. Morgan	Matron Butler Cottage			

Asylum (Children's Village from 1905 forward)				House of Reception		
Year	Last Name	First Name	Title	Last Name	First Name	Title
	Morgan	Mrs. W. N.	Matron Stuart Cottage			
	Pollard	Mrs. E. L.	Matron Rose Cottage			
	Sharp	Mrs. G. E.	Matron Hartley Cottage			
	Sheller	Mrs. John	Matron Lincoln Cottage			
	Strohm	Mrs. Eugene	Matron Russ Cottage			
	Virden	Mrs. Charles E.	Matron Dwight Cottage			
	Wilson	Mrs. James	Matron Smith Cottage			
	Worrall	Mrs. Fred	Matron Fanshaw Cottage			
	Wright	Miss Grace	Matron Crolius Cottage			
1917	**			Unknown	Unknown	Matron
1918	Atkinson	Mrs. J. E.	Matron Collins Cottage	Sanborn	Mrs. A. O.	Matron
	Baker	Mrs. Joseph	Matron Lord Cottage			
	Barrows	Mrs. F. J.	Matron Howard Cottage			
	Beckwith	Mrs. John H.	Matron Green Cottage			
	Brewer	Mrs. Catherine	Matron Russ Cottage			
	Burkill	Mrs. James F.	Matron Rhinelander Cottage			
	Butcher	Mrs. John F.	Matron Hartley Cottage			
	Colvin	Mrs. E. F.	Matron Wolfe Cottage			
	Cookson	Mrs. John F.	Matron Havens Cottage			
	Davis	Mrs. Lelah	Matron Williams Cottage			
	Hilles	Miss Anne F.	Matron Minturn Cottage			
	Holt	Mrs. F. R.	Matron Burr Cottage			
	Honeyman	Miss Caroline K.	Matron Willetts Cottage			
	Humphreys	Mrs. E. M.	Matron Scholes Cottage			
	Irvine	Mrs. Gordon	Matron Rose Cottage			
	Jackson	Mrs. A. H.	Matron Lincoln Cottage			
	Karch	Mrs. O. H.	Matron Van Horn Cottage			
	Lawver	Mrs. H. M.	Matron Cooper Cottage			
	Leighton	Mrs. A. B.	Matron Brown Cottage			
	Lyle	Mrs. Harry	Matron Stuart Cottage			
	McClure	Mrs. E. W.	Matron Smith Cottage			
	Steward	Mrs. Thomas L.	Matron Dwight Cottage			
	Woodward	Mrs. Lyle	Matron Kingsley Cottage			
	Worrall	Mrs. Fred	Matron Fanshaw Cottage			
	Wright	Miss Grace	Matron Crolius Cottage			

	Asylum (Children's Village from 1905 forward)			**House of Reception**		
Year	Last Name	First Name	Title	Last Name	First Name	Title
1919	**			Unknown	Unknown	Matron
1920	Atkins	Mrs. Jessie	Matron Williams Cottage	Leininger	Mrs. Fred	Matron
	Atkinson	Mrs. Clare	Matron Howard Cottage			
	Boucher	Mrs. Wilfred	Matron Russ Cottage			
	Brown	Mrs. E. J.	Matron Wolfe Cottage			
	Burkill	Mrs. James F.	Matron Rhinelander Cottage			
	Cookson	Mrs. John F.	Matron Havens Cottage			
	Davis	Mrs. Lelah	Matron Smith Cottage			
	Frantz	Miss Alice M.	Matron Willetts Cottage			
	Grant	Mrs. Theodore W.	Matron Burr Cottage			
	Hilles	Miss Anne F.	Matron Minturn Cottage			
	Humphreys	Mrs. E. M.	Matron Scholes Cottage			
	Irvine	Mrs. Gordon	Matron Rose Cottage			
	Jackson	Mrs. A. H.	Matron Lincoln Cottage			
	Lawver	Mrs. H. M.	Matron Cooper Cottage			
	Lyle	Mrs. Harry H.	Matron Brown Cottage			
	Milligan	Mrs. C. S.	Matron Stuart Cottage			
	Plimpton	Mrs. George F.	Matron Lord Cottage			
	Riddle	Mrs. Grover	Matron Dwight Cottage			
	Robbins	Mrs. Floyd B.	Matron Butler Cottage			
	Smith	Mrs. Charles E.	Matron Kingsley Cottage			
	Waterfall	Mrs. Arthur	Matron Collins Cottage			
	Worrall	Mrs. Fred	Matron Fanshaw Cottage			
	Wright	Miss Grace	Matron Crolius Cottage			
1921	Atkinson	Mrs. Clare	Matron Howard Cottage	Pearson	Mrs. A.	Matron
	Barrows	Mrs. F. J.	Matron Wolfe Cottage			
	Boucher	Mrs. Wilfred	Matron Russ Cottage			
	Burkill	Mrs. James F.	Matron Rhinelander Cottage			
	Curry	Mrs. George	Matron Havens Cottage			
	Edwards	Mrs. Fred	Matron Butler Cottage			
	Frantz	Miss Alice M.	Matron Willetts Cottage			
	Hilles	Miss Anne F.	Matron Minturn Cottage			
	Humphreys	Mrs. E. M.	Matron Scholes Cottage			
	Hyatt	Mrs. George F.	Matron Kingsley Cottage			
	Irvine	Mrs. Gordon	Matron Rose Cottage			

Asylum (Children's Village from 1905 forward)				House of Reception		
Year	Last Name	First Name	Title	Last Name	First Name	Title
	Jackson	Mrs. A. H.	Matron Lincoln Cottage			
	Lawver	Mrs. H. M.	Matron Cooper Cottage			
	Lyle	Mrs. Harry H.	Matron Brown Cottage			
	MacKenzie	Mrs. Donald	Matron Lord Cottage			
	Merriman	Mrs. E. J.	Matron Burr Cottage			
	Milligan	Mrs. C. S.	Matron Stuart Cottage			
	Riddle	Mrs. Grover	Matron Dwight Cottage			
	Turner	Mrs. H. E.	Matron Hartley Cottage			
	Worrall	Mrs. Fred	Matron Fanshaw Cottage			
	Wright	Miss Grace	Matron Crolius Cottage			

*Position was intermitted in the Spring due to small number of admissions. Girls, if any, were sent to Asylum weekly.
**Unable to locate copy of Annual Report to verify.

APPENDIX E

County Agents of the NYJA

Men known to be NYJA county agents in Illinois:[5]

Last Name	First Name	City of Residence and County of Service
Barnes	M. A.	West Urbana (now Champaign), Champaign County, Illinois (1859)
Beasley	John S.	West Urbana (now Champaign), Champaign County, Illinois (1859)
Chase	Cyrus B.	Bellefame, Tazewell County, Illinois (Known agent 1856-62)
Clark	R. F.	Carrollton, Greene County, Illinois (Known agent in 1859)
Dickey	Alexander	Sparta, Randolph County, Illinois (Known agent in 1859)
Folsom	Mr. A.	Pana, Christian County, Illinois (Known agent in 1858-9)
Fry	Daniel	Middleport, Iroquois County, Illinois ("Agt." written after his name)
Henry	Samuel Y.	Nashville, Washington County, Illinois (Known agent in 1859-60)
Holmes	Hartley	Tolono, Champaign County, Illinois (Known agent 1859-60)
Hynes	Reverend Mr. Thomas W.	Greenville, Bond County, Illinois (Known agent in 1861-67)
Jenkins	Ezra	Vandalia, Fayette County, Illinois (Known agent circa 1860)
Johnson	John R.	State Line City, Warren County, Indiana (Known agent from Jan. 1860—circa 1864)
Jomu	G. B.	Middleport, Iroquois County, Illinois ("Cor." written after his name)
Kingsbury	Reverend Mr. Enoch	Danville, Vermilion County, Illinois (Known agent in 1860)
Koon	H. G.	Kankakee, Kankakee County, Illinois (Known agent in 1861-62)
Laird	Reverend Mr. [J. H. L.]	Carlyle, Clinton County, Illinois ("Cor." written after his name)
Lanchbaugh	Thomas P.	Mt. Pulaski, Logan County, Illinois
Lee	Mr.	Aurora, Kane County, Illinois ("Agt." written after his name)
Lillio or Lillie	Mr. [Daniel A.?]	Aurora, Kane County, Illinois ("Cor." written after his name).
Link	N. or F. M.	Paris, Edgar County, Illinois (Known agent in 1856)
Lockhart	James	Elkhorn, Washington County, Illinois (Known agent 1859-67)
Mapes	Reverend Mr. E. L.	Assisted E. Wright with company of kids to Decatur, IL Sept. 9, 1880

Last Name	First Name	City of Residence and County of Service
Murphy	Mr. J. H.	Bloomington, McLean County, Illinois (Known agent in 1888)
Palmer	Reverend Mr. [George R.]	Middleport, Iroquois County, Illinois ("Cor." written after his name)
Pyle	W. H. K.	Mattoon, Coles County, Illinois
Ritter	R.	Havana, Mason County, Illinois (Known agent 1857-58)
Scroggs	J. W.	West Urbana (now Champaign), Champaign County, Illinois (Known agent in July 1859)
Shannon	Captain S. P.	Bloomington, McLean County, Illinois (Known agent 1869-71)
Skidmore	A. B. [Bolivar]	Carlyle, Clinton County, Illinois (Agent in 1860)
Staples	Reverend Mr.	Kankakee, Kankakee County, Illinois ("Cor." written after his name)
Swannell	W. G.	Kankakee, Kankakee County, Illinois ("Agt." written after his name)
Thomas	Reverend Mr. E. J.	Atlanta, Logan County, Illinois (Agent in 1856)
Wilsey	Mr. [James S.?]	Bellefame or Pekin, Tazewell County, Illinois (Known agent 1855-57)

APPENDIX F

Civil War Service Roster

Roster of known NYJA wards who served in the Civil War:[6]

Last Name	First Name	Regiment/Notes	Officers
Alberts	Henry	Co. K, 105th Reg't. Ills. Vols.	Col. [Daniel] Dustin & Capt. H. [Horace] Austin
Alberson or Alperson or Albertson	William	Co. D, 25th Reg't., Ills.	Col. [William N.] Coler & Capt. [William] Osborne
Anderson	James	Enlisted in Army in 1862.	
Anderson	William	Enlisted at Chicago, Illinois	
Axtell	George H. aka Henry	Co. A, 89th Ills. Vols.	
Badger	Richard		
Bartholomew	John	Co. B, 113 Reg't., Ills.	Col. [George Blaikie] Hoge & Captain [Cephas] Williams
Barton	James		
Battis	Edward	Co. D, 25th Ills.	
Bellinger	George	Lincoln Reg't. [52nd?] Ills. Vols.	
Bennett	Andrew	2nd Ills. Cavalry Co. B	Capt. James Ewart
Bishop	William	[Co. F], 10th Reg't., Mo.	Rev. Capt. [Andrew C.] Todd
Black	Peter	125th Ills. Vols.	
Blessing	Miles	Co. A, 79th Ills.	
Brennan alias Breman	Patrick	Co. D, 125th	
Bright	James	Co. G, 113th Reg't., Ills. Vols.	Col. [George Blaikie] Hoge, Lieut. Col. Paddock, & Capt. [John G.] Woodruff
Broderick	John		
Brown	Henry		
Brown	John	Thought to be in Civil War.	
Brown	Thomas	Co. A, (73rd or 76th?) Ills. Vols.	

Last Name	First Name	Regiment/Notes	Officers
Bryan	Robert	Co. G, 25th Reg., Ills.	Sigit's or Sigel's? Division
Bryant	John	Co. G, 13th Ills. Cavalry	
Buckhalter	John	Cavalry Co. at Cairo, IL and in [Co. F], 10th Reg't., Mo. Vols.	Capt. Walbridge (IL) and Rev. Capt. [Andrew C.] Todd (MO)
Burns	Edward	Just out of Army as of Sept. 30, 1865	
Burns	John	Co. G, 13th Reg't., Ills. Cavalry	
Burr	John		
Bush	Ralph	9th Ills. Cavalry Reg't., Co. M	
Bush	Ransom H.	34th Ills. Reg. Vols., Co. A	Capt. Peter Ege & Col. Oscar M. Van Tassal. Chaplain Rev. M. Decker
C.	F.	Deserted.	
Canfield	James	Co. C, 12th Reg't., Ills. Vols.	Col. Chetler
Carney	Henry		
Carroll	Hugh	Co. E, 143rd Ills. Vols.	
Carroll	James	Co. D, 35th Ills. Vols.	
Carroll	John W.	Thought to be in Civil War	
Cavanagh	William	Served four years and four months.	
Chambers	John		
Clark	Sylvester	Co. D, 35th Ills. Vols.	
Cogswell	John W.	10th Reg., Mo.	Rev. Capt. [Andrew C.] Todd
Corney	Alonzo R.		
Corrigan	William	89th Reg., Ills.	
Couchman	Charles Young	111th Reg., Ills.	
Crea	Samuel	Co. B, 15th Tenn. Reg't. Vols. "Rebel Army"	
Croney	William	Co. F, 35th Ills. Vols.	
Crowley	John Joseph	In the Army for "some time."	
Crygier	Isaac		
Cunningham	Joseph	5th Ills. Cavalry	
Curran	Joseph	Served from New York.	
Dale	Thomas J.	Co. D, 35th Ills. Vol. Inf.	
Davis	Henry E.	New York Cavalry Reg't.	
Daram	Alfred	Likely served from New York	
DeLaney	Bernard		
Dennison	John	(25th or 35th) Ills. Reg't. Vols.	Capt. Wall

Last Name	First Name	Regiment/Notes	Officers
Derringer	Otto		
Divine	James		
Doane	Patrick		
Donahue	Barney	[Co. F], 10th Reg't., Mo.	Rev. Capt. [Andrew C.] Todd
Donahue	Patrick	Co. E, 8th Reg., Maryland	Capt. C. T. Dixon
Donnelly	William	Enlisted in Washington, D.C. (musician in Marine Corps.)	
Donelson	Thomas	Drummer Boy	
Donnegan	William	Co. C, Ills. Vols. (Drummer)	Col. Loomis
Donovan	John F.	Co. C, 56th Ills Vol. Inf. Reg.	
Doonan	Thomas	Co. C, 60th Ills.	
Dougherty	James	111th Reg't. Co. B, Ills. Vols.	
Dougherty	Michael	111th Reg't. Co. B, Ills. Vols.	
Dougherty	Philip	30th Ills. Vols. (possibly in 8th Kansas as well)	
Duffy	Hugh	156 Ills. Vols., Co. E	
Duffy	John	28th Reg. N.Y.S.V.	
Dullar	Alfred A.		
Dunn	Bernard	Thought to be in Civil War.	
Elliot	John	Co. D, 111th Ills. Vols.	
Farmer	James	Co. D, 20th Ind. Vols.	
F. [Farrell?]	D. [Dennis?]	123rd Ills.	
Farrell	Dennis	Died in the War.	
Fay	Thomas	42nd Reg., Ills. Re-enlisted in Co. B, 5th Reg. Indiana Invalid Corps.	Douglas Brigade (St. Louis)
Ferguson	John	Co. I (or J?), 80th Ills.	
Fillony	James	35th Ills.	
Fisher	John	[Co. F], 10th Reg't., Mo.	Rev. Capt. [Andrew C.] Todd
Fox	Isaac	Co. D, 35th Ills. Vols.	
Furness	Charles H.	Thought to be in Civil War.	
Free	James	28th Reg. N.Y. Vols.	
Gales [alias Ganes?]	Oscar		
Gallagher	Hugh	Co. K, 37th Ills.	
Gallagher	Michael		
Gambling or Gamble	Jonathan aka Johnson	Co. E, 51st. Ills.	

Last Name	First Name	Regiment/Notes	Officers
Green	John		
Green	Thomas	Co. K, 105th Reg., Ills.	Col. [Daniel] Dustin & Capt. H. [Horace] Austin
Greves	John		
Greves	William		
Griffin	Robert B.	82nd Cavalry	
Hackmyer	William	Ills. Vols.	
Haley	John	Killed in the War.	
Hampton	Michael	Ills. Vols.	
Hanifen	Michael	1st N. J. Artillery, Battery "B," 2d Div., 3rd, Corps.	
Harbinson	George W.	Served from New York.	
Hardenburgh	Simon		
Harkins	Benjamin Franklin aka Franklin	Co. K, 75th Reg., Ills. (Drummer)	Col. Ryan & Capt. Roberts
Harris	Joseph	Co. H, 113th Reg., Ills.	Capt. Sutherland & General McClernand
Hart	Charles		
Hart	Peter	31st Reg't., Ills., then in 1st Reg't. Kansas Vols.	Logan's Reg't. (IL) & Col. Spicer (KS)
Hatch	Joseph Henry		
Hayes	Michael	Thought to be in Civil War from New Jersey	
Hearn	Alexander	100 days' service (in Navy)	
Hearn	David	51st? Reg't. Ills. Vols.	
Heeny	William	63rd Ills. Vols.	
Hendrickson	Charles		
Hennessy	William	Thought to be in Civil War.	
Henry	William	Drummer in Co. D, 130th Reg't., Ills. Vols.	
Herme	Charles August	Co. K, 67th Reg., Ills. S. V.	Capt. [S. W.] McKown
Herren	John	Served three years in Army.	
Higgins	Timothy		
Hill	George E.	Died shortly after returning from War	
Hobbie	William C. A.	22nd Iowa Inf.	
Holland	Peter		
Horan	William	Likely in New Jersey or Pennsylvania.	

Last Name	First Name	Regiment/Notes	Officers
Horton	Benjamin Franklin	[Co. F], 10th Reg't., Mo.	Rev. Capt. [Andrew C.] Todd
Howard	Edward	42nd Reg., Ills.	Logan's Reg't.
Hoyt	Alonzo W.	Likely in Maryland.	
Hubbard	Andrew	42nd Reg., Ills. Vols.	
Hudson	Henry E.	Corcoran Legion, N.Y.	
Hughes	James	Served in the Navy	
Hunter	Charles	Co. F, 8th Reg., Ills., then re-enlisted	
Hyde	Joseph	[Co. F], 10th Reg't., Mo.	Rev. Capt. [Andrew C.] Todd
James	Nathaniel	23rd Reg't. V. R. C.?	
Jones	Pierce	90th Reg't., N.Y. Vols.	
Jourdan	John	Was in the Army.	
Kane	John	Co. B, 25th Reg't. Ills. Vols.	
Kavanaugh	William	Was in the Army	
Kean	John		
Kelly	James	In Connecticut and then Co. A, 19th U.S. Regulars in Indiana	
Kennedy	John	Co. K, 12th Ills. Vols.	
Kenney alias McKenna	William	In the Cavalry.	
King	Andrew	142nd Ills Reg't.	
Lannehan or Lanahan	Michael	113th Ills. (supposedly)	
Latter	Alexander	Co. F, 125th Reg. Ills. Vol. Inf.	
Lawler	John		
Leek	Cornelius	Co. B, 134th Ills. 100 days' service.	
Leek	Henry	Co. I, 20th Ills. Vols.	
Lender	John A.		
Lenger alias Lange	Paul		
Lennox	John	Thought to be in "Rebel Army."	
Leonard	John		
Libert	Augustus	Co. E., 85th N. Y. Reg't.	
Lipman	Leon		
Long	Benjamin F.		
Loundsbury	William A.		Governor Yates' State Regiment

Last Name	First Name	Regiment/Notes	Officers
Lynch	Patrick	Co. I, 27th Ills.—3rd Brigade, 2nd Div., 4th A. Corps.	
Lyons	Daniel W.	51st Reg't, Ills. Vols.	Capt. Pett
Madden	Daniel D.	Unknown Reg't. first, then in 34th Ills. Reg't, Co., K	
Madden	Michael	Co. F, 35th Ills. Transferred to 8th Wisconsin Battery.	
Maiers	Louis	Co. F, 135th Ills. Vols.	
Mair	George Sidney	Co. B, 135 Ills. Vols. (100 days' men)	
Manlin alias Wiler or Weber	Valentine	16th Ills. Cavalry	
Manning	John	Lincoln Reg't. Ills. Vols.	
Manning	William	Co. C, 49th Reg't., Ills. Vols.	
Marr	Peter	Co. D, 55th Ills.	
McCabe	Philip		
McCannon or McCanna	Patrick		
McCrum	James	Possibly 40th Ills. Reg't.	
McCue	John		
McDonald	James	Enlisted in Stanton Legion Oct. 1, 1861 at Cairo, Illinois	
McDermott	Luke	Co. G, 13th Ills. Cavalry	
McGirty	Hugh		
McGrew	Neil	Mule Driver in the War.	
McGuire	James	13th Ills. Cavalry	
McKenna	William	17th Ills. Cavalry	
McKenzie	Joseph Oatwell	Enlisted about August 1862.	
McLaughlin	Jeremiah	Co. I, 35th Ills. Vols. (Drum Major)	
McLaughlin	William W.	Co. A, 85th Reg't., Ills. Vols. Re-enlisted in 150th Reg't.	
McMadden	Michael	35th Reg't., Co. D	
McMenomy	John		
Melville	John	Served in the "Regulars."	
Miller	George	Served three years in Army.	
Miller	Henry	Enlisted at Sterling, IL	
Mills	George	Co. D, 3rd Ills. Cavalry	
Milot	William R.		

Last Name	First Name	Regiment/Notes	Officers
Monahan	Henry	Co. F, 4th Ills. Cavalry	
Monahan	John	Co. I, 71st Ills. Reg't	
Moore	Seely	Co. G, 13th Reg't., Ills. Cavalry	
Moreno	Fernando A.	Served three years in Capt. Barnard's Co.	
Morris	John	Enlisted on March 16, 1865 in 28th Ills. Inf. (drummer boy). Mustered out March 15, 1866 in Brownsville, Texas.	
Morrison	Dennis	Co. B, 125th Reg't. Ills. Vols.	
Moses	George	31st Reg., Indiana	
Mosher	Albert	Thought to be in Civil War.	
Mullen	David E.	Lead Mine Reg't., Ill. Vols. and in 33rd Reg't, Mo. Vols.	
Mullen	James	Co. F, 8th Reg., Ills.	
Mulvain or Mulvane or Mulram	James	Co. F, 8th Reg., Ills.	
Murphy	James	Co. F, 8th Reg. Ills	
Murphy	Peter	Co. F, 35th Ills. Vols.	Capt. Kiser
Murray	William		
Myers	James	Co. F, 19th Reg., Ills.	
Nevens	John	Co. F, 26th Ills. Vols.	
Newburgh	Joseph		
Nolan	Peter	Stanton Legion N. Y. S. V.	
North	John	Co. B., 5th Ills. Cavalry	
Norton	James	Served from New York.	
Norton	Jacob	Badly wounded.	
Norton	John	Thought to be in Civil War.	
O'Neil	Francis	Enlisted in regular army.	
Parr	Daniel	Served in the Army.	
Parsloe	Franklin	Co. E, 10th Missouri Reg't.	
Perriton	John S.	Co. D, 145th Ills. Inf.	
Phillips	William	Likely served from Illinois.	
Porter	Samuel	In Army at least two years—may have re-enlisted.	
Powers	John Henry	Served in the Army.	
Powers	William	[Co. F], 10th Reg., Mo.	Rev. Capt. [Andrew C.] Todd

Last Name	First Name	Regiment/Notes	Officers
Pugh	John	Co. C, 11th Ills. Vols.	
Quevedo	John	Co. F, 10th Mo. Reg't.	Rev. Capt. [Andrew C.] Todd
Ray	Morris	14th Ills. and then re-enlisted.	
Reeves	Theodore W.	Co. D., 13 Reg't., Ills.	Taker of dispatches to Generals Curtis and Grant
Regan	Aaron	30th Reg't. Ills. Vols.	
Rhel	Charles	10th Legion, New York	Col. [Charles H.] Van Wyck & Capt. Frederick Decker
Rigney alias John McKay	Michael	Served in Indiana Vols. as a Drummer.	
Riker	Daniel	8th Reg't., New Jersey Vols.	
Riley	James	[Co. F], 10th Reg't., Mo. Vols.	Rev. Capt. [Andrew C.] Todd
Riley	Thomas	[Co. F], 10th Reg't., Mo. Vols.	Rev. Capt. [Andrew C.] Todd
Roberdee	William T.	Co. B, 75th Reg., Ills. Vols.	Col. Ryan & Capt. Whallon
Roberts	Charles Henry	In four battles as of Dec. 1862.	
Robertson	James	72nd Ills. Reg't.	
Rodden	Edward		
Rodh	Frank	Co. H, 113th Reg't., Ills.	Capt. Sullivan & Col. [George Blaikie] Hoge
Rogers	Charles	Unk. Company, then re-enlisted in Co. D, 33rd Ills.	
Rogers	William D.	13th Reg., Ills.	
Rooney	James	31st Reg., Ills.	
Rowe	John	15th Reg't., Ill. V. R. Corps.	
Rutherford	Justice		
Ryan	Daniel	9th Reg., Mo., then re-enlisted.	
Sadleir	William	Enlisted with his employer.	
Scattergood	Edwin F.	Killed while serving in Army.	
Scott	Thomas	Co. A, 25th Ills. Vols.	
Scott	Walter	Co. C, 73rd Ills.	
Shambark	John		
Shannessy	Thomas	5th Cavalry then re-enlisted in Co. D, 42nd Ills.	
Sharp	William	Co. F, 130th Ills. Vols.	
Shaw	Gustavus	Co. K, 37th Ills. Vols.	
Smith	Charles	Enlisted Sept. 1861	
Smith	Eugene		
Smith	James H.	17th Ills. Cavalry	
Smith	James W.	88th Reg't, Ills. Vols.	Capt. Chickering & Col. Frank Sherman
Smith	John	35th Ills.	

Last Name	First Name	Regiment/Notes	Officers
Smith	John A. E.	Stanton Legion N.Y.S.V.	
Smith	John H.	100 days' Co. B, 135th Ills. Vols.	
Snow	Barney	Possibly 76th Ills.	
Snow	John James		
Sommerkom	Emil	Capt. in Army—served from Connecticut.	
Stansberry	Theodore	[25th?] Reg't. Ills. Vols.	
Staurer	George	Served three months.	
Stebbing	Michael	Co. D, 28th Ills. Inf.	
Stewart	John	11th U.S. Infantry [from Indiana?]	
Stewart or Stuart	William aka John J.	21st Indiana Vols.	
Stokes	Henry	Served in Ills. Cavalry.	Capt. H. Fullerton
Sullivan	John	Co. K, 30th Reg't, Ills. Vols.	Capt John Nichols & Col. Shad [Warren Shedd]
Sullivan	Michael	Co. D, 35th Ills. Vols.	
Summerton	Daniel		
Taggart	David	Co. H, 123rd Ills. Vols.	
Talbott	John	37th Ills. Reg't.	
Terry	Jesse W.	Private, Co. D., 35th Ill. Vols.	
Thomas	Francis J.	54th Ind., then re-enlisted in 71st Ind. (later known as 6th Ind. Cavalry)	
Thompson	Israel E.	U. S. Regulars for three years	
Thompson	John	Thought to be in Civil War.	
Timpson	John	Co. A, 154th Ills. Infantry	Capt. Fithian
Travis	James	Thought to be in Civil War.	
Travis	Owen	Joined the 100 Days' Men.	
Turrell	John	31st Reg., Ills.	
U.	Andrew	Killed in the War.	
Valiant	Alonzo	Supposedly a drummer in a NY Reg't. after returning from West.	
Vanderbeck	Henry		
Von Glahn	Louis Frederick		
Von Glahn	William C.	100 days' service. Re-enlisted in [29th?] Ills.	
Wagner	William	39th Ills. Vols.	
Walker	George	Iowa Reg.	
Warren	Michael		

Civil War Service Roster

Last Name	First Name	Regiment/Notes	Officers
Waters	Frederick	Likely served from Connecticut.	
Webb	John	Co. C, 125th Ills. Vols.	
Weed	George Alonzo	Served from New York.	
Welch	Patrick	Co. C, 11th Ills. Vols.	Orderly for General Ransom
Walsh	Peter	Co. K, 37th Ills. Vols.	Three years in Gen. John Charles Black's Company C
Whalen	Frank aka Francis	8th Ills. Co. C	Col. William Gamble, Capt. D. D. Lincoln, Chaplain Rev. Spencer, and Ord. Sergt. Charles G. Gilbert
Whalen or Whelan	Patrick	Thought to be in Civil War.	
White	Robert G.	Thought to be in Civil War.	
Whiteley	James D.		
Whittle	Edward		
Willard	Charles	25th Ills.	
Williams	John A.	Co. E, 5th Ills. Cavalry	
Williams alias Henry Brown	Samuel	Thought to be in Civil War (Navy).	
Williamson	Edward	73rd Ills.	Col. [James F.] Jacques
Wilson	John	Co. E, 70th Ind.	
Wilson	William		
Woodhams	David	Co. F, 2nd Ills. Cavalry	Capt. [Melville H.] Musser
Woodruff	Theodore	19th Ills., then [re-enlisted?] in New York	Col. Turchin [19th Ills.]
Woolweaver	Augustus	Co. C, 49th Ills. Reg't.	
Young	Joseph	Co. K, 30th Reg't, Ills. Vols.	Capt. Alexander Johnson

APPENDIX G

Spanish-American War Roster

Former NYJA wards went off to war once again when the United States declared war with Spain on April 21, 1898. The following is a list of those known to have served.[7]

Last Name	First Name	Regiment	West Company Date/Notes
Auer	Robert	Regiment is not known.	May 6, 1889 Company. Died in Camp at Chickamauga.
Beekman	Arthur W.	Likely Illinois. Regiment is not known.	March 5, 1888 Company.
Beyersdorffer	John	Likely Illinois. Regiment is not known.	August 30, 1886 Company.
Carter	Edward	Co. G, 65th N. Y. Vol. Infantry	March 6, 1893 Company.
Day	Alexander	Likely Illinois. Regiment is not known.	October 19, 1874 Company. See NYJA Annual Report for the year 1906. Killed in action.
Du Crow	George	Company K, 4th Illinois Regiment	March 25, 1878 Company. He served between May 11, 1898 to May 5, 1899.
Duffner	William	1st Ill. Vol. Cavalry; Orderly	February 14, 1881 Company.
Freligh	Henry	Navy, Training Ship Newport	April 20, 1896 Company.
Hubbs	Edward	Likely Illinois. Regiment is not known.	March 12, 1894 Company.
McCall	James	Battery H, 2d U. S. Artillery	April 6, 1885 Company.
Palmatier	Charles (E. or F.)	Private, Co. K, 6th Ills. Vol. Infantry	September 5, 1887 Company.
Palmatier	William H.	Co. K, 6th Ills. Vol. Infantry	September 5, 1887 Company.
Roll	William	Navy. Was at Santiago bombardment.	October 29, 1888 Company.
Schultz	Herman	Likely Illinois. Regiment is not known.	October 18, 1880 Company.
Seffers	Henry	Likely Illinois. Regiment is not known.	October 5, 1891 Company.
Tierney	Fred	Co. H, 4th Ill. Vol. Infantry	April 8, 1895 Company.
Wood	Frank B.	Co. E, 1st Wisconsin Vol. Infantry	May 28, 1888 Company.

APPENDIX H
Admission Percentage Table

Year	England	Scotland	Ireland	Germany	France	Russia	Poland	Italy	Turkey & Syria	West Indies
1853	4.65	1.61	28.66	5.94	0.16	0	0.32	0.16	0	0.32
1854	2.86	0.76	29.33	4.19	0.19	0	0.19	0.57	0	0.19
1855	3.58	1.38	27.65	6.19	0.14	0	0.14	0.55	0	0.14
1856	3.77	0.55	21.51	4.1	0.89	0	0	0.11	0	0.33
1857	5.8	0.54	25.64	4.99	0.4	0	0	0.54	0	0
1858	3.59	1.28	22.02	4.87	0.51	0	0	0.13	0	0
1859	3.94	1.62	16.8	5.56	0.35	0	0	0.81	0	0.12
1860	5.33	1.39	15.3	4.75	0.35	0	0	0.7	0	0.23
1861	4.62	1	9.62	4.72	0.25	0	0	1.5	0	0.25
1862	3.34	1.15	6.73	3.87	0.25	0	0.1	0.31	0	0
1863	3.62	1.29	4.14	2.84	0.43	0	0.34	0.09	0	0
1864	2.25	0.68	2.93	3.94	0.23	0.11	0.23	0.11	0.11	0
1865	3.2	1.23	3.45	3.69	0.37	0	0.12	0.25	0	0
1866	3.73	0.59	3.28	1.76	0.47	0	0.35	0	0	0
1867	2.27	0.11	1.96	3.47	0.43	0.11	0.11	0.32	0	0.11
1868	1.76	0.23	2.11	2.93	0.47	0	0	0.32	0	0
1869	3.15	0.12	1.69	3.75	0.24	0.12	0	0.48	0	0.24
1870	3.78	0.28	1.68	3.92	0.28	0.14	0.14	0.28	0	0
1871	3.67	0.17	2.97	5.42	0.35	0	0	0.7	0	0.18
1872	4.94	0.37	3.66	4.39	0.55	0	0.18	0.73	0	0
1873	1.55	0.34	0.86	5.68	1.55	0.34	0.17	1.03	0.17	0
1874	3.2	1.02	1.89	4.22	0.73	0	0.29	2.33	0	0
1875	3.48	1.42	2.37	4.91	2.21	0	0.63	0.6	0	0
1876	3.86	1	1.62	6.11	0.87	0	0.25	1.5	0	0
1877	3.74	0.34	1.36	2.55	1.19	0	0	0	0	0.34
1878	3.91	0.17	0.68	4.42	0.34	0.17	0	0.34	0	0
1879	2.33	0	0.36	1.97	0.9	0.35	0.36	0	0	0.36

Year	England	Scotland	Ireland	Germany	France	Russia	Poland	Italy	Turkey & Syria	West Indies
1880	1.56	0.35	0.35	1.56	0.52	0	0.17	1.04	0	0
1881	2.69	0.15	0.59	4.33	0.75	0	0.59	1.64	0	0.45
1882	2.53	0.3	0.3	5.65	0.71	0.45	0.15	4.46	0	0.3
1883	1.55	0.14	1.55	4.36	0.14	0.56	0.42	6.61	0	0
1884	2.13	0.61	0.31	5.21	0.46	0.15	0.61	8.11	0	0.15
1885	1.4	1.86	1.25	7.34	0.31	0.31	1.09	6.56	0	0.16
1886	1.08	0.46	0.15	8.47	0.15	1.54	0.77	5.86	0	0.15
1887	2.29	0.43	0.43	4.44	0.43	0.57	1.15	12.04	0	0.72
1888	3.35	0.73	0.44	7.42	0.73	3.06	0.87	10.19	0	0
1889	2.98	1.45	0.33	9.87	0.29	2.19	1.16	7.12	0.31	0.29
1890	2.48	0.77	0.62	9.29	0.31	2.17	0.77	16.72	0	0
1891	1.95	0.49	0.65	5.21	0.49	4.89	0.49	16.12	0	0
1892	3.06	0.48	0.64	6.57	0.48	5.45	0.64	9.94	1.01	0
1893	2.28	1.41	0.35	5.1	0.53	5.98	0.88	12.65	2.64	0.18
1894	3.34	0.33	1	6.68	0	8.51	1.17	9.51	2.84	0.17
1895	3.33	0.74	0.55	3.51	0.55	11.83	0.74	9.24	0.74	0.74
1896	1.16	0.58	0.58	3.61	0.72	9.97	0.29	16.91	2.02	0.43
1897	0.76	0.55	0.21	3.82	0.44	12.44	0.22	21.29	2.62	0
1898	2.44	0.71	0.31	2.34	0.31	15.89	0.41	16.9	1.32	0.41
1899	2.21	0	0.33	2.87	0.11	18.78	0.22	9.28	1.88	0
1900	1.77	0.18	0.09	1.67	0.18	20.78	0.37	3.35	0.65	0.65
1901	1.78	0.09	0.39	1.37	0.39	16.47	0.19	1.47	0.29	0.29
1902	1.05	0.58	0.11	1.85	0.23	16.49	0	1.05	0.11	0.46
1903	1.09	0.02	0.15	1.86	0.15	10.87	0.15	0	0	0.15
1904	1.98	0.13	0.13	1.19	0	10.95	0	0.13	0	0
1905	0.96	0.15	0.38	2.64	0	2.64	0.38	0.28	0	0
1906	0	0	0.61	3.66	0	0	0	0	0	0
1907	0.43	0	0.86	4.3	0	0.43	0	0.86	0	0
1908	0.46	0.93	0.46	0	0	0	0	0	0	0
1909	0.43	0	0.43	1.28	0	0	0	0	0	0.43
1910	0	0	0	0.7	0	0.35	0	0	0	0.75
1911	0.43	1.29	0.43	0.86	0	0.43	0	0.86	0	0
1912	0	1.86	1.39	1.39	0	0	0	0.93	0	0.93
1913	12.2	0.41	0	1.22	0	0.41	0	2.05	0	0.82
1914	0.38	0.38	0	1.52	0	0.76	0	0.38	0.38	1.52

APPENDIX I

Nativity of Children in Foreign Countries Table

Year	Canada, Etc.	England	Ireland	Scotland	France	Germany	Hungary	Turkey and Syria	Russia	Poland	Norway	Denmark	Sweden
1853	7	29	180	10	1	37	0	0	0	2	0	0	0
1854	8	40	308	8	2	44	1	0	0	2	2	0	0
1855	6	26	201	10	1	45	0	0	0	1	0	0	0
1856	7	34	194	5	8	37	0	0	0	0	0	0	1
1857	11	43	190	4	3	37	0	0	0	0	0	2	0
1858	9	28	172	10	4	38	0	0	0	0	0	0	0
1859	6	34	145	14	3	48	0	0	0	0	0	1	0
1860	9	46	132	12	3	41	0	0	0	0	0	0	0
1861	9	37	77	8	2	35	0	0	0	0	0	0	2
1862	6	32	74	11	4	37	0	0	0	1	0	0	2
1863	13	42	48	15	5	33	0	0	0	4	1	0	0
1864	9	20	26	6	2	27	0	1	1	2	0	0	0
1865	8	26	28	10	3	30	0	0	0	1	0	0	0
1866	10	32	28	5	4	15	0	0	0	3	0	0	0
1867	9	21	18	1	4	32	0	0	1	1	0	0	0
1868	6	15	18	2	4	25	0	0	0	0	1	0	0
1869	14	26	14	1	2	31	0	0	1	0	0	1	0
1870	5	27	11	2	2	28	1	0	1	1	0	0	3
1871	3	21	17	1	2	31	1	0	0	0	0	1	0
1872	4	27	20	2	3	24	0	0	0	1	1	0	0
1873	7	9	5	2	9	33	0	1	2	1	0	2	0
1874	9	22	13		15	29	0	0	0	2	0	2	0
1875	1	22	15	9	4	31	1	0	0	4	0	0	0
1876	3	31	13	8	7	49	0	0	0	2	0	1	2
1877	0	22	8	2	7	15	2	0	0	0	0	1	1
1878	2	23	4	1	2	26	0	0	1	0	0	2	1
1879	2	13	2	0	5	11	0	0	2	2	0	0	1
1880	3	9	2	12	3	9	1	0	0	1	1	0	0
1881	2	18	4	1	5	29	0	0	0	4	1	0	0
1882	4	17	2	2	5	38	3	0	3	1	0	0	0
1883	3	11	11	1	1	31	3	0	4	3	0	0	0
1884	2	14	2	4	3	34	3	0	1	4	0	0	0
1885	2	9	8	7	2	47	1	0	2	7	0	2	1
1886	1	7	1	3	1	45	0	0	10	5	2	1	2
1887	7	23	3	3	3	31	4	0	4	8	0	0	0
1888	4	23	3	5	5	51	2	0	21	6	0	2	1
1889	1	19	2	10	2	63	5	2	14	8	0	2	0
1890	4	16	4	5	2	60	14	0	14	5	0	0	2
1891	2	12	4	3	3	32	3	0	30	3	1	0	3
1892	6	19	4	3	3	41	3	7	34	4	0	1	2
1893	3	13	2	8	3	29	4	15	34	5	0	1	0
1894	3	2	6	2	0	40	4	17	51	7	0	0	1
1895	4	18	3	4	3	19	9	4	64	4	0	2	0
1896	1	8	4	4	5	25	4	14	6	2	0	0	1
1897	4	7	2	5	4	35	2	24	104	2	0	1	3
1898	3	24	3	7	3	23	4	13	156	4	0	1	2
1899	2	20	3	0	1	26	9	17	170	2	2	0	3
1900	1	19	1	2	2	18	6	7	224	4	1	2	3
1901	2	11	4	1	4	14	7	3	168	2	0	0	4
1902	4	9	1	5	2	16	9	1	142	0	3	1	2
1903	2	7	1	4	1	12	3	0	70	1	1	0	2
1904	4	15	1	1	0	9	3	0	83	0	0	0	2
1905	0	1	1	2	0	7	0	0	7	1	0	1	3
1906	0	0	1	0	0	6	0	0	0	0	0	0	1
1907	0	1	2	0	0	9	0	0	1	0	0	0	1
1908	2	1	1	2	0	0	1	0	0	0	1	0	0
1909	0	1	1	0	0	3	3	0	0	0	0	1	1
1910	1	0	0	0	0	2	0	0	1	0	2	0	0
1911	0	1	1	3	0	2	0	0	1	0	0	0	2
1912	0	0	3	4	0	3	0	0	0	0	1	0	0
1913	0	3	0	1	0	3	1	0	1	0	3	0	1
1914	1	1	0	1	0	4	3	1	2	0	2	0	0
Total	**259**	**1,117**	**2,051**	**269**	**177**	**1,665**	**119**	**127**	**1,523**	**123**	**25**	**30**	**56**

Native born, 31,179; Foreign, 9,668; Unknown, 423. Total, 41,270.

Holland	Switzerland	Spain	Africa	Italy	Australia	St. Helens	W. Indies	S. America	At Sea	Austria	Jap-China	Asia	Total	Unknown
0	1	0	1	1	0	0	2	0	1	0	0	0	272	25
1	1	1	0	6	0	1	2	0	3	0	0	0	430	53
0	0	2	0	4	0	0	1	1	0	0	0	0	298	27
0	0	0	0	1	0	0	3	0	0	0	0	0	290	44
0	0	0	0	4	0	0	0	0	0	0	0	0	294	14
0	1	0	0	1	1	0	0	0	3	0	0	0	267	35
0	0	0	0	7	0	0	1	0	4	0	0	0	263	14
0	2	0	0	6	0	0	2	0	0	0	0	0	253	11
0	0	0	0	12	0	0	2	0	2	0	0	0	184	8
0	0	0	0	3	2	0	0	0	0	0	0	0	172	3
0	1	0	0	1	1	0	0	0	4	1	0	0	171	0
1	0	0	0	1	0	0	0	0	1	2	0	0	100	0
0	0	1	1	2	0	0	0	0	1	0	0	0	110	0
1	0	1	0	0	3	0	0	0	2	0	0	0	104	2
0	0	0	0	3	0	0	1	0	1	0	0	0	92	1
0	0	0	0	3	0	0	0	0	0	0	0	0	74	1
0	1	0	0	4	2	0	2	0	1	1	0	0	101	1
2	0	0	0	2	1	0	0	0	0	0	0	0	87	0
0	2	0	0	4	1	1	1	0	0	1	0	0	86	1
0	3	0	0	4	0	0	0	1	0	0	0	0	90	0
0	0	1	0	6	1	0	0	3	0	0	0	0	32	0
0	2	1	0	16	0	0	0	0	0	1	0	0	109	0
3	1	0	0	4	0	0	0	0	1	0	0	0	106	0
0	1	0	0	12	0	0	0	1	0	0	0	0	130	0
0	1	0	0	0	0	0	2	2	0	0	0	0	63	2
0	4	0	0	2	0	0	0	1	0	1	0	0	70	2
0	4	0	0	0	0	0	2	0	0	1	0	0	45	4
0	3	0	0	6	0	0	0	0	0	0	0	0	43	3
1	4	0	0	11	0	3	3	1	0	0	0	0	84	2
1	3	0	0	30	0	0	2	1	0	1	0	0	113	0
1	3	0	0	47	0	0	0	0	0	1	0	0	120	0
0	3	0	0	53	0	0	1	1	0	4	0	0	129	0
0	5	0	0	42	1	0	1	0	0	1	0	0	138	2
0	2	2	0	38	0	0	1	1	0	3	0	0	125	0
0	5	0	0	84	0	0	5	0	0	4	0	0	177	0
0	1	2	0	70	0	0	0	0	0	3	0	0	199	0
0	3	1	0	49	0	0	2	2	0	1	0	0	186	0
0	2	0	0	108	0	0	0	0	0	3	0	0	229	1
0	2	1	0	99	0	0	0	4	0	11	0	0	223	2
1	5	1	0	62	0	0	0	0	0	9	0	0	205	0
0	2	0	0	72	1	0	1	2	0	6	0	0	201	0
1	3	2	0	57	0	0	1	2	1	3	0	0	222	1
0	3	0	1	50	0	0	4	0	1	4	0	0	197	1
0	0	10	1	117	0	0	3	1	0	13	0	0	281	1
3	0	2	0	195	0	0	0	3	0	17	0	0	413	0
1	0	0	0	156	0	0	4	0	1	22	0	0	42	0
1	0	0	0	84	0	0	0	1	1	17	2	0	359	4
1	0	0	0	36	0	0	7	1	1	21	0	0	359	5
1	1	0	0	15	0	0	3	0	0	11	0	0	251	81
0	0	0	0	9	0	0	4	0	0	18	0	0	226	13
0	0	0	0	0	1	0	1	1	0	17	0	0	124	39
0	0	0	0	1	1	0	0	0	0	14	0	0	134	51
0	1	0	0	1	0	0	0	0	0	0	0	0	25	11
0	0	0	0	0	0	0	0	0	0	0	1	0	8	0
0	0	0	0	2	0	0	0	0	0	1	1	0	18	0
0	0	0	0	0	0	0	0	0	0	1	0	0	10	0
0	0	0	0	0	0	0	1	0	0	0	0	0	0	1
0	0	0	0	0	0	0	5	0	0	0	0	1	0	1
0	0	0	0	2	0	0	0	0	0	0	0	0	0	1
0	0	0	0	2	0	0	2	0	0	1	0	0	0	0
0	0	0	1	5	0	0	2	0	0	3	0	0	0	2
0	0	1	1	1	0	0	4	0	0	2	0	0	23	4
20	**75**	**20**	**6**	**1,613**	**16**	**5**	**76**	**13**	**29**	**219**	**4**	**1**	**9,668**	**432**

Nativity of Children in Foreign Countries Table

APPENDIX J
Nativity of Children in USA Table

Year	NY	NJ	PA	MA	CT	ME	NH	VT	RI	VA	MD	DE	DC	NC
1853	281	13	11	6	5	1	0	0	0	1	2	0	1	0
1854	505	20	16	10	3	2	0	0	1	1	2	0	1	0
1855	360	6	9	13	3	1	1	1	1	0	3	0	0	0
1856	505	22	10	14	5	1	0	2	0	1	0	0	2	0
1857	393	11	4	8	9	0	0	0	0	2	1	1	1	0
1858	422	8	16	11	5	0	0	0	4	3	1	1	0	0
1859	537	10	12	6	6	2	0	1	1	0	2	0	1	0
1860	554	11	8	10	5	0	0	1	2	0	2	0	1	0
1861	543	9	13	8	7	3	1	1	3	2	0	0	1	0
1862	694	21	17	22	8	0	1	3	2	3	1	0	0	0
1863	897	28	14	11	16	0	1	0	3	3	3	0	0	0
1864	714	30	9	11	6	1	1	1	1	4	1	1	2	3
1865	620	33	16	7	7	0	0	0	2	4	2	0	0	1
1866	656	28	15	11	7	2	1	0	2	6	2	0	0	0
1867	743	15	20	15	8	0	0	1	0	4	2	0	2	0
1868	686	31	16	15	8	2	0	4	2	1	1	0	3	0
1869	628	25	18	12	10	1	1	0	2	2	1	1	2	0
1870	553	22	9	12	6	1	1	0	0	3	0	0	2	2
1871	433	25	6	4	4	1	0	1	0	1	0	1	0	2
1872	402	21	8	3	6	0	0	0	0	4	2	1	0	1
1873	445	15	11	5	9	0	1	0	1	0	0	1	0	0
1874	526	15	8	6	5	1	0	0	0	1	0	0	2	0
1875	476	11	8	4	5	0	0	1	0	1	4	0	0	1
1876	623	18	5	6	7	0	0	1	0	3	2	0	1	2
1877	469	21	13	46	3	0	0	0	0	1	1	0	1	0
1878	476	13	4	5	5	0	0	0	0	1	2	0	1	0
1879	448	24	11	6	3	0	0	0	1	1	1	0	1	1
1880	483	12	7	12	4	0	0	0	0	0	3	0	0	0
1881	529	16	7	4	10	0	0	0	0	1	3	0	0	1
1882	482	25	12	2	5	1	1	0	2	6	1	0	6	1
1883	507	25	14	5	12	0	0	0	6	5	3	0	1	2
1884	471	16	10	4	5	1	1	0	1	5	3	0	0	1
1885	440	18	10	2	6	0	0	1	0	5	1	0	4	2
1886	459	22	12	6	3	0	0	0	0	11	3	0	1	1
1887	455	16	13	3	1	0	0	2	1	12	3	0	5	1
1888	436	20	11	1	5	0	0	0	0	6	0	0	2	0
1889	396	13	4	4	3	0	0	0	0	21	5	0	1	1
1890	363	10	11	5	6	0	0	0	1	9	1	0	2	1
1891	341	18	4	3	3	0	0	0	1	7	2	0	2	0
1892	358	13	8	4	2	0	0	0	0	7	6	0	1	0
1893	321	13	6	3	1	0	0	0	0	10	0	1	2	0
1894	334	12	3	2	2	0	0	0	3	9	1	1	0	1
1895	314	3	5	0	3	0	0	0	3	4	0	1	0	1
1896	368	10	5	2	2	0	0	0	0	6	0	0	0	3
1897	438	13	4	4	8	0	0	0	0	10	1	0	4	1
1898	503	11	10	2	3	0	0	0	1	14	2	0	1	2
1899	466	9	9	6	7	0	0	1	1	20	2	0	1	2
1900	69	14	15	5	5	2	2	0	3	17	2	0	4	2
1901	666	17	15	5	4	0	0	0	1	21	2	1	0	4
1902	525	19	12	7	5	0	0	0	1	10	1	0	0	8
1903	417	16	6	5	1	0	0	1	0	12	1	0	2	3
1904	497	22	15	4	3	0	0	2	1	8	2	0	0	4
1905	211	5	3	0	1	0	0	0	0	1	1	0	0	0
1906	144	6	1	0	1	0	0	0	0	1	0	0	0	0
1907	202	1	3	4	4	0	0	0	0	0	0	0	0	0
1908	202	0	1	0	0	0	0	0	0	0	0	0	0	0
1909	197	10	3	1	0	0	0	0	0	4	1	0	0	1
1910	247	4	1	2	3	0	0	0	0	2	0	0	0	5
1911	207	1	0	1	0	0	0	0	0	2	0	0	0	0
1912	184	7	0	5	0	0	0	0	0	1	0	0	0	0
1913	189	7	4	4	1	0	0	0	0	5	0	0	0	0
1914	199	9	1	2	0	0	0	0	1	3	2	0	1	3
	22,759	**949**	**552**	**364**	**290**	**27**	**13**	**25**	**55**	**308**	**90**	**11**	**65**	**64**

Appendix J

SC	GA	LA	MO	IL	OH	MI	IA	WI	CA	TX	FL	MN	TN	IN	Total.
1	0	1	0	1	1	0	1	0	0	0	0	0	0	0	326
1	0	2	0	0	1	1	0	0	1	0	0	0	0	0	567
0	0	1	0	0	1	2	0	0	0	0	0	0	0	0	402
1	1	2	0	0	0	0	0	2	0	0	0	0	0	0	568
0	0	0	0	0	0	2	0	0	0	1	0	0	0	0	439
0	0	3	1	2	1	0	0	0	1	0	0	0	0	0	478
1	1	3	0	0	1	1	0	1	0	0	0	0	0	0	589
0	0	2	0	1	1	0	0	0	1	0	0	0	0	0	599
0	0	3	0	0	1	3	0	0	0	0	0	0	0	0	602
1	0	1	0	4	2	1	2	0	0	0	0	0	0	0	783
1	0	3	0	0	4	2	0	0	0	0	3	0	0	0	983
3	0	1	1	0	1	0	0	0	0	0	0	0	0	0	794
1	0	0	1	0	4	1	1	1	0	0	0	0	0	0	709
4	0	2	0	0	3	0	0	1	4	0	0	0	0	0	749
0	0	1	0	3	3	5	0	3	3	0	1	0	0	0	829
2	1	4	0	0	1	0	0	1	1	0	0	0	0	0	774
0	3	4	3	3	5	1	1	0	2	0	0	0	0	0	720
0	1	0	3	2	5	0	1	0	3	0	0	0	0	0	627
2	0	2	1	1	1	0	0	1	0	0	0	0	0	0	485
2	0	0	1	4	1	0	0	0	0	0	0	0	0	0	456
0	3	2	1	0	3	0	0	0	1	0	1	0	0	0	499
2	1	0	1	1	2	2	0	0	2	0	1	0	0	0	578
0	0	0	4	3	2	0	0	2	0	0	1	0	0	0	526
0	0	0	0	0	1	1	1	1	0	0	0	0	0	0	672
2	0	2	0	1	0	0	0	0	1	0	3	0	0	0	523
0	0	0	1	3	1	1	1	0	1	0	1	0	0	0	519
3	2	1	1	2	1	0	0	0	1	1	0	0	0	0	509
2	0	1	0	7	1	0	0	1	1	0	0	0	0	0	534
1	2	1	0	3	2	1	0	0	1	0	1	0	0	0	583
2	0	2	0	3	3	0	0	1	1	2	0	0	0	0	557
0	0	2	2	2	1	1	0	1	2	0	0	0	0	0	591
1	1	1	2	0	1	0	0	0	1	0	0	0	0	0	524
0	1	0	0	3	0	0	2	0	1	1	1	0	0	0	500
0	1	0	1	2	2	0	0	0	0	0	0	0	0	0	524
1	2	0	0	1	1	0	0	0	2	0	2	0	0	0	521
1	0	0	1	2	0	1	0	0	2	0	0	0	0	0	488
0	0	0	0	1	0	1	0	1	1	0	1	0	0	0	452
2	0	0	1	0	2	0	0	0	1	0	0	0	0	0	416
1	1	1	1	2	0	1	1	0	2	0	1	0	0	0	391
4	2	0	0	6	2	0	1	0	2	0	0	0	0	0	417
0	0	0	1	3	2	0	3	1	1	0	0	0	0	0	368
1	0	0	0	2	1	0	0	2	0	0	0	0	0	0	376
1	1	1	1	0	0	1	0	1	3	0	1	0	0	0	343
3	3	3	1	1	2	0	0	0	0	0	0	0	0	0	410
4	1	1	1	3	0	4	0	0	2	1	0	0	0	0	503
0	0	0	0	5	2	0	0	0	0	0	2	0	0	0	556
0	2	0	1	6	3	0	0	0	4	0	0	0	0	0	542
3	3	4	2	3	1	1	0	1	2	1	0	0	0	0	709
3	5	0	2	0	1	0	2	0	1	1	1	0	0	0	751
1	2	1	2	4	1	2	0	0	2	1	1	0	0	0	604
3	4	0	1	4	1	0	0	1	1	0	0	0	0	0	481
5	4	0	0	2	0	0	0	3	0	1	0	0	0	0	573
0	2	0	2	1	1	0	1	0	0	0	0	0	0	0	226
0	1	0	0	0	0	0	0	0	0	0	0	1	0	0	155
0	0	0	0	0	1	0	0	0	0	0	0	0	0	0	0
0	0	0	0	0	0	0	0	0	0	0	0	0	1	0	0
1	2	0	0	2	0	0	0	0	0	0	0	0	0	0	222
4	1	0	0	3	0	0	0	0	0	0	0	0	1	0	27
3	0	0	0	0	0	0	0	0	0	0	1	0	0	1	216
0	0	0	0	0	0	0	0	0	0	0	0	0	0	0	197
6	1	0	0	1	0	0	0	0	0	0	0	0	3	0	222
4	3	0	2	1	1	0	0	0	0	1	1	0	0	0	233
84	**58**	**58**	**43**	**106**	**80**	**36**	**18**	**26**	**55**	**12**	**24**	**1**	**5**	**1**	**31,179**

Nativity of Children in USA Table

APPENDIX K

Whether Parents Are Living Table

Year	Both Parents Living.	Father only Living.	Mother only Living.	Both Parents Dead.	Unknown.	Totals.
1853	230	122	164	106	1	623
1854	323	210	238	185	94	1,050
1855	275	114	195	129	14	727
1856	374	124	241	152	11	902
1857	316	114	185	117	9	741
1858	342	114	213	103	9	781
1859	396	112	251	84	20	863
1860	373	125	256	90	19	863
1861	387	106	228	70	9	800
1862	449	141	264	96	7	957
1863	557	180	331	88	4	1,160
1864	424	121	272	66	5	888
1865	367	124	228	91	2	812
1866	378	118	231	123	3	853
1867	400	151	294	77	0	922
1868	368	151	256	79	0	854
1869	381	144	227	74	0	826
1870	320	136	205	51	2	714
1871	253	95	169	45	10	572
1872	246	94	161	36	9	546
1873	232	101	205	41	2	581
1874	271	129	233	44	10	687
1875	240	133	205	39	15	632
1876	310	178	252	47	15	802
1877	202	121	213	33	19	588
1878	220	117	198	36	17	588
1879	189	135	186	38	10	558

Year	Both Parents Living.	Father only Living.	Mother only Living.	Both Parents Dead.	Unknown.	Totals.
1880	218	125	193	33	8	577
1881	280	144	202	31	13	670
1882	256	150	210	41	15	672
1883	310	150	215	25	11	711
1884	282	139	194	25	13	653
1885	240	153	198	40	9	640
1886	273	131	193	34	18	649
1887	297	166	176	51	8	698
1888	286	149	193	46	13	687
1889	282	116	174	54	12	638
1890	330	108	149	54	5	646
1891	313	117	147	30	7	614
1892	285	121	168	39	11	624
1893	269	114	157	25	4	569
1894	291	118	151	30	9	599
1895	246	115	151	28	1	541
1896	371	118	160	39	4	692
1897	541	128	202	44	1	916
1898	686	95	164	33	5	983
1899	591	100	171	36	7	905
1900	742	114	180	31	6	1,073
1901	648	122	211	24	15	1,020
1902	547	100	151	34	29	861
1903	370	108	114	24	28	644
1904	422	122	138	39	37	758
1905	156	44	49	11	5	265
1906	68	48	39	7	1	163
1907	147	42	32	12	0	233
1908	105	44	53	11	1	214
1909	122	49	45	16	2	234
1910	122	82	62	19	0	285
1911	109	51	54	14	2	230
1912	109	43	49	13	0	214
1913	123	40	57	25	0	245
1914	123	42	67	24	1	257

APPENDIX L

Records of the NYJA and The Children's Village

Location of records:
Rare Book & Manuscript Library
Butler Library, 6th Floor
Columbia University
535 West 114th St.
New York, NY 10027
Telephone: (212) 854-5153

Call Number: MS1488
Bib ID: 6909466
117 linear feet/31 document boxes

The Medical Logs (Box 85, Folder 3 and Box 95, folder 1) are restricted. Researchers wishing to use the Medical Logs must sign a nondisclosure form certifying that they will not publish, or in any way disseminate, names or personally identifiable information from the Medical Logs. This collection is located onsite.

The rest of the collection consists primarily of ledgers used for record-keeping at the New York Juvenile Asylum and The Children's Village. The collection of ledgers, while large, is also fragmentary and represents a minority of the total volume of records NYJA produced. The majority of the ledgers document the movement of children through the asylum system, from arrival at the House of Reception to discharge to family or apprenticeship in the West. The ledgers also concern financial operations, committee minutes, and daily operations at the Asylum in Manhattan as well as at The Children's Village. Correspondence copybooks contain onionskin paper impressions of letters regarding institutional operations. Several of the ledgers contain papers and correspondence interleaved with the bound pages. Many are in fragile condition. A small number of reports and papers from a 1931 institutional survey are also included.

This collection has no restrictions.

APPENDIX M

Bibliography

Annual Reports:

New York Juvenile Asylum Annual Reports (1852-1921)
St. Christopher's School Annual Report (1970)
The Association for Improving the Condition of the Poor, First Annual Report (1845). Visitors' Manual.
Annual Report of the State Board of Charities of the State of New York (1885) and Volume 19 (1886)

Archival Resources:

NYJA records; Rare Book and Manuscript Library, Columbia University Library. Butler Library, New York City
National Orphan Train Complex, Concordia, Kansas
Library of Congress, Washington, D.C.

Books:

Avery, Gillian. *Nineteenth Century Children: Heroes and Heroines in English Children's Stories, 1780-1900*. London: Hodder & Stoughton, 1965.

Brace, Charles Loring. *The Dangerous Classes of New York and Twenty Years' Work among Them*. New York: Wynkoop & Hallenbeck, 1880.

Bremner, Robert H., et al. *Children and Youth in America: A Documentary History*, 3 vols. Cambridge, Mass.: Harvard University Press, 1970-74.

Brenzel, Barbara. *The Girls at Lancaster: A Social Portrait of the First Reform School for Girls in North America, 1856-1905*. Diss. Harvard University, 1978.

Charter and By-Laws of the The Children's Village, Dobbs Ferry. The Children's Village Press, 1931.

DeBow, J. D. B. *Mortality Statistics of the Seventh Census of the United States*, 33rd Cong., 2nd Sess., H.R., Ex. Doc. No. 98. Washington, D.C.: D. Nicholson, 1855.

Ernst, *Immigrant Life in New York City (1825-1863)*. Syracuse University Press, 1994.

General Catalogue of the Officers and Graduates of Williams College. Williams College, 1920.

Harris, Thomas L. *Juvenile Depravity and Crime in Our City*, New York, 1850.

Hart, Hastings. *The Extinction of the Defective Delinquent: A Working Program*. New York: Russell Sage Foundation, 1912.

Hart, Hastings. *Sterilization as a Practical Measure*. New York: Russell Sage Foundation, 1912.

Hurley, Daniel I. *A History of The Children's Home of Cincinnati 1864-1889*. Children's Home of Cincinnati, 1990.

Illinois State Gazetteer and Business Directory. Chicago: George W. Hawes & Co.

Kidder, Clark. *Orphan Trains and Their Precious Cargo: The Life's Work of Reverend Herman D. Clarke* (2nd Edition). Createspace, 2018.

Langsam, Miriam Z. *Children West—A History of the Placing-Out System of the New York Children's Aid Society 1853-1890*. State Historical Society of Wisconsin: Madison, 1964.

O'Connor, Stephen. *Orphan Trains—The Story of Charles Loring Brace and the Children he Saved and Failed*. Houghton Mifflin Co., 2001.

Picket, Robert S. *House of Refuge, Origins of Juvenile Reform in New York State, 1815-1857*. Syracuse University Press, 1969.

Proceedings of the Conference on the Care of Dependent Children. Sixtieth Congress, second edition, Senate Document No. 721, 8-14. Government Printing Office. Washington: 1909.

Proceedings of the National Conference of Charities and Correction, Ninth Annual Conference. Held at Madison, Wisconsin on August 7-12, 1882. Midland Publishing Co., 1882.

Rebecca. *Tramps in New York*. American Tract Society, 1863.

Report of the Joint Committee on Home-Finding Societies, Forty-eighth General Assembly, 1915. Springfield: Schnepp & Barnes, 1915.

Schneider, David M. and Albert Deutsch. *The History of Public Welfare in New York State 1867-1940*. Chicago, 1941.

Spann, Edward K. *The New Metropolis: New York City, 1850-1857*. New York: Columbia University Press, 1981.

von Hartz, John. *New York Street Kids—136 Photographs Selected by The Children's Aid Society*. New York: Dover Publications, Inc., 1978.

Welfare Bulletin No. 7. Illinois Dept. of Public Welfare, 1916.

Journals

The New England Journal of Medicine, 1904, 493. Quoting the *Boston Medical and Surgical Journal*, May 5, 1904. "New York: Cottage Colony for Juvenile Asylum."

Magazine Articles:

Finkelman, Paul. "The Protection of Black Rights in Seward's New York." *Civil War History*, Vol. 34 No. 3, 1988.

Dodge, Mary E. "A Day with Dr. Brooks." *Scribner's Monthly*, November 1870; Volume One, Number One, 36-58..

"The New York Association for Improving the Condition of the Poor: The Formative Years." *New York Historical Society Quarterly* (1959).

Wheeler, Leslie. "The Orphan Trains." *American History Illustrated*, December 1983, 10.

Newspapers:

Albany Evening Journal (Albany, New York)
Anaconda Standard (Anaconda, Montana)
Buffalo Evening News (Buffalo, New York)
Centinel of Freedom (Newark, New Jersey)
Central Illinois Gazette (West Urbana, now Champaign, Illinois)
Chicago Tribune (Chicago, Illinois)
Cleveland Herald (Cleveland, Ohio)
Cleveland Leader (Cleveland, Ohio)
Commercial Advertiser (New York City)
Daily Illinois State Journal (Springfield, Illinois)
Daily News Democrat (Huntington, Indiana)
Daily People (New York City)
Decatur Daily Republican (Decatur, Illinois)
Decatur Weekly Republican (Decatur, Illinois)
Dobbs Ferry Register (Dobbs Ferry, New York)
Duluth News Tribune (Duluth, Minnesota)
Evening Times-Republican (Marshalltown, Iowa)
Freeport Journal-Standard (Freeport, Illinois)
Gibson City Courier (Gibson, Illinois)
Joliet Weekly Sun (Joliet, Illinois)
Kansas City Times (Kansas City, Missouri)
Manchester Press (Manchester, Iowa)
Miami Herald (Miami, Florida)
Montgomery Advertiser (Montgomery, Alabama)
New-York Daily Tribune (New York City)
New-York Evening Post (New York City)
New York Herald (New York City)
New York Observer (New York City)
New-York Tribune (New York City)
People (New York City)
Pittsburg Dispatch (Pittsburg, Pennsylvania)
Plain Dealer (Cleveland, Ohio)
Repository (Canton, Ohio)
Saint Louis Dispatch (Saint Louis, Missouri)
Salt Lake Telegram (Salt Lake City, Utah)
Sangamo Journal-Illinois State Journal (Springfield, Illinois)
Springfield Republican (Springfield, Massachusetts)
Sterling Gazette (Sterling, Illinois)
Tacoma Daily News (Tacoma, Washington)
The Baltimore Sun (Baltimore, Maryland)
The Daily Long Island Farmer (Jamaica, Queens County, New York City)
The Decatur Herald (Decatur, Illinois)
The Duluth Evening Herald (Duluth, Minnesota)
The Evening Gazette (Monmouth, Illinois)
The Evening Telegram (New York City)
The Farmer's Review (Chicago, Illinois)
The New York Times (New York City)
The Ottawa Free Trader (Ottawa, Illinois)
The Pantagraph (Bloomington, Illinois)
The Pittsburgh Press (Pittsburgh, Pennsylvania)
The Portsmouth Journal of Literature and Politics (Portsmouth, New Hampshire)
The Puritan Recorder (Boston, Massachusetts)
The Quincy Daily Whig (Quincy, IL)
The Sabbath Recorder (New York City)
The Saratogian (Saratoga Springs, New York)
The Sun (New York City)
The Sun and New York Press (New York City)
The Syracuse Journal (Syracuse, New York)
The Times (Richmond, Virginia)
The Wheeling Daily Intelligencer (Wheeling, West Virginia)
True Republican (Sycamore, Illinois)
Vermilion County Press (Danville, Illinois)

Pamphlets:

Jewish Board of Guardians. "Hawthorne Cedar Knolls School."

Kingsbury, Fanny Goodwin. "The Church at Home and Abroad: Presbyterian Church," September 1896.

Odquiest, Maurice. "The History of Graham."

Williams, Mornay. "Memorandum as to the Development of the Asylum Work." New York: March 2, 1897.

Notes

Introduction

1. "During the last twenty years, a tide of population has settled towards those shores, to which there is no movement parallel in history. During the year 1852 alone, 300,992 alien passengers have landed in New York, or nearly at the rate of one thousand a day for every week day." *First Annual Report of the Children's Aid Society* (1854), 3-4.
2. John William Leonard, *History of the City of New York 1609-1909* (New York: Journal of Commerce and Commercial Bulletin, 1910), 539. According to Leonard, "The population of New York City in 1850 was, by Federal census, 515,477, and in 1860, 805,658." The 10,000 figure is given in *First Annual Report of the Children's Aid Society* (New York, 1854), 4.
3. Miriam Z. Langsam, *Children West—A History of the Placing-Out System of the New York Children's Aid Society 1853-1890*, (State Historical Society of Wisconsin, Madison, 1964), 2.
4. Documents Relative to the House of Refuge. Society for the Reformation of Juvenile Delinquents, (New York: Mahlon Day, 1832), 207.
5. New York State Senate, *Report of Select Committee Appointed to Visit Charitable Institutions Supported by the State, and All City and Country Work Houses and Jails*, doc. 8 (Jan. 9, 1857), 3-7.
6. Documents of the Senate of the State of New York, Volume 2, Issues 31-62. New York (State). Legislature. Senate. E. Croswell; Weed, Parsons and Company, State Printers (1880), 57.
7. "City Waifs on Western Farms," *Springfield Republican* (Springfield, Massachusetts), March 12, 1905, 17. "There are many thick volumes at the juvenile asylum made up of letters from youngsters who, on western farms, are gaining a firm foothold and a new outlook upon life."

Chapter 1 (pages 3-26)

1. The Panic of 1837 was one of America's first depressions, resulting in high unemployment and extensive bank failures. It featured a classic bubble at its start. The Panic of 1837 lasted about five years, although there was a brief upturn in 1839.
2. Year of organization and incorporation are in New-York Association for Improving the Condition of the Poor, *Sixth Annual Report* (1849). Title page. Visits and objective for doing so are in New-York Association for Improving the Condition of the Poor, *First Annual Report* (1845), 17.
3. New-York Association for Improving the Condition of the Poor, *First Annual Report* (1845). Visitors' Manual, 26.
4. Edward K. Spann. *The New Metropolis: New York City, 1850-1857* (New York: Columbia University Press, 1981), 262.
5. George W. [Washington] Matsell. Chief of Police in the New York City Police Department, *Semi-Annual Report of the Chief of Police from May 31 to October 31, 1849* (New York, 1850). Published as an appendix to Thomas L. Harris, *Juvenile Depravity and Crime in Our City*, New York, 1850, 14-15.
6. Charles Loring Brace. *The Dangerous Classes of New York and Twenty Years' Work among Them*, (New York: Wynkoop & Hallenbeck, 1880), 88-89; *First Annual Report of the Children's Aid Society*, 1854, 4.
7. Biographical Note, NYJA Records (The Children's Village), 1853-1954, Columbia University Libraries Collections; New York Juvenile Asylum, *Sixty-First Annual Report* (1912). Asylum Chronology (Appendix F), 76. The precise date was October 8, 1849.
8. New York Juvenile Asylum, *Sixty-Second Annual Report* (1913; printed 1914). Asylum Chronology (Appendix F), 78.
9. New York Juvenile Asylum, *First Annual Report* (June 10, 1853), 5-6.
10. "By Telegraph to the New-York Tribune: New York Legislature," *New-York Daily Tribune*, February 13, 1851, 7.
11. "Tribune's Special Dispatches: New-York Legislature," *New-York Daily Tribune*, March 18, 1851, 4; New York Juvenile Asylum, *Eighth Annual Report* (1860), 122.
12. *New-York Daily Tribune*, March 18, 1851, 4.
13. New York Juvenile Asylum, *Third Annual Report* (1854), 6.
14. Biographical Note, NYJA Records (The Children's Village), 1853-1954, Columbia University Libraries Collections; New York Juvenile Asylum, *Sixty-First Annual Report* (1912). Asylum Chronology, 76.
15. New York Juvenile Asylum, *First Annual Report* (1852), 4.
16. Ibid., 5.
17. New York Juvenile Asylum, *Sixty-First Annual Report* (1912). Asylum Chronology, 76; New York Juvenile Asylum, *First Annual Report* (1852), 6.
18. New York Juvenile Asylum, *First Annual Report* (1852), 9
19. Ibid., 6.

20 New York Juvenile Asylum, *Second Annual Report* (1853), 3; "Juvenile Asylum," *The Sabbath Recorder*, March 24, 1853, 162.
21 Cited in Ernst, *Immigrant Life in New York City, 1825-1863*. (Syracuse University Press, 1994), 140.
22 New York Juvenile Asylum, *Fifty-First Annual Report* (1902), 23.
23 New York Juvenile Asylum, *Second Annual Report* (1853), 15.
24 *In Memoriam. Apollos Russel Wetmore*, (New York, 1881), 5.
25 Ibid., 60.
26 Ibid., 7.
27 Ibid., 108.
28 Ibid., 10.
29 Ibid., 67.
30 Ibid., 109.
31 Ibid., 7, 20, 60.
32 "The New York Association for Improving the Condition of the Poor: The Formative Years," New York Historical Society Quarterly (1959), 319.
33 New York Juvenile Asylum, *Fifty-Fifth Annual Report* (1907). Asylum Chronology, 76.
34 New York Juvenile Asylum, *Third Annual Report* (1854), 7.
35 New York Juvenile Asylum, *Second Annual Report* (1853), 12.
36 Langsam, *Children West—A History of the Placing-Out System of the New York Children's Aid Society 1853-1890*, 5.
37 New York Juvenile Asylum, *Second Annual Report* (1853), 7, 14. Report of expenses: "Dec. 31. To Children's Aid Society, Expenses on Children placed in the Country: 129.00."
38 Ibid., 7.
39 NYJA records; Rare Book and Manuscript Library, Columbia University Library. Indentures-Case Files (Box 61), 1854-1888.
40 Ibid. An exact number is hard to determine because some children were picked up at different points on the way to Dowagiac.
41 E. P. Smith's journal, published in the *Third Annual Report of the Children's Aid Society*; (New York: M. B. Wynkoop), February 1856, 54-60.
42 Ibid.
43 Ibid. An exact number is hard to determine because some children were picked up at different points on the way to Dowagiac.
44 Ibid.
45 *Second Annual Report of the Children's Aid Society*; (New York: M. B. Wynkoop), February 1855, 16.
46 NYJA records; Rare Book and Manuscript Library, Columbia University Library. Indentures-Case Files (Box 61), 1854-1888.
47 New York State Census. Census of the Inhabitants in the 2nd Election District of the 19th Ward of New York in the County of New York, July 14, 1855.
48 Acreage size and purchase price is from New York Juvenile Asylum, *Sixty-First Annual Report* (1912). Asylum Chronology, 76.
49 New York Juvenile Asylum, *Fifth Annual Report* (1856), 12.
50 Correspondence. Indentures-Outgoing, 1868-70. Box 7. Orig. pp. 246-7. Report of Ebenezer Wright, Western Indenturing Agent.
51 "Our City Charities—No. II: The New-York Juvenile Asylum—Home Missionary Work: The Juvenile Asylum," *New York Times*, January 31, 1860; "Home Missionary Work: The Children of The Streets," *New-York Tribune*, February 18, 1860, 4; Opening day source: New York Juvenile Asylum, *Sixty-First Annual Report* (1912). Asylum Chronology, 76.
52 Mary E. Dodge, "A Day with Dr. Brooks," *Scribner's Monthly*, November 1870, Volume One, 50.
53 New York Juvenile Asylum, *Fiftieth Annual Report* (1901). Front matter features floor plan of building
54 Ibid.
55 NYJA records; Rare Book and Manuscript Library, Columbia University Library. Minutes of the Committee on Admissions, Indentures and Discharges (Box 1, Folder 1), 1853-1861. October 20, 1859 meeting, 355, 360.
56 Ibid., 370.
57 Ibid., 426.
58 Dodge, "A Day with Dr. Brooks," 48.
59 New York Juvenile Asylum, *Sixty-First Annual Report* (1912). Asylum Chronology, 76. Source for "three or four in a bed" is from NYJA records; Rare Book and Manuscript Library, Columbia University Library. Minutes of the Committee on Admissions, Indentures and Discharges (Box 1, Folder 1), 1853-1861. March 24, 1859 meeting, 261.
60 New York Juvenile Asylum, *First Annual Report* (1852), 19.
61 New York Juvenile Asylum, *Third Annual Report* (1854), 4-5.
62 Circulars of Information of the Bureau of Education, No. 6. Statements relating to the Reformatory, Charitable, and Industrial Schools for the Young, (Washington: Government Printing Office, 1875), 116.
63 NYJA records; Rare Book and Manuscript Library, Columbia University Library. Minutes of the Applications, House of Reception, Visiting Committee (Box 2, Folder 2), 1854-1863. March 1, 1855 meeting.
64 Rebecca, *Tramps in New York*. (American Tract Society, 1863), 99-100.
65 Circulars of Information of the Bureau of Education, No. 6. Statements relating to the Reformatory, Charitable, and Industrial Schools for the Young, (Washington: Government Printing Office, 1875), 116.
66 "Home Missionary Work: The Children of The Streets," *New-York Tribune*, February 18, 1860, 4.
67 "For the City's Waifs—The New York Juvenile Asylum Opens Its House of Reception," *The Sun* (New York), May 8, 1891, 9.
68 Ibid. The building was sold to Michael Coleman in February 1909, who in turn sold it to the Marmac Construction Company. Marmac sold it to a party that constructed a twelve-story loft building on Nos. 104 to 106 West Twenty-seventh street in 1909; "The Real Estate Market," *The Sun and New York Press* (New York), August 5, 1909, 9.
69 "A Fine House of Reception: The New-York Juvenile Asylum Opens Its New Building," *The Sun* (New York), May 8, 1891, 4.

70 "Midnight Alarm in 'A Boys' Asylum: Flames Bursting From an Occupant's Bedstead—Views of the Cause of the Fire," *New-York Daily Tribune*, July 15, 1878, 2.

71 Chapter 173, Laws of 1875, quoted in Robert Bremner et al., eds., *Children and Youth in America* (Cambridge: Harvard University Press, 1971), II, 281. Official criticism had come in the form of the Letchworth Report on Poorhouses and Almshouses in 1874. The New York Society for the Prevention of Cruelty to Children, founded in 1875, also pressed for more restrictive legislation.

72 *Annual Report of the State Board of Charities of the State of New York*; Volume 19 (1886), 173; David M. Schneider and Albert Deutsch. *The History of Public Welfare in New York State 1867-1940* (Chicago, 1941), 65: "Toward the end of 1874, there were 132 orphan asylums and homes for the friendless [in New York State] with a total population of 11,907 children under sixteen years of age. By 1885 there were 204 such institutions maintaining a total of 23,592 children."

73 Date of 1884 from *Welfare Bulletin No. 7* (Illinois Dept. of Public Welfare), 1916, 28: "The number of children increased from the time the law was enacted in 1875 to 1883, but it then declined because of the more rigid enforcement of the law following this inquiry [by commissioners of charities and correction]."

74 *Annual Report of the State Board of Charities of the State of New York*; Volume 19 (1886), 173.

75 "Report of State Board of Charities: Summary of Work of Year 1901 Transmitted to Legislature," *The Syracuse Journal*, March 18, 1902, 10.

76 Report on the Poorhouses of the Eighth Judicial District of New York by Commissioner Letchworth (In the Report of the New York State Board of Charities for 1896, 379-92. Transmitted to the Legislature February 25, 1897; also in pamphlet.)

77 The Charter for the Greater New York, And Acts Supplementary Thereto adopted by the State Legislature, as (Office of Publication: Eagle Building, Brooklyn: 1897). "The Charter of the City of New York as Adopted by the Legislature of 1901, with Amendments," 65. (Office of Publication: Eagle Building, Brooklyn); Brooklyn Eagle Library No. 54, Vol. XVI. No. 6, June 1901.

78 Mornay Williams. "Memorandum as to the Development of the Asylum Work," March 2, 1897, 5. Records of The Children's Village. The Memorandum was shared with other members of the board at the Asylum.

79 Ibid., 3.

80 NYJA records; Rare Book and Manuscript Library, Columbia University Library. Correspondence, Indentures-Outgoing (Box 7, Folder 1), 1868-1870. From the October 1870 monthly report of Ebenezer Wright, 501.

81 *Eighty-Third Annual Meeting of the Hebrew Orphan Asylum of the City of New York*, 1906 (New York: Stettiner Brothers), 59.

82 Ibid., 60.

83 Williams, "Memorandum as to the Development of the Asylum Work," 7.

84 Ibid., 3.

85 New York Juvenile Asylum, *Forty-Eighth Annual Report* (1899), 4.

86 New York Juvenile Asylum, *Fifty-Third Annual Report* (1904). Report of the Directors, 13.

87 Source for electric cars: New York Juvenile Asylum, *Fiftieth Annual Report* (1901). Front matter.

88 Williams, "Memorandum as to the Development of the Asylum Work," 7.

89 New York Juvenile Asylum, *Fiftieth Annual Report* (1901), 15.

90 Source of Northeast direction: "The Juvenile Asylum Buys A New Site," *The New York Times*, October 6, 1901, 5.

91 New York Juvenile Asylum, *Fifty-Third Annual Report* (1904). Report of the Directors, 11.

92 "The Juvenile Asylum Buys A New Site," *The New York Times*, October 6, 1901, 5.

93 For a full account, see Barbara Brenzel, *The Girls at Lancaster: A Social Portrait of the First Reform School for Girls in North America, 1856-1905*, (Diss. Harvard University, 1978).

94 Precedents such as Wichern's Rauhe Haus in Germany, De Meta's Ecole Agricole in France, and the Royal Philanthropic Society's Redhill School are surveyed in Brenzel's *The Girls at Lancaster*.

95 Maurice Odquiest, "The History of Graham" (pamphlet); "Hawthorne Cedar Knolls School," Jewish Board of Guardians (pamphlet); *St. Christopher's School Annual Report* (1970).

96 Annual Report of the State Board of Charities of the State of New York for the Year 1905, In Three Volumes, 286. Monroe County: Public Relief (Albany: Brandow Printing Company; State Legislative Printer, 1906).

97 Schneider and Deutsch, "*The History of Public Welfare in New York State*," 174-77.

98 Program for Architectural Competitive Bid: New York Juvenile Asylum, May 1902.

99 "Competition For Ideal Village Plans," *New-York Daily Tribune*, June 17, 1902, 7.

100 New York Juvenile Asylum, *Fifty-First Annual Report* (1902). "Report on Competitive Designs," Appendix B, 86.

101 NYJA records; Rare Book and Manuscript Library, Columbia University Library. General Correspondence, 1897-1903 (Box 7, Folder 3). Edwin C. Burdick to Henry E. Gregory, May 26, 1903, 345.

102 Ibid., July 9, 1903, 420.

103 New York Juvenile Asylum, *Fifty-Second Annual Report* (1903). Superintendent's Report, 22.

104 New York Juvenile Asylum, *Fifty-Third Annual Report* (1904), 27.

105 New York Juvenile Asylum, *Fifty-First Annual Report* (1902). "Proposed Sequel to a Work of Great Usefulness," (Appendix C), 89-90; Reprinted in the *New England Journal of Medicine*, Volume 150, 1904, 493: Quoting the *Boston Medical and Surgical Journal*, May 5, 1904. "New York. Cottage Colony for Juvenile Asylum."

106 New York Juvenile Asylum, *Fifty-First Annual Report* (1902). "Proposed Sequel to a Work of Great Usefulness," (Appendix C), 91.

107 New York Juvenile Asylum, *Fifty-Third Annual Report* (1904), 29-30. Brooks resided at 126 Chestnut Street in Springfield per an envelope addressed to Brooks from the NYJA, postmarked 1903, and offered for sale online in 2018. "Local Intelligence," *Springfield Republican*, December 20, 1904, 8.
108 New York Juvenile Asylum, *Fifty-Third Annual Report* (1904). Report of the Western Agency, 43.
109 New York Juvenile Asylum, *Fifty-Fourth Annual Report* (1905). "The Last Days on Washington Heights." Superintendent's Report, 1905, 21.
110 Ibid.
111 Ibid.
112 "Report of State Board of Charities: Summary of Work of Year 1901 Transmitted to Legislature," *The Syracuse Journal*, March 18, 1902, 10.
113 New York Juvenile Asylum, *Fifty-Fourth Annual Report* (1905). "The Last Days on Washington Heights." Superintendent's Report, 1905, 21.
114 "Thousand City Urchins at Big Christmas Party," *The Quincy Daily Whig* (Quincy, IL), December 18, 1904, 20.
115 New York Juvenile Asylum, *Fifty-Third Annual Report* (1904). Superintendent's Report, 28.
116 NYJA records; Rare Book and Manuscript Library, Columbia University Library. Correspondence, 1904-1908 (Box 10). Hilles to Blum, 49.
117 Ibid.
118 Proceedings of the Conference on the Care of Dependent Children: Held at Washington, D. C., January 25, 26, 1909 (Washington: Government Printing Office, 1909), 24.
119 NYJA records; Rare Book and Manuscript Library, Columbia University Library. Correspondence, 1904-1908 (Box 10). Hilles to Vaux, May 6, 1905.
120 New York Juvenile Asylum, *Fifty-Fourth Annual Report* (1905), 77.
121 Ibid., 20.
122 NYJA records; Rare Book and Manuscript Library, Columbia University Library. Correspondence, 1904-1908 (Box 10). Hilles to Wendell, May 19, 1905.
123 New York Juvenile Asylum, *Fifty-Sixth Annual Report* (1907). Asylum Chronology (Appendix C), 67.
124 New York Juvenile Asylum, *Fifty-Fifth Annual Report* (1906). Superintendent's Report, 31.
125 Dodge, "A Day with Dr. Brooks," 41.

Chapter 2 (pages 27-44)

1 New York Juvenile Asylum, *Third Annual Report* (1854), 21.
2 Dodge, "A Day with Dr. Brooks," 41. The article describes the founding, activities, and administration of the NYJA.
3 New York Juvenile Asylum, *Forty-Seventh Annual Report* (1898), 44-5.
4 "New-York Legislature: The New-York Juvenile Asylum," *New-York Daily Tribune*, January 28, 1856, 6.
5 NYJA Records; Rare Book and Manuscript Library, Columbia University Library. Case Registers-House of Reception,1878-1880 (Box 31, File 3). Unidentified newspaper clipping regarding the commitment of Charles Foster's two sons—glued to page at end of book.
6 NYJA records; Rare Book and Manuscript Library, Columbia University Library. Minutes Admissions, Indentures, Discharges with Invoices, 1873-1880 (Box 8).
7 *Charter and By-Laws of The Children's Village*, Dobbs Ferry: The Children's Village Press, 1931.
8 New York Juvenile Asylum, *Third Annual Report* (1854), 5
9 Ibid., 24.
10 New York Juvenile Asylum, *Sixty-Third Annual Report* (1914), 39-55.
11 Ibid.
12 New York Juvenile Asylum, *Twenty-Eighth Annual Report* (1879), 38.
13 Letter written from Kaseyville, Missouri dated January 5, 1899 from William Masterson to his sister, Ida. William was living in Pittsfield, Missouri at the time. Masterson Family Papers, MSN/CW 5109, Rare Books and Special Collections, Hesburgh Libraries of Notre Dame.
14 New York Juvenile Asylum, *Sixty-First Annual Report* (1913), 46.
15 "Dressing Up," *New York Herald Sun*, January 14, 1877, 6.
16 NYJA records; Rare Book and Manuscript Library, Columbia University Library. Case Registers-House of Reception, 1881-1883 (Box 132, Folder 1), 150.
17 Ibid., 153.
18 "Children of the Tenement Homes," *The Quincy Daily Whig*, (Quincy, IL), January 23, 1906, 2.
19 Ibid., 22.
20 "The Much Abused Street Boy," *Plain Dealer* (Cleveland, Ohio), February 19, 1905, 47.
21 "Children of the Tenement Homes," *The Quincy Daily Whig* (Quincy, IL), January 23, 1906, 2.
22 New York Juvenile Asylum, *Fifty-First Annual Report* (1902), 22-3.
23 NYJA Records; Rare Book and Manuscript Library, Columbia University Library; Parent Surrender Forms (1878-1880); Box 59; Folder 2; Admission Records—House of Reception (1878-1880), Box 13, Folder 3.
24 New York Juvenile Asylum, *First Annual Report* (1852), 21.
25 New York Juvenile Asylum, *Forty-Seventh Annual Report* (1898). Report of Louise A. Husted, M. D., 45.
26 Ibid., 44.
27 Ibid.
28 Ibid., 44-5.
29 New York Juvenile Asylum, *Twenty-Ninth Annual Report* (1880), 18.
30 NYJA records; Rare Book and Manuscript Library, Columbia University Library. Parent Surrender Forms, 1873-1875 (Box 59, Folder 1). Mrs. Murphy appeared on December 28, 1875.
31 New York Juvenile Asylum, *Sixty-Second Annual Report* (1913), 66. "Adequate Preparation for Life for Every Child"—an Address by Charles Dewey Hilles, at the New York City Conference of Charities and Corrections, May 15, 1913. He was quoting Thomas Arnold, headmaster of England's Rugby School from 1828-1841.
32 NYJA records; Rare Book and Manuscript Library, Columbia University Library. Correspondence. Guy Morgan to Mrs. Grace Waters, May 9, 1917.

33 "State Board of Charities Upheld," *Buffalo Evening News* (New York), December 23, 1901, 6.
34 "May Make Its Own Rules," *The Syracuse Journal*, October 8, 1902, 2.
35 NYJA records; Rare Book and Manuscript Library, Columbia University Library. General Correspondence, 1897-1903 (Box 7, Folder 3), 396.
36 Ibid., Burdick to Samuel Horowitz of New York City, 538.
37 Ibid., 585.
38 New York Juvenile Asylum, *Twenty-Eighth Annual Report* (1879), 37.
39 New York Juvenile Asylum, *Forty-First Annual Report* (1892), 43-4.
40 New York Laws, 1892, Ch. 217, amending section 291—New York Penal Code.
41 New York Laws, 1902, Ch. 590. The court was housed in the former Department of Public Charities building on Third Avenue and 11th Street.
42 "A Day in the Children's Court," *The Duluth Evening Herald*, April 1, 1905, 19.
43 Ibid.
44 "Children of the Tenement Homes," *The Quincy Daily Whig* (Quincy, IL), January 23, 1906, 2.
45 Ibid.
46 New York Juvenile Asylum, *Fifty-Second Annual Report* (1903), 17.
47 Extracts from Charter. A single sheet included with indentures. The particular indenture referenced in this case was that of Emma J. Westmen dated December 19, 1867. "The following are the Sections of the Charter of 'THE NEW YORK JUVENILE ASYLUM,' especially referred to in, and made a part of the foregoing instrument of indenture:"
48 Charters and by-laws of the New-York Juvenile Asylum, together with certain amendments and the by-laws of the Institution. (New York: A. J. Brady), 1859, 23.
49 Ibid., 11.
50 Ibid., 15.
51 New York Juvenile Asylum, *Second Annual Report* (1853), 12-3.
52 New York Juvenile Asylum, *Fourth Annual Report* (1856), 21.
53 New York Juvenile Asylum, *First Annual Report* (1852), 11.
54 New York Juvenile Asylum, *Fourth Annual Report* (1856), 48.
55 Ibid., 22.
56 NYJA records; Rare Book and Manuscript Library, Columbia University Library. General Correspondence, 1897-1903 (Box 7, Folder 3). Burdick to Clapsaddle, 316.
57 Extracts from Charter. A single sheet included with indentures. The particular indenture referenced in this case was that of Emma J. Westmen dated December 19, 1867.
58 Dodge, "A Day with Dr. Brooks," 40. New York Juvenile Asylum, *Twenty-Seventh Annual Report* (1878), 24: "By the Charter of the Asylum, the committing magistrate has power to discharge a child any time within twenty days after commitment. At the expiration of twenty days, sole authority over the children reverts to the Directors of the Asylum, who detain them until in their judgement it is proper to discharge them."
59 NYJA records; Rare Book and Manuscript Library, Columbia University Library. General Correspondence, 1897-1903 (Box 7, Folder 3), 302.
60 NYJA records; Rare Book and Manuscript Library, Columbia University Library. Minutes. Admissions, Indentures, Discharges with Invoices, 1873-1880 (Box 8).
61 New York Juvenile Asylum, *Forty-Seventh Annual Report* (1898). Report of Louise A. Husted, M. D., 46.
62 Ibid., 44.
63 NYJA records; Rare Book and Manuscript Library, Columbia University Library. General Correspondence, 1897-1903 (Box 7, Folder 3), Burdick to Gottlieb, 298.
64 Ibid. Burdick to Rosalsky, 332.
65 NYJA records; Rare Book and Manuscript Library, Columbia University Library. Correspondence, 1897-1903 (Box 7, Folder 3).
66 New York Juvenile Asylum, *Sixty-Ninth Annual Report* (1920). Report of Superintendent Guy Morgan, "Parole and After-Care," 20-1.
67 Various Annual Reports from The Children's Village, 1920-1930. The number placed on parole was given as a separate figure from those sent west in the annual report statistics.
68 New York Juvenile Asylum, *Forty-Seventh Annual Report* (1898), 17.

Chapter 3 (pages 45-60)

1 Robert S. Picket. *House of Refuge, Origins of Juvenile Reform in New York State, 1815-1857*. (Syracuse University Press, 1969), 2.
2 New York Juvenile Asylum, *Fiftieth Annual Report* (1901). Report of the Directors, 13.
3 New York Juvenile Asylum, *Sixty-First Annual Report* (1912). Asylum Chronology, 76.
4 J. D. B. DeBow, Mortality Statistics of the Seventh Census of the United States, 33rd Cong., 2nd Sess., H.R., Ex. Doc. No. 98 (Washington, D.C.: D. Nicholson, 1855), 180; Cited in Picket, *House of Refuge*, 5.
5 Percent of foreign admissions from *Plain Dealer* (Cleveland, Ohio), Sunday, February 19, 1905, 47. "The Much Abused Street Boy."
6 John von Hartz. *New York Street Kids—136 Photographs Selected by The Children's Aid Society*, (New York: Dover Publications, Inc., 1978), 39.
7 New York Juvenile Asylum, *Fifty-First Annual Report* (1902), 22.
8 Ibid.
9 New York Juvenile Asylum, *Fifty-First Annual Report* (1902). "Proposed Sequel to a Work of Great Usefulness," (Appendix C), 87-91.
10 NYJA records; Rare Book and Manuscript Library, Columbia University Library. Minutes of the Committee on Admissions, Indentures and Discharges (Box 1, Folder 1), 1853-1861, 526.
11 Ibid., 540.
12 Ibid., November 17, 1861, 549.

13 NYJA records; Rare Book and Manuscript Library, Columbia University Library. Minutes of the Committee on Admissions, Indentures and Discharges (Box 1, Folder 1), 1853-1861, 132.
14 Dodge, "A Day with Dr. Brooks," 46-7.
15 New York Juvenile Asylum, *Thirty-Seventh Annual Report* (1888), 25.
16 NYJA records; Rare Book and Manuscript Library, Columbia University Library. General Correspondence, 1897-1903 (Box 7, Folder 3), 328.
17 Ibid., August 15, 1903, 578.
18 New York Juvenile Asylum, *Fifty-Eighth Annual Report* (1909), 12.
19 Ibid., 21.
20 New York Juvenile Asylum, *Fifty-Ninth Annual Report* (1910). Superintendent's Report, 22.
21 New York Juvenile Asylum, *First Annual Report* (1852), 21.
22 Rebecca, *Tramps in New York*, 94-5, 104.
23 New York Juvenile Asylum, *Twenty-Ninth Annual Report* (1880), 18.
24 New York Juvenile Asylum, *First Annual Report* (1852), 21.
25 New York Juvenile Asylum, *Twenty-Ninth Annual Report* (1880), 19.
26 NYJA records; Rare Book and Manuscript Library, Columbia University Library. General Correspondence, 1897-1903 (Box 7), Burdick to Cohen, May 7, 1903.
27 New York Juvenile Asylum, *Forty-Eighth Annual Report* (1899), 5.
28 NYJA records; Rare Book and Manuscript Library, Columbia University Library. Correspondence (Box 10), 1904-1908. Hilles to Daniels, March 29, 1905.
29 New York Juvenile Asylum, *Fifty-Fifth Annual Report* (1906). Superintendent's Report, 26.
30 New York Juvenile Asylum, *Sixtieth Annual Report* (1911). Superintendent's Report, 24.
31 Letter written from Pittsfield, Missouri, dated May 1889 from William Masterson to his sister, Ida. William was living in Pittsfield, Missouri at the time. Masterson Family Papers, MSN/CW 5109, Rare Books and Special Collections, Hesburgh Libraries of Notre Dame.
32 New York Juvenile Asylum, *Sixty-First Annual Report* (1912). Superintendent's Report, 24-5.
33 NYJA records; Rare Book and Manuscript Library, Columbia University Library. General Correspondence, 1897-1903 (Box 7, Folder 3). Edwin C. Burdick to Samuel H. Goldberg, July 22, 1903, 472.
34 New York House of Refuge, Case Files, Series A2064, Vol. 20 (1851-52); Case 5423. New York State Library Archives, Cultural Education Center, Albany, New York.
35 New York Juvenile Asylum, *Fifty-Fourth Annual Report* (1905). Superintendent's Report, 28.
36 New York Juvenile Asylum, *Fourth Annual Report* (1856), 27-8.
37 New York Juvenile Asylum, *Third Annual Report* (1854), 8.
38 Ibid., 28.
39 "Juvenile Fugitives," *Commercial Advertiser* (New York), March 30, 1868, 4.
40 "From A Sixth Story Window," *The Sun* (New York), May 7, 1891.
41 "Boys in Asylum Break Out for Holiday," *Chicago Tribune*, November 3, 1902.
42 New York Juvenile Asylum records; Rare Book and Manuscript Library, Columbia University Library. General Correspondence, 1897-1903 (Box 7, Folder 3). Burdick to Henry E. Gregory (Vice Chairman of the A. I. & D. Committee), April 20, 1903, 248.
43 New York Juvenile Asylum, *Fifty-Fourth Annual Report* (1905). Superintendent's Report, 28.
44 Ibid.
45 New York Juvenile Asylum, *Fifty-Fifth Annual Report* (1906). Superintendent's Report, 26-7.
46 "Six Boys Flee in Pajamas," *The Daily Long Island Farmer* (Jamaica, Queens County, New York City), November 26, 1915, 4.
47 "Condensed Telegrams," *Norwich Morning Bulletin* (Connecticut), April 14, 1916, 2.
48 NYJA records; Rare Book and Manuscript Library, Columbia University Library. General Correspondence, 1897-1903 (Box 7, Folder 3). Burdick to Barrow, April 20, 1903, 247.
49 New York Juvenile Asylum, *Ninth Annual Report* (1861), 22-23; New York Juvenile Asylum, *Eighteenth Annual Report* (1870), 27.
50 Dodge, "A Day with Dr. Brooks," 41. Brooks' quote.
51 NYJA records; Rare Book and Manuscript Library, Columbia University Library General Correspondence, 1897-1903 (Box 7, Folder 3). Burdick to Rathbun, 324.
52 "The Very First Steps in Crime," *Anaconda Standard* (Montana), March 16, 1913, 1.
53 "Boy Scout Who Killed Chum Sent to Asylum," *The Evening Telegram* (New York), June 3, 1912, 1.
54 New York Juvenile Asylum, *Sixty-Sixth Annual Report* (1912), 10.
55 New York Juvenile Asylum, *Fifty-Sixth Annual Report* (1907). Superintendent's Report, 20.
56 New York Juvenile Asylum, *Sixtieth Annual Report* (1911), 13.
57 New York Juvenile Asylum, *Thirteenth Annual Report* (1865). Final report of George H. Allan, New York, December 31, 1864, 55.
58 "Miscellaneous," *Chicago Tribune*, January 4, 1864, 2.
59 New York Juvenile Asylum, *Twelfth Annual Report* (1864), 59-60.
60 New York Juvenile Asylum, *Fifteenth Annual Report* (1867), 45.
61 "Memorial Day Memoirs," *Tacoma Daily News*, May 26, 1906, 3.
62 New York Juvenile Asylum. *Eleventh Annual Report* (1862), 46.
63 New York Juvenile Asylum, *Forty-First Annual Report* (1892), 54; "Waifs Of A Great City Write From Western Farms," *Montgomery Advertiser*, March 12, 1905, 5.

Chapter 4 (pages 61-82)

1 Circulars of Information of the Bureau of Education, No. 6. Statements relating to the Reformatory, Charitable, and

1 Industrial Schools for the Young, (Washington: Government Printing Office, 1875), 117.
2 Ibid., 17.
3 New York Juvenile Asylum, *First Annual Report* (1852), 19.
4 Rebecca, *Tramps in New York*, 101.
5 Dodge, "A Day with Dr. Brooks," 46.
6 Ibid., 20.
7 Ibid., 46.
8 NYJA records; Rare Book and Manuscript Library, Columbia University. Visiting Minutes, 1897-1887 [sic], Box 3.
9 New York Juvenile Asylum, *Forty-First Annual Report* (1893), 33-6.
10 New York Juvenile Asylum, *Twenty-Eighth Annual Report* (1879), 14-5, 42-3.
11 New York Juvenile Asylum, *First Annual Report* (1852), 20.
12 Dodge, "A Day with Dr. Brooks," 51. Dodge was quoting the latest annual report of the NYJA.
13 Ibid., 50.
14 Circulars of Information of the Bureau of Education, No. 6. Statements relating to the Reformatory, Charitable, and Industrial Schools for the Young, (Washington: Government Printing Office, 1875), 117.
15 New York Juvenile Asylum, *Fourth Annual Report* (1856), 27.
16 New York Juvenile Asylum, *Forty-Eighth Annual Report* (1899), 19-20.
17 Mary E. Dodge, "A Day with Dr. Brooks," *Scribner's Monthly*, November 1870, 49.
18 NYJA records; Rare Book and Manuscript Library, Columbia University. General Correspondence, 1897-1903 (Box 7, Folder 3).
19 Dodge, "A Day with Dr. Brooks," 49-50.
20 Circulars of Information of the Bureau of Education, No. 6. Statements relating to the Reformatory, Charitable, and Industrial Schools for the Young, (Washington: Government Printing Office, 1875), 117.
21 New York Juvenile Asylum, *Twenty-Eighth Annual Report* (1879), 15.
22 "Our Industrial Schools," *New York Herald*, October 22, 1882, 19.
23 "The Juvenile Asylum Exercises," *New-York Tribune*, November 6, 1897, 5.
24 New York Juvenile Asylum, *First Annual Report* (1852), 19; New York Juvenile Asylum, *Second Annual Report* (1853), 11.
25 New York Juvenile Asylum, *First Annual Report* (1852), 16.
26 New York Juvenile Asylum, *Second Annual Report* (1853), 8.
27 New York Juvenile Asylum, *Fifth Annual Report* (1856), 20.
28 New York Juvenile Asylum, *Second Annual Report* (1854), 9-10; New York Juvenile Asylum, *Fifth Annual Report* (1857), 20.
29 Dodge, "A Day with Dr. Brooks," 56.
30 Ibid., 43.
31 NYJA records; Rare Book and Manuscript Library, Columbia University. Minutes of the Applications, House of Reception. Visiting Committee Minutes, 1864-1871. (Box 2, Folder 3), 158.
32 New York Juvenile Asylum, *Fifty-Third Annual Report* (1904). Superintendent's Report, 21. "About two years ago a drill squad was organized as an aid to discipline."
33 NYJA records; Rare Book and Manuscript Library, Columbia University Library. General Correspondence, 1897-1903 (Box 7, Folder 3), 524.
34 New York Juvenile Asylum records; Rare Book and Manuscript Library, Columbia University Library. General Correspondence. Hilles to Boyer, April 3, 1905.
35 New York Juvenile Asylum, *Sixty-First Annual Report* (1912). Superintendent's Report, 21.
36 New York Juvenile Asylum records; Rare Book and Manuscript Library, Columbia University Library. General Correspondence (Box 7, Folder 3), 1897-1903. Elbridge T. Gerry to Hon. H. G. Weaver, New York, April 12, 1897. Mr. Gerry was co-founder and Vice President of the New York Society for the Prevention of Cruelty to Children.
37 Ibid. Hilles to Henry E. Gregory, Vice Chairman of the Committee on Admissions, Indentures, and Discharges, April 23, 1903, 253.
38 New York Juvenile Asylum, *Fifty-Seventh Annual Report* (1908). Report of the Directors, 12.
39 New York Juvenile Asylum, *Forty-Ninth Annual Report* (1900), 14.
40 New York Juvenile Asylum, *Fifty-First Annual Report* (1902). Superintendent's Report, 19-20.
41 NYJA records; Rare Book and Manuscript Library, Columbia University Library. Correspondence. Hilles to Conroy, April 17, 1905.
42 New York Juvenile Asylum, *Fifty-Fifth Annual Report* (1906). Superintendent's Report, 30.
43 NYJA. Records of individual inmates. Cited in Matthew A. Crenson: *Building the Invisible Orphanage*, (Harvard University Press, 1998), 139.
44 New York Juvenile Asylum, *Sixty-Second Annual Report* (1913). Superintendent's Report, 28.
45 New York Juvenile Asylum, *Fifty-Eighth Annual Report* (1909), 14.
46 Ibid., 75.
47 New York Juvenile Asylum, *Fifty-Seventh Annual Report* (1908). Superintendent's Report, 23.
48 New York Juvenile Asylum, *Sixty-Third Annual Report* (1914), 13-14.
49 Dodge, "A Day with Dr. Brooks," 53.
50 Ibid.
51 Ibid., 51.
52 New York Juvenile Asylum, *Sixteenth Annual Report* (1868), 17.
53 Ibid.
54 "Sad Case of Drowning," *The Portsmouth Journal of Literature and Politics*, July 28, 1860, 1.
55 New York Juvenile Asylum, *First Annual Report* (1852), 20.
56 "Charity Feasts Among the Poor," *New-York Daily Tribune*, November 25, 1874, 3.
57 NYJA Visiting Committee, Books, 1897-1887 [sic], Box 3. December 31, 1883 meeting, 261-2.
58 NYJA Visiting Committee, Books, 1897-1887 [sic], Box 3. December 29, 1884 meeting, 346-7.

59 Circulars of Information of the Bureau of Education, No. 6. Statements relating to the Reformatory, Charitable, and Industrial Schools for the Young, (Washington: Government Printing Office, 1875), 117.
60 New York Juvenile Asylum, *Fifty-Fourth Annual Report* (1905). Official Staff listed in front matter.
61 New York Juvenile Asylum, *Forty-Ninth Annual Report* (1900), 28.
62 "Twelve Found Homes," *Manchester Press* (Iowa), September 20, 1900.
63 "Memories of Memorial Day—How Waifs of New York Juvenile Asylum Fought for Lincoln," *The Pittsburgh Press*, May 27, 1906, 5.
64 New York Juvenile Asylum, *Fifty-Seventh Annual Report* (1908), 58.
65 New York Juvenile Asylum, *Fifty-Eighth Annual Report* (1909), 22.
66 New York Juvenile Asylum, *Sixty-First Annual Report* (1912). Superintendent's Report, 25.
67 NYJA records; Rare Book and Manuscript Library, Columbia University Library. Minutes of the Visiting Committee, 1854-1863 (Box 2, Folder 2), 208 (officers' menu), 218-19 (children's menu).
68 NYJA records; Rare Book and Manuscript Library, Columbia University. Visiting Minutes, 1897-1887 [sic], Box 3.
69 Dodge, "A Day with Dr. Brooks," 51.
70 New York Juvenile Asylum, *Fifty-Seventh Annual Report* (1908). Report of the Directors, 12.
71 New York Juvenile Asylum, *First Annual Report* (1852), 20.
72 Ibid., 13.
73 Dodge, "A Day with Dr. Brooks," 53.
74 NYJA records; Rare Book and Manuscript Library, Columbia University. Visiting Minutes, 1897-1887 [sic], Box 3.
75 New York Juvenile Asylum, *First Annual Report* (1852), 20.
76 Rebecca, *Tramps in New York*, 102-3.
77 Dodge, "A Day with Dr. Brooks," 48-9.
78 "Rain Baths for Children," *Kansas City Times*, June 9, 1895, 18.
79 Dodge, "A Day with Dr. Brooks," 49.
80 Circulars of Information of the Bureau of Education, No. 6. Statements relating to the Reformatory, Charitable, and Industrial Schools for the Young, (Washington: Government Printing Office, 1875), 117.
81 NYJA records; Rare Book and Manuscript Library, Columbia University. Visiting Minutes, 1897-1887 [sic], Box 3.
82 Source of chapel seat capacity: "Twelve Found Homes," *Manchester Press* (Iowa), September 20, 1900.
83 Dodge, "A Day with Dr. Brooks," 39.
84 Ibid., 56-7.
85 Ibid., 44.

Chapter 5 (pages 83-94)

1 New York Juvenile Asylum, *Fifty-Eighth Annual Report* (1909), 12.
2 New York Juvenile Asylum, *Fifty-Ninth Annual Report* (1910). Superintendent's Report, 23.
3 New York Juvenile Asylum, *Sixtieth Annual Report* (1911). Superintendent's Report, 20.
4 New York Juvenile Asylum, *Sixty-First Annual Report* (1912), 11. Age of children is from: New York Juvenile Asylum, *Sixty-Second Annual Report* (1913), 14.
5 New York Juvenile Asylum, *Fifty-Eighth Annual Report* (1909), 13.
6 Hastings Hart. *The Extinction of the Defective Delinquent: A Working Program* (New York: Russell Sage Foundation, 1912), 5. It was Hart's assertion that the best way to limit procreation by the feebleminded was through institutionalization, while sterilizing only "rapists, sexual perverts or degenerates, confirmed masturbators and others whose sexual tendencies call for such action." Hastings Hart. *Sterilization as a Practical Measure* (New York: Russell Sage Foundation, 1912), 5.
7 Quoted in Schneider and Deutsch, "The History of Public Welfare in New York State," 241.
8 New York Juvenile Asylum, *Fiftieth Annual Report* (1901), 25.
9 New York Juvenile Asylum, *Sixty-First Annual Report* (1912), 14.
10 NYJA records; Rare Book and Manuscript Library, Columbia University Library Correspondence, 1904-1908 (Box 10). Hilles to Sawyer, April 13, 1905.
11 Ibid. Hilles to Dowling, March 29, 1905.
12 New York Juvenile Asylum, *Fifty-Fourth Annual Report* (1905). Superintendent's Report, 23.
13 Ibid., 23; New York Juvenile Asylum, *Sixty-Second Annual Report*. Superintendent's Report, 23.
14 "From Slum to Farm," *The Quincy Daily Whig* (Quincy, IL), July 1, 1906; 9.
15 Ibid. Front matter.
16 Ibid., 9.
17 Ibid.
18 NYJA records; Rare Book and Manuscript Library, Columbia University Library Correspondence (Box 7, Folder 3), 1897-1903. Edwin C. Burdick to S. E. Woodruff & Sons, April 10, 1903.
19 Ibid.
20 New York Juvenile Asylum, *Sixty-First Annual Report* (1912). Superintendent's Report, 27.
21 New York Juvenile Asylum, *Fifty-Ninth Annual Report* (1910). Superintendent's Report, 28.
22 NYJA records; Rare Book and Manuscript Library, Columbia University Library Correspondence, 1897-1903 (Box 7, Folder 3). Burdick to Davison, 1903, 360.
23 "Sporting Gossip: Matty a Poor Umpire," *The Saratogian* (New York), June 24, 1914, 6.
24 New York Juvenile Asylum, *Fifty-Fifth Annual Report* (1906). Superintendent's Report, 29-30.
25 New York Juvenile Asylum, *Fifty-Sixth Annual Report* (1907), 9-10.
26 "In What Is Known as Westchester's `Children's Village' About 300 City Waifs Are Learning to be Good Citizens—A Novel Settlement," *New York Times*, December 6, 1908, 11.
27 New York Juvenile Asylum, *Fifty-Sixth Annual Report* (1907). Superintendent's Report, 28.
28 New York Juvenile Asylum, *Fifty-Ninth Annual Report* (1910). Superintendent's Report, 30.

29 New York Juvenile Asylum, *Fifty-Fifth Annual Report* (1906). Report of the Directors, 11-12.
30 New York Juvenile Asylum, *Fifty-Seventh Annual Report* (1908). Report of the Directors, 13.
31 New York Juvenile Asylum, *Fifty-Fourth Annual Report* (1905). Superintendent's Report, 25.
32 New York Juvenile Asylum, *Fifty-Ninth Annual Report* (1910). Superintendent's Report, 22.
33 Ibid., 19.
34 New York Juvenile Asylum, *Sixty-Fourth Annual Report* (1915), 22.
35 "President Taft to Visit Here Tomorrow," *Dobbs Ferry Register* (New York), November 15, 1912, 1.
36 New York Juvenile Asylum, *Sixty-First Annual Report* (1912), 8-9. Hilles served as secretary from 1911 to 1913.
37 "The Great Work of New York's Juvenile Asylum," *Miami Herald*, December 1, 1912, 6.
38 Source of Taft quote: "New York's Unique Juvenile Settlement for Boys," *Salt Lake Telegram*, February 21, 1914, 8.

Chapter 6 (pages 97-112)

1   "Practical Benevolence," *The Ottawa Free Trader* (Illinois), September 22, 1855, 2.
2   New York Juvenile Asylum records; Rare Book and Manuscript Library, Columbia University Library. Minutes of the Committee on Admissions, Indentures and Discharges (Box 1, Folder 1), 1853-1861. October 23, 1855 meeting, 32.
3   Ibid.
4   Ibid., November 15, 1855, 36.
5   New York Juvenile Asylum, *Third Annual Report* (1855), 21-2.
6   Pearcy visit from: NYJA records; Rare Book and Manuscript Library, Columbia University Library. Minutes of the Committee on Admissions, Indentures and Discharges (Box 1, Folder 1), 1853-1861. June 18, 1857 meeting. In June 1857, Alexander C. Pearcy, Superintendent of the House of Reception, was dispatched to Maryland to check up on the children who were previously placed there.
7   NYJA records; Rare Book and Manuscript Library, Columbia University Library. Minutes of the Committee on Admissions, Indentures, and Discharges (Box 1, Folder 1), 1853-1861, 72.
8   Ibid., 74.
9   *Illinois State Gazetteer and Business Directory* (Chicago: George W. Hawes & Co.), 13.
10 "City Facts and Fancies," *Plain Dealer* (Cleveland, Ohio), Monday, March 12, 1855, 3 (quoting the *Express*).
11 "Practical Benevolence," *The Wheeling Daily Intelligencer* (West Virginia), September 20, 1855, 2 (quoting the *New-York Tribune*).
12 NYJA records; Rare Book and Manuscript Library, Columbia University Library. Indentures-Case Files (Box 61), 1854-1888.
13 "New York Children for The West," *Cleveland Herald*, March 26, 1856, 2.
14 "New York Juvenile Asylum," *New York Observer*, February 21, 1856, 2.
15 Ibid.
16 New York Juvenile Asylum, *Fifth Annual Report* (1856), 18.
17 "To Farmers," *Vermilion County Press* (Danville, Illinois), January 11, 1860, Column 1, 3. The article also mentions agent John R. Johnson of State Line City (now Illiana, Illinois).
18 "Novel Orphan Asylum," *The Puritan Recorder* (Boston), March 6, 1856, 40.
19 New York Juvenile Asylum, *Fifth Annual Report* (1856), 17.
20 "Children for the West," *New-York Tribune*, October 23, 1862, 3.
21 New York Juvenile Asylum, *Twelfth Annual Report* (1864). Final report of George H. Allan, New York, December 31, 1864, 51-2.
22 New York Juvenile Asylum, *Sixteenth Annual Report* (1868). Report of Western Agency by H. D. Perry, 43; Reverend Enoch Kingsbury died on October 2, 1868.
23 NYJA records; Rare Book and Manuscript Library, Columbia University Library. Minutes of the Committee on Admissions, Indentures, and Discharges (Box 1, Folder 1), 1853-1861, 261.
24 Ibid.
25 Ibid., 284-5.
26 NYJA records; Rare Book and Manuscript Library, Columbia University Library. Minutes of the Committee on Admissions, Indentures, and Discharges (Box 1, Folder 1), 1853-1861, 318.
27 Ibid.
28 New York Juvenile Asylum, *Eighth Annual Report* (1859), 40.
29 New York Juvenile Asylum records; Rare Book and Manuscript Library, Columbia University Library. General Correspondence, 1897-1903 (Box 7, Folder 3). A. [Aaron] P. Garrabrant to Mr. E. Wright, May 26, 1897, 41.
30 Society for the Reformation of Juvenile Delinquents in the City of New York and Nathaniel C. Hart, *Documents Relative to the House of Refuge [. . .] in 1824* (New York: Mahlon Day, 1832), 234. Author's own observation of the microfilmed case files of children at the New York House of Refuge.
31 "An Important Decision," *The Pantagraph* (Bloomington, Illinois), December 13, 1875, 3.
32 NYJA records; Rare Book and Manuscript Library, Columbia University Library. Minutes of the Committee on Admissions, Indentures, and Discharges (Box 1, Folder 2), 1862-1872, 149.
33 New York Juvenile Asylum. *Thirty-Sixth Annual Report* (1887), 50.
34 New York Juvenile Asylum. *Thirty-Third Annual Report* (1884), 42.
35 "Homes for Seven Children," *The Daily Review* (Decatur, Illinois), May 28, 1896. "It quite often happens, however, that the society has to take the children away before the contract is completed. Mr. Wright when asked about that thought that only a few more than half of the children staid out the full term."; "A Party of Youngsters," *Chicago Daily News* (Chicago, Illinois). September 20, 1882, 1. "If any just cause of complaint is found the boy's indentures are canceled and a new home found for him. About 40 per

36 cent of the boys serve out their apprenticeship. The remainder free themselves by running away."
36 NYJA records; Rare Book and Manuscript Library, Columbia University Library. Indentures-Case Files (Box 61), 1854-1888.
37 New York Juvenile Asylum, *Eighth Annual Report* (1859), 40-1.
38 NYJA records; Rare Book and Manuscript Library, Columbia University Library. Correspondence, Indentures-Outgoing, 1868-1870 (Box 7, Folder 1).
39 Ibid., 316-17.
40 "Asylum Children," *The Evening Gazette* (Monmouth, Illinois), September 26, 1887, 4.
41 NYJA records; Rare Book and Manuscript Library, Columbia University Library. Minutes of the Committee on Admissions, Indentures, and Discharges (Box 1, Folder 1), 1853-1861.
42 Ibid.
43 Ibid.
44 "Senate: Petitions," *Sangamo Journal-Illinois State Journal*, January 14, 1861, 2.
45 "Public Laws of Illinois," *Sangamo Journal-Illinois State Journal*, March 26, 1861, 3.
46 New York Juvenile Asylum, *Eleventh Annual Report* (1862), 37; Number signing petition from New York Juvenile Asylum, *Sixteenth Annual Report* (1868), 38.
47 Dodge, "A Day with Dr. Brooks," 40. "Through the suggestion of Dr. Brooks a Western Agency is now firmly established at Chicago."
48 NYJA records; Rare Book and Manuscript Library, Columbia University Library. Minutes of the Committee on Admissions, Indentures, and Discharges (Box 1, Folder 2), 1862-1872. February 4, 1867 meeting, 244.
49 Ibid. May 13, 1867, 254.
50 "New York Juvenile Asylum. *Ninth Annual Report* (1860), 15. We are indebted to Mr. Ebenezer Wright, who succeeded Mr. Pearcy as Superintendent of the House of Reception, in May last . . ."
51 Massachusetts State Census for 1855, Town of Monson, Hampden County, Massachusetts. Enumerated July 21, 1855. Inhabitants of the Almshouse in Monson, 17 (lines 1-5).
52 *Marriages Solemnized in Amherst, Hampshire County, Massachusetts during the year 1860*, Volume 4, 20. Marriage of Ebenezer B. Wright to Mary D. Cowls [*sic*]. Names of parents listed as "Ebenezer & Harriett (Goodale) [*sic*] Wright."
53 Ibid., August 5, 1867, 263.
54 Ibid., 274.
55 Dodge, "A Day with Dr. Brooks," 40.
56 NYJA records; Rare Book and Manuscript Library, Columbia University Library. Correspondence. Indentures-Outgoing, 1868-1870 (Box 7, Folders 1, 12, and 16). Reference to house number 611 on Fullerton Avenue is from page 297 of same record book. The area the house was located in was not annexed to the City of Chicago until 1889.
57 NYJA records; Rare Book and Manuscript Library, Columbia University Library. Minutes of the Committee on Admissions, Indentures, and Discharges (Box 1, Folder 2), 1862-1872. October 16, 1871 meeting, 437-8.
58 Ibid., March 17, 1872, 453.
59 "The City," *The Pantagraph* (Bloomington, Illinois), May 17, 1872, 4.
60 New York Juvenile Asylum, *Twenty-Sixth Annual Report* (1877), front matter.
61 Wright's Find A Grave Memorial (Number 144565293); "Normal [News]," *The Pantagraph* (Bloomington, Illinois), January 6, 1890, 4.: "Mr. E. Wright has purchased a house in Chicago and expects to move there soon."; NYJA records; Rare Book and Manuscript Library, Columbia University Library Correspondence (Box 7, Folder 3), 1897-1903. The address was 645 61st Street per letter to Ebenezer Wright regarding the quarantine at the NYJA, which was likely the address for the "rear house" referred to in some correspondence.
62 NYJA records; Rare Book and Manuscript Library, Columbia University Library. Minutes of the Committee on Admissions, Indentures, and Discharges (Box 1, Folder 3), 1889-1901, 278.
63 New York Juvenile Asylum, *Forty-Ninth Annual Report*, (1900), 18.
64 NYJA records; Rare Book and Manuscript Library, Columbia University Library. Minutes of the Committee on Admissions, Indentures, and Discharges (Box 1, Folder 3), 1889-1901, 289.
65 New York Juvenile Asylum, *Thirty-Seventh Annual Report* (1888), 53-4. Letter from Pauline Held: "I agree with you about including Iowa, because there are not places in Illinois for all of the children that come out West."
66 Ibid., 330.
67 "The Much Abused Street Boy," *Plain Dealer* (Cleveland, Ohio), February 19, 1905, 47.

Chapter 7 (pages 112-128)

1 NYJA records; Rare Book and Manuscript Library, Columbia University Library. Case Registers-House of Reception. 1871-3 (Box 131); Appendix.
2 NYJA records; Rare Book and Manuscript Library, Columbia University Library. Admissions, Indentures, Discharges with Invoices, 1873-1880 (Box 8).
3 NYJA records; Rare Book and Manuscript Library, Columbia University Library. Indentures-Case Files (Box 61), 1854-1888.
4 New York Juvenile Asylum, *Eighteenth Annual Report* (1870), 15, 22-23.
5 New York Juvenile Asylum, *Forty-Eighth Annual Report* (1899). Report of the Western Agency, 52.
6 New York Juvenile Asylum, *Fifty-Second Annual* Report (1903). Report of the Western Agency, 36.
7 NYJA records; Rare Book and Manuscript Library, Columbia University Library. Minutes of the Committee on Admissions, Indentures, and Discharges (Box 1, Folder 2), 1862-1872. March 8, 1867 meeting, 247-8.
8 New York Juvenile Asylum, *Eighth Annual Report* (1859), 37.

9. "To Farmers: Homes for Friendless Children," *The Greenville Advocate* (Greenville, Illinois), July 16, 1860.
10. NYJA records; Rare Book and Manuscript Library, Columbia University Library. Minutes of the Committee on Admissions, Indentures, and Discharges, 1889-1901 (Box 1, Folder 3), 92.
11. Ibid., 38.
12. NYJA records; Rare Book and Manuscript Library, Columbia University Library. Admissions, Indentures, Discharges with Invoices, 1873-1880 (Box 8).
13. Ibid.
14. Courtesy of Chuck Battey, a descendant of Thomas Oscar "Oscar" Westmen.
15. Rebecca, *Tramps in New York*, 99-100.
16. "New York Juvenile Asylum," *Commercial Advertiser* (New York, New York), September 13, 1860, 2.
17. "To Farmers," *Central Illinois Gazette* (West Urbana, now Champaign), July 13, 1859.
18. New York Juvenile Asylum, *Fiftieth Annual Report* (1901), 19.
19. "Children Going to the West," *New-York Tribune*, April 25, 1876, 2.
20. New York Juvenile Asylum, *Twenty-Sixth Annual Report* (1877), 37, 42; New York Juvenile Asylum, *Twenty-Seventh Annual Report* (1878), 61.
21. Quoted in Gillian Avery: *Nineteenth Century Children: Heroes and Heroines in English Children's Stories, 1780-1900* (London: Hodder & Stoughton, 1965), 101.
22. New York Juvenile Asylum, *Eighth Annual Report* (1859), 39.
23. NYJA records; Rare Book and Manuscript Library, Columbia University Library. Minutes of the Committee on Admissions, Indentures, and Discharges (Box 1, Folder 1), 1853-1861. March 12, 1856 meeting.
24. "Homeless Children," *Decatur Weekly Republican* (Decatur, Illinois), September 9, 1880, 5.
25. Dodge, "A Day with Dr. Brooks," 49.
26. New York Juvenile Asylum, *Eighth Annual Report* (1859), 64.
27. "Boys for the Country," *Albany Evening Journal* (New York), March 19, 1856, 2; "Boys For The Country," *Centinel of Freedom* (Newark, New Jersey), March 18, 1856, 2.
28. "New York Children for the West," *Cleveland Herald*, March 26, 1856, 2.
29. Kidder, *Orphan Trains and Their Precious Cargo*, 26.
30. NYJA records; Rare Book and Manuscript Library, Columbia University Library General Correspondence, 1897-1903 (Box 7, Folder 3), 217.
31. "Home Department: Migration of Children To The West," *Commercial Advertiser* (New York, New York), May 18, 1858, 2.
32. New York Juvenile Asylum, *Eighth Annual Report* (1859), 39.
33. Ibid.
34. Kidder, *Orphan Trains and Their Precious Cargo*, 26, 144-5.
35. Ibid., September 27, 1861, 2.
36. New York Juvenile Asylum, *Seventh Annual Report* (1858). "Reports of Western Trips" by the Superintendent of the House of Reception, 42-3.
37. *Cleveland Leader*, December 9, 1863, 4. "A Company for the West—Forty-two boys and girls from the New York Juvenile Asylum, arrived in our city last night, and proceeded to the New England House, where they spent the night,"
38. NYJA records; Rare Book and Manuscript Library, Columbia University Library. Indentures-Case Files (Box 61), 1854-1888.
39. New York Juvenile Asylum, *Thirteenth Annual Report* (1865), 61.
40. New York Juvenile Asylum, *Sixteenth Annual Report* (1868). Report of the Western Agency. List of railroads used as of 1868 as recognized by H. D. Perry, 47.
41. NYJA records; Rare Book and Manuscript Library, Columbia University Library. Minutes of the Committee on Admissions, Indentures, and Discharges (Box 1, Folder 2), 1862-1872. October 12, 1868 meeting, 305.
42. *Joliet Weekly Sun* (Illinois), September 20, 1879.
43. "Homes For Children," *Decatur Daily Republican* (Illinois), Friday, May 9, 1884, 2.
44. "The Dunlaps' Experience," *People* (New York, New York), February 9, 1901, 2.
45. "Children Given Away," *The Evening Gazette* (Burlington, Iowa), October 19, 1898.
46. "How I Found My Brother," *Star Tribune* (Minneapolis, Minnesota), November 27, 1910.

Chapter 8 (pages 129-152)

1. NYJA records; Rare Book and Manuscript Library, Columbia University Library. Correspondence, Indentures-Outgoing, 1868-1870 (Box 7, Folder 1), 354-5.
2. "Homes for Seven Children," *The Daily Review* (Decatur, Illinois), May 28, 1896.
3. NYJA records; Rare Book and Manuscript Library, Columbia University Library. Correspondence. Indentures-Outgoing, 1868-1870. Box 7, Folder 1, 462.
4. "The City: These New York Juvenile Asylum Children," *The Pantagraph* (Bloomington, Illinois), September 14, 1875, 3. The letter was dated "Normal [Illinois], September 13, 1875."
5. NYJA records; Rare Book and Manuscript Library, Columbia University Library. Indentures-Case Files (Box 61), 1854-1888.
6. New York Juvenile Asylum, *Third Annual Report* (1854), 16. Four Jews and ninety-nine "unknown" were admitted as well.
7. *Annual Report of the State Board of Charities for the Year 1885*, (New York), 166. The law was amended in 1878 and the age lowered to two.
8. "Homes for the Homeless," *The Ottawa Free Trader* (Ottawa, Illinois), September 12, 1885, 2.
9. "The Placing Out of Children," *New-York Tribune*, May 6, 1897, 8.
10. NYJA records; Rare Book and Manuscript Library, Columbia University Library. General Correspondence, 1897-1903 (Box 7, Folder 3), July 10, 1903, 427.
11. New York Juvenile Asylum, *Fiftieth Annual Report* (1901), 41.
12. New York Juvenile Asylum, *Forty-Sixth Annual Report* (1897), 19-20.

13 New York Juvenile Asylum, *Forty-Ninth Annual Report* (1900). Report of Western Agent James W. Shields, 51.
14 NYJA records; Rare Book and Manuscript Library, Columbia University Library. Indentures-Case Files (Box 61), 1854-1888.
15 "The New-York Juvenile Asylum," *New-York Tribune*, March 7, 1857, 7.
16 NYJA records; Rare Book and Manuscript Library, Columbia University Library. Indentures-Case Files (Box 61), 1854-1888.
17 New York Juvenile Asylum, *Eighth Annual Report* (1859), 41.
18 New York Juvenile Asylum, *Third Annual Report* (1854), 7.
19 New York Juvenile Asylum, *Eighth Annual Report* (1859), 42; Extracts from Charter. A single sheet included with indentures. The particular indenture referenced in this case was that of Emma J. Westmen dated December 19, 1867. "The following are the Sections of the Charter of 'THE NEW YORK JUVENILE ASYLUM,' especially referred to in, and made a part of the foregoing instrument of indenture: Sec. 24.—And it shall be the duty of the master or his assignee, to whom any such child shall be bound to service, and he shall, by the terms of the indenture, be required, as often as once in every six months, to report to the said board of directors the conduct and behavior of the said apprentice or child so bound to service, and, whether such apprentice is still living under the care of the person to whom he was originally bound and, if not, where else he may be."
20 NYJA records; Rare Book and Manuscript Library, Columbia University Library. Correspondence. Indentures-Outgoing, 1868-1870. Box 7, Folder 1, 446.
21 Ibid., 447.
22 Ibid., 432.
23 Ibid., 444.
24 New York Juvenile Asylum, *Eighth Annual Report* (1859), 43.
25 New York Juvenile Asylum, *Thirteenth Annual Report* (1865). Final report of George H. Allan, New York, December 31, 1864, 52-3.
26 NYJA records; Rare Book and Manuscript Library, Columbia University Library. Indentures-Case Files (Box 61), 1854-1888.
27 Ibid.
28 New York Juvenile Asylum, *Twentieth Annual Report* (1872), 47.
29 "Came for Children," *The Edwardsville Intelligencer* (Edwardsville, Illinois), May 29, 1896.
30 New York Juvenile Asylum, *Forty-Ninth Annual Report* (1900), 49.
31 New York Juvenile Asylum, *Fifty-Fifth Annual Report* (1906). Report of the Western Agency, 36.
32 New York Juvenile Asylum, *Thirty-Seventh Annual Report* (1888), 53-4.
33 New York Juvenile Asylum, *Fifty-Second Annual Report* (1903), 21.
34 "Harry Brooks of New York Makes Anxious Inquiry Concerning His Only Relative," *The Decatur Herald* (Decatur, Illinois), April 14, 1900, 9.
35 NYJA records; Rare Book and Manuscript Library, Columbia University Library. Indentures-Case Files (Box 61), 1854-1888.
36 "Separated from Kin 19 Years," *The Baltimore Sun* (Baltimore), May 19, 1907, 18.
37 "The Juvenile Asylum," *New-York Daily Tribune*, February 18, 1860, 5.
38 New York Juvenile Asylum, *Sixteenth Annual Report* (1868). Report of new western agent [Ebenezer Wright], 49.
39 Extracts from Charter. A single sheet included with indentures. The particular indenture referenced in this case was that of Emma J. Westmen dated December 19, 1867. "The following are the Sections of the Charter of 'THE NEW YORK JUVENILE ASYLUM,' especially referred to in, and made a part of the foregoing instrument of indenture:"
40 NYJA records; Rare Book and Manuscript Library, Columbia University Library. Correspondence. Indentures-Outgoing, 1868-1870. Box 7, Folder 1, 117.
41 New York Juvenile Asylum, *Forty-Eighth Annual Report* (1899). Report of the Western Agency, 60-1.
42 NYJA records; Rare Book and Manuscript Library, Columbia University Library. Correspondence, Indentures-Outgoing, 1868-1870, 276. Wright added, ". . . Poor success in placing this company has caused an unusually large board account, but as the names of children are not stricken from the Asylum board roll until they are placed in homes, an equivalent amount will accrue to the funds of the agency from the City Treasury," 280.
43 NYJA records; Rare Book and Manuscript Library, Columbia University Library. Correspondence. Indentures-Outgoing, 1868-1870 (Box 7, Folder 1), 144, 156.
44 New York Juvenile Asylum, *Sixteenth Annual Report* (1868), 41.
45 Extracts from Charter. A single sheet included with indentures. The particular indenture referenced in this case was that of Emma J. Westmen dated December 19, 1867. "The following are the Sections of the Charter of 'THE NEW YORK JUVENILE ASYLUM,' especially referred to in, and made a part of the foregoing instrument of indenture:"
46 NYJA records; Rare Book and Manuscript Library, Columbia University Library. Minutes of the Committee on Indentures and Discharges (Box 1, Folder 1), 1853-1861. November 19, 1857 meeting. 123-4; 1860 United States Federal Census, 1st Ward, City of Chicago, Cook County, Illinois, 205.
47 "Paxton [Illinois] Notes," *Gibson City Courier* (Illinois), May 28, 1880, 1.
48 "A Remarkable Case of Child-Birth," *The Pantagraph* (Bloomington, Illinois), April 23, 1884, 3.
49 NYJA records; Rare Book and Manuscript Library, Columbia University Library. Indentures-Case Files (Box 61), 1854-1888.
50 "Up from the Slum," *Daily Recorder* (Olympia, Washington), April 13, 1906, 4; NYJA records; Rare Book and Manuscript Library, Columbia University Library. Indentures-Case Files (Box 61), 1854-1888.

51 NYJA records; Rare Book and Manuscript Library, Columbia University Library. Indentures-Case Files (Box 61), 1854-1888; 832, 896.
52 NYJA records; Rare Book and Manuscript Library, Columbia University Library. Indentures-Case Files (Box 61), 1854-1888.
53 New York Juvenile Asylum, *Fifty-Third Annual Report* (1904). Superintendent's Report, 26.
54 NYJA records; Rare Book and Manuscript Library, Columbia University Library. Indentures-Case Files (Box 61), 1854-1888.
55 This anecdote was relayed to author Clark Kidder by one of Sarah's descendants via email in 2020.
56 "Charged with Serious Crime," *Evening Times-Republican* (Marshalltown, Iowa), October 7, 1901.
57 NYJA records; Rare Book and Manuscript Library, Columbia University Library. Indentures-Case Files (Box 61), 1854-1888.
58 Ibid.
59 Ibid.
60 Ibid.
61 Ibid.
62 Ibid.
63 Ibid.
64 "A Boy Fatally Injured," *The Pantagraph* (Bloomington, Illinois), February 8, 1876, 1.
65 New York Juvenile Asylum, *Twenty-Eighth Annual Report* (1879). Letters from Children, 52.
66 NYJA records; Rare Book and Manuscript Library, Columbia University Library. Indentures-Case Files (Box 61), 1854-1888.
67 "An Orphan Boy's Christmas," *The Times* (Richmond, Virginia), December 31, 1886, 1.
68 "Due to a Love Affair," *The Pantagraph* (Bloomington, Illinois), January 3, 1900, 5.
69 New York Juvenile Asylum, *Fifty-Fifth Annual Report* (1906). Report of the Western Agency, 36.
70 NYJA records; Rare Book and Manuscript Library, Columbia University Library. Correspondence. Indentures-Outgoing, 1868-1870. Box 7, Folder 1, 470.
71 NYJA records; Rare Book and Manuscript Library, Columbia University Library. Indentures-Case Files (Box 61), 1854-1888.
72 Ibid.
73 NYJA records; Rare Book and Manuscript Library, Columbia University Library. Correspondence. Indentures-Outgoing, 1868-1870. (Box 7, Folder 1), 123.
74 NYJA records; Rare Book and Manuscript Library, Columbia University Library. Correspondence. Indentures-Outgoing (Box 7, Folder 1), 1868-1870. Monthly Report of Western Agent (1869), 402-3.
75 NYJA records; Rare Book and Manuscript Library, Columbia University Library. Indentures-Case Files (Box 61), 1854-1888.
76 NYJA records; Rare Book and Manuscript Library, Columbia University Library. General Correspondence, 1897-1903 (Box 7, Folder 3), 447, 450-1.
77 "Ranaway," *Sterling Gazette* (Illinois), April 7, 1866, 4.
78 NYJA records; Rare Book and Manuscript Library, Columbia University Library. Minutes of the Committee on Admissions, Indentures, and Discharges (Box 1, Folder 1), 1853-1861. January 10, 1861 meeting. Rev. W. C. Van Meter was in charge of the Howard Mission and Home for Little Wanderers in New York City and often brought companies of children West on orphan trains, not only from his own Mission, but also on behalf of the CAS, NYJA, New York House of Refuge, and the Five Points Mission—all in New York City.
79 NYJA records; Rare Book and Manuscript Library, Columbia University Library. Correspondence. Indentures-Outgoing, 1868-1870. Box 7, Folder 1, 502.
80 "Tried to Kill Him," *Pittsburg Dispatch*, November 24, 1890, 2; "Seeking Revenge for her Child's Detention," *New-York Tribune*, December 5, 1890, 10; "Narrowly Escapes Assassination," *New York Herald*, December 5, 1890, 4.
81 New York Juvenile Asylum, *Fifty-Third Annual Report* (1904), 26-7.
82 "General Local Miscellany," *Freeport Journal-Standard* (Illinois), August 4, 1883, 4.
83 New York Juvenile Asylum, *Fifty-Eighth Annual Report* (1909), 54-5.
84 New York Juvenile Asylum, *Forty-Second Annual Report* (1893). "The Placing Out of Juvenile Offenders," by Superintendent Elisha M. Carpenter, October 24, 1893, 90-1.
85 NYJA records; Rare Book and Manuscript Library, Columbia University Library. Indentures-Case Files (Box 61), 1854-1888.
86 New York Juvenile Asylum, *Forty-Second Annual Report* (1893). "The Placing Out of Juvenile Offenders," by Superintendent Elisha M. Carpenter, October 24, 1893, 92.
87 Ibid., 90-1.
88 "John J. Brown of Vandalia Dies at Home," *Daily Illinois State Journal* (Springfield, Illinois), November 2, 1932, 2.
89 "Killed by an Engine," *True Republican* (Sycamore, Illinois), March 25, 1891, 4.
90 NYJA records; Rare Book and Manuscript Library, Columbia University Library. Indentures-Case Files (Box 61), 1854-1888.
91 "Where the Boys Get a Chance," *New-York Evening Post*, September 22, 1906, 8; New York Juvenile Asylum, *Fifty-Fifth Annual Report* (1906), 67. Extracts from 1906 Publications in reference to the work of the New York Juvenile Asylum.
92 NYJA records; Rare Book and Manuscript Library, Columbia University Library. Indentures-Case Files (Box 61), 1854-1888.
93 NYJA records; Rare Book and Manuscript Library, Columbia University Library. General Correspondence, 1897-1903 (Box 7, Folder 3), August 12, 1903, 571.

Chapter 9 (pages 153-165)

1 New York Juvenile Asylum, *Forty-Eighth Annual Report* (1899), 18-19.
2 New York Juvenile Asylum, *Forty-Ninth Annual Report* (1900), 17-18.

3 New York Juvenile Asylum, *Twentieth Annual Report* (1872), 53.
4 NYJA records; Rare Book and Manuscript Library, Columbia University Library. Minutes of the Committee on Admissions, Indentures, and Discharges (Box 1, Folder 3), 1889-1901.
5 Ibid. February 19, 1900 meeting, 386.
6 Ibid., 388.
7 Ibid., 418.
8 Ibid. December 3, 1900 meeting, 417.
9 "Advertisements," *The Farmer's Review* (Chicago, Illinois), May 5, 1904, 338.
10 NYJA records; Rare Book and Manuscript Library, Columbia University Library. Minutes of the Committee on Admissions, Indentures, and Discharges (Box 1, Folder 3), 1889-1901. December 3, 1900 meeting.
11 New York Juvenile Asylum, *Fiftieth Annual Report* (1901). Report of the Western Agency, 40-1.
12 Ibid., 37.
13 New York Juvenile Asylum, *Fifty-First Annual Report* (1902). Report of the Western Agency, 44-5.
14 New York Juvenile Asylum, *Fifty-Third Annual Report* (1904), 41.
15 New York Juvenile Asylum, *Fifty-Fifth Annual Report* (1906), 37.
16 New York Juvenile Asylum, *Fiftieth Annual Report* (1901). Report of the Western Agency, 42.
17 New York Juvenile Asylum, *Fifty-Third Annual Report* (1904). Report of the Western Agency, 43.
18 Ibid.
19 Ibid.
20 New York Juvenile Asylum, *Fifty-Second Annual Report* (1903), 21.
21 Ibid., 22.
22 "She Is Working for Homeless Children," *St. Louis Dispatch*, Thursday, June 14, 1906.
23 New York Juvenile Asylum, *Fifty-Third Annual Report* (1904). Report of the Western Agency, 44.
24 New York Juvenile Asylum, *Fifty-Fourth Annual Report* (1905). Report of the Western Agency, 41-2.
25 "Finding Waifs Homes," *New-York Daily Tribune*, June 17, 1906, 4.
26 New York Juvenile Asylum, *Fifty-Third Annual Report* (1904). Report of the Western Agency, 43-4.
27 "Finding Waifs Homes," *New-York Daily Tribune*, June 17, 1906, 4.
28 New York Juvenile Asylum, *Fifty-Sixth Annual Report* (1907). Superintendent's Report, 19-20.
29 Ibid.
30 Ibid. Report of the Western Agency, 34.
31 New York Juvenile Asylum, *Fifty-Seventh Annual Report* (1908), 39.
32 New York Juvenile Asylum, *Fifty-Eighth Annual Report* (1909). Front matter.
33 Ibid.), 33. "Placing-out Work" by Robert N. Brace, Superintendent of the Children's Aid Society. "Less than two years ago we agreed to undertake the work of finding homes for your children in the West, and during the year 1908 received from the Juvenile Asylum 42 children, and in the year 1909 one boy who, however, did not come directly from the Asylum."
34 New York Juvenile Asylum, *Sixty-Second Annual Report* (1913). "Placing-out Work" by Robert N. Brace, 39.
35 New York Juvenile Asylum, *Fifty-Seventh Annual Report* (1908), 33.
36 Ibid. Letters from Wards and Guardians, 58.
37 New York Juvenile Asylum, *Fifty-Ninth Annual Report* (1910), 42.
38 Langsam, *Children West—A History of the Placing-Out System of the New York Children's Aid Society 1853-1890*, 56.
39 *Proceedings of the National Conference of Charities and Correction* Ninth Annual Conference. Held at Madison, Wisconsin on August 7-12, 1882, (Midland Publishing Co., 1882); 147-8, 152.
40 Ibid.; Twelfth Annual Conference (1885), 204.
41 New York Juvenile Asylum, *Twentieth Annual Report* (1872), 48.
42 Source for new law: Schneider and Deutsch, "*The History of Public Welfare in New York State*," 169.
43 Daniel I. Hurley. *A History of The Children's Home of Cincinnati 1864-1889*; (Children's Home of Cincinnati, 1990), 64.
44 New York Juvenile Asylum, *Forty-Eighth Annual Report* (1899), 61.
45 "Farmed Out: Are Children From New York Asylum," *Repository* (Canton, Ohio) April 1, 1900, 9.
46 "Wholesale Kidnapping: Children Of The Poor A Subject Of Traffic," *Daily People* (New York), January 28 1901, 1.
47 Ibid.
48 *Proceedings of the Conference on the Care of Dependent Children*. Sixtieth Congress, second edition, Senate Document No. 721, 8-14. (Government Printing Office, Washington, 1909); "Best to Preserve the Family Ties," *Daily News Democrat* (Huntington, Indiana), January 26, 1909, 7.
49 Quoted in *Children and Youth in America: A Documentary History*, 3 vols., edited by Robert H. Bremner et al (Cambridge, Mass.: Harvard University Press, 1970-74), 2:365.
50 New York Juvenile Asylum, *Fifty-Ninth Annual Report* (1910), 15.
51 *Report of the Joint Committee on Home-Finding Societies, Forty-eighth General Assembly, 1915* (Springfield: Schnepp & Barnes, 1915), 39.
52 "Indentured Children," *Chicago Tribune*, March 19, 1926, 8.
53 Based on data compiled by the National Orphan Train Complex in Concordia, Kansas.
54 New York Juvenile Asylum, *Fifty-Second Annual Report* (1903), 37.
55 New York Juvenile Asylum, *Seventieth Annual Report* (1921). Superintendent's Report, 19.
56 Based on numbers sent West in the various NYJA annual reports available up to 1920.
57 New York Juvenile Asylum, *Seventieth Annual Report* (1921), 22-3.
58 Records compiled by the National Orphan Train Complex

59 in Concordia, Kansas. Cited in Stephen O'Connor: *Orphan Trains—The Story of Charles Loring Brace and the Children he Saved and Failed*, (Houghton Mifflin Co.), 2001, 309.
59 New York Juvenile Asylum, *Seventieth Annual Report* (1921). Asylum Chronology, 52.

Appendices (pages 167-218)

1 Various annual reports of the NYJA.
2 New York Juvenile Asylum, *Seventieth Annual Report* (1921), 15.
3 Ibid. Appendix C, 48.
4 New York Juvenile Asylum Annual Reports for each year listed.
5 Ibid., 211.
6 Most names from NYJA records; Rare Book and Manuscript Library, Columbia University Library. Indentures-Case Notes, Box 61, 1854-1888. The page is titled "Army List." Other names were gleaned from various NYJA Annual Reports.
7 New York Juvenile Asylum, *Forty-Seventh Annual Report* (1898), 56.

Index

A

Abrams, Elizabeth, Miss 181, 182, 183
Adams, Charles D. 171
Adams, John T. 171
Adams, Samuel 148
African American 22, 47
Agnew, Andrew Gifford 171
Agnew, George B. 171
Alberson/Alperson/Albertson, William 191
Alberts, Henry 191
Albertson/Alberson/Alperson, William 191
Allan, George H. 55, 56, 101, 103, 104, 108, 113, 124, 134
Allen, Horatio 171
A. L. O. E. (a lady of England) 119
Alvord, Franc, Miss 179, 180, 181
Amarosa Band 74
American Educational Aid Association 155
American Indian 31
American Tract Society 136
Anderson, James 191
Anderson, Pierson A., Mrs. 182
Anderson, William 191
Anthes, Minnie 31
Appley, Emma A., Mrs. 177
Army 191, 192, 194, 195, 197, 198, 199, 233
Arnold, Thomas 34
Arrighi, Antonio, Rev. 16
Arthur, W. R. 124
Astor, John Jacob, Jr. 171
Atkins, Jessie, Mrs. 186
Atkinson, Clare, Mrs. 186
Atkinson, J. E., Mrs. 185
Auer, Robert 201
Austin, Horace, Capt. 191, 194
Axtell, George H. aka Henry 191
Axtell, Henry aka George H. 191

B

Bacon, Elijah 142, 143
Badger, Richard 191

Bain, W. E. 155
Baker, Joseph, Mrs. 181, 182, 183, 184, 185
Baker, Josiah W. 171
Barnes, M. A. 189
Barrow, James T. 54, 67, 111, 171
Barrows, F. J., Mrs. 185, 186
Bartholomew, John 191
Barton, James 191
Bates, E. G. 133
Battis, Edward 191
Bayes, William R. 171
Beasley, John S. 189
Beck, Charles 126
Beck, George 126
Beckwith, John H., Mrs. 185
Beekman, Arthur W. 201
Beekman, Senator 4
Bellinger, George 191
Bennett, Andrew 191
Bennett, John 7
Beyersdorffer, John 201
Bigelow, Richard 171
Billotti, Annie 160, 161
Billotti, Giuseppe 160, 161, 162
Billotti, James 160, 161
Billotti, Rosie 160, 161
Bishop, Nathan 171
Bishop, William 191
Bixby, Judge 31
Black, John Charles, Gen. 200
Black, Peter 191
Bleekman, K. O., Miss 178, 179, 180, 181
Blessing, Miles 191
Blum, Adolph 22
Bombard, Mr. 69
Bonney, Benjamin W. 171
Boucher, Wilfred, Mrs. 186
Bower, Isaac N., Mrs. 182, 183
Brace, Charles Loring 6, 9
Brace, Charles Loring, Jr. 158
Brace, Robert N. 158, 159
Bradish, Luther 4, 5, 169, 171
Breman alias Brennan, Patrick 191
Brennan alias Breman, Patrick 191

Brewer, Catherine, Mrs. 185
Bright, James 191
Broderick, John 191
Brooks, Harry 139
Brooks, Samuel D., Dr. 11, 21, 26, 48, 54, 61, 68, 72, 73, 81, 108, 109, 119, 167
Brown alias Samuel Williams, Henry 200
Brown, E. J., Mrs. 186
Brown, F. Q., Colonel 90
Brown, George M., Mrs. 182, 183, 184
Brown, George, Mrs. 181
Brown, Henry 191
Brown, James 171
Brown, John 191
Brown, John J. 149, 150
Brown, Mr. 108
Brown, Stewart 4, 171
Brown, Thomas 191
Brown, William 149
Brown, William Harman 171
Bruce, Charles E., M. D. 66, 154, 167
Bryan, John A. 102, 107, 171
Bryan, Robert 192
Bryant, John 192
Buckingham, I. A. 139
Bulkley, Charles A. 68, 171
Bungay, Peleg 14
Burdick, Edwin C. 20, 44, 47, 52, 54, 70, 90, 91, 147
Burkill, James F., Mrs. 185, 186
Burns, Edward 192
Burns, John 192
Burr, John 192
Bush, Irene A., Mrs. 177
Bush, Ralph 192
Bush, Ransom H. 192
Butcher, John F., Mrs. 185
Butler, Benjamin F. 4, 5, 61, 171
Butler, Benjamin F., Jr. 171
Butler, Willard Parker 171
Byers, John 171

C

Calla, Christina 7
Canada 122

Canfield, James 192
Cannon, George S. 31
Canton, John 72
Carmer, Mary 5
Carney, Henry 192
Carpenter, Elisha M. 30, 115, 147, 148, 149, 167
Carpenter, J. C., Mrs. 177
Carroll, Hugh 192
Carroll, James 192
Carroll, John W. 192
Carter, Edward 201
Carter, Peter D. 172
Carter, Robert 119
Cavanagh, William 192
Chambers, John 192
Chapin, Henry, M. D. 172
Chase, Cyrus B. 98, 99, 189
Chetler, Colonel 192
Chickering, Capt. 198
Children's Village
    Andrew H. Green Cottage 89, 178, 180, 181, 182, 183, 184, 185
    athletic field 90
    band room 86
    barber shop 86
    baseball 90
    "B" Cottage 182, 183
    Boys' dining room 87
    boys' fire brigade 88
    Bradish Cottage 88, 178, 179, 180, 181, 183, 184
    Brown Cottage 183, 184, 185, 186, 187
    Burr Cottage 184, 185, 186, 187
    Butler Cottage 25, 179, 180, 181, 182, 183, 184, 186
    "C" Cottage 182
    Collins Cottage 25, 180, 182, 183, 184, 185, 186
    Cooper Cottage 178, 180, 182, 183, 184, 185, 186, 187
    Crolius Cottage 183, 184, 185, 186, 187
    Dwight Cottage 179, 180, 181, 182, 183, 184, 185, 186, 187
    Fanshaw Cottage 183, 184, 185, 186, 187
    garden 88, 89, 90
    Green Cottage 179
    Hartley Cottage 178, 179, 180, 182, 183, 184, 185, 187
    Havens Cottage 183, 184, 185, 186
    honor cottage 93
    Howard Cottage 179, 180, 181, 182, 183, 185, 186
    Intelligence Quotation Testing 85
    Intelligence Quotient Testing 83
    Kingsley Cottage 93, 178, 179, 180, 181, 182, 183, 184, 185, 186
    Lenox Cottage 178, 179, 180, 182, 183, 184
    Lincoln Cottage 182, 183, 184, 185, 186, 187
    Lord Cottage 183, 184, 185, 186, 187
    Minturn Cottage 184, 185, 186
    nurse 88
    physician 88
    Reception Cottage 87, 88
    Rhinelander Cottage 71, 185, 186
    Rose Cottage 178, 179, 180, 181, 182, 183, 184, 185, 186
    Russ Cottage 178, 179, 180, 181, 182, 183, 185, 186
    Scholes Cottage 179, 180, 181, 182, 183, 184, 185, 186
    "S" Cottage 179, 180, 181
    silver cup 90
    Smith Cottage 184, 185, 186
    Stuart Cottage 178, 179, 180, 181, 182, 183, 184, 185, 186, 187
    "T" Cottage 180, 181, 182
    "U" Cottage 180, 181, 182
    uniforms 93
    Van Horn Cottage 183, 184, 185
    "V" Cottage 181, 182
    "W" Cottage 180, 181, 182
    Wetmore Hall 83, 86
    Willetts Cottage 178, 179, 180, 181, 182, 183, 184, 185, 186
    Williams Cottage 182, 183, 185, 186
    Wolfe Cottage 183, 184, 185, 186
    "X" Cottage 182, 183
Civil War ix, 143, 191, 192, 193, 194, 197, 199, 200
    Battle of Antietam 59
    Battle of Bull Run 59
    Battle of Chancellorsville 59
    Battle of Chickamauga 201
    Battle of Chickasaw Bayou 59
    Battle of Fort Donelson 59
    Battle of Fredericksburg 59
    Battle of Gettsburg 59
    Battle of Malvern Hill 59
    Battle of Stone River 57
    Battle of Wilson's Creek 59
    Corcoran's regiment 59
    Douglas Brigade 193
    First New Jersey artillery 58
    Fort Hill 59
    Governor Yates' State Regiment (Illinois) 195
    Grand Army of the Republic 58, 74
    Irish brigade 59
    Lead Mine Regiment 59
    Lincoln rifles 59
    Logan's Regiment 194, 195
    Louisiana
        Battle of Ponchatoula 59
    Lyon, General 59
    Stanton legion 59
Clarke, Herman D., Reverend Mr. 122
Clark, George R. 109
Clark, Helen F. 47
Clark, R. F. 189
Clark, Sylvester 192
Coates, Joseph H. 172
Cochran, Thomas 126
Coffin, George B. 104, 105
Cogswell, John W. 192
Cohen, J. Moe 50
Colburn, Elizabeth T., Miss 178
Colegrove, Charles H. 145, 146
Coleman, Michael 220
Coler, William N., Col. 191
Collins, George C. 172
Collins, Joseph B. 4, 172
Collins, William 159
Colvin, E. F., Mrs. 178, 179, 180, 181, 182, 183, 184, 185
Conference on the Care of Dependent Children 162, 163, 164
Connecticut 17, 116
Cook, Allanson 135
Cookson, John F., Mrs. 185, 186
Cooper, Adeline 139
Cooper, Peter 4, 5, 172
Cornell Agricultural College 88
Corney, Alonzo R. 192
Corrigan, William 192
Cortwright, Capt. 52
Cottage plan 19, 20
Cotton, Jerry 138
Cotton, Nancy 138
Couchman, Charles Young 192
Couper, Henry J. 88
Couper, Henry J., Mrs. 178, 179
Cox, Dr. 5
Cox, Henry, Mrs. 181
Crea, Samuel 192
Crocker, Charles A. 139
Crolius, Clarkson 172
Cronein, Mary 131, 154
Croney, William 192
Cross, Orville C. 74
Crowley, John Joseph 192
Crygier, Isaac 192
Cuba
    30
Cunningham, Joseph 192
Curran, Joseph 192
Curry, George, Mrs. 186
Curthworth, Catharine 177
Curtis, Cyrus 172

Curtis, General 198
Cushman, James S. 172

D

Dale, Thomas J. 60, 192
Daly, May, Miss 181
Dana, Richard P. 172
Daram, Alfred 192
Daughters of the American Revolution 74
Davenport, John 172
Davis, Bessie, Miss 181, 182, 183
Davis, Henry E. 192
Davis, Lelah, Mrs. 179, 180, 181, 182, 183, 184, 185, 186
Davison, Halsey 90
Day, Alexander 201
Day, Joseph P. 172
Dean, George Hamilton 90
Decker, Frederick, Capt. 198
Decker, M., Reverend Mr. 192
Dee, Jennie J. 143, 144
DeLaney, Bernard 192
Dennison, John 192
Denny, Thomas 4, 172
Denny, Thomas, Jr. 172
Dermitt, Jane, Miss 181
Derringer, Otto 193
Devoe, Frederick W. 169, 172
DeWees, Roy H., Mrs. 182
Dick, E. A., Miss 178
Dick, Eliza, Miss 179, 180
Dickey, Alexander 189
District of Columbia
    Washington 193
Divine, James 193
Dixon, C. T., Capt. 193
Doane, Patrick 193
Dodge, Mary E. 26
Donahue, Barney 193
Donahue, Patrick 193
Donaldson, Laura J., Mrs. 156, 157
Donelson, Thomas 193
Donnegan, William 193
Donnelly, William 193
Donovan, John F. 143, 144, 193
Doonan, Thomas 193
Dorman, Richard A. 172
Dougherty, James 193
Dougherty, Michael 193
Dougherty, Philip 193
Dowd, William 172
Du Crow, George 201
Duer, John 4, 172
Duffner, William 201
Duffy, Hugh 193
Duffy, John 193
Dullar, Alfred A. 193
Duncan, George 7

Dunham, E. W., Mrs. 183
Dunlap, John 124
Dunlap, N. J., Mrs. 177
Dunn, Bernard 193
Dustin, Daniel, Col. 191, 194
Dwight, Edmund 169, 172
Dwight, Edmund, Sr. 69, 172
Dwight, Mr. 68
Dwight, Theodore W. 172

E

Early, Thomas 7
Edmonds, John W. 4, 172
Edwards, Fred, Mrs. 186
Edwards, Henrietta, Miss 180, 181
Ege, Peter, Capt. 192
Elliot, John 193
Elmore, Andrew E. 159
Ely, Charles 172
England
    London 150
    Marylebone 119
    School
        Rugby 34
Everett, Mrs. 130
Ewart, James, Capt. 191
Ewing, Thomas 172

F

Farmer, James 193
Farmer, William M. 149
Farrell, Dennis 57, 193
Farrell, Johanna 108
Faulkner, Leon, Col. 167
Fay, Thomas 193
Ferdon, Edna, Miss 179
Ferdon, Edna, Mrs. 178
Ferguson, John 193
Ferguson, W. K., Miss 178
Field, Frank Harvey 172
Field, Joel E. 155
Fillony, James 193
Fisher, John 193
Fisk, Wilbur C. 172
Fithian, Captain 199
Fitzgerald, John 7
Flara, Rosina 7
Flynn, John 126
Flynn, Richard 140
Folsom, A., Mr. 189
Fox, Isaac 193
France 51
Franky, Mary 117
Frantz, Alice M., Miss 186
Frash, George 51
Free, James 193
Freligh, Henry 201
Fremer, John J. 72
Friedman, Jacob 42

Fry, Daniel 189
Fryer, Kevin 120
Fullerton, H., Capt. 199
Furness, Charles H. 193

G

Gales, Oscar 193
Gallagher, Hugh 193
Gallagher, Michael 193
Gallaway, Robert M. 172
Gamble, William, Col. 200
Gambling or Gamble, Johnson aka Jonathan 193
Gambling or Gamble, Jonathan aka Johnson 193
Gardner, William F. 133
Garrabrant, Aaron P. 52, 64, 103, 167
Garth, Horace E. 172
Gaston, Mr. 141
Geer, Joseph, Mrs. 181, 182
Geissenhainer, Frederick W., Jr. 172
Germany ix
Gerry, Elbridge Thomas 36
Gibson, Isaac 172
Gilbert, Albert, Hon. 4, 172
Gilbert, Charles G., Sergeant 200
Giles, Hiram H. 159
Gillan, Michael 7
Gilman, William C., Jr. 172
Gilman, William C., Sr. 172
Gilmartin, Bridget 7
Glossop, George 150
Gloss, Sarah 148
Goddard, Henry 83
Goeller, Robert 172
Goodell, Harriet 109
Goodrich, Samuel G., 2nd 172
Gottlieb, Morris H. 44
Gould, E. R. L. 173
Gould, J. W. DuBois 173
Graham, John A. 173
Grant, General 59, 74, 198
Grant, Theodore W., Mrs. 181, 182, 183, 184, 186
Gray, Father 130
Gray, John 7
Green, Andrew H. 173
Green, John 194
Green, Thomas 194
Gregory, Henry E. 91, 131, 173
Greves, John 194
Greves, William 194
Griffin, Robert B. 194
Griggs, Maitland F. 173
Groharing, Richard 126
Groharing, William 126
Guest, Mr. 10
Guynne, Harry, Mrs. 184

Index   237

H

Hackmyer, William 194
Hadden, Alexander M. 173
Hadden, Alexander, M. D. 173
Hale, Grace E., Miss 183
Haley, John 194
Haley, Peter 9
Hall, Richard 145
Halsey, Ada, Miss 179
Hammond, C. G. 124
Hammond, John H. 173
Hampton, Michael 194
Hanaway, Frank, Mrs. 182
Hanifen, Michael L. 58, 194
Hanlon, Peter S. 64
Harbinson, George W. 194
Hardenburgh, Simon 194
Harkins, Benjamin Franklin aka Franklin 194
Harkins, Franklin aka Benjamin Franklin 194
Harriman, Charles 31
Harrington, John 140
Harris, Joseph 194
Hart, Charles 194
Hart, Hastings Hornell, Dr. 37, 85, 148, 155, 156, 157, 162, 164
Hartley, Joseph W. 173
Hartley, Robert Milham 4, 173
Hart, Peter 194
Hasbrouck, James 161
Hasbrouck, Joseph, Dr. 91
Hatch, Joseph Henry 194
Havens, Rensselaer N. 4, 102, 173
Hawk, William S. 169, 173
Hayes, Michael 194
Hearn, Alexander 194
Hearn, David 194
Heeny, William 194
Held, Pauline 137
Hendrickson, Charles 194
Hennessy, John C. 130
Hennessy, William 194
Henninger, William 149
Henry, Samuel Y. 189
Henry, William 194
Herme, Charles August 194
Herren, John 194
Herring, Silas C. 4, 173
Hickey, Christian 51
Hickey, Joseph 51
Higgins, Timothy 194
Hilles, Anne F., Miss 182, 183, 184, 185, 186
Hilles, Charles Dewey 21, 22, 26, 34, 50, 52, 55, 70, 71, 93, 121, 167, 169, 173
Hill, George E. 194
Hills, Gilbert H. 72
Hills, Henry F. 173

Hobbie, William C. A. 194
Hoge, George Blaikie, Col. 191, 198
Holden, Daniel J. 173
Holland, Peter 194
Holly, William H. 72
Holmes, Hartley 189
Holt, Charles J., Mrs. 35
Holt, F. R., Mrs. 183, 184, 185
Honey, Anna M. 7
Honeyman, Caroline K., Miss 180, 181, 182, 183, 184, 185
Hood, Katherine, Miss 183
Hoover, Alexander 126
Hoover, George S. 147
Hoover, Theresa 126
Hopper, Isaac T. 4, 173
Horan, William 194
Horton, Benjamin Franklin 195
Hosler, Ada, Miss 179
Hosler, C. O., Mrs. 178, 180, 181
Howard, Edward 195
Howard, Frank 145
Howard, Mrs. 146
Hoyt, Alonzo W. 195
Hubbard, Andrew 195
Hubbard, C. B. 155
Hubbard, Elbert 127, 128
Hubbard, Judge 143
Hubbs, Edward 201
Hudson, Henry E. 195
Huff, Henry 72
Hughes, Bridget 104, 105
Hughes, James 195
Humphrey, Henry M. 67, 111, 173
Humphreys, E. M., Mrs. 185, 186
Humphries, E. M., Mrs. 183, 184
Hunter, Charles 195
Hunter, John 150
Hurry, Randolph 173
Husted, Louise A. 33, 44
Hyatt, George F., Mrs. 186
Hyde, Joseph 195
Hynes, Thomas W., Reverend Mr. 189

I

Iles, Belle S., Mrs. 178, 179, 180
Illinois 9, 21, 22, 30, 56, 58, 59, 60, 98, 99, 101, 106, 107, 112, 122, 129, 132, 136, 147, 149, 155, 160, 161, 162, 165, 189, 197, 201
    Aledo 129
    Almshouse 147
    Annawan 114
    Aurora 146
    Bellefame 99
    Belleville 108
    Bernardsville 140
    Bloomington 110, 111, 127, 130, 190

    Bond County
        Greenville 189
    Brookville 148
    Cairo 58, 59, 196
    Carthage 127
    Cedarville 148
    Centralia 143
    Champaign City 59
    Champaign County 59, 144
        Tolono 189
        West Urbana (now Champaign) 117, 189, 190
    Chester 150
    Chicago 109, 122, 123, 148, 153, 154, 155, 161, 165, 191
        Dearborn Station (railroad depot) 123, 124
        Great Chicago Fire 110
        Illinois Central Depot 110
        Massasoit House Hotel 110
        Union Depot (aka Illinois Central) 110
    Christian County
        Pana 189
    Clinton County 107
        Carlyle 108, 189, 190
    Coles County
        Mattoon 190
    Coles Station 143
    Cook County 161
    Danville 97, 99, 116
    Decatur 106, 124, 189
    DeKalb County 101
    Dixon 119
    Du Quoin 156
    Edgar County
        Paris 142, 189
    Edwardsville 136
    Englewood 112, 123, 153, 155, 156
    Fayette County 149
        Vandalia 9, 149, 150, 189
    Ford County 145
    Fountain Creek 148
    Galva 150
    Gibson 118, 143
        Burwell House (hotel) 118
    Grand Prairie 97
    Greene County
        Carrollton 189
    Grundy County 146
    Havana 123
    Hudson 127
    Illinois Children's Home and Aid Society 22, 85, 148, 155, 156, 157, 158, 162, 165
    Iroquois County 160, 161
        Gilman 161
        Middleport 190
    Joliet 124, 130

Prison 143
  St. Nicholas hotel 124
Kane County
  Aurora 189
Kankakee County
  Kankakee 145, 189, 190
Kenwood 109
Kinmundy 143, 144
LaGrange 148
Lakeview township 109
LaSalle 130
LaSalle County 130
Lee County 101
Legislature 107, 108, 165
Lincoln 134
Livingston County 144
Loda 151
Logan County
  Atlanta 190
  Mt. Pulaski 189
Macon County 145
Malone Township 99
Mason County
  Havana 190
McDonough County 141
McLean County
  Normal 110, 111
Metamora 134
Monmouth 107
Monticello 144
National Children's Home Society 155
Normal 229
  State Normal University 111
Norton Township 145
Ocoya 145
Ogle County 101, 144
Ottawa 129, 131
Peoria 99
Peotone 145
Peru 130
Pontiac 145
Randolph County 145
  Sparta 189
Rantoul 156
Shelbyville 156
Southern Illinois Penitentiary 150
Springfield 107
Sterling 147
St. Mary's Academy 130
Tazewell County 132, 151
  Bellefame 98, 189, 190
  Pekin 190
Vermilion County 99
  Danville 60, 97, 99, 189
  The Vermilion County Juvenile Aid Society 97, 102
Warren County 141

Washington County 107, 140, 145
  Elkhorn 189
  Nashville 189
Wesleyan University 149
Whiteside County 101
Yates, Governor 107, 108
Young America 125
Indiana 97, 100, 112, 160, 198, 199
  Covington 97
  Delphi 139
  Wabash 97
  Warren County
    State Line City 189
Iowa 9, 22, 111, 112, 144, 154, 155, 156, 160, 199
  Burlington 127
  Independence 155
  Legislature 154
Ireland ix
Irvine, Gordon, Mrs. 185, 186

J

Jackson, A. H., Mrs. 185, 186, 187
Jacques, James F., Colonel 200
James, D. Willis 131
James, Nathaniel 195
Jarvis, Maitland 55
Jefferson, George Washington 133
Jenkins, Ezra 189
Jenner, Solomon 4, 173
Jesup, Charles M. 71, 173
Jesup, Richard M. 173
Jewell, Mary S. 156
Johnson, Alexander, Captain 200
Johnson, Boy 41
Johnson, Frederick 7
Johnson, John E. 173
Johnson, John R. 189
Johnson, S. M., Miss 178, 179
Jomu, G. B. 189
Jones, Pierce 195
Jourdan, John 195
Joy, Joseph F. 173

K

Kane, John 195
Kansas 21, 60, 111
  Governor 21
  Riley 74
  State Agricultural College 60
Karch, O. H., Mrs. 185
Karr, John 145
Kavanaugh, William 195
Kean, John 195
Kellogg, Mr. 108
Kelly, James 4, 7, 173, 195
Kenmore, James 145
Kennedy, David S. 4, 173

Kennedy, John 195
Kenney alias McKenna, William 195
Kimmel, Matilda aka Tillie 136, 138
Kingsbury, Enoch, Reverend Mr. 97, 98, 99, 100, 101, 102, 142, 189
Kingsley, Ezra M. 16, 74, 169, 173
Kingsley, William M. 173
King, William V. 173
Kirkbride, Franklin B. 173
Kiser, Captain 197
Klein, John 156
Knight, Henry 7
Koon, H. G. 189
Kornmann, Frederick W. 29
Krech, Lucy, Miss 182
Krieg, J. K. 65

L

La Bruce, E. L., Miss 178
Laird, J. H. L., Reverend Mr. 189
Lambert, William 173
Lanahan or Lanahan, Michael 195
Lanchbaugh, Thomas P. 189
Lange alias Lenger, Paul 195
Lannehan or Lanahan, Michael 195
Larkin, Michael 7
Latter, Alexander 195
Lawhead, Charles A. 161
Lawler, John 195
Lawrence, Justice 160, 161
Lawver, H. M., Mrs. 185, 186, 187
Lawyer, Glen A., Mrs. 180
Leake, Eugene 7
Leek, Cornelius 195
Leek, Henry 195
Lee, Mr. 189
Leighton, A. B., Mrs. 185
Leininger, Fred, Mrs. 186
Lender, John A. 195
Lenger alias Lange, Paul 195
Lenhart, May, Miss 179, 180
Lennox, John 195
Leonard, John 195
Libbey, Nellie M., Mrs. 177
Libert, Augustus 195
Lillio or Lillie, [Daniel A.?], Mr. 189
Lincoln, Abraham 55, 56, 58, 60, 62, 91
Lincoln, D. D., Captain 200
Lindsay, Alexander 130
Lindsley, J. W. 139
Link, F. M. or N. 189
Link, N. or F. M. 189
Lipman, Leon 195
Lockhart, James 189
Lockwood, Joseph B. 74, 173
Lockwood, Roe 173
Long, Benjamin F. 195
Long, Hannah 7

Loomis, Colonel 193
Louisiana Purchase Exposition 150
Loundsbury, William A. 195
Lovell, Leander N. 174
Low, Benjamin R. C. 174
Lowenstein, Solomon 18
Lowery, John 174
Lunger, John B. 174
Lyle, A. J., Mrs. 178, 179, 180, 181, 182, 183, 184
Lyle, Harry H., Mrs. 186, 187
Lyle, Harry, Mrs. 183, 184, 185
Lynch, Patrick 196
Lyons, Daniel W. 196

M

MacDonald, H. M. 178
MacKenzie, Donald, Mrs. 187
Madden, Daniel D. 196
Madden, Michael 196
Maiers, Louis 196
Mair, George Sidney 196
Maley, Mr. 108
Manlin alias Wiler or Weber, Valentine 196
Manning, John 196
Manning, William 196
Mapes, E. L., Reverend Mr. 189
Marks, Isaac 51
Marling, Alfred E. 112, 174
Marr, Peter 196
Martin, Michael 7
Maryland 9, 98, 193, 195
Massachusetts
    Boston
        New England Home for Little Wanderers xi
    Lancaster 20
    Ludlow 109
    Monson 109
        State Reform School 109
    Springfield 21
    State Farm School 68
    State Industrial School for Girls 20
Master, Miss 75
Masterson, Ida 30, 50
Masterson, William 30, 50, 222, 224
Mathewson, Christy 91
Matsell, George Washington ix, 3, 5
Mayo, Justice 55
McCabe & Duffy 21
McCabe, Philip 196
McCall, James 201
McCanna or McCannon, Patrick 196
McCannon or McCanna, Patrick 196
McClernand, General 194
McClintock, C. E., Mrs. 182, 183, 184
McClure, E. W., Mrs. 184, 185
McColen, Caleb 7

McCrum, James 196
McCue, John 196
McDermott, Luke 196
McDonald, James 196
McDonough, George, Mrs. 182, 183
McDonough, John T. 131
McGirty, Hugh 196
McGrew, Neil 196
McGuire, James 196
McIntosh, Joseph 161
McKay alias Michael Rigney, John 198
McKenna alias Kenney, William 195
McKenna, William 196
McKenzie, Joseph Oatwell 196
McKown, S. W., Captain 194
McLaughlin, Jeremiah 196
McLaughlin, Mary 7
McLaughlin, Mary Ann 7
McLaughlin, William W. 196
McMadden, Michael 196
McMenomy, John 196
McNeil, Godfrey aka Godfried 159
McNeil, William 159
McNeir, George 174
McPherson, William 126
McQuinn, Thomas 7
McTaggart, Mrs. 116, 117
Meagher, James 7
Meltz, Albertina 106
Melville, John 196
Merrill, J. M., Mrs. 184
Merriman, E. J., Mrs. 187
Michigan 9, 47, 160
    Detroit 7
    Dowagiac 7
Miles, Emma V., Miss 178
Miller, George 196
Miller, George H. 106
Miller, Henry 196
Miller, Lilly, Mrs. 184
Miller, Walter T. 174
Milligan, C. S., Mrs. 186, 187
Mills, Ella B., Miss 180, 181, 182
Mills, George 196
Milot, William R. 196
Minnesota 160
Mins, Linda 138
Minturn, Robert B. 4, 174
Mississippi
    Jackson 57
    Vicksburg 59
Missouri 60, 112, 155, 160
    St. Louis 193
        World's Fair 150
Moffitt, Burt J. 74
Monahan, Henry 197
Monahan, John 197
Moore, Orville, Mrs. 184
Moore, Seely 197

Moreno, Fernando A. 197
Morgan, B. T. 28
Morgan, Guy 48, 167
Morgan, Morgan, Mrs. 184
Morgan, W. N., Mrs. 185
Morris, John 197
Morrison, Dennis 197
Morrison, James M. 174
Morris, William 7
Moses, George 197
Mosher, Albert 197
Most, Harry 51
Moulton, Franklin W. 112, 174
Mullen, David E. 197
Mullen, James 197
Mulvain/Mulvane/Mulram, James 197
Mulvane/Mulvain/Mulram, James 197
Munger, Isaac E. 7
Murphy, Catherine 34
Murphy, Edward 7, 34
Murphy, James 197
Murphy, J. H. 190
Murphy, Martha 34
Murphy, Peter 197
Murray, Henry, Justice 113, 114
Murray, William 197
Musser, Melville H., Captain 200
Myers, James 197

N

National Conference of Charities and Correction 25, 85, 160
National Conference on the Education of Delinquent, Truant, and Backward Children 25
National Prison Reform Conference 159
Navy 194, 195, 200, 201
Nebraska 159, 160
Nelson, General 59
Nevens, John 197
Newbold, Clayton 174
Newburgh, Joseph 197
New Jersey 47, 83, 194, 198
    Jersey City 31, 120, 121, 122
    Palisades 10
    Vineland 83, 85
        Training School for the Feeble-Minded 83
New York 3, 4, 17, 19, 31, 47, 99, 100, 130, 145, 146, 147, 148, 149, 162, 194, 200
    Almshouse 17
    Board of Charities 17, 34, 55, 70
    Bridgehampton 135
    Brown, Governor 131
    Buffalo 123
    Chauncey 19, 20, 50, 58, 150
        Railroad Station 25
    Children's Law 17

commission ix
Commissioners of Public Charities 69
Disorderly Child Act ix
Dobbs Ferry 19, 20, 21, 22, 44, 48, 50, 52, 75, 77, 83, 89, 150, 165
   St. Christopher's Home 20, 75
Dunkirk 100, 123
East Rockaway 41
Elmira Reformatory 44
Fordham 35
   St. James Rectory 35
Genesee River 123
Harlem River 10, 72
Hastings 50, 53
   Country Fair 75, 90
Hastings-on-Hudson 20
   New York Orphan Asylum 20
Hawthorne 20
   Cedar Knolls School 20
   Hawthorne School 20
Hope Farm
   School 157
Hornellsville 123
Hudson 22
   House of Refuge for Women 22
Hudson River 10, 19, 48, 54, 58, 72, 121, 123
Industry 20
Kensico
   Brace Farm School 22, 131, 159
Legislature ix, 4, 17, 20, 107, 130, 162
Long Island 47
   Mineola 157
      Children's Home 157
Long Island Sound 10
Manhattan 21, 22
New York City ix, 19, 20, 30, 47, 160, 161, 162
   Almshouse ix, 30
   American Female Guardian Society and Home for the Friendless 11
   Architects
      Butler & Rodman 20
      Howells & Stokes 20
      Parish & Schroeder 20
      Thomas & Son 9
      Walker & Morris 20
      York & Sawyer 20
   Association for Improving the Condition of the Poor 3
   Association of Ladies for an Asylum 4, 5
   Asylum for Friendless Boys 4
   baseball team
      New York Giants 91
   bootblacks 32, 33
   Bronx 34
   Brooklyn 36, 113
      Brooklyn Bridge 32
      Children's Aid Society 131
      Children's Court 37
      Industrial School Association 11
   Castle Garden 45
   Catholic Home Bureau 22
   Catholic Protectory 48, 70, 130, 132
   Children's Aid Society 6, 8, 9, 97, 107, 122, 129, 131, 157, 158, 159, 160, 165
   Children's Court 36, 38, 55, 83, 165
   Colored Orphan Asylum 22
   Commissioners of Charity 28
   Conference of Charities and Correction 34
   court magistrates 38
   Department of Public Charities 17, 35, 132, 157
   East River 5
   Five Points House of Industry 22
   Five Points Mission 231
   Fort Washington
      Railroad depot 72
   German immigrants ix
   Hebrew Orphan Asylum 18, 22
   Hebrew Sheltering Guardian Society 22
   High Bridge 9, 25, 47, 50
   Howard Colored Orphan Asylum 22
   Immigrants ix
   Inwood 75
   Irish immigrants ix, 100
   Isaac Newton (steamship) 7
   Jefferson Market Police Court 31
   Jumel Mansion 74
   Leake & Watts Orphan Asylum 10
   Longacre Square (now Times Square] 150
   Madison Square church 117
   Mayor William L. Strong 67
   Mayor Woodhull 3
   newsboys 33
   Newsboys' Lodging House 147, 150
   New York House of Refuge ix, 4, 16, 20, 22, 39, 44, 51, 52, 53, 70, 71, 141, 231
   New York Society for the Prevention of Cruelty to Children 35, 36, 38, 154
   Old Greenwich Village 140
   peddlers 32
   Poorhouse ix
   Protestant Half-Orphan Asylum 22
   Randalls Island 20, 22
   Theological Seminary 31
   Tombs (Prison) 3, 35
   truant schools 70
   United Hebrew Charities 22
   vagrant children ix
   Van Cortlandt Lake 77
   Washington Heights 9, 11, 19, 20, 21, 22, 50, 52, 74, 148
   Washington Market 132
   Workhouse ix
North River 121
Poorhouses 17
Portage 123
Prison
   Sing Sing 31
Prison Association 4
Ramapo River 123
Rochester 20, 22
   State Industrial School 20
Society of St. Vincent De Paul 160
State Board of Charities 17, 131
State Industrial School 22
Staten Island
   Nursery and Hospital 47
State Training School for Girls 22
Supreme Court 161
Valhalla 158
Vassar College 20
Westchester County 19
   Cochrane Estate 19
   Dobbs Ferry 19, 25, 26
   Echo Hills 19
   Saw Mill river valley 25
   Villard Estate 19
White Plains 70
   Westchester Temporary Home 70
Yonkers 74
   Leake & Watts Orphan Asylum 20, 74
Nichols, John, Captain 199
Nolan, Peter 197
North, John 197
Norton, Jacob 197
Norton, James 197
Norton, John 197
NYJA. See New York Juvenile Asylum

O

Oberlin College 155
O'Brien, Daniel 126
O'Connor, Celia 67
O'Conor, Charles 4, 174
Ohio 100
   Ashtabula County

Index

Andover 9
Cleveland 99, 123
Oklahoma 157
O'Neil, Francis 197
Opdycke, Leonard E. 174
Orphan Train Movement 165, 167, 169
Orphan trains 112, 162, 165, 231
    county agents in Illinois 189
    prejudices against New York boys 129
    railroad fares 99, 106, 107
Osborne, William 191
Osborn, William C. 131

P

Paddock, Lieutenant Colonel 191
Palliser, George 87
Palmatier, Charles E. or F. 201
Palmer, George R., Reverend Mr. 190
Palmer, Grace O. 136, 138
Parkin, William W. 174
Parr, Daniel 197
Parsloe, Franklin 197
Partridge, Charles 4, 174
Patterson, Mary 151
Patterson, Mr. and Mrs. 106
Payne, Charlotte, Miss 180
Pearcy, Alexander C. 28, 100, 102, 109, 123
Pearson, Mrs. A. 186
Peck, Charles C. 174
Pedersen, Julius, Mrs. 184
Pell, Mr. 10
Perriton, John S. 197
Perry, H. D. 108, 124, 126, 142, 143
Pett, Captain 196
Phillips, William 197
Plimpton, George F., Mrs. 186
Plummer, John F. 174
Pointon, George F. 7
Pollard, E. L., Mrs. 178, 179, 180, 181, 182, 183, 184, 185
Porter, Samuel 197
Potter, Martha 142
Powel, Robert J. H. 174
Powers, John Henry 197
Powers, William 197
Price, Miss S. M. 177
Pugh, John 198
Punch, Patrick Philip 7
Pyle, W. H. K. 190

Q

Quevedo, John 198
Quincy, John W. 174

R

Railroad
    Baltimore and Ohio 110
    Burlington & Quincy 124
    Chicago, Alton and St. Louis Railroad 124
    Chicago, Burlington and Quincy 124
    Chicago & North Western 124
    Chicago & Western Indiana 123
    Cleveland, Cincinnati, Chicago & St. Louis 111
    Erie 100, 122, 123, 124
        express trains 121
        Long Dock 123
        Pavonia Ferry 121, 122
        Susquehanna ferry boat 121
    Illinois
        Chicago & Alton 111
        Englewood 111
        Galena & Chicago Union 110
        New York Central Railroad 111
        Rock Island 140
    Illinois Central 124
    Iowa Central 121
    Lake Shore and Michigan Southern 123
    Lake Shore and Rock Island Railroad 123
    Minneapolis & St. Louis 121
    New York
        Putnam Railroad 19
    Nickel Plate 111
    Pennsylvania 111
    Rock Island and Pacific Railroad 111
Railway
    Chicago, Milwaukee & St. Paul 122
    Erie 121
    Erie (depot) 120
    Manhattan Elevated Railway 19
Ransom, General 200
Rathbun, William H. 7
Rathburn, Minnie M. 54
Ray, Morris 198
Rector, Walter, Mrs. 180, 181
Redfield, James S. 174
Reese, Clarence 33
Reese, Laura 33
Reese, Lewis 33
Reeves, Theodore W. 198
Regan, Aaron 198
Rhel, Charles 198
Richey, Eugene, Mrs. 183
Richey, Mrs. Eugene 182
Riddle, Grover, Mrs. 186, 187
Riggin, Fannie, Mrs. 179, 180, 181
Rigney alias John McKay, Michael 198
Riker, Daniel 198
Riley, James 198
Riley, Thomas 198
Ritter, R. 190

Robbins. Floyd B., Mrs. 186
Robb, J. Hampden 174
Roberdee, William T. 198
Roberts, Captain 194
Roberts, Charles Henry 198
Robertson, James 198
Robnett, J. M. 143, 144
Rodden, Edward 198
Rodgers, James M. 108
Rodh, Frank 198
Roe, Frank O. 174
Rogers, Charles 198
Rogers, William D. 198
Roll, William 201
Rooney, James 198
Roosevelt, Theodore, President 162, 163, 164
Root, Herbert T. 156
Rose, H. E., Mrs. 181
Rose, Jack 54
Rosenbaum, Morris 53
Rouse, Dennis 60
Rowe, John 198
Rubendahl, Uriah 148
Russ, John D. 4, 5, 41, 167, 174
Rutherford, Justice 198
Ryan, Colonel 194, 198
Ryan, Daniel 198
Ryan, Mary 14
Ryer, George 135

S

Sackey, E. A., Mrs. 178, 179, 180, 181, 182, 183, 184
Sadleir, William 198
Sanborn, A. O., Mrs. 185
Sandford, Emily, Miss 81
Sanford, Daniel R. 142
Scanlan, Michael J. 160
Scattergood, Edwin F. 198
Scheurman, Mary T., Miss 181
Schultz, Herman 201
Schultz, Ruthella, Miss 177
Schwab, Gustav H. 174
Schwartz, Charles 29
Scott, David B. 9
Scott, Thomas 198
Scott, Walter 198
Scroggs, J. W. 117, 190
Seffers, Henry 201
Seidemann, Julius 69
Sell, Fannie J. 177
Sells, Ione B., Miss 182
Shad, Col. 199
Shambark, John 198
Shannessy, Thomas 57, 198
Shannon, S. P., Captain 190
Sharp, G. E., Mrs. 185
Sharp, William 198

Shaw, Amelia 177
Shaw, Gustavus 198
Shedd, Warren 199
Sheffold, George, Mrs. 178, 179, 180, 181, 182, 183
Sheller, John, Mrs. 184, 185
Sherman, Benjamin B. 174
Sherman, Frank, Colonel 198
Sherman, General 59
Sherman, William Watts 174
Shields, James W. 121, 136, 154, 155, 156, 161
Siebert, Edward 113, 114
Siebert, Mary A. 113, 114
Sigel, General 59
Sigel or Sigets, Mr. 192
Sigits or Sigel, Mr. 192
Silvester, Florence, Miss 182
Simon, August 130
Simon, Louis 130
Skidmore, A. Bolivar 190
Slade, Francis Louis 174
Slade, John M. 174
Sloan, William 74
Smith, Charles 198
Smith, Charles E., Mrs. 186
Smith, Edward Parmelee 7, 8
Smith, Eugene 198
Smith, Father 130
Smith, James 7
Smith, James H. 198
Smith, James W. 198
Smith, John 7, 198
Smith, John A. E. 199
Smith, John H. 199
Smith, Mrs. 43
Smith, Orison B. 174
Smith, William W. 174
Sneider, John 7
Snow, Barney 199
Snow, John James 199
Society of Friends 4
Somers, Sophia, Miss 179, 180, 181, 182, 183, 184
Sommerkom, Emil 199
South Carolina 108
    Fort Sumter 108
Spain 201
Spalding, A. M. 115
Spanish-American War 201
    Cuba
        Santiago bombardment 201
Speer, Robert E. 174
Spencer, P. A., Mr. 97
Spencer, Reverend 200
Spicer, Colonel 194
Stanford University 83
Stansbery, Theodore 199
Staples, Reverend Mr. 190

Staurer, George 199
Steamer
    Santiago de Cuba 113
Stebbing, Michael 199
Stevens, Mr. 145
Steward, Thomas L., Mrs. 185
Stewart, John 199
Stewart or Stuart, William aka John J. 199
Stewart, T. M., Mrs. 179, 180, 181
St. Ives 79
Stockin, Gordon, Mrs. 184
Stokes, Anson G. P. 174
Stokes, Henry 199
Stokes, J. G. Phelps 175
Straight, David L. 145
Stratton, Robert M. 4, 175
Strohm, Eugene, Mrs. 185
Strong, Theron G. 174
Strong, William K. 174
Stuart or Stewart, John J. aka William 199
Sturges, Isaac, Rev. 16
Sullivan, Captain 198
Sullivan, John 108, 199
Sullivan, Michael 199
Summerton, Daniel 126, 199
Summerton, James 126
Sutherland, Captain 194
Sutton, George D. 175
Swannell, W. G. 190
Sweetser, Joseph A. 175
Swensky, Samuel 147
Sweyer, Minnie, Miss 180, 181

T

Taft, William Howard, President 93, 94
Taggart, David 199
Talbert, Joseph T. 175
Talbott, John 199
Talmadge, Henry 175
Taylor, William B. 175
Taylor, Zachariah 147
Tennessee 59
    Shiloh 59
Terry, Jesse W. 199
Texas 157, 159
    Hunt County
        Greenville 139
    Lampasas 159
        Oak Dale Ranch 159
    Sulphur Springs 165
Therman, Lewis 83
Thiel, Frank 120
Thomas, E. J., Reverend Mr. 190
Thomas, Francis J. 199
Thompson, Israel E. 199
Thompson, John 9, 52, 199
Thurston, Henry W. 157

Tierney, Fred 201
Tifft, Henry N. 175
Tillon, Francis R. 4, 175
Timpson, John 199
Todd, Andrew C., Reverend Captain 59, 60, 191, 192, 193, 195, 197, 198
Townley, Thomas T. 143
Townsend, Charles Collins 7
Townsend, Howard 36, 38, 175
Travis, James 199
Travis, Owen 199
Trow, John F. 175
Truax, John E., Dr. 67
Truax, John G., M. D. 175
Trump, William 7
Tucker, Charlotte Maria 119
Turchin, Colonel 200
Turner, H. E., Mrs. 187
Turrell, John 199

U

U., Andrew 199
Underhill, Samuel 125
Underwood, William Henry 108

V

Valiant, Alonzo 199
Van Amringe, Guy 175
Van Brunt, E. M., Mrs. 178, 179
Van Buren Arsdale, Martin, Reverend Mr. 155
Vanderbeck, Henry 199
Van Loon, Ida 147, 148
Van Loon, Sophia 147
Van Meter, William C. 147
Van Pelt, Camilla, Miss 182, 183
Van Pelt, Miss Camilla 181
Van Schaick, Myndert 4, 175
Van Tassal, Oscar M., Colonel 192
Van Wagenen, William F. 175
Van Wyck, Charles H., Colonel 198
Venette, George 148
Vermilye, Jacob D. 175
Vermont
    Poultney 54
Verplanck, William E. 175
Virden, Charles E., Mrs. 185
Virden, Charles F., Mrs. 184
Virginia
    Centreville 59
Von Glahn, Louis Frederick 199
Von Glahn, William C. 199

W

Wagner, William 199
Walbridge, Captain 192
Wald, Lillian D. 164
Walker, George 7, 199
Walker, Thomas 7

Wallace, Charles 131
Wallace, Eliza 139
Wallace, William 139
Wall, Captain 192
Walsh, Peter 200
Ward, John Seeley, Jr. 67
Ward, John Seely 175
Ward, Lebbeus B. 175
Warren, Charles Elliot 175
Warrens, H. C. 151
Washington, George 91
Waterfall, Arthur, Mrs. 186
Waters, Frederick 200
Weaver, Miss C. L. 178
Webber, Mrs. R. T. 178
Webb, John 200
Webster, Vernon, Mrs. 184
Weed, George Alonzo 200
Weiner, William 145, 146
Welch, Patrick 200
Wells, Gertrude 130
Wells, Nannie 130
Wemple, Christopher Y. 4, 175
Wendell, Evert Jansen 131, 175
West, Cornelia B., Miss 178
Westmen, Emma Jane "Jennie" 116
Westmen, Mary 116
Westmen, Thomas Oscar \"Oscar\" 116
Wetmore, Apollos R. 4, 6, 42, 46, 74, 100, 119, 169, 175
Wetmore, David 5
Whalen, Frank aka Francis 200

Whalen or Whelan, Patrick 200
Whallon, Captain 198
Wheelock, William E., M. D. 175
Whelan or Whalen, Patrick 200
White, Emil aka "Lafe" 126
Whiteley, James D. 200
Whitney, E. L., Mrs. 47
Whittle, Edward 200
Wicks, James 126
Wilcox, William G. 175
Wilder, John 143
Wiler or Weber alias Manlin, Valentine 196
Wilkin, Judge 37
Willard, Charles 200
Williams alias Henry Brown, Samuel 200
Williams, Cephas, Captain 191
Williams, E. H. 124
Williams, John A. 200
Williams, Leighton 74, 175
Williams, Mornay 17, 18, 19, 25, 31, 46, 67, 70, 88, 91, 112, 131, 162, 164, 169, 175
Williams, Nathaniel J. 7
Williamson, Edward 200
Wills, Charles T. 21
Wilsey, Mr. 190
Wilson, James, Mrs. 183, 184, 185
Wilson, John 200
Wilson, William 200
Winston, Frederick S. 4, 175
Wisconsin 9, 112, 159, 165, 201

State Board of Charities and Reform 159
Wolcott, Frederick H. 5, 175
Wood, Frank B. 201
Woodhams, David 200
Woodhouse, Lorenzo G. 175
Wood, Oliver E. 175
Woodruff, John G., Captain 191
Woodruff, S. E. 90
Woodruff, Theodore 200
Woodward, Lyle, Mrs. 185
Woolweaver, Augustus 200
Worrall, Fred, Mrs. 181, 182, 183, 184, 185, 186, 187
Worth, J. L. 175
Wright, Charles S. 136, 161
Wright, Ebenezer 18, 103, 106, 109, 110, 112, 129, 130, 136, 140, 141, 142, 143, 146, 147, 153, 160, 161, 189
Wright, Ebenezer Bert, Reverend Mr. 109
Wright, Ebenezer, Mrs. 154
Wright, Grace, Miss 183, 184, 185, 186, 187
Wyckoff, J. Edwards 175

Y

Yerkes, Mr. 70
Young, Joseph 200

Z

Ziegler, Philip 52

How sweet 'twill be at evening,
If you and I can say,
"Good Shepherd, we've been seeking
The lambs that went astray;
Heart-sore, and faint with hunger,
We heard them making moan –
And lo! we come at nightfall
Bearing them safely home!"

—A chorus line in the hymn "The Lost Sheep," ca. 1843

About the Author

Clark Kidder resides in Wisconsin. He is a freelance writer for international publications and has authored several books, including *Marilyn Monroe UnCovers* (Quon Editions, 1994); *Marilyn Monroe—Cover to Cover* (Krause Publications, Inc., 1999); *Marilyn Monroe Collectibles* (Harper Collins, 1999); *Orphan Trains and Their Precious Cargo* (Willow Bend Books, 2001; 2nd edition via CreateSpace, 2019); *Marilyn Monroe Memorabilia* (Krause Publications, Inc., 2001); *Marilyn Monroe—Cover to Cover*, 2nd Ed. (Krause Publications, Inc., 2003), *A Genealogy of the Wood Family* (Family Tree Publishers, 2003); *Emily's Story: The Brave Journey of an Orphan Train Rider* (Bookmasters, 2007, 2014); *A History of the Rural Schools of Rock County, Wisconsin* (CreateSpace, 2014), and *A History of the One-Room Schools of Dane County, Wisconsin* (CreateSpace, 2016).

Kidder's magazine articles have appeared in *History Magazine*, *The Wisconsin Magazine of History*, *Family Tree Magazine*, and *National Genealogical Magazine*.

Kidder won the 38th Annual William Best Hesseltine Award for his article titled "West by Orphan Train" in the *Wisconsin Magazine of History* (Winter 2003-2004).

Kidder has been interviewed by numerous reporters for articles in such newspapers as the *Los Angeles Times* and *Chicago Tribune*. His television appearances include MSNBC, PAX, WGN, Wisconsin Public Television, and Iowa Public television. He has been interviewed on numerous radio shows around the nation, including Wisconsin Public Radio and Iowa Public Radio. Kidder was host of his own television show called "Book Talk" on JATV, in Janesville, Wisconsin. In addition, he has provided consultation and photographs for documentaries and television shows produced by CBS and by October Films in London, England.

Kidder co-wrote and co-produced a documentary film based on his book *Emily's Story: The Brave Journey of an Orphan Train Rider*. It was released in 2014 and is titled *West by Orphan Train*. The film won two national awards in 2015: a Leadership in History Award from the American Association for State and Local History, and a Clarion Award. On October 3, 2015, it won an Upper Midwest Regional Emmy Award.

In 2016 the National Orphan Train Complex in Concordia, Kansas, presented the Charles Loring Brace Award to Mr. Kidder. The award recognizes the person who has helped preserve knowledge of the Children's Aid Society's participation in the Orphan Train Movement.

Contact information for Mr. Kidder:
Email: cokidder@hotmail.com
New York Juvenile Asylum Research website:
   www.newyorkjuvenileasylum.com

Other Works by the Author

Names of Children in the Records of the New York Juvenile Asylum (1853-1923). This book consists of a list of over 37,000 names of children gleaned from the surviving records of the New York Juvenile Asylum. Available online.

Emily's Story: The Brave Journey of an Orphan Train Rider. Available online.

Orphan Trains and Their Precious Cargo: The Life's Work of Reverend Herman D. Clarke, 2nd edition. Available online.

West by Orphan Train: A Documentary. DVD available at westbyorphantrain.com and Amazon.com.

A History of the Rural Schools of Rock County, Wisconsin
- Volume One: Avon, Beloit, Bradford, and Center Townships
- Volume Two: Clinton, Fulton, and Harmony Townships
- Volume Three: Janesville, Johnstown, and LaPrairie Townships
- Volume Four: Lima, Magnolia, and Milton Townships
- Volume Five: Newark, Plymouth, and Porter Townships
- Volume Six: Rock, Spring Valley, Turtle, and Union Townships

Available online

A History of the Rural Schools of Dane County, Wisconsin
- *Albion Township*
- *Dunkirk Township*
- *Pleasant Springs Township*

Available online.

www.ingramcontent.com/pod-product-compliance
Lightning Source LLC
Chambersburg PA
CBHW080546230426
43663CB00015B/2735